1992
Year C

AN ALMANAC OF PARISH LITURGY

SOURCEBOOK

FOR SUNDAYS AND SEASONS

G. Thomas Ryan

Peter Scagnelli · Timothy Fitzgerald · Mary Beth Kunde-Anderson · David Anderson
Illustrations by Steve Erspamer

LITURGY TRAINING PUBLICATIONS

Foreword

MANY of you who are reading these words (and readers of forewords are a rare breed) are old friends of *Sourcebook for Sundays and Seasons.* You have seen it grow from a 36-page supplement to *Celebrating Liturgy, 1985* (now called *Workbook for Lectors*) into the 200-plus page book you have in your hands. Many authors, artists, designers and editors have touched this book as it has developed over the years, and their fingerprints are still evident throughout it. In turn, many of you have told us here at LTP that *Sourcebook* has touched your community's worship. And many of you have influenced the book through suggestions and stories.

■ THIS YEAR'S *SOURCEBOOK* is similar in many ways to the 1991 book. The basic design has been kept, with a few modifications, particularly on the pages where prayer texts are printed. You may notice that these pages have only two columns, which allows for some of the prayers to be printed in sense lines. The type is also a bit larger on these pages than it was last year.

G. Thomas Ryan once again has served as the principal author and compiler for this year's book. Tom is a priest of the archdiocese of Boston and the liturgist for Holy Cross Cathedral. Tom often writes on liturgical subjects; his work has included *From Ashes to Easter* and *The Saint Andrew Bible Missal.* He is also a vast storehouse of liturgical and calendar information and an inveterate maker of charts.

Peter Scagnelli has once again provided many of the original prayer and ritual texts provided here, as well as translations of texts from other sources. Peter is a priest of the diocese of Providence and director of the Office of Worship for that diocese. He is also a linguist, a poet and a consultant for the International Commission on English in the Liturgy. Peter served for several years as principal author and compiler of *Sourcebook.* Much of his original work continues in these pages.

The artwork of Steve Erspamer, a Marianist brother and artist from St. Louis, again graces these pages and the cover. Fourteen new pieces have been added inside the book, most of them on Sundays within the liturgical seasons; new medallions depicting the liturgical and natural seasons in contemporary Christians' lives have been added to the cover design.

■ NEW TO THIS YEAR'S BOOK are the general intercessions composed or compiled by Timothy Fitzgerald. Tim is a priest of the diocese of Des Moines. He serves as staff resource person in adult education at St. Joseph Educational Center in West Des Moines, Iowa. Tim is a frequent author for LTP; his works include *Confirmation: A Parish Celebration.*

Mary Beth Kunde-Anderson and David Anderson provided the musical expertise for this year's book. Mary Beth is director of music for the Office for Divine Worship for the archdiocese of Chicago. David is music director for the Church of the Ascension, a Catholic parish in Oak Park, Illinois. Both are fine musicians with extensive pastoral experience.

■ MUCH IS OWED to the people behind the scenes. Copy editing and general editorial assistance was provided by Theresa Pincich, who navigates all of LTP's projects through the countless steps each one goes through. Lorraine Schmidt, the editorial department secretary, checked corrections, tracked down addresses, made endless telephone calls, and worked the copy machines into a frenzy.

LTP's graphics department takes all these words and makes them into a thing of beauty. Jane Kremsreiter, a former staff member, designed the 1991 book and the modifications for this year's book. Ana Aguilar-Islas, also a former staffer, designed the cover. Mary Bowers did the layout, and Mark Hollopeter did the typesetting.

Work on the 1993 book has already begun, but we are interested in hearing your comments and suggestions at any time.

Victoria M. Tufano,
Editor

Welcome to 1992!

THE Easter Triduum, the culmination of the entire liturgical year, occurs this year on April 16–19. The preparation for this preeminent celebration, and especially for the "mother of all vigils" (an ancient phrase; cf. *General Norms for the Liturgical Year and Calendar,* #21), should be at the top of the liturgical agenda. As in 1991, Western Christians observe their paschal festival on the same weekend that their Jewish sisters and brothers begin Passover. Eastern Christians celebrate Easter one week later.

■ SUNDAYS: The 52 Sundays of 1992 must also be at the center of our consciousness as we move into still another year of the Lord. Two of the Sundays in Ordinary Time will be replaced by important feasts—the Presentation on February 2 and All Saints on November 1.

Since it is Year C in the Sunday lectionary, the evangelist Luke will be our principal guide. Depending on the selection of options for three late-Lent Sundays and Easter Day, Luke may be read on as many as 39 Sundays this year. Because of his account of Jesus' nativity, he is also the favored gospel writer for the Christmastime feasts each year.

Homilists and those who plan the liturgy would do well to spend some time early in 1992 looking at their favorite commentaries on Luke. Two major sections of the gospel are most important this year:

- It has been 20 years since the issuance of our current lectionary, and this is the first time in all these years that the winter Ordinary Time of Year C has been long enough to read all the excerpts from the Sermon on the Plain.

- When the semicontinuous proclamations from Luke are resumed after the solemnity of The Body and Blood of Christ, we turn to the story of the Journey to Jerusalem and continue to read from this section of Luke until late October.

The other book of particular importance in 1992 is Revelation. From it, readings will be taken for all the Eastertime Sundays, and then for 12 weekdays at the very end of the liturgical year.

■ SEASONS: Lent will be later in 1992 than in the last four years, with Ash Wednesday falling in March. The great day of Pentecost and the solemnities that are positioned after it are all celebrated in June. Those who prepare the liturgy often wish for more time between Christmas and Lent; this later configuration comes about once every five years—enjoy! Christmastime ends a day earlier than last year and Christmas Day itself has moved one more day away from the Fourth Sunday of Advent, to Wednesday. Decorators, rejoice!

■ FEASTS "LOST": Each year certain feasts are "lost" because of the precedence of Sunday, the Triduum and the days immediately surrounding it. This year four feasts give way to the Octave of Easter and to Sundays: Mark, Philip and James, Visitation, and the evangelist of the year, Luke. About 25 memorials (such as Ambrose and Francis of Assisi) are omitted for the same reason this year. While we might miss these "eclipsed" days, the principle of the precedence of Sunday is central to our Christian tradition—after all, what saint or angel would not gladly give way to the paschal banquet of the Lord's Day?

■ FEASTS "FOUND": Well over a hundred observances from the "proper of saints" remain in liturgical year 1992. The Immaculate Conception is moved to Saturday, December 7 (and in most of the world it loses its "obligation" status). The Assumption falls on a Saturday, the only case this year of back-to-back days of obligation. Two feasts will receive greater prominence this year: The Presentation, with its wonderful procession of candlelight, and All Saints will be celebrated on Sundays. All but one of the observances particular to the dioceses of the United States are on unimpeded weekdays. One of them might be the best date to celebrate a service of reconciliation commemorating the fifth centenary of the first voyage of Christopher Columbus to the Americas (see page xiii). The greatest of these national days, the feast of Our Lady of Guadalupe (December 12), will fall on a Saturday in late 1992. This placement might prompt planners to schedule the penance service for that date.

Many days on the universal Roman calendar are listed as "optional memorials." Each parish should review these days and decide which will be observed this year. To these universal and national feasts, those who prepare the liturgy also must add the parish's own local festivals (see pp. 213–18) and any ember days (p. 221).

■ WEEKDAYS: This is Year II in the weekday lectionary, the year when we hear the story of Job (September 28 and following). We also hear more prophetic books and more New Testament letters than in Year I. Each week should be previewed:

> The continuous reading during the week is sometimes interrupted by the occurrence of a feast or particular celebration. In this case the priest, taking into consideration the entire week's plan of readings, is allowed either to combine omitted parts with other readings or to give preference to certain readings. (*General Instruction of the Roman Missal,* #319; see also the introduction to the lectionary, #82 in the 1981 edition.)

This *Sourcebook* includes notes at the beginning of weeks so affected.

■ OTHER CHARACTERISTICS OF 1992:

- Three distinctly American days coincide in a fruitful way with the liturgical calendar. As in 1991, the holiday of Martin Luther King, Jr., is on a martyr's day—this time St. Sebastian or St. Fabian. Memorial Day falls within the Easter season, allowing paschal images to shape Christians' entry into that day's memories. Thanksgiving Day will, as is often the case, be on the third-to-last day of the liturgical year, allowing appreciation for the harvest to mesh with eschatological hope.

- Labor Day and the often related opening of schools are as late as they ever get. Many people will feel like there's an extra week to summer. Liturgists will have to adjust the related blessings of students and of catechists.

- Christopher Columbus arrived in the Americas 500 years ago this year. See page x and following for suggestions concerning this anniversary.

- National elections will take place in the United States in early November, with primaries and political conventions occupying the consciousness of all citizens throughout the year. Debates about justice and national purpose, about society and rights, are never far from the church's mission. Liturgical ideas are outlined on page 166.

Using this Sourcebook

THIS book is a humble tool pointing to the riches of the Roman Catholic liturgical tradition. It is not a substitute for the official liturgical books or for the grand tradition of the liturgies we share. Rather, this book offers assistance on the way a parish might receive and celebrate this tradition. Its value is to be measured by how fully it enables a parish to implement the great treasure of Catholic liturgy.

■ CONTENTS: This book begins with general ideas and resources to be used throughout the year. Then the liturgical seasons and the weeks of Ordinary Time between them are introduced. A final section gives guidance on the all-too-often-ignored feasts of the local church.

■ ART: As it was last year, *Sourcebook* is graced with block-print art by Steve Erspamer, SM. These beautiful prints can be used as clip-art by a parish for its bulletins, worship folders and other handouts. This art may not be used, however, for commercial purposes.

■ INTRODUCTION TO EACH SEASON: The introductory material with each season gives those who prepare the liturgy an opportunity to consider an overall approach to a season while at the same time calling attention to the options in our ritual books, especially the sacramentary and lectionary. Here also are discussions of the groundwork that may be required to prepare the parish to keep a particular season with vigor. The music sections are the work of Mary Beth Kunde-Anderson and David Anderson.

■ CALENDAR: A day-by-day calendar appears immediately after each seasonal overview—helping the reader in the task of celebrating the season on each day within it. These suggestions presume that one has read the seasonal introductions first. Rarely are ideas suggested just for one day. Rather, the goal is that texts and music and ritual order will have a certain consistency throughout the season. Note that this year's calendar includes the liturgical colors for each day.

■ TEXTS FOR LITURGICAL USE: Sample prayer texts follow each seasonal calendar. The intercessions (models, not prescriptions) were composed by Timothy Fitzgerald or selected by him from one of these sources: *Intercessions for the Christian People* by Gail Ramshaw (New York: Pueblo Publishing Co., 1988), *The Book of Common Prayer,* the Divine Liturgy of St. John Chrysostom, the Divine Liturgy of St. James of Jerusalem and the Liturgy of St. Basil the Great. The prayers for each Sunday may serve as the conclusions of the intercessions. They are from the International Committee on English in the Liturgy (hereafter referred to as ICEL) or from Peter Scagnelli, who composed some and translated others from European sacramentaries. Unless otherwise noted, the other texts provided are translated or composed by Peter Scagnelli.

Scheduling

P ERHAPS the single most important part of incorporating the church's calendar into the life of a parish (and a crucial part of using this book) is the scheduling of feast days and liturgies. The times of Masses, the sacraments, the liturgy of the hours and other gatherings are most important. Every pastoral leader has a story about a parish torn apart by cancellations of "favorite" Mass times, of fights over tickets for limited seating on Christmas Eve, of stand-offs in the parish center as two groups claim the same space at the same time, or some other scheduling horror. In a more positive vein, every Catholic cherishes those memories of an entire parish gathered for a great event—the Vigil, a ground-breaking or an episcopal visitation. These "plenary" assemblies are not just impressive and grand, they are expressive and formative of the given local church.

■ SEASONS FOR THE WHOLE CHURCH: Liturgical planners must do more than wring their hands at how few people observe these days of rejoicing. First of all, of course, these leaders must be convinced that the keeping of set days and seasons by a local community is important.

Once this basic assumption is allowed to permeate local decision making, scheduling will be different: The Triduum will be listed at the top of every parish society's calendar, the days at the end of Lent and the Easter octave will be free

of business-as-usual, the great feasts will become the "magnet" dates for traditional parish socials, and liturgies such as Evening Prayer will be seen as the preferred format for regular prayers before parish meetings (for example, Evening Prayer may be scheduled at 7:00 each night, before the various meetings fill the parish center rooms at 7:30).

■ SEASONS' LENGTH: Once the priority of the church's feasts begins to affect schedules, each parish community will have to become equally convinced that it must keep these days and seasons in concert with ancient tradition and with other local churches. The *General Norms for the Liturgical Year and the Calendar* are exact concerning when seasons begin and end. American parishes must pay close attention to keeping Advent as Advent, to the length and end of Christmas, to the unity of the Triduum and to the length and unity of the Easter Season. In this season-setting, ancient tradition sets the agenda: The linkage of solar seasons, agricultural cycles, urban memory-keeping of holy men and women, established times for remembering the Christian mysteries and the customs of our parents cannot be invented or transformed in one lifetime or one century. Nor should they be. Festivals celebrate mysteries that transcend local boundaries. Keeping festival together across these boundaries forms us into a community of shared memories and visions, hopes and dreams, emotions and desires.

■ SUNDAYS:

▪ As few Sunday Masses as possible should be scheduled in each parish. The Catholic way is to gather the entire parish in as few assemblies as possible—ideally, *one*—so that every segment of the body can join with the other parts, making Sunday's eucharist a truer symbol and source of unity. In contrast, convenience and custom call for multiple Masses even when the building and people's schedules would allow one gathering. Courageous (and wise) indeed are those pastoral leaders who have declared that their parish gathers at 10:00 AM, and all should shape their Sundays to be able to be at *the* eucharist. Of course this is ideal, but some trimming of the schedule in many parishes is in order. And certainly no special groups should be gathering for their own Sunday Masses apart from the parish assembly.

▪ Various sacraments may be scheduled from time to time at the Sunday Mass: infant baptism, communal anointing of the sick, catechumenal rites, blessings, marriages *(yes!)*, and both confirmation and first communion during the Easter Season.

- The *Liturgy of the Hours* (#207), echoing the fondest hope of the Second Vatican Council (*Constitution on the Sacred Liturgy*, #100), calls for every parish to celebrate Evening Prayer every Sunday. This is not just a special event for one or two evenings a year. It is part of the way every parish should do Sunday.

- Other sacraments and rites raise special concerns: Infant baptisms should be celebrated on Sunday at Mass or at their own liturgy (*Rite of Baptism for Children*, #9); marriage celebrations should take the Sunday texts into account (*Rite of Marriage*, #11); confessions are not to be heard in the church while Mass is being celebrated; parishes should consider celebrating the other hours of the liturgy of the hours (especially Saturday night vigils).

- Social and catechetical gatherings for all ages should be a regular part of parish life. They allow those gathered for Mass or the hours to prolong their time together and deepen their unity. Fewer and more widely spaced Masses would allow for this.

- The entire Lord's Day, from Evening Prayer I at sunset on Saturday until late Sunday night should be kept sacred. This is not done by one Mass alone. Whether Mass is scheduled Saturday at 4:00 PM or Sunday at 6:00 AM, the other hours of the Lord's Day are to be kept holy—through participation in the liturgy of the hours, through domestic prayer and through gatherings for meals and shared reflection.

■ EASTER VIGIL:

- The entire Easter Vigil is to take place at night. "This rule is to be taken according to its strictest sense. Reprehensible are those abuses and practices that have crept into many places in violation of this ruling, whereby the Easter Vigil is celebrated at the time of day that it is customary to celebrate anticipated Sunday Masses." (*Circular Letter Concerning the Preparation and Celebration of the Easter Feasts*, #78.)

- See page 122 of this book for suggestions if one Vigil cannot accommodate the entire parish.

- Decisions must be made long before Easter concerning which rites will take place during and after the Vigil: adult initiation, reception into full communion, infant baptism, food blessing and/or refreshments for all. This night is not just another entry on the schedule; it is the primary gathering of the entire body.

■ THE REST OF THE EASTER TRIDUUM:

- Easter Day is to be kept sacred (as is every Sunday). This holds even for those who participated in the Vigil and do not return for a morning eucharist. Participation in the liturgy of the hours, in domestic prayer and in ecclesial social gatherings should mark the entire day as the Lord's. Few members will attend every event on the Easter schedule, but every member should be provided with the texts, schedule and inspiration to keep the entire day at home and at church.

- See the chapter on the Triduum for specific suggestions.

■ CHRISTMAS:

- See page 33 for a full discussion of the Christmas schedule and the legitimate desire of communities to have a "nocturnal experience" on Christmas.

- This is one of the two days besides Easter (Pentecost is the other) when our tradition encourages every parish to have some form of Vigil service (see page 35).

- As on Sundays, there should be as few Masses as possible, one being the ideal.

- The other hours of the festival are to be kept sacred by all. Whether there is one Mass or several, most parishioners will participate in just one. As on Easter and on Sundays, members are to be equipped and inspired to keep all the hours holy through liturgy of the hours celebrations, domestic prayer and social gatherings.

1492–1992
Christopher Columbus

THE NEED FOR RECONCILIATION

THE year 1992 marks the 500th anniversary of the first voyage of Christopher Columbus to this continent and its nearby islands. Some people say that this is a tremendously sad anniversary, calling to mind the turmoil brought about by the arrival or invasion of the European peoples. Others see it as a grand and welcome opportunity to celebrate Italian or Spanish roots and to honor Columbus. The year 1492 was a turning point. Depending on one's vantage point and ethnic background, it was a signal either of doom or of a new beginning for humanity. Many Mexicans, for example, see the resulting intermarriages as the foundation of their identity.

These divergent views are not cited to lull Americans into thinking that this anniversary is "whatever you want it to be." The renowned Harvard historian, Samuel Eliot Morison, who wrote the most definitive study of Columbus said that "the cruel policy initiated by Columbus and pursued by his successors resulted in complete genocide." The death of Native American peoples cannot be ignored, even in communities drawn to Columbus as a holy and noble hero. In these communities the question is most clear: How does any American parish observe the anniversary?

■ CHURCHES RESPOND: The U.S. bishops, in concert with the other episcopal conferences of the American continents, are asking parishes to commemorate Columbus' arrival by reflecting on 1492 as the beginning of evangelization in the Americas. It is envisioned that these reflections will give rise to liturgical celebrations, praising God for the gift of the gospel in the Americas. Liturgical texts (presidential prayers, entrance and communion antiphons, scriptural citations) have been approved by the bishops and are published in *Heritage and Hope* (Washington DC: United States Catholic Conference [USCC], 1991).

The National Council of Churches (NCC), through a resolution of its governing board, said that "this is not a time for celebration but a time for a committed plan of action ensuring that this *kairos* moment in history not continue to cosmetically coat the painful aspects of the American history of racism" (See *Origins* 20:171 [August 16, 1990]).

Neither response frames a completely adequate agenda for the sensitive pastor and pastoral planning group. A parish might want to celebrate the beginnings of the gospel here, but a liturgical forum for expressing genuine lament seems to be equally as necessary. Those who heed the NCC resolution for a committed plan of action cannot live by words and ideals alone; communal gatherings to hear God's word and to form both plans and hearts in that light are also needed. Following this section of *Sourcebook,* an outline for a penitential or reconciliation service is presented.

Through the vocabulary of repentance, we come closest to the Christian response to painful history. Such penitence is neither morbid, accusatory nor unbecoming for a national jubilee or anniversary. Penance does more than point to sins of the past; it lets the gathered community praise the God of all mercies and gifts. It frames the assembly in the image world, the hymns and

the prayers that let them be pulled to the New Jerusalem, the time of fullness when all will be in harmony. As stated in the introduction to the *Rite of Penance,* penitential services invite parishes to conversion and renewal of life. They announce our freedom from sin through the death and resurrection of Christ (#36).

Americans may go to civic events celebrating Columbus, but when the Christians of the Americas gather as Christians, they must turn to God as the source of freedom, to the blood of the cross as our reconciliation. The service outlined here may be celebrated as a service of the word alone, but with only slight adaptations it could allow time for individual confession and absolution.

The year 1992 may not turn out to be a *kairos* moment—that is, a moment of extraordinary grace—in the history of many towns and parishes, but the time spent marking the anniversary should allow for the tragedies of the past to be lamented, the joys of the present to be celebrated and the future of fullness to unite us all.

THE ARRIVAL OF COLUMBUS AND THE SPANISH

The history of the time between Columbus and the independence of the United States is as ambivalent as that of any other three centuries. These centuries carry happy memories even as they nearly overwhelm us with the tragedies of racism. The tragedy of these centuries is the annihilation of the Native American populations. The joy rests in the formation of our identity as an American people.

The Spanish were the first Europeans to come in large numbers to the Americas. From California to Florida and throughout the lands further south, residents carry Spanish blood and language. Two other groups came to these same regions of the Americas: The Portuguese settled in Brazil, and the Russians settled along the west coast of North America, bringing Orthodox Christianity to this land.

■ ROLE OF THE CHURCH: With the first settlers and military came the first missionaries. While diocesan priests cared for the liturgical and pastoral needs of the immigrants, Jesuits and Franciscans came to convert the native population. The early, frequent and sustained abuses heaped on the native people (and on imported slaves) were overlooked by patriotic, complacent clergy. While some leaders did speak and act in condemnation of these sins, it is no secret that the Jesuits owned slaves and that the missionaries erased a way of life that was, in many ways, more deeply religious than their own. As Virgilio Elizondo has noted, the missionaries (even the kindly ones) were more dangerous and violent than the conquistadors, for they were attacking the very core of native Mexican existence. (*La Morenita, Evangelizer of the Americas,* p. 64. See the bibliography at the end of this section.) From 1519–1521, the missionaries were accomplices in the total destruction of the Mexican way of life.

In 1537, Pope Paul III issued a decree championing the rights of Native Americans and condemning their disenfranchisement and enslavement. Wise missionaries continued to foster the rights of Indians, to learn their languages and to adopt their ways. People in Arizona cherish the memory of such men as Father Eusebio Francisco Kino, a defender of the natives and a world-class scholar.

■ OUR LADY OF GUADALUPE: The single greatest joy of the Spanish areas comes from outside Mexico City—pointedly on the outskirts, which even then were away from the centers of civil and episcopal power. In 1531, Mary appeared to Juan Diego on a hill known previously for the appearances of a serpent woman, a woman of wisdom and peace (for Mexicans, serpents were symbols of life and perfection). Despite some Spaniards' apprehensions about the image of Our Lady of Guadalupe, millions found legitimacy and faith itself in responding to the image of Mary as both an Indian and a cosmic power.

■ A TRADITION HANDED ON: While cherishing the heritage of devotions that accompanied the spread of the gospel, Catholics throughout the United States praise God for their regions' "first Masses" and early Catholic foundations: for the first Catholic parish in St. Augustine, for the strong witness of early and vital catechumenates and for the first confirmation celebration on Easter (cf. Ellis, p. 40. See the bibliography at the end of this section). Early missionaries in Texas showed their respect for the adult natives by declining their request for immediate baptism and by bringing them into a catechumenate (Ellis, p. 78).

■ RECONCILIATION: Each of the dioceses within the lands colonized by Spain can bring its own

memories to a service of reconciliation—the first martyr, Juan de Padilla (1542), in eastern Kansas; the venerable histories of such cathedrals as San Juan and St. Augustine; the missions of California and the Southwest. With trembling and awe, with tears and with the sure hope of renewal, in union with the Virgin of Guadalupe, we can cry out for reconciliation.

THE ARRIVAL OF COLUMBUS AND THE FRENCH

Soon after the confrontation between Spanish Catholics and native peoples, French explorers came, mostly to the north of the Spanish areas. The French missionaries' works were not accompanied by the massive slaughter that marked Mexico, but tragic confrontations were spawned by cultural arrogance. One example is the pitiable story of Jacques Cartier transporting Native Americans to France in 1534 to inspire the citizens to work for the conversion of "savages" (Ellis, p. 126). Slavery was as prevalent in French Louisiana as it was in Spanish South America.

The painful recollections of this post-Columbian period are accompanied by the stories of such giants as Isaac Jogues (see page 196) and Kateri Tekakwitha (page 180), by the regional memories throughout the Midwest and Northeast of "first Masses" and liturgical beginnings. Local memories of evangelization, mission-building, martyrdom and exploration should frame parish and diocesan celebrations of the 1992 anniversary. Catholics in the northern regions can turn to "Good St. Anne," the patron of their traditional American base, Quebec. Her shrine east of Quebec City draws Native Americans and European descendants together in daily prayer for reconciliation. Americans distant from such devotions need the same awareness that we inherit a troubled history.

THE ARRIVAL OF COLUMBUS AND THE ENGLISH

The Fifth Centenary will awaken memories in residents of the 13 original colonies of their own colonization. These recollections will be most intense for Catholics in Maryland and Pennsylvania, for here the heritage of our sacraments goes back to the first immigrants. In every state along the Atlantic, parishes need to include prayers for the Native Americans so conveniently forgotten or politely used to name ponds and suburban shopping malls.

■ THE FIRST CATHOLICS OF THIS REGION, particularly Maine and New York, were the natives who readily embraced the gospel preached by the French. When Catholics were finally allowed to hold liturgies in Boston (well after the Revolutionary War), their first priests went "on mission" to Maine. They were stunned and moved to tears as they walked through the forest, approached the "savages," and heard from a distance the liturgical chants and fervent Catholic prayers of natives who had been catechized 150 years earlier! Even today, the suffering and spirituality of the natives and of the descendants of black slaves can and should inspire whites and Hispanics.

■ ECUMENICAL CONCERNS: The memories of the colonial region bring ecumenical concerns to the foreground. Inter-Christian prejudices and discriminiatory laws fostered misconceptions and inflicted deep wounds that still mar entire communities. The Quakers of Philadelphia must be thanked for their early hospitality to Catholics. The earliest framers of the United States documents should be praised for their openness to Catholic presence. Then all Christians ought to kneel in humble prayer before the sight of abolitionist museums and Civil War memorials, to gather in repentance for all that our history tells us. From such penitence, renewal can spring.

RESOURCES

Those who prepare the liturgy in the parish may consult with local librarians for assistance in reconstructing the early history of Native Americans, of Europeans and of Christianity in their town or city. General studies include:

Ahlstrom, Sydney, *A Religious History of the American People* (New Haven: Yale University Press, 1972).

Ellis, John Tracy, *Catholics in Colonial America* (Baltimore: Helicon Press, Inc., 1965). A state-by-state summary, well worth the search.

Elizondo, Virgilio, *La Morenita: Evangelizer of the Americas* (San Antonio: Mexican American Cultural Center, 1980). A thorough study of Our Lady of Guadalupe and of post-Columbian history from the vantage point of the oppressed.

Goodpasture, M. McKennie, *Cross and Sword: An Eyewitness History of Christianity in Latin America* (Maryknoll NY: Orbis Books, 1989).

Morison, Samuel Eliot, *Admiral of the Ocean Sea: A Life of Christopher Columbus* (New York: The Atlantic Monthly Press, 1942). The classic.

Penitential Rite for the Fifth Centenary of Columbus and the Evangelization of the Americas

DATE FOR LOCAL OBSERVANCE

PLANNERS of local celebrations need to know the colonial and precolonial history of their town, state and region. They should be aware of the beginnings of Christianity and particularly of Catholicism in their area. The date for a parish celebration of reconciliation should be selected with these questions in mind: Which date and time would allow the greatest number of children and adults to participate? Which date already turns local residents' attention to their own history? Which date carries memories that need to be reconciled, or that most shape the local understanding of what it means to be American? Will other churches in town be marking the anniversary? When? Is there a local saint or blessed whose day would be appropriate?

If these considerations do not suggest a date, then Monday, October 12, 1992, which is, happily, both Columbus Day "traditional" and "observed," may be the best date. Otherwise, the day when most religious education classes meet could be selected, drawing the youth and adults into a common celebration of heritage and mercy.

INTRODUCTORY RITES

- *Opening Hymn and Processional:* Liturgy is not the place for patriotic music. The opening hymn should be a piece that unites the congregation and invites the vigorous participation of all voices.

Hymnal indices for "reconciliation" or "penitence" or "church" can be consulted. Content that is most broadly communal should be selected: This is not a service for "my" re-alignment with God, it is the gathering of church to remember and to dream precisely as church. This hymn may be accompanied by a procession of ministers—pastoral leader, lectors, choir, assistants. The parish pastoral council could be included, highlighting this as a gathering of the entire local church with all its diversity and ministries.

- *Sign of the Cross*

- *Greeting:* "May the grace, peace and mercy of God, from whom we have the remission of all our sins, be with you all."

- *Introduction:* Noting the significance of the date and mindful of local history, the leader of prayer may introduce the anniversary of Columbus with words such as these:

> The anniversary of Christopher Columbus's first voyage to the Americas reminds us of the Native Americans Columbus met, of the continual waves of immigrants after him, of the displacement and tragedy that followed. This observance calls to mind our own histories and the struggles between peoples that led to the United States as we now know it.
>
> The anniversary also reminds us of the arrival of the first missionaries and of the sacramental life passed on to us here. This day should inspire us to thank God, whose power is most at work when forgiveness is given.
>
> We gather here as church today because of our share in the ministry of reconciliation. We come, too, as sinners, to pray for forgiveness and restoration. Christ is peace itself. Divisions and sins are washed away by his blood. We find forgiveness in the power of the cross. Let us lead our cities and communities to the Lamb of God who takes away the sin of the world, who grants us peace amidst all our troubled memories.

- *Prayer:* From the *Rite of Penance,* #97–100, or from the sacramentary: the first opening prayer from the Mass for July 4, Independence Day, or, preferably, from Masses and Prayers for Various Needs and Occasions, 17. For the Nation. In the various seasons, an opening prayer from the Mass for one of the following days may be selected: Advent, Friday of the First Week; Christmas, Tuesday after January 1; Lent, Friday of the Second Week; Easter, Friday of the Octave.

LITURGY OF THE WORD

- *First reading:* Jonah 3:1—4:11 or shorter forms (3:1–10 or 4:1–11). These two passages, which preferably can be read in tandem, are found in the lectionary at #462–63.

- *Responsorial psalm:* The psalmist sings the verses and all sing the refrains for part or all of Psalm 51. Certain verses are collected in the lectionary at #175 (seasonal psalm for Lent) and #227. The appendix of the current U.S. lectionary ("Votive Mass for Thanksgiving Day") contains two excellent alternatives. Psalms 67 and 113 both praise God as the source of all nations. In Eastertime, any of these psalms may be enhanced by alleluia refrains.

- *Second reading:* Galatians 5:13–26 or a shorter form (5:18–25) found at lectionary #469.

- *Gospel acclamation:* A setting of the alleluia or of a lenten acclamation may be combined with a verse from the appendix of the lectionary (Note the fourth alleluia verse given there, with its expression of the international character of reconciliation). In Lent, use one of the verses at #224. In Eastertime, see #889.3.

- *Gospel:* Luke 11:29–32 (lectionary #467)—"Sign of Jonah," the assigned reading (by chance) for Columbus Day, 1992.

- *Homily:* These scripture texts are rich sources for communal interpretation. A few homily starting points:

> *Nineveh and national conversion:* The book of Jonah is one of the greatest stories in the Bible (indeed in all of human literature). It tells of an entire city repenting. The conversion of the Ninevites was total—it even involved the cattle and sheep. All the beasts and every human put on sackcloth and cried to the Lord.
>
> Even in a religiously pluralistic society such as Nineveh, such as the United States, conversion is of a whole people. This does not mean that we must get every American to convert to Catholicism, but it does mean that our message of reconciliation must be shared and made effective in every corner of the land. We do not preach only private forgiveness. We preach of total transformation, of a new world order.
>
> *Jonah, preachers and catechists:* Chapter 4 of Jonah is the least read but most important chapter in the book. Everyone knows about the whale. Many know of the swift repentance of the Ninevites. But these parts of the story lead to the great confrontation under the gourd plant in chapter 4. Early Christian images of Jonah often depict him sulking under the plant, upset that his enemy has converted, that God's ways are so merciful.
>
> We, too, are called upon to preach and teach reform, but God mysteriously pulls us beyond

our preconceived ideas and established categories. The missionaries and catechists who followed Columbus were at their best when they let God's power and love be seen by all peoples. They were at their worst when they were annoyed by the success of Native Americans, when they were reluctant to make Indians Catholics, or when they preached with guns pointed at slaves and the oppressed. Like Jonah, too many were more concerned with their own comfort and their own ideas of God, not with the truth and power of an all-merciful God.

Nineveh, Iraq: Nineveh was located on the banks of the Tigris River across from what is now Mosul (one of the principal cities of Chaldean Christians) in northeast Iraq. Though Nineveh was destroyed before the birth of Christ, sites in both Nineveh and in Mosul are still linked with Jonah and his big fish. Jonah's "tomb" is honored there and a mosque enshrines a skeleton reputed to be the big fish. In 1991, such places in Iraq took on an added significance. Here in the cradle of civilization, here in the land of Eden and of Abraham, of the flood and the Exile, stand the sites of the greatest national conversion. This conversion was preceded by a time of great decadence and oppression in Nineveh. No wonder Jonah did not want to go there! Yet, from such troubled history came such conversion!

Looking at our own continent's history of invasion, we can allow great reconciliation and conversion to flow from God's hands. In the shadow of war, we can pray for international reconciliation to flow from the turmoil in Mesopotamia. Without attention to the sign of Jonah, "the citizens of Nineveh will rise along with the present generation, and they will condemn it" (Luke 11:32).

In the seasons of Lent and Easter: The relationship of the story of Jonah and these paschal days can be highlighted. The "sign of Jonah" includes messages of repentance and openness to foreigners, but it also includes the link to Christ's three days in the tomb.

Freedom for service: The letter to the Galatians, read during the week of Columbus Day in 1992, invites us to reflect on that highly regarded American value, freedom. As Christians understand it, freedom is more than constitutional rights: It involves love, life in the Spirit, the crucifixion of passions and desires. This crucifixion is not a denial of passion but a purification or transformation of it. Liturgies such as this penitential gathering are opportunities to train our desires in the Lord, to hold them up to the judgment of God's word and our liturgical tradition.

- *Examination of Conscience:* This can be introduced at the conclusion of the homily. Such an introduction seems preferable to a long list of probing questions. Silence or instrumental music should last for several minutes.

PENITENTIAL ACTION

- *Litany:* The litany can be taken from the texts in the *Rite of Penance,* #204–5. The acclamations should each be followed by a sung response. See also the fine litany in the *Book of Blessings,* #1212; it is particularly fitting in the seasons of Advent, Christmas and Easter. The petitions in the *Book of Blessings,* #1674, can be extended for a lenten service. These petitions should be supplemented by locally composed invocations: for example, petitions for the healing of memories (such as local tragedies associated with European supremacy), for an end to racism, in thanksgiving for the local beginnings of evangelization, in hope of certain transformations needed by this local church. Exact names and incidents can be mentioned, especially those from the colonial era; the history of salvation and of sin is not abstract. It is local and universal. After the litany, one of the following actions takes place:

Laying on of hands: All are invited to come forward for a laying on of hands by pastoral leaders. This is done in silence, or with song, but without verbal interchange between those laying on hands and the other members of the assembly.

Or:

Signing with baptismal water: (Especially appropriate in the Easter season, but possible anytime except Lent.) All go to the baptismal font, dip their hands in the water and then trace the cross on the foreheads of those next to them. During this action, a strong baptismal or church unity hymn is sung by all.

Or:

Lighting of candle: (During Advent and Christmas season) All go to the Advent wreath or Christmas tree and there receive and light individual candles (electric lights are dimmed throughout the building). Standing around the emblems of the season (wreath, manger, tree or decorated ambo), the congregation holds candles and sings a seasonal carol that praises the God of mercy, and of the hopes and fears of all the years.

- *Lord's Prayer:* Introduced with words such as those in the *Book of Blessings,* #1675.

CONCLUDING RITES

- *Proclamation of praise:* The Canticle of Jonah (2:3–10) is sung by all. Or, if the service takes place in one of the seasons, sing the canticle most associated with those days: the Magnificat in Advent, the Canticle of Zachary in Christmastime, 1 Peter 2:21–24 in Lent, Revelation 19 in Eastertime.

- *Prayer:* Use the wonderful text by the first American bishop, John Carroll, in the *Book of Blessings,* #1965 (entire prayer or just paragraphs A and E). Or adapt the first prayer after communion found in appendix X.6 of the 1985 sacramentary (note that "eucharist" becomes "reconciliation service").

- *Blessing:* This should be in keeping with the time of year. For Ordinary Time, consider *Book of Blessings,* #471 (if the stress has been on evangelization) and #1214. Also see the solemn blessing in appendix X.6 in the sacramentary. In Advent, use the solemn Advent blessing; in Christmastime, the Epiphany blessing; in Eastertime, the Holy Spirit solemn blessing: These are located after the Order of Mass in the sacramentary. In Lent, use the new Lenten blessing at #5 in appendix II of the *Book of Blessings.*

- *Dismissal*

- *Closing Hymn*

Bibliography

RITUAL BOOKS

I. *The Roman Missal* has been published in several parts, mostly to distinguish the various ministries. These volumes form the core of any parish's liturgical library:

A. *Sacramentary:* The 1985 edition must be used (The Liturgical Press, Catholic Book Publishing Company).

> Complementary volumes:
>
> *The Book of the Chair* (various publishers, originally Australian) contains the portions of the sacramentary used at the presider's chair on Sundays.
>
> Especially for Saturdays in Ordinary Time, see the *Collection of Masses of the Blessed Virgin Mary:* partial English edition 1988, complete edition due in 1991 or 1992 (Catholic Book Publishing Company).

> Forthcoming publication:
>
> In the near future, look for a two-volume revision of the sacramentary, with revised translations from the Latin and many original texts. *(As the* Sourcebook *goes to press, exact dates for the publication of the revised sacramentary and other titles listed here as "forthcoming" have not yet been determined.)*

B. *Lectionary for Mass:* The 1970 edition is still in use (various publishers, some with individual volumes for each year of Sundays).

> Complementary volumes:
>
> A new lectionary was published in Latin in 1981; its introduction is published in English (USCC, also in Liturgy Training Publication's [LTP] collection, *The Liturgy Documents.*).
>
> Work continues on future publication of a lectionary for Masses with children, but meanwhile "approved" excerpts from the complete lectionary are *Lectionary for Masses with Children* (3 vols., Pueblo Publishing Co.) and *Weekday Lectionary for Masses with Children* (Costello Publishing, Inc., E. J. Dwyer).
>
> *The Book of Gospels:* The gospels from the 1970 lectionary have been published separately (Collins Publishers, Catholic Book Publishing Company).
>
> The *Simple Gradual* was published in English in 1968, and its collection of psalms has made its way into many available hymnals.
>
> Forthcoming publications:
>
> A revised lectionary for the United States should contain the revised *New American Bible* text with sense-lines for ease of proclamation, with additions and emendations from the 1981 Latin edition, and with American adaptations.
>
> *Lectionary for Masses with Children:* Long-awaited by catechists and pastoral liturgists, this new lectionary will make use of a completely new translation prepared by the American Bible Society.

II. *The Liturgy of the Hours:* 1975 (4 vols., Catholic Book Publishing Company; 2 vols., Daughters of Saint Paul). A treasure for all Catholics.

Complementary volumes:

Christian Prayer is a one volume excerpt from the full collection. (Catholic Book Publishing Company)

Shorter Christian Prayer (Collins Publishers, Catholic Book Publishing Company) is a simplified, pocket-size edition to help introduce the assembly to this form of liturgical prayer.

A *Supplement* with new memorials to be observed in the United States was published by Catholic Book Publishing Company in 1987.

Musical resources for the hours are listed on page xxi.

III. *The Roman Ritual,* published in one volume before Vatican II, has since been published in different volumes, one for each sacrament or rite. The increased number of options and adaptations made this necessary. Every parish, every presider and every planning group needs a full set of the current editions at hand (with the possible exception of the *Rite of Religious Profession*). These books are to be treated with care and reverence. For the celebration of the rites, beautifully bound editions of these books, which convey the dignity of the assembly and its worship, are to be used. Paperback editions are published for study and preparation only.

A. *Rite of Christian Initiation of Adults:* 1988 (LTP, The Liturgical Press, USCC, Catholic Book Publishing Company). This includes the rite for the Reception of Baptized Christians, formerly published in a separate booklet. Study editions are available from The Liturgical Press and LTP.

B. *Rite of Baptism for Children:* 1970 (The Liturgical Press, Catholic Book Publishing Company). The Canadian bishops published a handsome edition of this book with separate rites "within Mass" and "outside Mass." Copyright restrictions prohibit bulk sales in the United States, but individual copies can be obtained from the Canadian Catholic Conference.

C. *Rite of Marriage:* 1970 (The Liturgical Press, Ave Maria Press, Catholic Book Publishing Company). The Canadian edition (Canadian Catholic Conference) includes suggested texts for the rite of reception at the entrance and other texts which make it the best volume currently available.

Forthcoming publication:

The Vatican, ICEL, and the U.S. bishops' conference are working on a new edition, with suitable adaptations for the United States This will probably be the next section of the ritual to be published.

D. *Order of Christian Funerals:* The 1989 edition must be used. (LTP, The Liturgical Press, Catholic Book Publishing Company) A study edition of the entire rite and ritual editions of the wake and rite of committal are also available from LTP.

E. *Rite of Penance:* 1975 (The Liturgical Press, Pueblo Publishing Company, Catholic Book Publishing Company). Published in both "sanctuary size" for penance services and "confessional size" for individual penance.

F. *Pastoral Care of the Sick: Rites of Anointing and Viaticum:* The 1983 edition must be used. (LTP [Spanish and English], The Liturgical Press, Catholic Book Publishing Company). Published in "sanctuary" and "pocket" sizes.

G. *Holy Communion and Worship of the Eucharist Outside Mass:* 1974 (Catholic Book Publishing Company).

H. *Rite of Religious Profession:* 1988 (LTP).

I. *Book of Blessings:* 1989 (The Liturgical Press, Catholic Book Publishing Company). This book includes several rites once published separately: the orders for crowning an image of the Blessed Virgin Mary, for the commissioning of extraordinary ministers of the eucharist, for the installation of a pastor.

Complementary volumes:

Catholic Household Blessings and Prayers: 1988 (USCC). This is the first attempt by the U.S. bishops since *A Manual of Prayers,* issued by the Baltimore Council of 1888, to provide a standard prayer book for the whole country.

Shorter Book of Blessings: 1990 (Catholic Book Publishing Company). An abridged form of the *Book of Blessings,* it contains most of the blessings that take place outside of Mass.

Forthcoming publication:

"Public Prayer after the Desecration of a Church," a supplement to the *Book of*

Blessings, will be released by the Vatican. In the meantime, helpful descriptions of this rite appear in the *Ceremonial of Bishops.*

IV. The *Roman Pontifical* includes those rites normally celebrated by a bishop. The *Blessing of Oil and Consecration of Chrism* has been included in the sacramentary. The rites for confirmation and for a church dedication, at least, should be in every liturgical library:

A. *Roman Pontifical, Part I:* 1978 (ICEL). Contains the now outdated rites of initiation, the institution of readers and acolytes, the various ordination rites, and several blessings of persons (blessing of an abbot/abbess and consecration to a life of virginity).

> Complementary volumes:
>
> *Confirmation:* 1973 (USCC; included in the ICEL pontifical).
>
> Forthcoming revision:
>
> Rome is revising the ordination rites.

B. *Dedication of a Church and an Altar:* the current edition was published in 1989 (USCC). An important resource for parishes undergoing renovation or construction; useful for parishes preparing for each year's anniversary.

V. Other official books:

The Ceremonial of Bishops: 1989 (The Liturgical Press). While not a liturgical book of texts, it is an official compilation of rubrics and of emendations made since the various ritual books were published. The notes are useful for charting celebrations for every parish.

> Forthcoming publication:
>
> Within a few years, the Vatican hopes to publish a ceremonial for parish churches.

LITURGICAL DOCUMENTS

The Code of Canon Law (Canon Law Society of America, 1983) contains a significant amount of legislation pertaining to the celebration of the liturgy. Pastoral decisions can be enhanced by knowledge of the appropriate canons.

Documents on the Liturgy, 1963–1979: Conciliar, Papal and Curial Texts (Collegeville: The Liturgical Press, 1982). A fine translation and compilation of everything official. The massive index makes this a goldmine of information.

Liturgy Documentary Series, #6: Norms Governing Liturgical Calendars (USCC, 1984). The "General Norms for the Liturgical year and Calendar" are accompanied by the official commentary released by the Vatican in the early 1970s, by the principles for particular calendars and by clarifications issued by the Vatican.

The Liturgy Documents (LTP, 1991 edition). The most recent translations of Roman liturgical documents are included along with documents of the Bishops' Committee on the Liturgy.

Roman Calendar: Text and Commentary (USCC, 1976). This official commentary, released by the Vatican, lists many of the principles used in preparing the current calendar.

ON THE REFORMS
OF THE ROMAN RITE

Botte, Bernard, *From Silence to Participation: An Insider's View of Liturgical Renewal* (Washington DC: The Pastoral Press, 1989). Particular attention is paid to the European liturgical movements before Vatican II.

Bugnini, Annibale, *The Reform of the Liturgy, 1948–1975* (Collegeville: The Liturgical Press, 1990). A thorough insiders' guide to the reform of the liturgical rites.

Chupungco, Anscar J., *Liturgies of the Future: The Process and Methods of Inculturation* (Mahwah NJ: Paulist Press, 1989). An important history of the reform of the liturgical books and insightful views of the future.

Finn, Peter C., and Schellman, James M., *Shaping English Liturgy: Studies in Honor of Archbishop Denis Hurley* (Washington DC: The Pastoral Press, 1990). A history of ICEL, of language, of lectionary and of culture, and their relationship within ritual reform.

Hughes, Kathleen, ed., *How Firm a Foundation, Volume I: Voices of the Early Liturgical Movement* (LTP, 1990). A study celebrating the early prophets and pioneers of the liturgical movement.

Krosnicki, Thomas A., *Ancient Patterns in Modern Prayer* (Washington DC: The Catholic University of America Press, 1973). A study of the prayers after communion and their reform.

Tuzik, Robert, ed., *How Firm a Foundation, Volume II: Leaders of the Liturgical Movement* (LTP, 1990). A review of the lives and work of 40 leaders of the last three generations.

White, Susan J., *Art, Architecture and Liturgical Reform: The Liturgical Arts Society, 1928–1972.* (New York: Pueblo Publishing Co., 1990).

HISTORY AND OBSERVANCE OF THE LITURGICAL YEAR

Works that treat specific seasons are found on page 12 (Advent-Christmas) and on page 85 (Lent-Triduum-Eastertime). Works on Ordinary Time and Sunday are listed at page 60.

Adam, Adolf, *The Liturgical Year: Its History and Its Meaning After the Reform of the Liturgy* (New York: Pueblo Publishing Co., 1981). One of the best studies available.

Alexander, J. Neil, *Time and Community* (Washington DC: The Pastoral Press, 1990). Serious essays on such topics as the lenten lectionary in the fourth century, the origins of candlemas, and "seeing liturgically."

Bishops' Committee on the Liturgy Secretariat, National Conference of Catholic Bishops, *Study Text 9: The Liturgical Year: Celebrating the Mystery of Christ and His Saints* (USCC, 1984).

Bishops' Committee on the Liturgy Secretariat, National Conference of Catholic Bishops, *Holy Days in the United States: History, Theology, Celebration* (USCC, 1984). With additional notes on the days in the American proper calendar as of 1984.

Carroll, Thomas, and Halton, Thomas, *Liturgical Practice in the Fathers* (Wilmington DE: Michael Glazier, Inc., 1988). Carefully chosen quotations and commentary on the various seasons and feasts as they developed in the first centuries.

Christ Our Light: Readings on Gospel Themes, 2 vols. (Ambler PA: Exordium Books, 1985). Wonderful quotations from early Christian sources on seasonal themes and the Sunday gospels.

Cobb, Peter, G., "The History of the Christian year," in Jones et al., *The Study of Liturgy* (London: SPCK, 1978).

Donovan, Kevin, "The Sanctoral," in Jones et al., *The Study of Liturgy* (London: SPCK, 1978).

Jounel, Pierre, see the Martimort listing to follow.

Klauser, Theodore, *A Short History of the Western Liturgy* (New York: Oxford University Press, 1979).

Martimort, A. G., et al., *The Church at Prayer* vol. 4, The Liturgy and Time (Collegeville: The Liturgical Press, 1986). See especially the essays by Pierre Jounel on Sunday and the year. All four volumes of this comprehensive, scholarly series are highly recommended. The first three volumes cover general principles, the eucharist and the sacraments.

Merton, Thomas, *Seasons of Celebration* (New York: Farrar, Straus and Giroux, 1983).

Nocent, Adrian, *The Liturgical Year,* 4 vols. (Collegeville: The Liturgical Press, 1977). Excellent commentaries on the liturgical seasons and scriptures.

Parsch, Pius, *The Church's Year of Grace,* 5 vols. (circulating in various editions, most notably: Collegeville: The Liturgical Press, 1957). These volumes comment on the old calendar and rites, but they still offer enormous assistance to contemporary readers, especially when looking for guidance to the previous generations' approach to the seasons and saints.

Perham, Michael, *The Communion of Saints: An Examination of the Place of the Christian Dead in the Belief, Worship and Calendars of the Church* (London: Alcuin Club/SPCK, 1980).

Power, David, ed., *The Times of Celebration,* Concilium, #142 (New York: Seabury Press, 1981). Groundbreaking essays on time, seasons, Sundays and local calendars.

Talley, Thomas J., *The Origins of the Liturgical Year* (New York: Pueblo Publishing Company, 1986). Greatly rewarding for the serious reader.

Thurston, Herbert, and Attwater, Donald, *Butler's Lives of the Saints,* 4 vols. (Westminster MD: Christian Classics, 1981). The only complete and reliable publication on the saints in English. Invaluable for researching additions to the litany of the saints and for discovering traditional days to celebrate titular festivals.

Weiser, Francis X., *Handbook of Christian Feasts and Customs* (various editions, including: New York: Paulist Press, 1963). Often available in libraries and used books stores; invaluable for its references to once-popular traditions.

Wegman, Herman, *Christian Worship in East and West* (New York: Pueblo Publishing Co., 1985).

Wilde, James A., ed., *At That Time: Cycles and Seasons in the Life of a Christian* (LTP, 1989).

LITURGICAL/PREACHING HELP

See page 60 for references on Luke, this year's evangelist.

Bishops' Committee on the Liturgy, National Conference of Catholic Bishops, *God's Mercy Endures Forever: Guidelines on the Presentation of Jews and Judaism in Catholic Preaching* (USCC, 1988).

Brown, Raymond, et al. *The New Jerome Biblical Commentary* (Englewood Cliffs NJ: Prentice Hall, 1990). The one volume on all the scriptures that should be in every Catholic library.

Ford, J. M., *Revelation,* Anchor Bible #38, (Garden City: Doubleday, 1975). This book of the Bible appears throughout Eastertime this year and on the last two weeks of the year.

Marcheschi, Graziano, and Marcheschi, Nancy Seitz, *Workbook for Lectors and Gospel Readers* (LTP, annual). Contains the lectionary texts with notes to help in understanding and proclaiming them.

Pawlikowski, John T., and Wilde, James A., *When Catholics Speak about Jews* (LTP, 1987. Notes for homilists, catechists and intercession writers—arranged by the liturgical year.

The Saint Andrew Bible Missal (Brooklyn: William J. Hirten Co., 1982). Contains insightful introductions to the liturgical seasons and to the readings, as well as attention to Christian initiation. The finest English missal available.

MUSIC RESOURCES

I. Hymnals

Cantate Domino (New York: Oxford University Press, 1980). The European ecumenical hymnal (the first edition was produced in the 1920s). An invaluable resource.

Cantemos Al Señor (Miami: Archdiocese of Miami, 1987) Liturgical music of Hispanics in Miami; relies heavily upon the style and rhythms of Cuba.

Catholic Book of Worship II (Ottawa: Canadian Conference of Catholic Bishops, and Toronto: Gordon V. Thompson, Limited, 1980). The Canadian national Catholic hymnal; currently undergoing revision.

The Catholic Liturgy Book (Baltimore: Helicon Press, Inc., 1975). A fine, early attempt at a service book, well edited.

The Collegeville Hymnal (Collegeville: The Liturgical Press, 1990). Contains new seasonal psalm settings and contributions by many Benedictine authors and composers.

Flor Y Canto (Portland: Oregon Catholic Press, 1990). Compiles music from the liturgical traditions of the European, Caribbean and American Spanish-speaking cultures.

Gather (Chicago: GIA Publications, Inc., 1988). The "contemporary" companion to *Worship*.

The Hymnal 1982 (New York: The Church Pension Fund, 1985). The Episcopalian hymnal. There's more chant in this volume than in any Catholic hymnal.

Hymnal for Catholic Students (Chicago: GIA Publications, Inc., and LTP, 1988). A basic book for grade-school students in parochial schools and religious education programs. Children can learn this repertoire and then carry this repertoire with them throughout their lives. The *Leaders' Manual* of this book is fundamental reading for anyone interested in public worship.

Hymnal for the Hours (Chicago: GIA Publications, Inc., 1989). A goldmine of hymnody.

Hymns, Psalms and Spiritual Canticles (Belmont MA: BACS Publishing Co., 1983). The great Theodore Marier's vision. It is idiosyncratic but spectacular.

ICEL Resource Collection (Chicago: GIA Publications, Inc., 1981). Hymns in the public domain and settings of service music for the rites by contemporary composers.

Lead Me, Guide Me, A Hymnal for African American Parishes (Chicago: GIA Publications, Inc., 1987). Many good selections, although some tend to emphasize an individualistic approach to salvation and redemption.

Lutheran Book of Worship (Minneapolis: Augsburg Publishing House, 1978). Very well-rounded. Classic chorale tunes often have been restored to their original rhythms.

Peoples Mass Book (Schiller Park IL: World Library Publications, Inc., 1984). A basic collection with lots of Lucien Deiss.

The Summit Choirbook (Summit NJ: The Dominican Nuns, Monastery of Our Lady of the Rosary, 1983). Wonderful tunes and texts, many from

WELCOME, YULE!
ADVENT AND CHRISTMASTIME 1991–1992

PASCHAL MISSION
LENT ★ TRIDUUM ★ EASTERTIME
March 1, 1992 to June 7, 1992

Use *Welcome, Yule!* in your parish

- To bring Christian meaning to the many traditions of the season
- As a gift to families, shut-ins, patients and inmates
- For prayer and discussion in the catechumenate, Bible study, religious education and parish renewal groups
- As a decorative reminder of all that these seasons bring

Your supply of *Welcome, Yule!* will be shipped to arrive before the First Sunday of Advent, December 1, 1991. It will be wrapped in multiples of 100 copies of each handout ready to be given to each household as folks leave church on Sundays or for ministers to take or send to those who cannot be present. A Poster/Calendar and a "How to Use" book with additional suggestions for use will be included with each order.

How much does it cost?

Welcome, Yule! is available in bulk. For example, if you order 500 copies you get 5 packages of an informative introduction to the season, 5 packages of 100 handouts for each of the seven Sundays, 5 packages of 100 prayer cards, and a **double order** (10 packages) of special handouts for Christmas to take care of extra attendance. (Sorry, we cannot provide packages of less than 100 or fill orders for individual Sundays.) The price is $50 per 100. An *Individual Packet* containing one of each handout, a poster and a "How to Use" guidebook is available for $5.00.

What is it?

PASCHAL MISSION lets Lent *be* Lent and Easter be a full fifty days. The series begins on the Sunday before Ash Wednesday with a handout that invites all to enter Lent seriously and joyfully. Then, every Sunday through Lent and Easter and all the way to Pentecost has a handsome leaflet with a calendar, reflections and seasonal activities for home and community.

How is it used?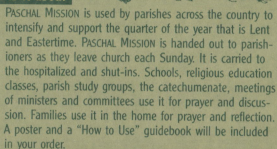

PASCHAL MISSION is used by parishes across the country to intensify and support the quarter of the year that is Lent and Eastertime. PASCHAL MISSION is handed out to parishioners as they leave church each Sunday. It is carried to the hospitalized and shut-ins. Schools, religious education classes, parish study groups, the catechumenate, meetings of ministers and committees use it for prayer and discussion. Families use it in the home for prayer and reflection. A poster and a "How to Use" guidebook will be included in your order.

How much is it?

PASCHAL MISSION is available by the set (17 different handouts) in lots of 100. The cost is about 5¢ per family each Sunday — less than a handout you would print yourself. The price is $80 per 100.

A packet containing one of each handout is also available for $5.00.

ORDER EARLY!
Lent begins March 4, 1992.

PASCHAL MISSION for 1992 will be available for shipment December 1, 1991.

SAVE!

Order bulk quantities of both *Welcome, Yule!* **and** PASCHAL MISSION **at the same time** and save 15% off the total cost. See LTP catalog (page 21) for details.

Order now from:

Liturgy Training Publications
1800 North Hermitage Avenue
Chicago IL 60622-1101

Phone: 1-800-933-1800
FAX: 1-800-933-7094

To inquire about orders or payments, call
1-800-933-4779.

ORDER FORM

Welcome, Yule! 1991–1992

Send ____ **Welcome, Yule!** for ____ families = _____

Send ____ Individual Packet(s) at $5.00 ea. = _____
(one of each leaflet)

Send ____ Calendar-posters at $2.00 ea. = _____

Welcome, Yule! Total = _____

PASCHAL MISSION 1992

Send ____ PASCHAL MISSION for ____ families = _____

Send ____ Individual Packet(s) at $5.00 ea. = _____
(one of each leaflet)

Send ____ Calendar-posters at $2.00 ea. = _____

PASCHAL MISSION Total = _____

If ordering both:
Welcome, Yule! Total _____ plus PASCHAL MISSION **Total** _____ = _____ **ORDER TOTAL**

Read carefully and choose your method of payment.

$ _____ Full payment enclosed. If sending full payment with order, add 5% for shipping and handling (10% for Canada; 15% for all other countries). Minimum of $2.00 U.S. fund only.

$ _____ Bill me. Minimum "bill me" order is $20. 10% for shipping and handling will be added to the bill. (15% for Canada; 20% for other countries.)

Bill to _____ Account # _____

Street address _____
(We ship UPS. Give street address. No PO boxes.)

City, State, Zip _____

Phone _____ Date ordered ___/___/___

If additional instructions are needed, please attach separate sheet. Keep a copy of your order for future reference.

304

THANK YOU FOR YOUR ORDER.

PASCHAL MISSION
LENT ★ TRIDUUM ★ EASTERTIME
March 1, 1992 to June 7, 1992

PASCHAL MISSION is the annual series of 17 bulletin inserts/
wrap-arounds for each week from the Sunday before
Ash Wednesday through Pentecost.

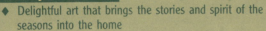

Each week you will find:

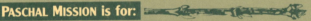

- ◆ Delightful art that brings the stories and spirit of the
  seasons into the home
- ◆ Stimulating meditations on the Sunday scripture
  readings
- ◆ Questions for all ages that invite discussion and
  reflection
- ◆ A calendar for customs and ideas for keeping Lent
  and Eastertime

Prayer cards for home use during the weeks of Lent and
Eastertime are included.

PASCHAL MISSION is for:

- ◆ Parishes that want Lent to be a strong time of initiation and renewal leading to the Easter Triduum
- ◆ Parishes that want help in welcoming catechumens
- ◆ Parishes that want Eastertime to be a season of
  enthusiastic celebration that lasts until Pentecost
- ◆ All parishioners each Sunday and for small groups as
  well: renewal programs, prayer groups, Bible study
  groups and gatherings of catechumens and sponsors

Use this card to order PASCHAL MISSION 1992.

WELCOME, YULE!
ADVENT AND CHRISTMASTIME 1991–1992

A gift for each household

The annual series of beautiful handouts to bring home the
seasons of Advent and Christmastime in your parish. Plan
now to provide your parish families with these handouts
for the coming Advent/Christmas season.

What's in *Welcome, Yule?*

- ◆ Reflections on the comfort and joy of the Sunday
  scriptures
- ◆ Beautifully illustrated blessing prayers for wreath, food,
  lights, tree, crèche, home and new year
- ◆ A weekly calendar full of customs, seasonal lore and
  ideas for sharing charity and hospitality
- ◆ The week's scripture citations and songs to sing
  at home

How many different handouts?

Ten! An introduction to the seasons and their observance.
A leaflet for each of the Sundays of Advent and Christmastime. Prayer cards to use at the dinner table. We even
include **a double order** of the Christmas leaflet so you
can give something special to the many people who
attend this day.

Use the other side to order Welcome, Yule!
from Liturgy Training Publications.

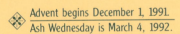
Advent begins December 1, 1991.
Ash Wednesday is March 4, 1992.

Liturgy Training Publications
1800 North Hermitage Avenue
Chicago IL 60622-1101

| Place |
| 19¢ Postage |
| Here |

◀ **Use this card to
ORDER NOW!**

☎ **Phone Orders
Welcome:
1-800-933-1800**
🖷 **or FAX:
1-800-933-7094**

Liturgy Training Publications
1800 North Hermitage Avenue
Chicago IL 60622-1101

the richly imaginative "office hymns." The non-inclusive language is puzzling, however. A fine choirbook.

Worship, Third Edition (Chicago: GIA Publications, Inc., 1986). Well-rounded American Catholic service book and hymnal. Leans heavily on English hymnody.

II. Musical Resources for Liturgy of the Hours

Throughout this *Sourcebook* there are references to parish celebrations of the Liturgy of the Hours. The publications listed here provide full settings. Titles listed in the "hymnals" section may also offer orders of service, prayer texts, and musical settings of invitatories, office hymns, psalms, intercessions and canticles.

Christian Prayer, organ accompaniment. Various composers (Washington DC: ICEL, 1978).

Holden Evening Prayer. Marty Haugen (Chicago: GIA Publications, Inc., 1990).

Hymnal for the Hours (Chicago: GIA Publications, Inc., 1989).

Light and Peace (Morning Praise and Evensong). David Haas (Chicago: GIA Publications, Inc., 1986).

Nightsong: Music for Evening Prayer. Howard Hughes, SM (Chicago: World Library Publications, 1989).

O Joyful Light. Michael Joncas (Phoenix: North American Liturgy Resources, 1985).

Praise God in Song: Ecumenical Daily Prayer. Compiled and edited by John Allyn Melloh, SM, and William G. Storey with original music by David Clark Isele, Howard Hughes, SM, and Michael Joncas (Chicago: GIA Publications, Inc., 1979).

Praise God in Song: Ecumenical Night Prayer. Compiled and edited by John Allyn Melloh, SM, and William G. Storey with original music by David Clark Isele, Howard Hughes, SM, and Michael Joncas (Chicago: GIA Publications, Inc., 1982).

Worship, Third Edition Liturgy of the Hours Leaders' Edition (Chicago: GIA Publications, Inc., 1989).

III. Psalm Resources

These collections of responsorial psalmody are available as individual publications. Many contain reprintable refrains, allowing a parish to expand the assembly's possibilities for psalmody by purchasing one book for cantor and one for the accompanying instrument.

The Gelineau Gradual. Responsorial psalms for the lectionary for Mass for the Sundays and principal feasts of the liturgical year. (Chicago: GIA Publications, Inc., 1977).

The Gelineau Gradual, Volume II. Responsorial Psalms from the lectionary for Mass for the rites of the church. (Chicago: GIA Publications, Inc., 1979).

The Grail Gelineau Psalter. 150 Psalms and 18 Canticles (Chicago: GIA Publications, Inc., 1972).

Grail Psalms Inclusive Language Version (text only) (Chicago: GIA Publications, Inc., 1983).

ICEL Lectionary Music. Psalms and alleluia and gospel acclamations for the liturgy of the word. Various composers (Chicago: GIA Publications, Inc., 1982).

PsalmBook. Various composers (Phoenix: Epoch/NALR, 1991).

Psalms and Selected Canticles. Robert Kreutz (Portland: Oregon Catholic Press, 1983).

Psalms for All Seasons: From the ICEL Liturgical Psalter Project. Various composers (Washington, DC: NPM Publications, 1987).

Psalms for the Cantor, Volumes I–VII. Various composers (Schiller Park: World Library Publications, 1985-1987).

Psalms for the Church Year. Marty Haugen and David Haas (Chicago: GIA Publications, Inc., 1983).

Psalms for the Church Year, Volume II. Marty Haugen (Chicago: GIA Publications, Inc., 1988).

Psalms for the Church Year, Volume III. David Haas and Jeanne Cotter (Chicago: GIA Publications, Inc., 1989).

Psalms for the Church Year. David Clark Isele (Chicago: GIA Publications, Inc., 1979).

Psalms for Feasts and Seasons. Christopher Willcock, SJ. (Melbourne: Dove Communications, 1977; distributed by Cooperative Ministries).

Psalms for Singing. Stephen Somerville. (Schiller Park: World Library Publications, 1976).

Psalms for Sundays and Seasons. Twelve psalms for soloist, choir and congregation. Jim Hansen (Waco: Chancel Music, 1984; distributed by Oregon Catholic Press).

Psalter. Steven Warner (Chicago: GIA Publications, Inc., 1990).

Respond and Acclaim, Cycle C. Owen Alstott (Portland: Oregon Catholic Press, 1991).

Salmos. Manuel F. Garcia (Portland: Oregon Catholic Press, 1984).

Service Music for the Mass, Volumes 1–5. Various composers (Schiller Park: J.S. Paluch Company, Inc., 1988–1989).

PERIODICALS

Assembly (Notre Dame: Center for Pastoral Liturgy). Five times a year. Each issue explores the tradition, meaning and practice of some aspect of the liturgical event in order to help the community and its ministers enter more deeply into the spirit of the liturgy.

Bishops' Committee on the Liturgy Newsletter (USCC). Ten times a year.

Catechumenate: A Journal of Christian Initiation (LTP). Six times a year. Each issue contains pastoral and scholarly writing on the topics concerning initiation.

Environment & Art Letter (LTP). Twelve times a year. Explores the issues concerning the environment for worship, both permanent and seasonal.

Liturgy (Washington DC: The Liturgical Conference). Quarterly. The Journal of The Liturgical Conference, an ecumenical organization. Each issue explores a single aspect of liturgy, usually taking in many disciplines and many church traditions. Back issues are available and are excellent resources.

Liturgy 90 (LTP). Eight times a year. Features articles on the seasons and sacraments, regular columns on music, environment and art, questions and answers.

National Bulletin on Liturgy (Ottawa: National Liturgical Office, Canadian Catholic Conference). Four times a year. Each issue explores one topic in detail, often with extensive bibliographies. Many of the "thematic" back issues of this fine journal are still available.

Pastoral Music (Washington DC: National Association of Pastoral Musicians). Six times a year.

Often contains several major articles on a single theme together with reviews and announcements. Centers on music but touches on all areas of liturgy.

Worship (Collegeville: The Order of St. Benedict). Six times a year. Scholarly journal which, since 1926, has been the primary support of liturgical renewal throughout the English-speaking world. Order from The Liturgical Press.

Addresses of Publishers

Archdiocese of Miami
9401 Biscayne Boulevard
PO Box 382000
Miami FL 33238-2000

Augsburg Publishing House/Fortress Press
426 South 5th Street
Box 1209
Minneapolis MN 55440
(one among many locations)

Ave Maria Press
Notre Dame IN 46556

(BACS) Boston Archdiocese Choir School
34 Mt. Auburn Street
Cambridge MA 02138

Canadian Conference of Catholic Bishops
90 Parent Avenue
Ottawa, Ontario K1N 7B1, Canada

Canon Law Society of America
Catholic University of America
Washington DC 20064

Catholic Book Publishing Company
257 West 17th Street
New York NY 10011

Catholic University of America Press
620 Michigan Avenue, N.E.
Washington DC 20064

Center for Pastoral Liturgy
PO Box 81
Notre Dame IN 46556

Christian Classics, Inc.
Box 30
Westminster MD 21157

Church Hymnal Corporation
800 Second Avenue
New York NY 10017

Collins Liturgical Publications
187 Piccadilly
London W1V 9DA England

Cooperative Ministries
PO Box 4463
Washington DC 20017

Daughters of St. Paul
50 St. Paul's Avenue
Boston MA 02130

Doubleday
Division of Bantam Doubleday Dell
Publishing Group, Inc.
666 Fifth Avenue
New York NY 10103

Exordium Books
PO Box 20840
Riverdale MD 20840

Farrar, Straus & Giroux, Inc.
19 Union Square, West
New York NY 10003

GIA Publications
7404 South Mason Avenue
Chicago IL 60638

Michael Glazier, Inc.
1935 West Fourth Street
Wilmington DE 19805

William J. Hirten Company
6100 17th Avenue
Brooklyn NY 11204

ICEL (International Committee
on English in the Liturgy)
1275 K Street NW
Suite 1202
Washington DC 20005-4097

The Liturgical Conference
1017 12th Street NW
Washington DC 20005

The Liturgical Press
St. John's Abbey
Collegeville MN 56321

Monastery of Our Lady of the Rosary
Morris and Springfield Avenue
Summit NJ 07901

NALR (North American Liturgy Resources)
10802 North 23rd Avenue
Phoenix AZ 85029

NPM (National Association
of Pastoral Musicians)
225 Sheridan Street NW
Washington DC 20011

Order of St. Benedict
St. John's Abbey
Collegeville MN

OCP (Oregon Catholic Press)
5536 NE Hassalo
Portland OR 97213

Oxford University Press
200 Madison Avenue
New York NY 10016

Pastoral Press
220 Sheridan Street NW
Washington DC 20011

Paulist Press
992 Macarthur Boulevard
Mahwah NJ 07430

Prentice-Hall
Division of Schuster, Inc.
The Simon & Schuster Building
1230 Avenue of the Americas
New York NY 10020

Pueblo Publishing Company
(Now published by The Liturgical Press)

The Seabury Press
℅ Harper and Row Publishers, Inc.
10 East 53rd Street
New York NY 10022

SPCK (Society for Promoting Christian
Knowledge)
(Alcuin Club)
Sheldon Press–Triangle Trade Enqueries
Holy Trinity Church
Marlebone Road
London NW1 England

Twenty-third Publications
185 Willow Street
PO Box 180
Mystic CT 06355

USCC (United States Catholic Conference)
3211 Fourth Street, NE
Washington DC 20017-1194

World Library Publications
3815 North Willow Road
Schiller Park IL 60176

ADVENT

*December is the time for expressing the hope and strengthening the dreams that
will carry us through the year. Advent is the way we as church express our hopes.
Prophetic visions and prayers calling for the Lord to come put us in touch
with the most profound levels of human hoping. Advent lets us do what most others do in
December—but to see in the coming Lord the answer to our dreams.
In our Catholic tradition, keeping Advent means singing the songs of
expectation—savoring our hopes and longing before we enter into the full-throated praise
of Christmas carols.*

Images of the Season

Advent has a twofold character: as a season to prepare for Christmas when Christ's first coming to us is remembered; as a season when that remembrance directs the mind and the heart to await Christ's second coming at the end of time. Advent is thus a period for devout and joyful expectation. (*General Norms for the Liturgical Year and Calendar,* #39)

ALL humans cherish hope. They possess a natural inclination to desire transformation, fullness and peace. Urban parishioners pray daily for an end to violence on the streets. Citizens everywhere long for an economy that gives them their fair share. The disenfranchised, the sick and all who are sensitive to the imperfections of our world want justice and peace. No matter how blessed we are, we always want and need more.

These inclinations are right at the surface of expression in December in most Western societies. They find imperfect but real outlets in the cultural practices of the holiday season. December is a season of hope not just inside those Christian churches that keep Advent; it is a privileged and much-loved time for expressing hope in public, for working to restore others' hopes, for strengthening the dreams that carry us through the entire year. We can recognize even in the rush to the shopping malls a certain impetus, the urge of nature craving light, grace, gifts and beauty.

■ STRUCTURE FOR OUR HOPING: In the midst of the hopes and dreams of our society, Advent is passed on to us as our church's way to express our dreams. The language-world of Advent, the scriptures, prayers and hymns, can inform and inspire all who come to liturgy. Before we approach the tasks of planning the catechetics and liturgies for this month, we must know Advent's power to structure our dreams of transformation. We must be convinced that the prophets, the eschatological visions and the expectation of salvation put us in touch with the most profound levels of human hoping. Advent lets us do what most others do in December— but it invites us to see in the coming Lord the answer to our dreams.

This invitation into Advent requires a certain distance from rampant commercialism and hedonism. Ranting against the department stores' excesses produces little; we would do better to focus our efforts—over the years and with great respect—on helping the people with whom we celebrate the sacraments to recognize the transformation they seek, to see what "wanting more" really means.

Keeping Advent also implies a sense of timing different from the rest of our society, indeed a sense of the season quite different from that held by many Christian communities. To hear the sounds of hoping and dreaming, the Catholic tradition says that we must discipline ourselves in our liturgical gatherings and in our households. The wisdom of our ancestors is that we must savor the longing for weeks before we jump into the full-throated praise of the incarnation. The gentle singing of our dreams, the repeated invocations ("Come, Lord Jesus!"), the attention given to the "end-time" all need their own space and time. Appeals not to spoil Christmas by "jumping the gun" phrased in authoritarian or negative language are both trite and counterproductive. It is not Christmas that we must worry about, rather it is that Advent will be spoiled and its treasures missed.

This patient "holding back," this exorcism of crass materialism, this call to Christian hope shape our affections and form us as a people who find light and grace in the Lord. This is what the liturgy of Advent means. The liturgy never can be reduced to a set of paragraphs on the liturgical books. The liturgy of Advent becomes most fully realized when the liturgical tradition and its books are opened in the midst of a catechized, faithful people.

■ STRUCTURING THE SEASON: The liturgical books, especially the sacramentary, the lectionary and the *Liturgy of the Hours,* give words and images to Advent. They do this in terms of the two comings of Christ mentioned in the *General Norms.* Hope in these two comings provides two distinct periods in Advent: From December 17 until Christmas Eve, the texts focus more on the coming at Bethlehem; that is, they "serve to prepare more directly for the Lord's birth" (*General Norms for the Liturgical Year and Calendar,* #42). Earlier in Advent, the coming of the Lord in glory, the fullness of our hope for the future, provides many of the words for our assemblies. Yet these two comings—and these two parts of Advent—cannot be seen in isolation. Expectation is the natural response to the approach of Christmas, which, in turn, awakens in Christians a vibrant anticipation of the final coming.

Thomas Merton, in one of the essays collected in *Seasons of Celebration,* reviewed the way Bernard of Clairvaux approached the comings of Christ. The first advent was Christ's birth. The other will be at the end of time. Faith in these two stimulates recognition of a third, the advent of Christ in our church now, today.

Viewed from this perspective, the Advent liturgy is neither a romantic return to the Old Testament while we wait for the baby at Bethlehem, nor is it an exercise in expressing hope for an ever-receding parousia. The Advent liturgy is neither nostalgic nor illusory. When parish communities take the tradition and enter it fully, they "become" Advent, the people in and through whom Christ comes.

■ THE SAINTS IN ADVENT: Joining us in this season are the saints whose memories and stories are kept during these December days. Our Advent tradition gives a special place of honor to the Blessed Virgin Mary. We celebrate the great solemnity of the Immaculate Conception, this year transferred to December 7. Catholics in the United States observe a feast from the Mexican tradition, Our Lady of Guadalupe, on December 12. The last Sunday of Advent focuses on her role in salvation history. It is a season singularly suited to veneration of the Mother of God; in it, we see her role in the preparation for the first coming and her keeping vigil with us before the final coming. The traditional images of the Immaculate Conception and of Our Lady of Guadalupe are remarkably eschatological. We could not ask for more fitting pictures for Advent—a woman clothed in the sun and stars, striking out at evil.

Other saints' days during Advent are fewer in number than during the rest of the year. Liturgical reformers, both after Vatican II and at earlier periods in the church's history, have tried to keep Advent, Christmastime, Lent, Triduum and Eastertime as free from saints' days as possible. If saints are honored during these weeks, it should be in the spirit of the season. The *cultus* of the saints (that is, liturgical and devotional memory-keeping) can sharpen our longing for the heavenly Jerusalem and help us enter into Advent's grand image-world of light and darkness.

Preparing the Parish

You have many things to do as fall passes and December becomes marked by ever-more frenetic activity. *Sourcebook* can help you prepare liturgical gatherings for your parish.

In these assemblies, we will have the awesome task of retraining our desires, of reshaping our expectations, of modifying our affections. This task is ours throughout the year, but Advent lets us become more explicit and more intense about this aspect of our life together.

Our Advent tasks begin outside the sanctuary. Our parish schools, parish halls and all the homes of parishioners should reflect Advent's sober patience. This demands a lot of catechesis on the value of giving Advent and its traditions their own time before the quite different sounds of Christmas. This is another way of calling for us to reclaim our Catholic calendar. Until the calendar we keep at worship becomes the calendar we live by, our worship will be but a shadow of what it can be. The year-in, year-out witness of care and patience best teaches Advent's values. We must gradually fix the calendar items over which we have control: one year saving the parish's Christmas party until after December 25, the next year moving the pageant or the lessons and carols to the Epiphany.

■ RELIGIOUS EDUCATION: Parishioners who grew up with a full Advent season and who have successfully waited for Christmas in their own homes may write brief testimonies for the Sunday bulletin or speak to religious education gatherings. People can share family or ethnic Advent customs. Because the Advent wreath is essentially a home custom, it is wise to help all parish households keep this custom by teaching people about it during November and asking artisans to show examples.

■ MATERIALS FOR THE HOME: Advent is a good season to make *Catholic Household Blessings and Prayers* available for purchase. Additional home prayer materials could include a sheet or booklet typed up with weekly Advent prayers (perhaps chosen from the sacramentary collects), or LTP's little pocket prayer book, *Keeping Advent and Christmastime,* as well as its annual series of Sunday handouts for Advent and Christmastime, *Welcome, Yule!* An *Advent*

Sourcebook, a wonderful treasury of seasonal lyrics, poetry and prose for day-by-day reading and reflection, also is published by LTP.

The Mass

INTRODUCTORY RITES

THE Advent liturgy may begin with the usual procession to and reverencing of the altar: While the opening antiphon and psalm or the opening hymn is sung, the presider and ministers make a profound bow before the altar and the presider goes to the altar and kisses it. The music continues as the altar is honored with incense; the Advent wreath also may be incensed.

An alternative structuring of the opening rites can be considered for the season, especially if the Advent wreath is in the entranceway or hanging over the assembly. The liturgy would begin with a call to face the wreath (with the ministers standing near the wreath, perhaps with the processional cross and incense held underneath it). Then the sign of the cross, the greeting and introductory words and even the penitential rite are sung or said, followed by the incensing of the wreath and the people, then the procession to the chair. The incensation and procession are accompanied by the entrance psalm or hymn. At the chair, the presider proclaims the opening prayer.

■ PUBLIC LIGHTING OF THE WREATH: Whatever pattern is outlined for your community, the perspective of chapter 47 of the *Book of Blessings* must be adopted. On the First Sunday of Advent, the wreath's first candle is lit after the blessing of the wreath—which takes place after the general intercessions. Regarding the following Sundays, the *Book of Blessings* states: "When the Advent wreath is used in church, on the Second and succeeding Sundays of Advent, the candles are lighted either before Mass begins or immediately before the opening prayer; no additional rites or prayers are used" (*Book of Blessings,* #1513). This is meant as a corrective to those places where the lighting of the wreath took on too much prominence.

■ SELECTING TEXTS: While decisions about the ritual order are important, considerable care also is required when framing the texts for Advent's Sundays and feasts. One greeting, selected from the sacramentary or from the *Book of Blessings* (#1549 or #1577), should be used at all major assemblies during the season. Invocations C*ii* of the penitential rite (in the sacramentary) are appropriate for the Sundays of Advent and can be chanted throughout the season. They blend well the three comings we think of during this season—past, present and future. The musical setting of the penitential rite for the Sundays of Advent (GIA, G-3099) by Robert Hutmacher is well worth preparing. Other ideas for these texts are found on page 18.

LITURGY OF THE WORD

The lectionary is replete with Isaiah's images during these weeks. Other prophets are read during Advent, but none with the same frequency. Biblical commentaries that identify the different parts of Isaiah, each part with its unique approach, should be high on the reading lists of liturgical planners and preachers during Advent. (Several helpful commentaries are listed on page 12 under "Liturgical/Preaching Help.") Yet scholarly reviews must never eclipse our ability to proclaim and to hear the wondrous dreams, our ability to be stirred and inspired, to be shaped by the sure hope in the future coming.

■ INTERVALS OF SILENCE: The brevity and simplicity of the introductory rites direct attention to how the scripture passages are proclaimed. The introduction to the lectionary (#28) suggests a period of quiet settling in before the readings begin, then silence again after the readings and again after the homily:

> The liturgy of the word must be celebrated in a way that fosters meditation; clearly, any sort of haste that hinders reflectiveness must be avoided. The dialogue between God and God's people taking place through the Holy Spirit demands short intervals of silence suited to the assembly as an opportunity to take the word of God to heart and to prepare a response to it in prayer.

■ INTRODUCTIONS: Each liturgy of the word can begin with a brief and poetic introduction, drawing the congregation into the context of the scriptures about to be proclaimed. These introductions are not to become additional sermons before each reading, nor may they narrow the rich images into a single lesson we are supposed to draw from what we are about to hear. The U.S. appendix to the *General Instruction of the Roman Missal* (printed at the front of the sacramentary) includes a fuller description of what such introductions can be (#11).

■ THE PSALM: The seasonal responsorial psalms and the seasonal psalm responses often bring us to the heart of a season. As listed in #174–75 of the lectionary, they chart the church's journey through the paschal mystery. Advent's seasonal psalm response picks up on the prophetic call, "Come, O Lord, and set us free." Sung with each Sunday's proper psalm, this urges us into an attitude of watchful supplication. Even when other options are selected for the psalms, this sentence can become our Advent companion, whispered and sung and breathed through these dark days.

The two seasonal psalms listed are equally evocative. Psalms 25 and 85 call on the Lord with sure confidence. Taken together, these treasures from the *Book of Psalms* help us read the other scriptural passages and liturgical texts with our hearts attuned to their message of wondrous hope. This Advent, Psalm 25 is recommended for use throughout the season. It appears as the proper psalm for the First Sunday of Advent, December 16 and December 23. A few recommended musical settings for Psalm 25 include:

- James Chepponis, "Lord, I give myself to you," verses 1, 2 and 4 (*Psalms for All Seasons:* From the ICEL Liturgical Psalter Project, NPM)
- Marty Haugen, "To you, O Lord" (*Psalms for the Church Year,* GIA, G-2664)
- Robert E. Kreutz, "Come, O Lord" (*Psalms and Selected Canticles,* Oregon Catholic Press)
- Fintan P. O'Carroll, "Psalm 25: Make me know your ways" (*The Collegeville Hymnal*)
- Christopher Willcock, "To you, O Lord" (*Psalms for Feasts and Seasons,* Cooperative Ministries)

■ GOSPEL ACCLAMATIONS: At #193 and #202, the lectionary contains small treasures for catechists and liturgical planners, indeed for anyone who wants to learn the words of the season. Twenty-one verses from the scriptures and from our ancient traditions are listed as gospel acclamations for the weekdays of Advent. They also provide a compendium of the season, gems for meditation and sources for our daily prayer. The seven listed for late Advent are the revered

"O Antiphons," borrowed from the evening prayer celebrations of the week before Christmas. A parish may select a few of these for this Advent, repeating them often to facilitate a true "learning by heart."

■ SUNDAY GOSPELS IN ADVENT: Year C is the year of Luke; three of the Sundays' gospel passages are taken from this gospel. As explained in the introduction to the lectionary (#93):

> Each gospel reading has a distinctive theme: the Lord's coming at the end of time (First Sunday of Advent), John the Baptist (Second and Third Sunday) and the events that prepared immediately for the Lord's birth (Fourth Sunday).

■ THE WEEKDAY LECTIONARY, read continuously except on December 7 and 12, also is described in the introduction (#94):

> In the first part of Advent there are readings from Isaiah, distributed in accord with the sequence of the book itself and including salient texts that are also read on the Sundays. For the choice of the weekday gospel, the first reading has been taken into consideration.
>
> On the Thursday of the second week the readings of the gospel about John the Baptist begin. The first reading is either a continuation of Isaiah or a text chosen in view of the gospel.
>
> In the last week before Christmas the events that immediately prepared for the Lord's birth are presented from Matthew (chapter 1) and Luke (chapter 1). The texts in the first reading, chosen in view of the gospel reading, are from different Old Testament books and include important messianic prophecies.

■ THE PRESENTATION OF JEWS AND JUDAISM: These references to the first reading in the light of the gospel, and vice versa, should alert sensitive homilists to the relationship between what we call the Old and the New Testaments. The Jewish Scriptures never can be seen as a mere prelude to Christ's coming. The prophetic passages should be read with a full appreciation of their promise to all of us. In 1988, the United States Bishops' Committee on the Liturgy issued a powerfully worded booklet on the presentation of Jews and Judaism in Catholic preaching, *God's Mercy Endures Forever.* Available from the United States Catholic Conference (USCC) Publications Office, it draws from the wisdom of earlier statements from the Holy See's Commission for Religious Relations with the Jews. It is well worth reading, discussing and internalizing, because the work of shaping a parish's experience of Advent never can be far from its concerns. Its remarks about Advent (#11) are worth quoting as an example:

> The lectionary readings from the prophets are selected to bring out the ancient Christian theme that Jesus is the "fulfillment" of the biblical message of hope and promise, the inauguration of the "days to come" described, for example, by the daily Advent Masses, and on Sundays by Isaiah in Cycle A and Jeremiah in Cycle C for the First Sunday of Advent. This truth needs to be framed very carefully. Christians believe that Jesus is the promised Messiah who has come (see Luke 4:22), but also know that his messianic kingdom is not yet fully realized. The ancient messianic prophecies are not merely temporal predictions but profound expressions of eschatological hope. Since this dimension can be misunderstood or even missed altogether, the homilist needs to raise clearly the hope found in the prophets and heightened in the proclamation of Christ. This hope includes trust in what is promised but not yet seen. While the biblical prophecies of an age of universal *shalom* are "fulfilled" (i.e., irreversibly inaugurated) in Christ's coming, that fulfillment is not yet completely worked out in each person's life or perfected in the world at large (1974 *Guidelines* II). It is the mission of the Church, as also that of the Jewish people, to proclaim and to work to prepare the world for the full flowering of God's Reign, which is, but is "not yet" (cf. 1974 *Guidelines,* II). Both the Christian "Our Father" and the Jewish *Kaddish* exemplify this message. Thus, both Christianity and Judaism seal their worship with a common hope: "Thy kingdom come!"

■ DISMISSAL OF THE CATECHUMENS: If catechumens are present in your assembly, they can be sent forth with words of dismissal that allude to this season of our dreams. (See the sample text on page 18.)

■ GENERAL INTERCESSIONS: A set of intercessions for Advent is given on page 18. These, like all those offered in this book, are proposed as a pattern, not as a prescription. They should be repeated each week of Advent, sometimes with weekly adaptations, sometimes exactly the same. They also must be adapted to each community's setting. Too often a lack of understanding of these prayers leads them to become anything but general. The specific needs of local concern and immediate interest must find a place in the explicit prayer of the parish, but these should be within the wider context of the world, the church and the poor. Of course, a careful balance is called for here: On the one hand, universal needs cannot be forgotten and, on the other hand, communities need direct references and prayers for those who, for example, are living with AIDS, preparing for first eucharist or celebrating wedding anniversaries. The prayers in this book can provide a seasonal and universal skeleton for adding local flesh.

LITURGY OF THE EUCHARIST

■ EUCHARISTIC PRAYER: The preface during most of the season (until December 16) is Advent Preface I. As the season moves toward the birth of Christ (December 17–24), the more urgent and emotion-filled words of Advent Preface II are used. For the rest of the eucharistic prayer, care must be taken in the selection and in the week-by-week consistency of the prayer. Many parishes select the second Eucharistic Prayer for Reconciliation for all of Advent. This is a powerful text when proclaimed well. Its conclusion is a celebration of the gathering of all creation into the messianic banquet.

■ COMMUNION RITE: During the seasons of Advent, Christmas, Lent and Easter, this rite can take on a seasonal tone, explicitly expressing the church's journey through the year. See page 20 for examples: an introduction to the Lord's Prayer, a prayer at the peace greeting and an invitation to communion.

"My soul in stillness waits" by Marty Haugen (GIA, G-2652) and Jacques Berthier's "Wait for the Lord" (Taizé; GIA, G-2778) are effective for the communion procession; this also can be a place to use "O come, O come, Emmanuel" and responsorial-style settings of the Magnificat such as "Magnificat" by James Chepponis (GIA, G-2302) and "Our Lady's song of praise" by Richard Arnandez, a chantlike setting found in the J. S. Paluch *We Celebrate* hymnal.

CONCLUDING RITE

■ DISMISSAL OF MINISTERS BEARING THE EUCHARIST FOR THE HOMEBOUND: This can take on a seasonal form as noted in the texts for the eucharistic assembly, page 20.

■ BLESSING AND DISMISSAL: Let one Advent blessing and one dismissal be chosen and memorized by the presider and deacon for all the Sunday Masses of the season. Solemn Blessing 1 from the sacramentary would be appropriate

throughout the season. See the other example on page 20.

MUSIC

■ THE SOUND OF ADVENT: What does "devout and joyful expectation" sound like in our assemblies? We can hear it for ourselves when texts, melodies, arrangements and performance styles during Advent allow those gathered to express their faith, trust and hope in the promise of Christ's coming.

■ KEEPING THE TREASURES: When those in leadership roles pay attention and listen to what the assembly is saying through the quantity and quality of its participation, the decision of what music to keep from one Advent to the next and what to revise becomes easier. A wealth of songs, psalmody and hymnody is available for this brief season, and the temptation to prepare a new set of Advent music for each year is great. Our pastoral sense must remind us that a worthy piece, well performed, can bring people into the spirit of the season year after year.

With this principle in mind, consider again the traditional chant, "Conditor alme siderum." Several translations are available; see "Creator of the stars of night" in *Worship* (GIA) and *The Collegeville Hymnal* (LP). The translation in the *Hymnal for the Hours* (GIA) is poetic and effective, but omit verse five unless used for the Evening Prayer.

A fresh, engaging Advent text wedded to a lively tune ("Gaudeamus pariter") is "When the king shall come again" in *Worship* (GIA). The images in verse three are sure to bring delight. Worthy and refreshing imagery is also the strength of "People look east," set to a lilting traditional French tune that is easily learned and remains enjoyable throughout the season.

The text of "Savior of the nations, come," found in different translations and with various verses in several hymnals, refers to the three comings of Christ that we encounter this season; *The Collegeville Hymnal* allows this melody ("Nun komm, der heiden heiland") to move through the Christmas season by offering alternate verses for the Epiphany and the Baptism of the Lord. The Taizé ostinato refrain "Wait for the Lord" also can be effective in unifying the season as well as the assembly.

■ O COME, O COME EMMANUEL: Finally, as we listen and decide what music should remain consistently in the parish Advent repertoire, and where there is room for expression, we are sure to find "O come, O come Emmanuel" in the balance. This is a well-known and time-honored sound of Advent, to be sure, but not the only sound! "O come, O come Emmanuel" need not be sung every Sunday; it probably is best reserved for the last week of Advent when the O Antiphons are properly used as a final preparation for the great feast of Christmas.

Other Ritual Prayer and Sacraments

ADVENT'S extraordinary power and emotion —nor that of any season—cannot be released solely in the weekly eucharistic gathering. Gatherings for other liturgical forms, domestic prayer and public devotions are but a few of the activities we should be fostering in a Christian community. Even though people are unusually busy at this time of year, they are hungry for an antidote to the shopping season. Consider ways that the prayer of this season may be nurtured outside of the Mass.

LITURGY OF THE HOURS

■ RESTORING THE HOURS: Vespers (Evening Prayer) is becoming more a part of the worshiping community's life in many parishes, especially on Sundays and during the preparatory seasons. Much of Advent's prayer seems to arise within the darkness of a wintry evening; Vespers provides a perfect context for the ritual candle lighting that the Advent wreath invites. The liturgy of Evening Prayer can become a regular part of the parish's life, scheduled every day or every Sunday throughout the year or every Sunday in the preparatory and festive seasons. The prayer should not be scheduled just for "theme days" that may draw a crowd. They must become a part of the regular fabric of parish life.

Many in our midst hope for the day when the entire schedule of the liturgy of the hours, or at least Morning Prayer and Evening Prayer, becomes a part of parish life. Then this ancient

liturgy, the very breath of the church, will be rescued from its often narrow audience and its all-too-frequent degradation to a privately read exercise by observant clergy and perhaps a small number of the laity.

Once the regular schedule of Evening Prayer has taken root on Sunday, parishes can begin to extend its familiar format to other special days. The memorial of Lucy (December 13, a Friday this year) and the feast of Our Lady of Guadalupe (December 12) are appropriate days for special evening celebrations—perhaps followed by Advent music concerts or other festivities honoring the virgin martyr of Advent or the "Virgin Mother of the Americas."

■ BLESSING THE WREATH: The *Book of Blessings* (BB), in chapter 47, suggests Evening Prayer I of the First Sunday of Advent as an appropriate setting for the blessing of the Advent wreath and the lighting of its first candle. The liturgy of Evening Prayer, modified to include these elements, looks like this:

- introduction (but not a *lucernarium*), hymn, psalmody, reading (perhaps of Isaiah as in BB, #1526), homily, silence, responsory, gospel canticle (Magnificat), all as usual
- intercessions (BB, #1530)
- Lord's Prayer (as introduced in BB, #1531)
- prayer of blessing (BB, #1532 or #1533)
- lighting of the first candle
- concluding rite (BB, #1534)

Parishes that regularly begin the celebration of Evening Prayer with a service of light *(lucernarium)* may use the prayer of blessing from the *Book of Blessings* and light the first candle at the start of the celebration. Then the first Advent candle will be the light praised in hymn and thanksgiving. (In subsequent weeks, at Evening Prayer the Advent candles would be used for this *lucernarium*.)

■ OFFICE OF READINGS (VIGILS): The practice of keeping vigil together, recommended in earlier *Sourcebooks* at least for the solemnities of the year, has much to offer a parish. People who join in worship on the eve of great feasts or on Saturday nights during the seasons can be formed in the spirit of the church. The liturgy of the Office of Readings (Vigils) may seem new, but it is more ancient than Christianity. The calendar need not be filled with these vigils. A season's Saturdays or a few solemnities can be selected at first. Bible study groups or other groups of parishioners may want to move their meetings to Saturday or to the eves of solemnities on these occasions. The *Liturgy of the Hours* gives this description:

> As with the Easter Vigil, it was customary to begin certain solemnities (different in different churches) with a vigil. Among these solemnities, Christmas and Pentecost are preeminent. This custom should be maintained and fostered, according to the particular usage of each church. Where it seems good to celebrate other solemnities or occasions of pilgrimage with a vigil, the general norms for celebrations of the word should be observed (#71, #73).

> Again, since in the Roman rite the Office of Readings is always of uniform brevity, especially for the sake of those engaged in apostolic work, those who desire to extend the celebration of the vigils of Sundays, solemnities and feasts in accordance with tradition should do as follows.

> First, the Office of Readings is to be celebrated as in the *Liturgy of the Hours* up to the end of the readings. After the two readings, and before the *Te Deum,* canticles should be added from the special appendix in the *Liturgy of the Hours.* Then the gospel should be read; a homily on the gospel may be added. After this, the *Te Deum* is sung and then the prayer.

> On solemnities and feasts the gospel should be taken from the lectionary for Mass; on Sundays it should be taken from the series of gospels on the paschal mystery in the appendix to the *Liturgy of the Hours.*

Even well-versed liturgists and pastors may have missed this opportunity. If you are unfamiliar with the format of a vigil, review appendix I of the *Liturgy of the Hours.* Canticles and paschal gospels are given for each of Advent's four Sundays, for the Immaculate Conception and for the commons of saints whose memorials fall in Advent. Consider gathering part of the parish for Saturday nights in Advent or for the eve of your local solemnity if your parish is named after Francis Xavier or Lucy or one of the other saints of Advent.

COMMUNAL PENANCE

John the Baptist's call to conversion rings through Advent. While not officially described as a penitential season (which distinguishes it from Lent), it is still a season for ongoing conversion. If you schedule a communal celebration of reconciliation, appendix II of the *Rite of Penance* provides a complete service for Advent.

COMMUNAL ANOINTING OF THE SICK

Sickness knows no seasons. People are in need of this sacrament throughout the year. When calendars are charted for the year, parish communal anointing services may be scheduled periodically, perhaps at a Sunday eucharist (although many of those who would avail themselves of a communal anointing service may find Saturday morning convenient). Sundays in Ordinary Time, and especially those with pericopes about healing, would seem to be the best Sundays for this. If the need arises for anointing within Mass on an Advent Sunday, the ritual Mass is excluded by the norms. However, one of the scriptures from the *Pastoral Care of the Sick* can be used, perhaps as a second reading, so that the great prophetic voices of Advent are not eclipsed. At a communal anointing in Advent, one of the three Isaiah passages in the rite may be used. The last of these is similar to the passage given for the Third Sunday of Advent. Other prayer texts can be found on page 22 for the reception of the sick and for the prayer after anointing.

FUNERALS

Funeral Masses are not allowed on the Sundays of Advent. Whenever they are celebrated, however, the spirit of Advent can permeate these assemblies. Here of all places we can see and shape personal icons of Advent, of eschatological hope. Psalm 25, one of the common psalms for Advent, also may be chosen for funerals during these 24 days. The readings of the Advent weekday, with their words of intense hope and expectation, may be used for funerals.

The sacramentary's presidential prayers for the days of Advent should not be overlooked. While the *Order of Christian Funerals* (OCF) multiplies our available opening prayers, we still need more options for the prayer over the gifts and the prayer after communion. The Advent prayers often work for this purpose. In a similar vein, the traditional music for Advent, its psalms and hymns, generally known to many of the faithful, expresses well the intensity of human emotion present at funerals. "O come, O come, Emmanuel" is particularly appropriate and familiar. Its lyrics are a plea for God to save us from death.

MARRIAGES

When a marriage is celebrated during Advent or Lent or on other days of penance, the parish priest should advise the couple to take into consideration the special nature of these times. (*Rite of Marriage, #11*)

What does this mean? On Advent Sundays, it means that all the Mass texts must be from the current Sunday of Advent. Surely, it also means a respect for the way the parish community has decorated the space for Advent. Perhaps the presence of a beautiful Advent wreath will serve to underscore the redundancy of "marriage candles." (Be sure to light the appropriate number of candles in the Advent wreath for all gatherings, including weddings and funerals.)

The readings of the day, especially if they reflect on the prophetic images of God marrying God's people, should be considered for days other than Sunday as well. The pericope from the Song of Songs is traditionally associated with Advent. Intercessions and music also must be arranged with an awareness of Advent's character: Christmas carols do not belong at an Advent Saturday wedding any more than they belong in an Advent Sunday Mass.

RITE OF CHRISTIAN INITIATION OF ADULTS

The Rite of Acceptance into the Order of Catechumens and the Rite of Welcoming Candidates are *not* prescribed for the First Sunday of Advent. These powerful rites are better celebrated on Sundays in Ordinary Time. Liturgies of the word and other prayers celebrated with catechumens and candidates outside the Sunday assembly should be prepared with Advent in mind.

The Worship Environment

THE *Ceremonial of Bishops, #236*, succinctly summarizes our challenge:

During Advent, the playing of the organ and other musical instruments as well as the floral decoration of the altar should be marked by a moderation that reflects the character of this season but does not anticipate the full joy of Christmas itself.

This moderation, with a proper, seasonal expression of joyful expectation, demands great discipline and prudence. One can neither jump ahead and decorate with evergreens and flowers nor decide that a bare church with a purple cloth is enough.

■ ADVENT WREATH: This circle of greens with four candles is meant to be a simple foretaste of the evergreens of Christmas—and this means not using evergreens anywhere else during Advent except within the wreath. Local communities can select from the current options for color—four violet, three violet and one rose, or four white candles. (See *Book of Blessings, #1510–11*.)

If the Advent wreath is to be used in church, it should be of sufficient size to be visible to the congregation. It may be suspended from the ceiling or placed on a stand. If it is placed in the presbyterium, it should not interfere with the celebration of the liturgy, nor should it obscure the altar, lectern or chair. (*Book of Blessings, #1512*)

■ MARIAN SHRINE: The Advent wreath may hang here or other candles and flowers can be kept nearby. If there is more than one image of Mary in the church and environs, this is an opportunity to consult with art historians or iconographers. What images do you have? Some are obvious: the Immaculate Conception stepping on the snake, or Our Lady of Guadalupe clothed with the sun. If these are present, pay attention to them on their Advent feasts. Other images are less evident in their heritage, but all have a story to tell. A related task is the awkward but important one of being sure that the local diocesan norms for art and for not multiplying images are respected.

■ OTHER IMAGES: The eschatological and preparatory qualities of Advent have found expression in many other images: statues or windows of John the Baptist (important in places as diverse as Quebec and Puerto Rico), images of Isaiah or one of the other prophets (this is the year when we hear from the greatest number of prophets on the Sundays—Jeremiah, Baruch, Zephaniah and Micah) or the "Jesse Tree." (The most ancient renderings of this Christian interpretation of the Hebrew Scriptures show pictures of the various offspring of Jesse—not arcane symbols that must be explained.) If your church has these images or any others appropriate to the season, attention can be given to them with candles or by reproductions of them on Advent handouts. If not, local artists may create one for the entranceway this year.

■ OUTDOORS: Our Catholic tradition that gives Advent its own sounds, smells and sights should be expressed in the face we show our neighbors as they drive by the church building. Outdoor mangers and lit trees can be blessed with caroling and festivity in the days just before Christmas or on the eve or on the day itself. Our desire to allow Advent its own expressions needs creative adaptation in each community—how can our longings and readiness be expressed in color and other embellishments? Purple strips of cloth? An outdoor tree with "Jesse" figures?

■ VESTURE is customarily fashioned in shades of violet and purple, or slate, sarum and other deep shades of midnight blue; trims and ornament are in silvers, whites, dark blue and grays—the colors of winter. Care should be taken to ensure that the vesture used in Advent is different from that used during Lent and that this vesture returns year after year. Avoid purple vesture with passion symbols.

Resources

THE following bibliography is useful for both Advent and Christmastime. Together, these two seasons constitute a single season; they must be discussed and prepared together.

HISTORICAL BACKGROUND

Several of the general studies listed on page xix provide sections on Advent and Christmas. See especially Adam, Bishops' Committee on the Liturgy *Study Text 9*, Carroll and Halton, Cobb, Martimort, Nocent, Parsch and Talley.

LITURGICAL/PREACHING HELP

See the general anthologies or works listed under this heading on page xx—especially the ones by Merton, Nocent (vol. 1, "Advent," 27–167; "Christmas," 181–247; "Epiphany," 257–326).

Brown, Raymond. *A Coming Christ in Advent* and *An Adult Christ at Christmas* (Collegeville: The Liturgical Press, 1988 and 1977). An excellent condensation of his epic work, *The Birth of the Messiah*.

Brueggeman, Walter. *The Prophetic Imagination* (Philadelphia: Fortress, 1978). In popular, converstional style, this book gives an excellent overview of the prophetic vision.

Hopko, Thomas. *The Winter Pascha* (Crestwood, New York: St. Vladimir's Seminary Press, 1984). Although references are to the Byzantine pre-Nativity observance, much of this material is valuable to Christians of the Western rites.

Irwin, Kevin. *Advent and Christmas: A Guide to the Eucharist and Hours* (New York: Pueblo Publishing Co., 1986). An exhaustive guide to every day and every liturgical text in these seasons.

Lawrence, Emeric, OSB. *Jesus Present and Coming* (Collegeville: The Liturgical Press, 1982). The author sets the scriptural texts within the liturgical context in a readable and concise way.

O'Gorman, Thomas, ed. *An Advent Sourcebook* (Chicago: LTP, 1988). Texts of all kinds from over the centuries to enliven the many separate moments in Advent and the season's overall development.

Simcoe, Mary Ann, ed. *A Christmas Sourcebook* (Chicago: LTP, 1984). A treasury of texts from various traditions and churches. Extensive attention to the *comites Christi* and to all the days between Christmas and Epiphany.

Simcoe, Mary Ann, ed. *Parish Path through Advent and Christmastime* (Chicago: LTP, 1983). Each chapter looks at one element of the liturgy, such as the lectionary, music and environment.

Vawter, Bruce. "Introduction to Prophetic Literature" in *The New Jerome Biblical Commentary* (Englewood Cliffs NJ: Prentice Hall, 1990, 186–200). The most concise and enlightening summary of current scholarship on the prophets. See also the various commentaries on the prophetic books used in Advent.

December

Lectionary #3 violet
First Sunday of Advent

■ ADVENT EVE: The beginning of the season deserves attention, and evening seems the finest time of day to celebrate. Some parishes begin to announce well in advance that the Saturday evening liturgy for the First Sunday of Advent is their principal Mass that weekend and then give this Mass extra attention. Others schedule a special celebration of Evening Prayer (see page 9 regarding an outline for blessing the Advent wreath at Evening Prayer) or a vigil of Advent readings, psalms and hymns (see appendix I in the *Liturgy of the Hours*).

■ INTRODUCTORY RITES: Either opening prayer is fitting this day, but the first prayer is less wordy. The order for the opening rites can take on a seasonal quality this weekend and can be kept the same for the other three Sundays (see page 5).

■ THE LITURGY OF THE WORD: Each year Advent begins with a gospel proclamation of the end-time. This year we open Luke for the first time and hear two paragraphs from his account of Jesus' preaching in Jerusalem, a ministry exercised just before the fateful days of the passion. In Luke, these words are weighted with much solemnity and with an awareness of the paschal mystery about to unfold in the person of Jesus. By placing this passage at the start of the liturgical year, the church starts with the end, both in terms of Jesus' final message to his listeners and in terms of the Day of the Lord.

Preachers and listeners have wrestled with these eschatological (end-time) messages in every generation. The power of the words is ill-served by treating them merely as a condemnation of indulgence, drunkenness and worldly cares. The great day will indeed "close in like a trap," but the faithful should "stand up straight and raise [their] heads, for [their] ransom is near at hand." With the paradox of sin and salvation, we enter into the annual passage through the paschal mystery.

One way for preachers and planners to respect this paradox and to be true to our ever-evolving Catholic tradition is to read the passages from early church leaders found in each season's Office of Readings. Today's passage by Cyril of Jerusalem, Tuesday's by Gregory Nazianzen and this Thursday's from Ephrem are particularly evocative of Advent's spirit and meaning.

The *Book of Blessings* (chapter 47) has texts for blessing the wreath after the homily if this has not been done at Evening Prayer. Advent psalm antiphons or other short refrains, such as "Prepare the way of the Lord" (Taizé, GIA), "My soul in stillness waits" (Haugen, GIA) or "A voice cries out in the wilderness" (Joncas, NALR), effectively add assembly participation to rituals like this. One song written specifically for the lighting of the Advent wreath (which does not assign an artificial significance to each candle) is "Wait for Messiah" from the *Hymnal for Catholic Students* (GIA and LTP).

MON 2 #176 violet
Advent Weekday

■ HANUKKAH: Our Jewish neighbors begin celebrating Hanukkah today. This eight-day feast of lights brings all religious peoples a message of light and fidelity. It also invites us to pray for the people of the covenant. Hebrew tradition tells how, at the rededication of the Temple after the tyrant Antiochus left Jerusalem in ruins, the Jews found only a small portion of oil for the sacred lamp. Miraculously, the lamp burned for eight days until new oil could be prepared. The lessons of this festival include the dangers of cultural assimilation and the consequences of abandoning religious tradition.

TUE 3 #177 white
Francis Xavier, priest
MEMORIAL

He was one of the initial group who joined Ignatius Loyola to become Jesuits. Like John the Baptist for the people of Judea, he was the precursor to Christ for the peoples of Japan and India. Use the readings for the weekday with another marvelous passage from Isaiah. The proper prayers for the saint bring us references to the eternal life toward which we stretch with special fervor in Advent. The intercessions may well include the well-being of Catholics in India, especially around Goa, many of whom can trace their spiritual history to this baroque Baptist.

WED 4 #178 violet
Advent Weekday

John Damascene, priest and doctor, optional memorial/white. ▪ The proper prayer for this saint, with its reference to light, may serve as the conclusion of the general intercessions if not used as the opening prayer of the Mass.

T
H
U
5 #179   violet
Advent Weekday

F
R
I
6 #180   violet
Advent Weekday

Nicholas, bishop, optional memorial/white. ▪ While we know for sure only that Nicholas was an early bishop of Myra (now part of Turkey), the stories about him have multiplied over the centuries. Especially in the eastern churches, he is one of the most beloved figures in history. Whether he actually did all that has been said of him or not, he has become an icon of generosity. We would do well to help children learn once more about the linkage with Santa Claus—not to complicate little children's dreams, but to help older children appreciate the origins of this archetypal figure.

Nicholas is equally revered in other nations as a defender of orthodoxy (against Arianism), as the patron of Russia (and frequently invoked these days as religion undergoes a rebirth there) and as the patron of children. Many aspects of his story help frame brief weekday homilies and intercessions.

The readings for Mass are from the seasonal weekday. The nations along the eastern Mediterranean always have been in ferment. The ancient words of Isaiah still can express our own hopes: "Lebanon shall be changed into an orchard. . . ." Nicholas taught the people of his diocese, located just north of Lebanon, how to make this hope their own. No matter how far we are from the promised orchard, the hopes of Isaiah and Nicholas should be ours as well. Our very world will be transformed!

S
A
T
7 #689   white
Immaculate Conception
SOLEMNITY

In this celebration, we affirm that the Blessed Virgin Mary was filled with God's grace at the moment of her conception. This dogma was proclaimed by Pope Pius IX in 1854, although the feast of the conception of Mary in her mother's womb is very ancient. Under this title, Mary is patroness of the United States. This designation, made soon after the papal proclamation, was not just an arbitrary decision by the bishops. Many of the Catholic peoples migrating to this land, and prominent missionaries such as Marquette had a special love for Mary under this title.

▪ IMMACULATE CONCEPTION OR VIRGIN BIRTH? A special introduction after the sign of the cross and greeting would be helpful today, if only to clarify the confusion that still exists in most people's minds —complicated by today's gospel reading—between the "immaculate conception" of Mary and the "virgin birth" of Jesus. One possibility:

Today we honor holy Mary,
and celebrate the day
she was conceived
   in the womb of her mother.
(Mary is called the
   Immaculate Conception
and by this title we honor her
   as patroness of our nation.)
Praising God,
who kept her sinless from the
   first moment of her life,

and who is gracious and quick
   to forgive,
let us humbly acknowledge
   our sins.

▪ MAINTAIN THE ADVENT SPIRIT. Because the angel's message and Mary's response perfectly match the expectancy of the season, let almost everything stay the same as worship on Sunday. The alternative opening prayer not only helps us to consider the meaning of the feast, it also links our prayer to the season ("Prepare once again a world for your Son"). A few adaptations to the seasonal order may be: a sung Gloria, a petition for the rights and dignity of all the people of the United States, some Marian music that fits the mood of Advent ("O Sanctissima," for example), floral and candle arrangements near the image of Mary—although attention to this image is fitting throughout the season. In the solemn blessing printed with today's texts in most editions of the sacramentary (solemn blessing #15), "humanity" would be more inclusive than "mankind." The seasonal blessing used on other Advent days, however, would be appropriate today as well.

▪ THE *LITURGY OF THE HOURS,* appendix I, provides Marian canticles and a gospel to add to the Office of Readings that can be used to create an extended vigil for the gathered assembly. Parishes that carry the title of the Immaculate Conception should give this vigil serious consideration. Parish leaders can share resources with their communities to enrich domestic prayer on this day. This could be part of an overall Advent booklet, using material found in *Catholic Household Blessings and Prayers* (p. 184).

■ TRANSFERRED SOLEMNITY: This festival has been moved back one day this year (Advent Sundays take precedence) and so many places leave aside the "holy day of obligation" status. This decision, made with an eye to avoiding confusion, may have the opposite result. In any event, we should recognize the importance of this day and encourage people to remember to honor Mary in their private and domestic prayer on this day and, perhaps, to participate in the daily eucharist, if one is normally is scheduled on Saturday.

This seems to be the last time that we in the Roman rite will move a solemnity back one day. Recently announced changes to the *General Norms for the Liturgical Year and the Calendar,* #5, will mean that solemnities occurring on the Sundays of Advent, Lent and Easter will be moved ahead to the next available day. This will be seen next in 1995 (St. Joseph moved to March 20) and then in 1996 (Immaculate Conception moved to December 9).

✵8 #6 violet
Second Sunday of Advent

The appearance of John the Baptist in the liturgy this Sunday and next, and in the weekday gospels beginning this Thursday, is central to Advent. He comes to us in scripture, prayer texts and hymns to bring us with him to the River Jordan and the manifestation there of Jesus as the Son of God. His prophetic preaching brings us to the Jordan today, now. Advent

does not just open for us the mysteries of the past. It pulls us all to the great future, to the glory of the Lord.

MON 9 #182 violet
Advent Weekday

Blessed Juan Diego, optional memorial/white. ▪ This Native American is now honored as more than just the one who saw Our Lady of Guadalupe. Recognition of his own holiness has led to his recent beatification. This is the first time that this optional memorial can be celebrated in the United States. As is the case with other festivals added to the calendar since the current sacramentary was printed (1985), the proper texts often are hard to find. The scriptures, as usual, are from the seasonal weekday. The commons (for this day, the commons of holy men and women) may be used if you have not received the proper texts through your diocesan worship office.

TUE 10 #183 violet
Advent Weekday

WED 11 #184 violet
Advent Weekday

Damasus I, pope, optional memorial/white. ▪ Biographies of this fourth-century pope describe his work to foster devotion to martyrs. His witness, his proper prayer and the reading from Augustine in today's Office of Readings invite us to increase our own devotion to ancient and current martyrs.

THU 12 #707–712 white
Our Lady of Guadalupe
FEAST

■ CELEBRATING AN IMAGE: Many Catholics need to be reacquainted with images. There seems to be some antagonism to statues, icons and images in general. Perhaps our contemporary iconoclasts are tired of the cheap materials and poor art used in many representations. Or perhaps the popular attention given to saints, to the apparent exclusion of the paschal mystery, disturbs sensitive pastoral ministers. These realities should be troubling. Yet we all must internalize the proper respect for images that is part of the authentic tradition of our paschal-centered liturgy.

In other words, we should be able to enjoy the witness this feast gives. Here we have a premier American day given over to a wonderful image—and a wonderful story about the image's origins. In 1531, Mary appeared to the Mexican Indian, Juan Diego, at Tepeyac, a hill northwest of Mexico City. She left with him a picture of herself on his cloak—as an Indian herself, pregnant and shining like the sun and moon together. Under this image, Mary is patroness of the Americas. The image brings us the good news it brought to Juan Diego: Christianity is not alien to this continent; Mary is not just from the eastern Mediterranean.

■ CELEBRATING A PEOPLE: This feast also allows the church in the United States to celebrate the contributions of Mexican Americans. They were among the first Catholics in this land, building communities and architectural monuments throughout the area that is now the southwest United States. Baltimore may be our primatial see, but Mexico was our font of faith even earlier.

■ LECTIONARY: The scriptures of this day are to be drawn from the Commons of the Blessed Virgin Mary. One of the passages from the prophetic books (there are three from Isaiah, one from Micah and one from Zechariah) would help link this day to the Advent season that envelops it. Either of the passages from Luke 1 are traditional for Advent.

■ PRAYER TEXTS: The proper prayers for this feast were issued too recently to be part of the 1985 edition of sacramentary. The presidential prayers for Mass can be found on page 21. The solemn blessing of the Blessed Virgin Mary (#15) can be used at any celebrations this day, eucharistic or otherwise. The blessing found in the *Book of Blessings* at #1289 also can be used.

■ OTHER TIMES FOR PRAYER: New texts for the *Liturgy of the Hours* for this day have been published in English by the Bishops' Committee on the Liturgy (see the BCL *Newsletter* March/April, 1989). They include an account of the visions from the sixteenth century, a message from Pope Paul VI and intercessions that are both evocative and American. This also may be a day to prepare for the attention to be given in 1992 both to Christopher Columbus and to the fifth centenary of the evangelization of the Americas. This may mean bulletin notices, or this may be the occasion for the first of several penitential services to mark the anniversary (see page xiii).

F
R
I
13 #186   red
**Lucy,
virgin and martyr**
MEMORIAL

Planners and presiders may want to use the option (mentioned in the introduction to the lectionary and in the *General Instruction of the Roman Missal)* to adjust the weekday pericopes if there are

interruptions to the continuity of the readings caused by feasts and solemnities. The readings that would have been used on Thursday, if it were not the 12th, begin the lengthy series of passages about John the Baptist. That gospel may be added to the verses given for today.

Lucy is the perfect Advent saint. Her name means "light." Although she was martyred in Sicily, she is venerated with great solemnity in places as diverse as Venice and Sweden. Like St. Nicholas Day, this is a great day on which to schedule Advent concerts. There is a great body of music relating to Lucy, to legends about her and to light in general.

S
A
T
14 #187   white
**John of the Cross,
priest and doctor**
MEMORIAL

John's *The Dark Night of the Soul* gives us at least one clue as to how to receive him and celebrate his memory in an Advent manner: In darkness, in the pain of the cross, we find light.

⚙ **15** #9   violet or rose
**Third Sunday
of Advent**

It is Gaudete Sunday, the day traditionally called "rejoice." This title comes from the first word of the Latin entrance antiphon. The first and second readings bring rejoicing into the heart of the liturgy of the word.

■ PRAYER TEXTS: The alternative opening prayer contains a rare reminder, "the earth rejoices" that Christ comes to set all creation free. The first opening prayer and the prayer after communion offer the imprecise word "birthday" as a translation for the Latin "day of birth." That's an enormous difference! In both prayers, "birthday" should read "birth." What is at stake here is an understanding of a Christian festival as something far more than a historical commemoration. In our Christmas—as in all our festivals—we enter the mystery of God's own timelessness, where we can declare in truth: Today is born our Savior, Christ the Lord.

M
O
N
16 #188   violet
Advent Weekday

T
U
E
17 #194   violet
Advent Weekday

The second part of Advent, when the liturgy leads us to Bethlehem and to the coming of God in the flesh, begins today. Most noteworthy about these days are the "O Antiphons"—found as the antiphons for each day's Evening Prayer and given as the gospel acclamation verses at Mass (see lectionary #202). They are set metrically in the hymn "O come, O come, Emmanuel." Appropriate verses may be sung during the gospel acclamation at Mass or at any gathering this week. With these antiphons come other less familiar images and words. The prayers and scriptures found in the sacramentary and lectionary constitute a rich diet for our gatherings this week. This is one more positive reason for postponing the Christmas carols and festivities until Christmas—the treasury of our images of longing deserve their own time.

WED 18 #195 violet
Advent Weekday

THU 19 #196 violet
Advent Weekday

FRI 20 #197 violet
Advent Weekday

SAT 21 #198 violet
Advent Weekday

Peter Canisius, priest and doctor, optional memorial. ▪ No color is listed for this optional memorial, because the days immediately before and after Christmas take precedence (see *General Instruction of the Roman Missal, #316a*). Thus, Germany's "second apostle" can receive only a commemoration. For example, parishes with German roots may use his proper prayer to conclude the general intercessions.

▪ LECTIONARY OPTIONS: Choosing the Song of Solomon passage instead of Zephaniah gives communities a rare opportunity to hear from this book and to recognize the presence of God in sexual love. The gospel for today also will be read tonight and tomorrow. To avoid this duplication, some parishes may wish to substitute Luke 1:46–56 today (from lectionary #199).

✳ 22 #12 violet
Fourth Sunday of Advent

The first opening prayer is a rewrite of the old Angelus collect, although hard to recognize in this version. It is an admirable joining of the incarnation and paschal mystery. The older translation:

> Pour forth, we beseech thee,
>   O Lord,
> thy grace into our hearts:
> that we, to whom the incarnation
>   of Christ thy Son
> was made known by the message
>   of an angel,
> may, by his passion and cross,
> be brought to the glory
>   of the resurrection:
> through the same Christ
>   our Lord. Amen.

▪ WINTER SOLSTICE: This weekend marks the winter solstice. *Christmas Sourcebook* from LTP begins with several reflections on the change of seasons, many of them relating Christ to the Sun of righteousness. More and more frequently, liturgical publishing houses are including such dates on their calendars, helping users make connections between secular, cosmic and Catholic observances. This openness to the world works if we follow our early Christian ancestors in seeing our scriptures and faith tradition as giving the seasons their true significance. See Talley's *The Origins of the Liturgical Year*, pages 92–96, or Carroll and Halton's anthology, page 151 (both on the resources list, page xix). They describe the origins of Christmas as being independent of solar symbolism—even if cosmic language became attached to Christmas because of the proximity of its date to the solstice festivals.

MON 23 #200 violet
Advent Weekday

John of Kanty, priest, optional memorial. ▪ Once again, these late Advent days allow for only brief commemorations of this Polish priest and professor. Pray for that nation and for all universities in the intercessions.

TUE 24 #201 violet
Advent Weekday

The liturgy for this short liturgical day, ending before Evening Prayer I, includes an opening prayer that could serve as the perfect expression of the community's thoughts and dreams. It begins, "Come, Lord Jesus, do not delay"—unusual because it is addressed to Christ, not to the first person of the Holy Trinity as most opening prayers are.

INTRODUCTORY RITES

Greeting

From the Christ who was, who is, and who is
    to come:
grace, light and peace be with you all.

Invitation to Penitence

[My brothers and sisters:]
coming together to the table of word
    and eucharist
let us be alert to the advent of our God
and prepare the Lord's way by turning
    from our sins,
embracing justice and truth,
and finding comfort in the Christ who
    promises peace.

Penitential Rite:

Form Cii in the sacramentary, or:

You came as Redeemer to announce glad
    tidings of salvation:
Lord, have mercy.

You come as Shepherd to gather
    and feed us:
Christ, have mercy.

You will come as judge to establish a new
    heaven and earth:
Lord, have mercy.

LITURGY OF THE WORD

Dismissal of Catechumens

My dear friends: With the assurance of our loving support, this community sends you forth to reflect more deeply upon the word of God we have shared. Our Advent prayer is that God may bless you with every spiritual gift and strengthen you with the comfort of glad tidings, so that in due time you may share fully at the Lord's table and be found blameless on the day when Christ comes in glory.

General Intercessions

Invitation to prayer

The Lord comes to save us and to establish the kingdom: let us give voice in our prayer to the longings of all the human race, especially those who are poor and forgotten.

For the church

For the church throughout the world,
that we faithfully announce peace
and work for justice
until the Lord comes in glory:
let us pray to the Lord.

For the church throughout the world,
that we hear the word of God
and put it into practice:
let us pray to the Lord.

For the world

For the prophets who proclaim
the reign of God,
that their words and deeds
turn us from violence,
let us pray to the Lord.

For peace among the nations,
that the poor may be fed
and the refugees find a home,
let us pray to the Lord.

For various needs

That God who is comfort
may hear the cries of all who are in need,
let us pray to the Lord.

For missionaries and all who share
the good news with the poor,
let us pray to the Lord.

For the local community

For those awaiting the birth of a child,
that their hearts be filled with peace
and their fears be turned to joy,
let us pray to the Lord.

For the good earth which God has given us,
and for the wisdom and will to conserve it,
let us pray to the Lord.

Attuned to the Sunday readings

For peace within the walls of Jerusalem,
that all nations and peoples
may unite there in praising God,
let us pray to the Lord.

For catechumens, candidates and inquirers

For the catechumens
and the candidates of the church,
that they may grow in faith, hope and love
as they ponder God's word,
let us pray to the Lord.

For the catechumens and candidates
of the church,
that their eyes be opened and their hearts
set free
by the good news of Christ,
let us pray to the Lord.

For the departed

For those who have fallen asleep
in the hope of rising to everlasting life,
let us pray to the Lord.

Concluding Prayers for the General Intercessions

FIRST SUNDAY OF ADVENT:
God our Savior,
you utter a word of promise and hope
and hasten the day of justice and freedom,
yet we live in a world forgetful of your word,
our watchfulness dulled by the cares of life.

Keep us alert.
Make us attentive to your word,
ready to look on your Son
when he comes with power and great glory.
Make us holy and blameless,
ready to stand secure
when the day of his coming shakes
the world with terror.

We ask this through him whose coming
is certain,
whose day draws near:
your Son, our Lord Jesus Christ,
who lives and reigns
[with you in the unity of the Holy Spirit,
one God] for ever and ever.
—© ICEL

SECOND SUNDAY OF ADVENT:
God of our salvation,
you straighten the winding ways
of our hearts
and smooth the paths made rough by sin.

Make our conduct blameless,
keep our hearts watchful in holiness,
and bring to perfection the good you have
begun in us.

We ask this through him whose coming
is certain,
whose day draws near:
your Son, our Lord Jesus Christ,
who lives and reigns
[with you in the unity of the Holy Spirit,
one God] for ever and ever.
—© ICEL

THIRD SUNDAY OF ADVENT:
Almighty God,
you send your Son into a world
where the wheat must be winnowed
from chaff
and wickedness clings even to what is good.

Let the fire of your Spirit
purge us of greed and deceit,
so that, purified, we may find our peace
in you
and you may delight in us.

We ask this through him whose coming
is certain,
whose day draws near:
your Son, our Lord Jesus Christ,
who lives and reigns
[with you in the unity of the Holy Spirit,
one God] for ever and ever.
—© ICEL

FOURTH SUNDAY OF ADVENT:
Who are we, Lord God,
that you should come to us?
Yet you have visited your people
and redeemed us in your Son.

As we prepare to celebrate his birth,
make our hearts leap for joy at the sound
of your word,
and move us by your Spirit to bless your
wonderful works.

We ask this through him whose coming
    is certain,
whose day draws near:
your Son, our Lord Jesus Christ,
who lives and reigns
[with you in the unity of the Holy Spirit,
one God] for ever and ever.

— © *ICEL*

LITURGY OF THE EUCHARIST

Introduction to the Lord's Prayer

God so loved the world that he sent his only Son to be our Savior: let us, therefore pray with confidence for the coming of the kingdom, as Jesus taught us:

Prayer for Peace

Lord Jesus Christ, whose first coming we bless and whose final coming we long for as the advent of perfect peace: look not on our sins, but on the faith of your church, and grant us the peace and unity of your kingdom where you live for ever and ever.

Invitation to Communion

This is the Lamb of God who takes away the sins of the world: the Savior who is to come. Happy are those who are called to his supper.

CONCLUDING RITE

Dismissal of Eucharistic Ministers

Go forth in peace to the sick and homebound of our community, bearing the word of life and the Body of Christ together with the assurance of our love and concern. Be to our brothers and sisters heralds of glad tidings and ministers of Christ's abiding presence.

Blessing

May the Sun of Righteousness shine upon you and scatter the darkness from before your path; and may almighty God bless you . . .

Dismissal

Go in peace to prepare the way of the Lord.

TEXTS FOR MASS WITH CHILDREN

These texts have been translated by Peter Scagnelli from the Italian sacramentary.

Opening Prayer

Lord,
you have given us a mind to think,
the strength to love,
and the joy to give.
Help us to be always ready and eager
to welcome Jesus every day
until at last he comes to call us home
    to himself.
We ask this through Christ our Lord.

Prayer over the Gifts

Accept, O Lord, this bread and wine,
our precious gifts to you.
Change them for us
into your most precious gift of all:
Jesus Christ our Lord,
who lives and reigns for ever and ever.

Prayer after Communion

Let your bread of life, O Lord,
strengthen us for our journey
until we come to the happiness
of our heavenly home.
We ask this through Christ our Lord.

The liturgical celebration of Mary under the title of Our Lady of Guadalupe was raised to the level of feast and given new texts in the dioceses of the United States of America after the current sacramentary was printed.

Entrance Antiphon

A great sign appeared in the sky, a woman clothed with the sun, with the moon under her feet, and on her head a crown of twelve stars. *(Revelation 12:1)*

Opening Prayer

God of power and mercy,
you blessed the Americas at Tepeyac
with the presence of the Virgin Mary
    of Guadalupe.
May her prayers help all men and women
to accept each other as brothers and sisters.
Through your justice present in our hearts
may your peace reign in the world.
We ask this through our Lord Jesus Christ,
    your son,
who lives and reigns with you and
    the Holy Spirit,
one God, for ever and ever. Amen.

Lectionary Readings

Any readings from the *Lectionary for Mass,* nos. 707–12, may be used. Especially appropriate are Zechariah 2:14–17 (707.11) or Revelation 11:19, 12:1–6, 10 (708.2) and Luke 1:39–47 (712.4).

Prayer over the Gifts

Lord,
accept the gifts we present to you
on this feast of Our Lady of Guadalupe
and grant that this sacrifice
will strengthen us to fulfill your
    commandments
as true sons and daughters of the
    Virgin Mary.
We ask this through Christ our Lord. Amen.

Eucharistic Prayer

Preface of the Blessed Virgin Mary I or II
(P 56 or P 57)

Communion Antiphon

The Lord has cast down the mighty from their thrones, and has lifted up the lowly. *(Luke 1:52)*

Or:

God has not acted thus for any other nation; to no other people has he shown his love so clearly. *(See Psalm 147:20.)*

Prayer after Communion

Lord,
may the Body and Blood of your Son,
which we receive in this sacrament,
reconcile us always in your love.
May we who rejoice in the holy Mother
    of Guadalupe
live united and at peace in this world
until the day of the Lord dawns in glory.
We ask this through Christ our Lord. Amen.

Introduction/Reception of the Sick

We have come together in this Advent season to celebrate the sacraments of anointing and eucharist. The prophet Isaiah sang of a day when the desert would blossom and the parched land exult, a day when weary bodies and frightened hearts would find fresh strength and new courage, a day when the Lord, like a shepherd, would gather the lambs in his arms and speak tender words of healing and comfort. May Christ draw near to us now in these sacraments, as once he came among us, the good physician of souls. May Christ ever be the health and strength of all who look forward to the day when he will come again in glory.

Prayer after Anointing

Strong and gentle God,
with justice for the afflicted
    you come to save us;
with healing for the weary
    you draw near to comfort us.
To those whom we have anointed
grant courage and strength.
Preserve them whole and entire,
    spirit, soul and body,
irreproachable for the coming
    of our Lord Jesus Christ,
who lives and reigns for ever and ever.

CHRISTMAS

*"Ox and ass before him bow, for he is in the manger now: Christ is born today!" Early
Christians pictured these animals by the manger because they knew that, according to
Isaiah, their presence would point to the Messiah, to the One who was to come.
The animals and the manger not only point to the lowliness of the birth; they call us to rise
up in splendor, to shout "Glory!" This is not a feast of the romantic past. The manger
invites us forward to eat the bread of life. The New Jerusalem calls all creation—
dromedaries, magi and ourselves—to a sure and full future.*

Images of the Season

Next to the yearly celebration of the paschal mystery, the church holds most sacred the memorial of Christ's birth and early manifestations. This is the purpose of the Christmas season. (*General Norms for the Liturgical Year and Calendar,* #32)

WE like to tell our children that Christmas is Jesus' birthday. The celebration of Jesus' birth, however, should not look or feel like any birthday party that we have ever attended. This is not just an anniversary of something that happened long ago. Nor is it a party to honor one person. As precious as the baby Jesus is, as much as we like to visit historical representations of the manger, this is not a season simply to go back in time to honor a baby. We set up manger scenes, we light Christmas trees and we cry, "Today!" We sing, "Ox and ass before him bow, for he is in the manger now: Christ is born today! Christ is born today!" As the liturgical texts of these days put it, the Word of God humbled himself to share in our humanity that he may enable us to share in his divinity—today!

This word "today" *(hodie)* is a key to entering into the mystery of Christmastime. If Christ is born today, then we can be born with him, we can see and touch and hold Christ. If Christ is alive in our midst, then truly the reign of God has begun, the reign in which the very rocks of the earth cry out for justice and compassion, acclaiming the coming of the Lord. The decorations of Christmas, especially the lighted tree, are more than signs of a birthday. They are emblems of eternity, of the tree of life, of health and wholesomeness and the endless delight of heaven itself. On the final day of the season, Gregory Nazianzus is featured in the Office of Readings. His sermon calls us to go down into the waters with Jesus, to rise with him, to be radiant lights beside his light—this day, *today!*

■ HISTORY OF THE SEASON: Teachers and preachers often tell their listeners of the origins of the Christmas festival in the late Roman Empire's solstice celebrations. Christmas was, it would seem, the Christians' attempt to counteract pagan homage to the returning sun. The Sun/Son of Righteousness was commemorated then—because we had no idea when Jesus was born—and the celebrations were marked by lights and evergreens, copying and transforming Roman customs. So the explanation goes, and up to a point it is correct.

Other reasons seem to lie behind the placement of Christmastime in the days after the solstice. As noted briefly under the remarks in the previous section at December 22, Thomas Talley (in *The Origins of the Liturgical Year,* pages 92–96), who has collated current scholarship, indicates that Christmas' date was set independent of solar symbolism. What follows is a very brief summary of that point of view.

First, the ancient world tended to place the beginning and the end of an important person's life on the same date. Jesus was believed to have been crucified on March 25 or April 6 (this varied according to geographic area, prevalent calendars and systems of computation). His conception was believed to have been on the same date, thus placing his birth on December 25 or January 6.

Second, the revelation regarding the conception of a son to Zechariah during his priestly duties at Yom Kippur places the conception of John the Baptist in September and his birth in June. Gabriel told Mary that Elizabeth was "in her sixth month;" this places the conception of Jesus in March and his birth in December.

These scholarly reconstructions of our earliest celebrations help us appreciate Christmas as part of the overall story of salvation, as intimately related to the forerunner John and as a foreshadowing of the passion. However the date was first set, the proximity of the pagan festivals of light helped the Nativity and Epiphany feasts become filled with cosmic and solar symbolism.

■ NOT JUST FOR ROMANTICS: Pastors and liturgical planners wear themselves out trying to celebrate this season well. Yet our efforts often are made more difficult by the belief that the season is about "good" or "warm" feelings. As the great Roman liturgist Adrian Nocent puts it:

> The introduction of the crèche and all the Christmas folklore has been a good thing, and neither can nor should be simply rejected. We must admit, however, that the injection of these elements, especially at a time when both the liturgy and the knowledge of scripture were in decline, has turned Christmas, for many, into the feast of tender pity; midnight Mass is the most important thing to these Christians, and the feast has no further influence on their lives. The mistake is to have focused the celebration too much on the birth at Bethlehem and to have turned the object of the feast into a moving story. (*The Liturgical Year* vol. 1, p. 191)

Sentimental tendencies have their place, but they are not the goal of pastoral work. Rather, we must all be engaged in the hard work of restoring the full observance of Christmas—its pathos, its praise of salvation and sure promise of the eternal kingdom, its remembrances and its celebration of "today!"

■ NOT JUST FOR ONE DAY: Those responsible for worship cannot prepare Christmastime without preparing the parish through education and outreach. Some people of goodwill strip their homes of celebration on December 26 or January 2 or January 6. In our tradition, the high time of Christmas continues through the Epiphany celebration—this year on Sunday, January 5—and then the Roman Rite continues the festivity up to the Baptism of the Lord (this year on January 12). We must vigorously address the incompatibility of our Catholic calendar with the commercial calendar. Through all these 19 days, Christmastime should keep its splendor—shining with the angels on Christmas, beaming with the stars at Epiphany, glistening in the waters on the Baptism of the Lord.

The texts of the liturgy (especially the sacramentary and the *Liturgy of the Hours*) can help us appreciate this length of time and the interrelationship of Nativity, Epiphany and Baptism. For example, the antiphons given for the introductory rites of the Mass on the days between Epiphany and the Baptism of the Lord link these two aspects of the same mystery. The readings from early Christian sources in the Office of Readings for the days between Epiphany and the Baptism of the Lord form a rich treasury for understanding these connections. All three aspects of Epiphany—the magi, the Baptism and the miracle at the wedding in Cana—are announced in the antiphons for the gospel canticles at Morning Prayer and at Evening Prayer II on Epiphany itself.

These three aspects are more fully examined by Peter Chrysologus in the selection from his writings given in the Office of Readings on the following day. The relationship of Christmas, Epiphany and the Baptism of the Lord are examined by Proclus of Constantinople on Wednesday of the week after Epiphany. Finally, Maximus of Turin on Friday of the same week addresses the issue most explicitly—"Reason demands that this feast of the Lord's baptism, which I think could be called the feast of his birthday, should follow soon after the Lord's birthday, during the same season, even though many years intervened between the two events."

■ STRUCTURE OF THE SEASON: The conviction of our ancestors that we have a season and not just a day brought us a whole series of festivals. The greatest days—Christmas Day; Mary, Mother of God; Epiphany; Baptism of the Lord—define the phases of our season. The days from December 25 to January 1 have a high liturgical ranking;

they form an octave of celebrating the birth and its consequences. The days between January 1 and Epiphany (three weekdays this year) center on the manifestation stories told by John. The days from Epiphany to the Baptism of the Lord broaden our appreciation of this manifestation and link it to our own baptism.

■ THE SAINTS IN CHRISTMASTIME: During the days of Christmas, Mary is seen as the glorious mother, the Seat of Wisdom presenting the redeemer to all nations. While some seasonal texts and the feast of the Holy Family show Mary in a more familial, domestic setting, the dominant image is one of public glory.

The saints of these weeks take on a similar cast. The observances immediately following Christmas Day have been gathering images of the manifestation to themselves for centuries. These are the days celebrating the *comites Christi,* the first companions of the Christ. In the dioceses of the United States, a cluster of saints proper to our country surrounds Epiphany. The gospel acclamation verses given for St. John the apostle (". . . your glorious band of apostles extols you.") and Holy Innocents (". . . the radiant army of martyrs acclaims you.") illustrate the way we see all of these saints in the light of Christmas.

Preparing the Parish

CATHOLICS must learn from one another ways to keep the festival through Epiphany and on to the Baptism of the Lord. They do not need to be told that they are "doing it all wrong," nor do they need extensive written notes on the "real length" of Christmas. Positive encouragement is much more fruitful in helping people keep these days. A parish can support the keeping of the season, for example, by scheduling its traditional Christmastime "open house" or other seasonal parties closer to January 5, not during Advent. Older parishioners can share with youngsters the remembered customs of Epiphany, when people from places such as Puerto Rico sing their songs of the Three Kings, when a carolsing or pageant unfolds on the weekend between Christmas and New Year's Day, when local churches offer "First Night" gatherings of their

own. This is education through scheduling and peer support.

While some classroom-centered catechesis may be suspended, other forms of religious education will continue and should reflect the light of these days. Catechumens will go on with their formation during these weeks, with the rite of dismissal and discussions of the manifestation of Christ in their lives. Those who meet in preparation for the other sacraments will hear the Christmas story in terms of their own approach to the sacramental manifestation— their infant's baptism, their marriage, their loved one's funeral, their anointing in the Lord, their ordination to service.

■ DOMESTIC PRAYER: To help the parish's households observe the entire season, texts from *Catholic Household Blessings and Prayers* can be shared with all. The blessing of a Christmas tree, the blessing of a manger, table prayers for Christmas, the blessing of a new year and the blessing of homes at Epiphany provide a rich treasury for every parish home.

The Mass

INTRODUCTORY RITES

JUST as care is needed for the simple introductory rites of Advent, so it must be given to the ordering of those rites during Christmastime. Every entrance rite is about the assembly entering into its liturgy. The presider's and ministers' entrance into the sanctuary may be one of the things that happen, but the purpose of these rites is to bring all the people together into their deeds of word and eucharist.

The liturgical texts for Christmastime, beginning on page 42, include a greeting and penitential invocations. The seasonal greetings from the *Book of Blessings* (#1549, #1577) also are appropriate for these 19 days. Other invocations for the penitential rite are found at form C*iii* in the sacramentary. The rite of sprinkling can be used on Holy Family, Epiphany and the Baptism of the Lord. This would resonate with the practice in Eastern churches of blessing baptismal water on Epiphany. Manifestation images are sparse in the prayers in the sacramentary for the blessing of water, so a sample text appears on page 42.

■ GLORY TO GOD: This is the season to highlight the Gloria; this song of the angels should be chosen for its strength and attractiveness, and enhanced with vocal harmonies, handbells, flute or whatever is available. The familiar "Gloria in excelsis Deo" refrain from "Angels we have heard on high" becomes the assembly's refrain in two settings: the "Christmas Gloria" by Daniel Laginya (GIA, G-2971), for cantor and congregation, and the "Gloria for Christmastime" by Richard Proulx (GIA, G-3085), for two-part mixed voices, cantor and congregation (and flute/oboe *obligato*). Two settings by Benedictine composers are, like the Laginya, effective for cantor and congregation alone, but invite creativity when used with choir and/or instruments: the Gloria by Columba Kelly in *The Collegeville Hymnal* (The Liturgical Press) and the "Glory to God" from Becket Senchur's "Mass of Hope" in *People's Mass Book* (World Library Publications). These refrains can be made more festive by the imaginative use of handbells and the verses divided between the men and the women of the choir.

LITURGY OF THE WORD

■ THE SCRIPTURES: The forthcoming edition of the lectionary will have more readings for Years B and C for the feasts of the Holy Family and the Baptism of the Lord. Meanwhile, those who proclaim the gospel must be especially familiar with the exalted language of the first chapter of John's gospel. It appears frequently in the Roman rite's passage from the Christmas octave to Epiphany.

■ THE PSALM: Psalm 98 is the appointed common seasonal psalm for Christmas and it is appropriate from Christmas Day to the Baptism of the Lord. A few suggested arrangements:

- Robert Leaf, "The ends of the earth have seen the victory of our God" (*Psalms for All Seasons:* From the ICEL Liturgical Psalter Project, NPM)
- Richard Proulx/Joseph Gelineau, "All the ends of the earth" (*Worship,* third edition, Lectionary Accompaniment/Cantor Book, GIA)
- Bob Hurd, "All the ends of the earth" (OCP, #9107)
- David Haas and Marty Haugen, "All the ends of the earth" (GIA, G-2703)

■ GOSPEL ACCLAMATIONS: The eight verses for chanting before the gospel, listed in the lectionary at #212 and #219, supplement the proper verses listed with the several solemnities and feasts of this season. One or two of them may be spread over all the days and featured in any seasonal handouts, allowing the faithful to commit them to memory.

■ AFTER THE HOMILY: When catechumens are dismissed, an appropriate seasonal dismissal text may be used. See the example on page 42. The profession of faith, highlighted on Christmas by genuflecting at the remembrance of the incarnation, should be said or sung in the most solemn way known by the parish. Choose a set of general intercessions to be used throughout Christmastime, with one or two variable petitions befitting the emphasis of each day within the season. See the suggestions in the appendix to the sacramentary (#4 for the Christmas season) and also on page 42 in this *Sourcebook.*

LITURGY OF THE EUCHARIST

■ EUCHARISTIC PRAYER: Six prefaces are designated for these 19 days—some specific to a day and four others evoking more general themes of the Christmas-Epiphany continuum. Eucharistic Prayer I has special inserts for Christmas Day and its octave as well as for Epiphany. If the eucharistic acclamations during Advent have been sung very simply, consider "dressing them up" for the Christmas season. Festive settings that employ a call and response between the cantor and assembly, such as Howard Hughes's "Mass of the Divine Word," (GIA, G-2415) facilitate participation and are a sign of hospitality to visitors during this season. The Vermulst "People's Mass" is widely known; consider the fine arrangement by Richard Proulx of this Holy and the "Danish Mass" memorial acclamation and Amen (World Library Publications).

The value of seasonal familiarity should not be forgotten. The acclamation settings do not have to change partway through the season. All six prefaces do not have to be used in the same year. Note, especially, that the sanctoral days use the prefaces of the season, not of martyrs nor of holy women.

■ COMMUNION RITE: To help our prayers at communion express the intensity of the season, sample texts for the introduction to the Lord's

Prayer, the prayer for peace and the invitation to communion are given on page 44. They are followed by a wonderful image: people processing to the Lord's table singing "tidings of comfort and joy." Carols, particularly those with refrains, are appropriate throughout this season. "What child is this" and "We three kings" are good Epiphany choices.

CONCLUDING RITE

■ ANNOUNCEMENTS: On Christmas and New Year's Day, the good wishes of the pastoral staff may be given following the prayer after communion and before the final blessing. Announcements and messages of gratitude need careful wording: Who is thanking whom? Pastoral leaders may want to thank all the workers in the name of the entire assembly.

■ BLESSING AND DISMISSAL: As eucharistic ministers are sent from the assembly to the homebound and sick, a seasonal text for that dismissal may be used (see page 44). Texts for the solemn blessing during the Christmas season are found in the sacramentary: #3 for January 1 (but #10 may be a better choice for it echoes the first reading or #15 for feasts of Mary), #4 for Epiphany, #2 for Christmas Day and all other days in the season. Another blessing and a sample dismissal text are found on page 45.

MUSIC

■ FAMILIARITY: Consistency in musical choices is one of the best ways to demonstrate and foster the unity of the Sundays and solemnities of Christmastime. In this liturgically intense and compact season, you should expect to hear the same Gloria, psalm setting, acclamations, intercessions and Lamb of God five times in two and a half weeks. The music selected should sparkle and delight like the season itself; this way the repetition will not become dull or burdensome.

■ HYMNODY: The gathering and closing music may vary for the various celebrations of this season, but planners need not search for thematic selections for each feast, particularly if these hymns are unfamiliar or not related to the Christmas season. Hymns appropriate for celebrations of baptism, for example, do not speak of the manifestation of Christ as God's son and are, therefore, out of step with the Baptism of the Lord. On the feast of the Holy Family, texts found in an index under "Family Life" shift our focus away from the ongoing celebration of the Christmas message.

Christmas carols, both by their poetry and their immediate association in peoples' minds and hearts with the festivity of the season, serve best from Christmas eve through the Baptism of the Lord.

If the parish's repertoire of carols seems too limited to sustain the season, consider that some of the carols not commonly sung in church have been playing in shopping malls, workplaces and homes; imagine people learning religious music outside of church! Remember, too, that one new carol learned this year can be sung for many Christmas seasons to come.

Other Ritual Prayer and Sacraments

LITURGY OF THE HOURS

IF Morning or Evening Prayer has been kept during Advent, this observance should not end at Christmas. These hours can be embellished with caroling and other rituals. They are particulary apt times for the blessing of the parish Christmas tree or manger on Christmas itself. If a small group gathers for these celebrations over the following days, they may be seated near one of these emblems of paradise.

Appendix I of the *Liturgy of the Hours* includes material for extended vigils on the eves of Christmas Day, Holy Family, January 1, Epiphany and the Baptism of the Lord. See the notes on page 35 for a Christmas Eve vigil. Texts also are provided in the *Liturgy of the Hours* commons for any local titular solemnity if, for example, your parish is named after John the Evangelist or Elizabeth Ann Seton. The traditional service of lessons and carols is actually a vigil service, held before any major festival, and Christmastime is full of festival days. But these services should not be merely concerts with a few ritual elements added. The music of a lessons and carols service can shine in a vigil service format, with the addition of psalmody and perhaps a *lucernarium*.

COMMUNAL ANOINTING OF THE SICK

The ritual Mass for the anointing of the sick is not permitted on Christmas Day, on January 1 or on Epiphany. Throughout Christmastime, however, celebrations with the sick, both in small groups and in the parish assembly, can draw on the season's messianic and manifestation images. The three scripture passages from Isaiah in the rite are appropriate, as they were in Advent. The reading from 1 John fits with the others from this letter throughout the season. The passage about Jesus and John the Baptist (Luke 7:18–23) brings the sick into the image-world of Christmas—their health and the providence of God are as central to the season as crèches are, for the sick and the suffering are living icons of the epiphany of God. See page 50 for a seasonal introduction and a prayer after anointing.

FUNERALS

Funeral Masses are not permitted on Christmas Day, on January 1 or on the Epiphany. When mourners gather with the parish for Christmastime funerals, the season's excerpts from Isaiah and 1 John are appropriate. The readings from any of the days, often vividly presenting the paschal mystery, also can be used. "Hark the herald angels sing" is a fitting carol for inclusion in the funeral liturgy, as is "Good Christian friends." Pretending it is not Christmastime at a funeral is impossible in a church full of poinsettias—homilists must face this and speak of the paschal mystery revealed in the images of Christmastime. Christmas is the time for the church to tell stories about the Holy Innocents, the sword of sorrow piercing Mary, the flight into Egypt, the death we all face.

MARRIAGES

The ritual Mass for marriage cannot be used on Christmas Day, on January 1 or on Epiphany. As noted in #11 of the introduction to the marriage rite, one of the proper readings from the rite of marriage can be integrated into the day's texts on Holy Family and the Baptism of the Lord. On these same two days, nuptial Masses that are not parish Masses can use the full set of marriage texts. This notation presumes that at least some marriages are celebrated at parish Masses!

Within the marriage lectionary, the Song of Songs, 1 John (2 options) and the wedding feast at Cana (John 2:1–11) are traditional and beautiful both for weddings and for this time of year. The Cana event is central to the celebration of Epiphany. This "first miracle" is one of the great manifestation stories. It expresses well the messianic fullness entered into at Christmas—and at weddings.

OTHER PUBLIC ASSEMBLIES

A parish with a school can gather that community for eucharist, a prayer service or a catechetical assembly on a weekday after school has reopened. (See the resources starting on page 74 in the *Leader's Manual of the Hymnal for Catholic Students*.) Be sure the school's Christmas decorations are still up when the children return. A school assembly during Christmastime is far better than staging a "Christmas" Mass the day before school vacation begins, when children are flying higher than Rudolph and the liturgy should be drawing us into the O Antiphons and the expectation of Mary. If the school does not seem quite ready for this, then be creative: Use Advent's vesture and music, focus any "pageant" on the annunciations to Mary and to Joseph, on the visitation and on the journey to Bethlehem (the gospels of the final week of Advent).

■ BLESSING OF A CHRISTMAS MANGER: The *Book of Blessings* (chapter 48) has an order for gathering by the manger, listening to the word of God, singing carols, offering intercessions and blessing the manger and all who look on it. This can take place on Christmas Eve or on the evening of Christmas Day, perhaps at a gathering of families after Christmas dinner (led by one of the parents) or as part of the prayer before a meal for the homeless or infirmed people served at the church hall. These texts unite the crèche to the paschal mystery and the liturgy.

■ BLESSING OF A CHRISTMAS TREE: The same *Book of Blessings* (chapter 49) provides an outline and texts for a parish assembly to bless a Christmas tree and to light it for the first time. The texts point to the history of the Christmas tree as a tree of paradise. This is also an opportunity for parish members to gather in prayer with those who are associated with the parish, but who do not usually share in its liturgical life (day-care workers and their families or self-help programs that rent space, for example). If the parish has a large outdoor tree lit for the season, it is an incredible and primitive experience to stand under a tree in the darkness of a winter's night, singing carols and invoking God and watching the lights go on for the first time. Even in areas where street violence mars the beauty of the season, the parish can light an evergreen tree and shine forth a promise of the fullness Christmas offers.

The Worship Environment

THE first manger, obviously, was in Bethlehem, and early Christians went there in pilgrimage. Not much time passed before the manger of clay was replaced with one of silver and the grotto encased in an enormous basilica. Such changes were not universally applauded. A few centuries later, pilgrims went to the basilica of St. Mary Major in Rome to venerate relics of the manger. These Christians also decorated worship spaces with representations of the nativity—Jesus in a manger between an ox and an ass. Then the custom received the form as we know it when St. Francis of Assisi and his community set up mangers with live animals.

While we may laud Francis for popularizing the custom, we need not follow his practice of setting up the manger at the altar. He lived at a time of confusion between sentimental devotions and liturgy, of private prayer occupying the assembly while the priest "said Mass," of pageants and dramas becoming more prominent on feasts than the eucharist. As the *Book of Blessings* envisions it, the manger may be set up outdoors—all the better for live animals! "If the manger is set up in the church, it must not be placed in the presbyterium [sanctuary]. A place should be chosen that is suitable for prayer and devotion and is easily accessible by the faithful" (#1544). This can be a place to visit before or after worship.

The traditional animals should not be forgotten in the planning of the parish's manger. There should be sheep, and the ox and ass have a very long tradition. Our earliest ancestors

placed them at Bethlehem to fulfill Isaiah 1:3, to show that this, indeed, was the Messiah. The presence of the animals and the manger itself are not signs of poverty. Even if room had been available at the inn, there would have been animals inside.

■ OTHER INTERIOR DECORATIONS: Poinsettias, greens and other flowers should be planned with three additional concerns: First, the floral decor must never obscure the altar, ambo and presider's chair. In their own spaces, the font and tabernacle must be seen. A tree cannot be placed between the lector and the assembly, nor between the presider and the assembly, nor in front of the font. Equally as important, the ambo must continue to look like a reading table. The altar still should be seen as a table. No matter how beautiful a garland of greens or a pyramid of poinsettias may be, it must not obscure these focal points in our worship.

The local fire marshal or civic regulations may have to be consulted. What space is needed for the safe evacuation of the assembly? Are cut trees and real greens allowed? How do we place lit candles in relationship to these and to straw? Even if we were not caught up in an overly litigious society, we would not want our liturgy to bring the potential for danger. If we do not like the answers we receive from the fire marshal and if we are sure that other answers respect both the liturgy and public safety, then it is time for representatives of the parish or the diocesan liturgical commission to see the boards or officials responsible.

■ OUTDOORS: What are you putting outdoors to announce the good news to all your neighbors? A flag? A weatherproof banner? Lights on a large evergreen tree? A manger? Garlands over the entries? *Luminarias* along the parish walkways, lit at night on Christmas and Epiphany? Words of greeting on the parish sign? Lights on the steeple or tower? One huge wreath on the tower or around a rose window?

Look at the property and the architecture, and do something you can afford that is in scale and that can be seen. Then keep it in place until the Baptism of the Lord. On the last days of Christmastime, people will wonder why you have not yet taken down your decorations, thus providing the perfect opportunity to do some informal catechesis on why Christmastime lasts as long as it does.

December

W E D **25** #13–16 white
Christmas
SOLEMNITY

GENERAL NOTES FOR ALL MASSES OF CHRISTMAS

■ HOSPITALITY: Why not have refreshments available for all after worship? Even if space is not available in nearby halls, hot cider or eggnog served on the way to the parking lot or on the front plaza of an urban church may be most welcome and well worth the time it takes in preparation. With or without refreshments, many parishes provide brass ensembles playing carols outdoors as people enter and leave.

This hospitality is further enhanced by a careful approach to the liturgy's music. How different the assemblies on this day are from those on most Sundays of the year! Some of the "regulars" have traveled to spend the holidays with family and some are hosting relatives and other visitors; many who are not regular church-goers are drawn to Christmas services. Keeping the nature of these assemblies in mind will help to encourage participation in Christmas worship. Besides the implications of music choices noted elsewhere, hospitality requires that both words and music are printed in a worship aid or service book; it cannot be assumed that service music or song or acclamation is known by all who gather today.

Even pastors and pastoral associates who experienced many hectic Christmas liturgies, with strangers demanding the best seats and silent crowds waiting to be impressed, still find it difficult to resist scolding (mock or serious). This is the most difficult assignment given to pastoral workers every Christmas and Easter. Even good-natured ribbing directed at twice-a-year worshipers reduces them to outsiders and works against their becoming anything more than twice-a-year worshipers. Our best welcoming efforts —without any tone of condescension—must be put forward.

■ MUSIC: The expectant sounds of Advent find fulfillment in this feast of new birth. Keep in mind the effect of Christmas's candles and lights, lavish greens and bountiful feasting. Our songs and the way we sing them also should be bright, fresh and lively, and another mirror of God's abundant goodness. On this feast, worship deserves the very best that the music ministers (and here we include the presider and assembly) can produce. Success is not measured by the degree of difficulty; choose music everyone can perform well and enjoy at the same time.

When you have a tentative plan for the Christmas music, it is helpful to review all the texts together to make sure that the historical aspect of Christmas is not the overwhelming focus of what will be sung at this celebration.

■ ETHNIC CUSTOMS: Feel free to adapt and improve on any of the ethnic traditions of this season. Many of these traditions changed as they crossed the Atlantic or Pacific and met Santa Claus in America. Search out the ancient

form of a custom—often a mystical reinterpretation of common liturgical practice, such as the lighting of the Christmas tree, which is a *lucernarium* at heart— and reincarnate the ethnic tradition into a form that makes sense in our liturgy. Sometimes this takes a bit of genius, and certainly it takes a sense of wonder.

■ CHANTING THE GOSPEL: Chanting the gospel can add to the festivity if it is sung well and with clarity. Two traditional Roman tones from the *Liber usualis* are outlined in the Episcopal altar missal, and more elaborate and challenging settings of this and other festal readings are available through GIA.

■ DRAMATIZING THE GOSPEL: If "pageants" are not customary in your parish, do not rush to begin one. They are extremely difficult to integrate properly into the liturgy. Whenever a dramatic action is planned at any liturgy, whether it is a dramatization of Luke 2 this night or a play depicting the parish's origins on its dedication anniversary, several principles are useful to remember.

Be sure the selection of players does not divide the parish. Find or create a script—one that uses the biblical texts, not a paraphrase— that allows for the participation of crowds of children if many sign up for the event. Every religious educator who has worked with children knows how to create crowds of angels and shepherds. Be sure that the hour before the liturgy is not a confusion of last-minute practices and distractions for leaders and assembly. Utilize the whole worship space for this gospel action. Begin with a gospel procession that includes the gospel book, incense and candles and is accompanied with singing. Have the shepherds' field in one part of the building, the manger area in another. Write in some processions of characters—from Nazareth to Bethlehem, from the field to the manger, from Arabia to Jerusalem to the manger—accompanied by more congregational singing. Avoid crowding all the action "up front" around the ambo.

Most importantly, do not let the dramatics of an acted-out gospel overwhelm the Mass. We do not gather just to watch the children, even though their innocence and their portrayal of the primordial story never fails to melt hearts. But we cannot let the emotions just sit there and "resume" Mass after it. We bring those emotions to the table and translate them into the act of praising God.

Some ways to keep the "pageant" appropriate to the liturgy include: a strong proclamation of the first reading followed by powerful psalm-singing by all; the use of a gospel book (with all the ceremonies it normally receives on Sunday) for the narrator; the inclusion of a sung alleluia before and joyous carols by all both during and especially after the piece; a homily that brings the drama into the eucharistic image-world and intercessions that join this congregation in solidarity with the whole world and its dependence on the all-powerful God. In short, the "pageant" must be brief, participatory for all and placed into the context of a strong, active rite.

■ THE PROFESSION OF FAITH: A genuflection is made during the profession of faith on this day at the words "by the power of the Holy Spirit." Introduce the creed in a way that cues the community to this change, then slow the recitation (or singing) of the text and execute the genuflection in a way that clearly manifests reverence.

SCHEDULING

■ RECENT YEARS: This is one feast where much of the celebrating happens between Evening Prayer I and Morning Prayer. Liturgists and pastors wrestle with the growing participation at Eve Masses and the drastic decline in Christmas Day participation. In many communities, 90 percent of the worshipers come on the Eve. Liturgists and diocesan offices often have reacted with warnings about not losing the sense of Christmas Day. They also have insisted, in terms even stronger than the principles of the lectionary, that the genealogy passage from Matthew must be read at all Masses of the Eve—even if these have large numbers of children attending, even if everyone wants to hear the story from Luke 2 at their one liturgical event of the feast. Some perspective and solutions may flow from the earliest centuries of Christmas-keeping.

■ THE HISTORY OF SEVERAL MASSES ON CHRISTMAS: As explained by Pierre Jounel in the volume edited by Martimort (see the resources list on page xix), multiple Masses on the feast originated in the city of Rome around the sixth century.

For a few centuries before this time, the only Mass was celebrated during the day. When a replica of Bethlehem's manger was built near the basilica of St. Mary Major, pious residents and visiting pilgrims asked for a nocturnal liturgy like the one at Bethlehem, celebrated close to the time when it was said that Jesus was born. The liturgical practices of Jerusalem and Bethlehem and their environs were enormously influential during those centuries. The people of Jerusalem were able to be a bit more literal in their references to the mysteries of the Lord's life, often pointing to the places where the events happened. This literalism generated new feasts, led to the manger in Rome and, thus, was indirectly responsible for the Roman Mass during the night.

Even before December 25 came to be observed as the Nativity, St. Anastasia (whose name means "resurrection") had long been commemorated on that day in her basilica in Rome. This observance was particularly cherished by the Byzantine authorities who lived in that district of Rome. To honor them, the popes began going to the liturgy commemorating her on their way to the Day Mass of Christmas. After some generations, the stop at the basilica of St. Anastasia continued, but texts relating to the Nativity crept in, reducing Anastasia's texts to a commemoration. A reference to her remained in the Dawn Mass of Christmas until just a few decades ago.

This system of three Roman Masses was not invented to "follow the sun," but as it spread to other urban areas without mangers or basilicas of St. Anastasia, the texts for each Mass began to take on images appropriate to the sun's position and its passage from night into day.

■ CHRISTMAS EVE OR CHRISTMAS DAY? How many times will the parish gather to celebrate the Nativity of the Lord from the evening on the 24th through the evening on the 25th? The liturgy of the hours and the various Masses make the answer complicated.

The reason given by so many for the shift from Day Masses to overcrowded Eve Masses is "convenience." But there seems to be a deeper reason—the need for a nocturnal liturgy at Christmas. Although the liturgy in Rome was held during the day, instincts in Bethlehem and at St. Mary Major pressed for a nocturnal celebration of the birth of Christ. The search for this nighttime celebration certainly caused many to attend the Midnight Mass in the centuries before Vigil Masses. Now that Masses are scheduled at an earlier hour, and sunset in most areas of the Northern hemisphere is quite early, parents are able to bring their small children soon after sunset and celebrate a "nighttime" liturgy as a family. Senior citizens often also find an earlier time more suitable.

The actual liturgical title of the Mass in Latin is "Night" not "Midnight." And while generations have been thrilled to hear the bells peal the passing of December 24 into December 25, the "liturgical day" of Christmas begins at sundown, as do all our principal festivals. The gulf between "vigil" and "night" should not be dug too deeply. All four Christmas Masses listed in the sacramentary are equally festive. One does not have to wait until midnight to be festive. As on Saturday evenings all year, this is a festival, not a penitential wait for midnight. As noted in the Vatican commentary on the Roman Calendar:

> The medieval notion of a vigil as a day of penance before a feast has been completely abolished. With the exception of the Easter Vigil which is celebrated sometime during the night, the term "Mass of the Vigil" now refers to the Mass which can be celebrated in a festive way in the evening, before or after Evening Prayer I of certain solemnities. (p. 23)

Recognizing this history and the shift to the Eve observance, one need not defend Christmas Day as the only proper time for celebrating the eucharist. Those who prefer to celebrate after dark, whether early in the evening or toward midnight, are not to be berated as if they were forgetting the day. They may well be holding to a tradition as ancient as the feast itself.

The entire time span that we are discussing is sacred and is Christmas. No part of this time is to be consigned to a liturgyless realm. Even if the eucharist is celebrated by most on the Eve, domestic prayer and ecclesial gatherings for the liturgy of the hours keep the whole feast holy. Schedule framers can set up Evening Prayer I, the Office of Readings, Morning Prayer, Evening Prayer II and the various celebrations of the eucharist. Parish announcements of these liturgies may include suggestions on how they may be part of a family's keeping the feast. Meanwhile, every household in the parish can be supplied with resources to assist them in shaping domestic prayer on Christmas Day and throughout the season. If the household goes to church for Mass early in the Eve hours, the manger can be blessed or the tree lit for the first time later that night. The prayers at table on the day itself may be more extensive and intense.

EVENING PRAYER I

Large parishes or parishes that implemented the liturgy of the hours should consider at least a simple Evening Prayer celebration. If the clergy and choirs and lay ministers are busy preparing for the Masses, then the leadership and planning of this liturgy may best be performed by a community of religious living in the parish or by a few households who will take on this responsibility. This celebration could include the blessing and first lighting of the parish's Christmas tree (see the *Book of Blessings*).

MASS IN THE EARLY EVENING

■ SELECTION OF TEXTS: The whole ensemble of texts from the lectionary and the sacramentary should be evaluated for its appropriateness to this evening. The presidential prayers designated for the Vigil Mass are most appropriate, but the alternative opening prayer of the Mass at Midnight is strongly "vigil" in content. The Acts reading for the Vigil Mass is strongly linked with Matthew's genealogy. All three of the readings presume that the assembly is awaiting Christmas and the implication seems to be that the assembly will reconvene later at night or in the morning. This may be the case in certain communities, but in most parishes this will be the one and only liturgical event of the festival. In that case, a strong pastoral case can be made for proclaiming the story of the nativity as found in Luke 2.

The approach to selecting readings is closely related to the issue of scheduling the times of liturgies. Pastors and committees do not just set up schedules. Most parishes have more than one time when the eucharist is celebrated, and those who assemble regularly on Sundays develop patterns of celebration. It may be that the early evening Mass has many children attending, or perhaps this is a time favored by senior citizens, or there may be a mixture of young families and elderly persons.

If there are many children in the assembly, texts should be selected with the norms in the *Directory for Masses with Children* in mind. The beauty of the *Directory* is that its principles for children so often engender a gracious, beautiful and deeply liturgical style of celebration for all ages in the assembly. The *Directory* does not encourage childish talk; rather it calls for strong, clear actions and music that enable all children and adults to enter into the sacrament.

■ BLESSING THE MANGER: The blessing of the parish's Christmas manger is a compelling action this evening, particularly if the assembly or at least the children process there with joyous song. The rite for this blessing during Mass is simple as outlined in the *Book of Blessings,* but it can become more elaborate with such a procession, with sung intercessions at the manger and with some of the figures for the scene being carried in the procession. Whereas a dramatization of the gospel this evening can drown other aspects of the liturgy, this blessing seems more in scale with the liturgy.

VIGIL/OFFICE OF READINGS

This is not the Vigil Mass but the Office of Readings extended into a vigil service, a liturgy encouraged for Sundays and certain solemnities. Christmas and Pentecost are considered the most important opportunities for this. Based on the norms from the *Liturgy of the Hours* (#71 and #73 and the rubrics of the Christmas Office of Readings) and specifications made in the *Ceremonial of Bishops* (#238), this vigil may take one of these forms before the late-night Mass.

■ TRADITIONAL ROMAN OPTION: For those communities familiar with the *Liturgy of the Hours* and used to combining certain hours with the Mass, and for those who want to use the customary Roman form:

- Opening procession. (Same order as the opening procession at Mass.)

- Greeting and opening dialogue. (From the ordinary of the Office of Readings.)

- Hymn.

- Psalmody, sung. (The proper psalms for the Christmas Office of Readings are Psalms 2, 19a and 45. Proper antiphons are proposed for each.)

- Verse. (Proper to Christmas.)

- Reading: Isaiah 11:1–10.

- Responsory, sung. (Text given in the Office of Readings.)

- Sermon of St. Leo the Great. (Found in the Office of Readings. This is one of the best passages of our tradition on the mystery of the incarnation.)

- Responsory, sung. (Text given in the Office of Readings.)

- Antiphon for the Christmas vigil, sung. (From appendix I of the *Liturgy of the Hours.*)

- One, two or three canticles, sung. (Found in appendix I of the *Liturgy of the Hours.* The proper ones are all from Isaiah this night.)

- The proper vigil antiphon is sung again to conclude the canticles.

- Reading: Matthew 1:1–25 or 1:18–25 (the genealogy of Jesus), proclaimed by the deacon or assisting presbyter, with candles and incense.

- Gloria, sung by all in its Christmastime setting.

- Opening prayer of Midnight Mass.

- The liturgy of the word and the rest of the Mass as usual.

■ OPTION WITH SERVICE OF LIGHT AND CAROLS: The pattern for this vigil is similar to the pattern of the Easter Vigil. This is adapted from outlines present in earlier editions of the *Sourcebook,* which are rooted in the practices of the Ambrosian rite:

- Entrance procession, including the presider and all the ministers of the Mass, accompanied by strong instrumental music. During the entrance procession, the invitatory from the *Liturgy of the Hours* may be sung ("Christ is born for us; come let us adore him"). The church is in darkness, and ministers in the procession carry lit candles. Use the large candles from the Advent wreath or Christmas tree to lead the procession if these candles can be detached. The procession pauses once or twice and stops at the wreath or tree so that the ministers can pass their light to members of the assembly near them. When the procession arrives at the altar, many candles are lit there and throughout the space, such as pew candles or the consecration candles on the walls.

- Greeting. The sung dialogue on light, found in many liturgical resource books (for example, *Worship*).

- Hymn or carol with references to light such as "O little town of Bethlehem" or "O come, divine Messiah."

- Thanksgiving for light sung by cantor, deacon or priest. As the community sings its Amen to conclude this thanksgiving, a few lights may be turned on and the assembly may extinguish its candles.

- Introduction or welcome to the vigil.

    In this vigil we celebrate the dawn of our salvation in the birth of our Lord Jesus Christ, the Father's only-begotten Son, born for us of the Virgin Mary. With gratitude let us recall his humanity and the life he shared with the children of the earth, praying that the power of his divinity may enable us to answer his call to forgiveness and life.

- Readings and carols. Select several of these five readings suggested by tradition:

- Reading I: Genesis 15:1–12, 17–18 (lectionary #373)

- Psalm and/or carol, followed by a prayer (prayer texts for each of these five readings are found on page 45).

- Reading II: 1 Samuel 1:9–20 (lectionary #306)

- Psalm and/or carol, followed by a prayer.

- Reading III: Isaiah 7:1–9 (lectionary #390) or 7:10–14 (lectionary #10)

- Psalm and/or carol, followed by a prayer.

- Reading IV: Judges 13:2–7, 24–25 (lectionary #196)

- Psalm and/or carol, followed by a prayer.

- Reading V: An excerpt from a Christmas homily by St. Leo the Great (from the Office of Readings).

- The Proclamation of the Birth of Christ, sung by the cantor. (See pages 46–47.) As the proclamation concludes, the rest of the lights in the space may be turned on. The traditional processional carol for Christmas, "O come, all ye faithful," may well be missed. It can be sung at the Preparation of the Altar.

- Gloria, sung by all in its Christmastime setting.

- Opening prayer of Mass.

- The liturgy of the word and the rest of Mass continue as usual.

MASS IN THE NIGHT

If you do not schedule a vigil for the hour or half hour before Mass, think long and hard before scheduling some other, nonliturgical format. Is a choir concert needed now? Does it help the assembly enter into the liturgy? We need great choirs, and their performance of certain selections lends richness to a liturgy, but it can be devastating to communal participation to begin Mass with a concert. If a choir *tour de force* is

deemed appropriate, then at least include carols for all.

■ THE PROCLAMATION OF THE BIRTH OF CHRIST (pp. 46–47) can be used just before the processional hymn—a prayerful way to signal the beginning of Mass.

MASS AT DAWN

Many times older people attend this early Mass, or those whose children are grown and have moved away and whose grandchildren are miles apart. Music at all the usual times certainly must be present here. The alternative opening prayer is clear and beautiful. Remember the genuflection during the creed. There is the inaccurate word "birthday" in the prayer after communion: "Birth" is the more precise translation.

If a number of folks who live alone participate in this early morning Mass, a breakfast gathering immediately after Mass may be fitting.

MORNING PRAYER

Who will come? The folks for whom the parish gathering is the high point of their Christmas Day may appreciate Mass at 7:00, breakfast at 8:00 and Morning Prayer at 9:00. Or Morning Prayer can be the first liturgy of the day—it is, after all, the church's daily "sunrise service." For families who celebrated the eucharist in the evening, this briefer time of liturgy may be a welcome greeting to the festival day. A starting time of 9:00 will seem like midday to families with small children!

MASS DURING THE DAY

Everything about the church this day should proclaim what the entrance antiphon puts into words: "A child is born for us, a son given to us; dominion is laid on his shoulder, and he shall be called Wonderful-Counselor!" "Humankind" and "us" are more inclusive than "man" and "him" in the first opening prayer.

Although rubrics permit the interchangeable use of the four sets of Christmas readings, the prologue to John's gospel is a venerable tradition at this Mass during the Day. It speaks of light, the brightness of the noonday sun now streaming in the windows. As Jounel notes,

> The high point of the Christmas liturgy is the reading of the Prologue of St. John in the daytime Mass: "And the Word became flesh and dwelt among us; . . . we have beheld his glory" (John 1:14). All the other readings lead up to this one or echo it. . . . In accordance with their varied literary genres, all of them proclaim the dogmas of Nicaea, Ephesus and Chalcedon, in the light of which the feast was born and developed.

CHRISTMAS DAY AFTERNOON

Try to leave the church open throughout the day. Announce it at all Masses as an invitation to return. You would be surprised how many households may enjoy stopping in with their guests to show off their parish home. It may be necessary to have volunteers stay in the church in some neighborhoods.

EVENING PRAYER II

While some liturgical leaders have traveled far to be with friends or family, others are in town. Many parishioners are looking for a way to get out of their houses and bring a public breath of air into the day. Just witness the lines of cars this evening circling on those streets reputed to be the best lit. Note the long lines at movie houses and the full arenas at major-league hockey and basketball games. This desire can easily be translated into an ecclesial spirit through the celebration of Evening Prayer on Christmas Day. The canticle from Colossians and the reading from 1 John help put the assembly in touch with the many levels of meaning of Christmas—in ways far more poetic than the best sermons.

THU 26 #696 red
Stephen, first martyr
FEAST

"Come, let us worship the newborn Christ who has given the glorious crown to St. Stephen." So begins the *Liturgy of Hours* for this day, and in the same spirit the great season of Christmas envelops each saint's day. These are days for carols, extra hospitality, gift giving, extra solemnity even for the daily Mass. Ritual details planned for the Masses of Christmas can continue through the Baptism of the Lord.

Other liturgical texts for St. Stephen reflect the invitatory antiphon with which the day begins. The prayer after communion links Jesus' birth and Stephen's martyrdom. The sermon by Fulgentius of Ruspe and its responsory in the Office of Readings provide inspiration for any homilist. The intercessions for Evening Prayer form an amazing compendium of

Christ's life and the paschal mystery seen from the light of Christmas (and can be used at daily Mass).

■ *COMITES CHRISTI:* Pius Parsch wrote in the decades before Vatican II about this day and the next two days:

At Bethlehem God's kingdom came into existence. But how did it fare? Who were responsible for its extension? And what aided most in its development?

The feast of St. Stephen contributes one very important answer. In order to flourish, God's kingdom requires martyrs. In the gospel Christ points to a list of divinely commissioned [people], from Abel down to the present, who were put to death. It is ever the same with God's kingdom on earth. The feast of St. John gives further information on what is needed. For membership, there are two requirements: God's call and people's wholehearted compliance. John heads the list of Christ's friends, those who are called "great in the kingdom of heaven." The Holy Innocents, too, by liturgical standards are Christian heroes. Thus as the King proceeds, he is not alone; he is followed by the glorious retinue of his kingdom. *(The Church's Year of Grace,* vol. 1, p. 215)

FRI 27 #697 white
John, apostle and evangelist
FEAST

"Come, let us worship the Lord, the King of apostles" (invitatory antiphon). Again, today's liturgical texts are excellent examples of observances of the saints set in a seasonal context.

SAT 28 #698 red
Holy Innocents, martyrs
FEAST

"Come, let us worship the newborn Christ who crowns with joy these children who died for him" (invitatory antiphon). If there is a developing tradition in the parish of observing ember days, see *Catholic Household Blessings and Prayers* (p. 189) for ideas on this day. Once more the paschal quality of Christmas presents itself to us. Sacrifice is a fruit of the incarnation.

☀ 29 #17 white
Holy Family
FEAST

Don't make unnecessary work for yourself. First and foremost, this is a Christmastime celebration. The liturgy for this Sunday does not fixate on the word "family," and neither should you. Both today and January 1 are Christmas liturgies, with the entire parish's involvement required, with the regular ministers functioning, with Christmas readings, prayer texts, melodies and environment—and after-worship hospitality.

Making a special effort to choose only nuclear families (father, mother, children) today to act as liturgical ministers (preparing the gifts, offering hospitality) runs the risk of excluding many households in the parish. Scheduling a "blessing of families" or a "renewal of vows" by all married couples brings excessive focus on "family" and presumes forethought and readiness on the part of the congregation that may be hard to muster a few days after Christmas. Blessing families and couples is an admirable liturgical practice at the right place and time. See the *Book of Blessings* for appropriate rites that would best be used in Ordinary Time and when groups have time to prepare and to decide whether to step forward for the blessing.

Today's first opening prayer is succinct. "Humanity" and "people" would be more inclusive than "man" and "men" in the alternative opening prayer.

In some parts of the world and in some ethnic groups in the United States, many people bring devotional objects to church today, seeking a blessing for them. Parishes may well plan a brief blessing for those who want to stay after the recessional. Those who bring such Christmas gifts then may gather by the manger and a priest or deacon could use chapter 44 of the *Book of Blessings* (see the shorter form for use just after Mass).

Be sure to place the statues of the magi somewhere in the church heading toward the manger. Keep a few vigil lights burning around them and a few Christmastime flowers nearby. Then day by day move them closer to the manger until they arrive on Epiphany. This simple practice can be further embellished by asking groups of children or families to help in the moving each day.

M O N 30 #204 white Sixth Day in the Octave of Christmas

The Presentation of the Lord is not a feast of the Christmas season as such, but the event and its memory are always part of telling the infancy story of our beginnings. The gospel about the meeting with Simeon, assigned to the

Fifth Octave Day, was skipped because of Sunday, so it can be joined to today's story about Anna. Or the briefer passage about the meeting with the woman of many days can stand as this season's reminder of that mystical meeting.

T U E 31 #205 white Seventh Day in the Octave of Christmas

Sylvester I, pope, optional memorial / white. ▪ Sylvester's feast is one of the oldest in the Roman rite. The passage from Eusebius in the Office of Readings offers a nice glimpse of his era. The opening prayer for the memorial can be used as such or with the intercessions; other texts are from the season.

January

W E D 1 #18 white Mary, Mother of God SOLEMNITY

Octave of Christmas. ▪ *New Year's Day.* ▪ *World Day of Prayer for Peace.* ▪ This day always has been rich in titles and allusions. The circumcision (biblically set on the eighth day), the Holy Name of Jesus and the motherhood of Mary are all biblical themes that developed from early Christians' Christmas piety. More recently, popes have invited all local churches to keep the intentions of peace close to the heart of the assembly on this day.

▪ NEW YEAR'S EVE: From the very first century, these themes unfolded against the backdrop of New Year's Day, but many ecclesiastical leaders warned their congregations against the day's secular observances—drunkenness, immoral parties, idolatry. While we are more familiar with the connection of this solemnity with January 1, and while most New Year's Eve festivities are more hollow than immoral, Christian communities would do well to integrate any parish New Year's customs into an explicitly Christmas spirit. We have better icons for temporal transitions than "Father Time." The communion antiphon today offers the beginning of a hymn for New Year's: "Jesus Christ is the same yesterday, today and forever."

▪ WATCH-NIGHT SERVICE: Some Catholic parishes have coupled a New Year vigil ("watchnight") with festivity. They have borrowed the idea from certain Protestant churches as a chance to praise God for the blessings of the old year and to ask God for blessings in the new. Such a vigil in a Catholic church must take full account of the season and feast. This can be accomplished with one or more of these resources for guidance:

- The Episcopal *The Book of Occasional Services* offers "A Service for New Year's Eve."

- The *Liturgy of the Hours,* in appendix I, gives canticles and a gospel to extend the Office of Readings into an extended vigil.

- *Catholic Household Blessings and Prayers* (p. 121) has a brief service for blessing the new year.

▪ MASS ON THE DAY: As is true every day, the liturgy calls for the sign of the cross and a greeting in the Lord's name and peace. No "Happy New Year" can substitute. The words of introduction after the cross and liturgical greeting may include such warm wishes —phrased as our wishes for each other, not just as "father's greeting." The alternative opening prayer successfully weaves together several aspects of this day. The intercessions should include peace and justice throughout the world. The collect prayer of the intercessions can be the opening prayer from the Masses and Prayers for Various Needs and Occasions, 24. Beginning of the Civil Year.

#206   white
T H U 2 Basil the Great and Gregory Nazianzen, bishops and doctors
MEMORIAL

These learned men of the fourth century, who lived in what is now Turkey, were influential throughout all the churches of the world. Together with Basil's younger brother, Gregory of Nyssa, they are remembered as the most important teachers ("doctors") of the faith in their time. Their feasts were joined and moved to this day a few years ago, a day closer to their death anniversaries and closer to the East's January 1 feast in honor of Basil.

The Office of Readings has a sermon by Gregory in which he describes his friendship with Basil; it contains wonderful sentences for greeting cards to friends at this season. While the readings and prayers would best be from the Christmas season, the saints' prayer can be used as the opening prayer or as the collect to intercessions. The antiphon to the canticle of Zechariah at Morning Prayer begins the work of integrating the saints into this joyous week of Epiphany: "Those who are learned will be as radiant as the sky in all its beauty; those who instruct the people in goodness will shine like the stars for all eternity."

The gospel passages for these three days between January 1 and Epiphany are all from John 1. They contain John the Baptist's testimonies about himself and about Jesus, forming a nice connection between Advent and the manifestation of Epiphany. We have organized the liturgical seasons along certain lines and tend to think of John the Baptist as an "Advent" saint, but the biblical narratives do not put any such limits on John. He is just as much a Christmas and manifestation saint as he is a herald of the coming end time.

#207   white
F R I 3 Christmas Weekday

Christmastime continues all week. Keep the statues of the magi marching through the church to Bethlehem.

#208   white
S A T 4 Elizabeth Ann Seton, religious
MEMORIAL

This is a particularly American memorial. With Elizabeth on Saturday and with Blessed André Bessette on Monday, we frame this year's Epiphany celebration with bright American lights. We know that the mystery of the manifestation of God in the flesh was not just in ancient Palestine. It is on our continent, *hodie*.

Elizabeth was a widow with several children who founded the first American religious community, the first Catholic parish school and the first Catholic orphanage— first at least for the states that were then forming into the United States. We must not forget the older Mexican Catholic presence in the areas that eventually became states.

The readings listed in the sacramentary (the current lectionary was printed before her canonization) are to be used only in

those communities where her memorial is celebrated as a solemnity, for example, in a parish that carries her title. Otherwise, use the proper presidential prayers for her day and Christmastime texts at all other points. Her texts for the *Liturgy of the Hours* are in appendix V of the newest editions.

#20   white
☀5 Epiphany
SOLEMNITY

IMAGES OF THE DAY

Three mysteries have been a part of this holy day over the centuries: Today, the star leads the magi to the infant Christ; today, water is changed into wine for the wedding feast; today, Christ wills to be baptized by John in the River Jordan to bring us salvation (see the antiphons for the gospel canticles at Morning Prayer and Evening Prayer II).

Just as in the West the conception of John the Baptist at Yom Kippur (the Jewish Day of Atonement) may have formed the chronological anchor for figuring out the date of the Nativity of Jesus (see p. 26), different methods of calculating Jewish and secular dates in the East led to January 6 as the Nativity festival date. In both western and eastern churches, the winter solstice and the returning sun filled the Incarnation festivals with solar symbolism. In the East, this cosmic sense was further deepened by pagan beliefs that on this day the rivers run red with wine. Thus, the manifestation stories of the baptism of the Lord making the Jordan sacred and the turning of water into wine picked up ancient themes and gave new meaning to them.

This triptych of mysteries—the magi, Cana and the baptism of Jesus—does not come close to exhausting Epiphany's meaning. See, for example, the first reading from Isaiah, a passage long linked with Epiphany in the churches' lectionaries. Here the "ingathering" theme is struck, inviting all to see the new Jerusalem pulling in the nations, the dromedaries, the rulers. Faced with such richness, do not try to explain or contain the celebration by focusing exclusively on only one particular aspect of the feast.

The rubrics again free us from other concerns. Ritual Masses are forbidden for marriages and communal anointings. (This is one of those days that would best be marked on the parish calendar as inappropriate for weddings.) Funerals may not be celebrated today at Mass. See the seasonal introduction for notes about the blessing of homes that may take place on this day.

The Christmastime worship environment remains; the magi and their retinue arrive at the manger. The *Ceremonial of Bishops, #240*, calls for "a suitable and increased display of lights"—a curious translation, but a reminder nonetheless that this is the season for candlelight.

MASS

■ INTRODUCTORY RITES: Today is the most ancient Christian feast of God's reign; this is reflected in the assigned antiphon. As a general rule for such festivals, if a "suitable hymn" is sung instead of the antiphon, planners should

at least refer to these lines (previously called the "Introit") during their preparations. Festival after festival, they provide marvelous summaries of the feasts, setting just the right tone for the moment.

Children may be invited to take part in the entrance procession, perhaps carrying silver stars on sticks and wearing halos of garland in their hair. In every Mass with children, they should be drawn into the celebration. Sometimes this means explicit greetings or words, sometimes not. But it always demands that presiders and planners think of the entire assembly. This Sunday and next, use the rite of blessing and sprinkling. Note the text on page 42. The alternative opening prayer contains the important word "today," as well as the ugly phrase "resplendent fact." ("People" would be more inclusive than "men.") The first prayer is ancient and direct.

■ LITURGY OF THE WORD: The *Ceremonial of Bishops* (#240) institutionalizes a tradition long advocated in this *Sourcebook:*

> After the singing of the gospel reading, depending on local custom, one of the deacons . . . or someone else, vested in cope, will go to the lectern (ambo) and there announce to the people the movable feasts of the current year.

The traditional use of copes by all ministers is a fascinating subject in itself, but not one to be pursued here. This directive indicates, even in its reference to vesture, this rite's importance. For a sung text, see pages 48–49.

Homily and intercession ideas for today can be found on pages 35 and 44 in *When Catholics Speak about Jews* (see resources list).

■ LITURGY OF THE EUCHARIST: The proper preface is a gem. Note that there is a proper insert to Eucharistic Prayer I.

■ CONCLUDING RITE: Handing out parish calendars, a complement to the chanted dates, can be carried out with style. Think ahead and wrap the calendars in festive ribbons. (Perhaps the religious education program students or the senior-citizens' club could do this.)

EVENING PRAYER II

This is one Sunday when you especially will rejoice if you have established Sunday Vespers as a regular part of ecclesial life. This is also a grand night for the parish Christmas choir concert. Precede it with Evening Prayer and many carols for everyone to sing—and maybe a visit from the magi themselves! Epiphany is a fine day for one of several annual parish potluck suppers.

MON 6 #213 white
Christmas Weekday

Blessed André Bessette, religious, optional memorial/white. ▪ The dioceses of the United States share this observance with Canada. Parishes, especially in the Northeast, are well advised to observe his memory. Such local witnesses to holiness help us realize that "sacred" is not just far away and long ago. Born near Montreal in 1845, André worked as a young adult in the French-Canadian communities of Rhode Island and Connecticut. On returning to the province of Quebec, he entered the Holy Cross brothers and became the famous "man of prayer on the mountain." He inspired many with a love of St. Joseph, became renowned for his healings and instigated the building of an important shrine on the hillside where he lived in Montreal. His simple and rather unsophisticated approach to Catholicism still causes some controversy in his native region, but the liturgy today lets us praise the manifestation of God through André, through devotion to Joseph and through a commitment to the poor and afflicted.

The gospel this day, and throughout the week, turns our attention to the first manifestations and ministerial actions of Jesus—cures, miracles, teaching in the synagogue.

TUE 7 #214 white
Christmas Weekday

Raymond of Penyafort, priest, optional memorial/white. ▪ If the memorial is observed, the texts for today's saint, a Dominican general, canonist and commentator on the sacrament of penance, would best be integrated into this seasonal framework: Use the readings and prayers of the Tuesday after Epiphany with Raymond of Penyafort's prayer (so evocative of his life) at the intercessions.

WED 8 #215 white
Christmas Weekday

As noted in the seasonal introduction (p. 26), the Office of Readings passage from Proclus of Constantinople examines the connections between the feasts of Christmas, Epiphany and the Baptism of the Lord.

THU 9 #216 white
Christmas Weekday

FRI 10 #217 white
Christmas Weekday

Once again, the Office of Readings excerpt from early Christian literature answers those who wonder why the Baptism of the Lord is connected to Christmas.

SAT 11 #218 white
Christmas Weekday

The gospel today, like tomorrow's feast, brings us back to John the Baptist decreasing so that Christ may increase. The Advent-Christmas passage comes full circle.

☼ 12 #21 white
Baptism of the Lord
FEAST

The baptismal font may be decorated today. Some parishes position the Christmas manger in the baptistry so that this underlying connection is evoked each year—perhaps you can consider this for next Christmas. What is not advised is the setting up of a temporary font or additional display of water by the crib on this day. The font is one and should be permanent. Keep the Christmas order of rites and prayer texts. The rite of sprinkling could be used at Mass today (see the text on page 42). Do not stop singing carols: Christmas light now glistens in the waters of the Jordan and in the parish font. Evening Prayer II (with more carols and perhaps an "undecorating party") can bring Christmastime to a close.

Homilists would do well to imitate the homily found in the Office of Readings. Gregory of Nazianzus calls the community to the "now" of this feast, to the necessity of entering into the river of new life with Christ.

INTRODUCTORY RITES

Greeting

The peace and love of God our Father, manifested in Christ who was born for our salvation, be with you all.

Rite of Blessing and Sprinkling of Holy Water

Dear brothers and sisters: let us implore the blessing of God our Father that this rite of sprinkling water may revive in us the grace of baptism through which we have been immersed in the redeeming death of the Lord, the Word made flesh and the Son of Mary, that we might rise with him to new life.

O God our Father,
by your voice thundering over the waters
    of the Jordan,
you proclaimed Christ as your beloved Son
and summoned us to place our faith in him.

R. Cleanse and bless your church, O Lord!

[Or: Glory and praise to you, O Lord!]

[Or: Glory to God in the highest!]

O Christ, beloved Son,
by your baptism you sanctified the waters
    of the Jordan
and unsealed for your church the fountain
    of baptism,
the cleansing flood of health and
    holiness. [R]

O Holy Spirit,
you descended upon Christ in the form
    of a dove,
confirming the Father's witness,
anointing Jesus with the oil of gladness,
and inviting us to become his disciples. [R]

Great are you, Lord God, enthroned above
    the flood forever,
yet choosing to make your dwelling
    in our midst
through Christ, your Word made flesh.

Bless this water as you did the waters
    of the Jordan,
and let the power of baptism so inundate
    our souls
that by the witness of our words and deeds
your saving power may be proclaimed to
    the ends of the earth.

We ask this through Christ our Lord.
—*Text adapted from the Byzantine Rite*

Invitation to Penitence

In these shining days of Christmas,
as we celebrate the mystery of God with us,
let us turn to the Lord
and ask God's gracious mercy.

Penitential Rite:

Form Ciii in the sacramentary, or:

Eternal Word, through whom all things were made: Lord, have mercy.

True Light, enlightening everyone born into the world: Christ, have mercy.

Son of God, made flesh in the womb of the Virgin Mother: Lord, have mercy.

LITURGY OF THE WORD

Dismissal of Catechumens

Dear catechumens: with the assurance of our loving support, this community sends you forth to reflect more deeply on the word of God we have shared. Our prayer for you in this season of Christmas joy is that the mystery of the Word made flesh may strengthen your resolve to embrace Christ as your Savior and lead you to share fully with us at the Lord's table as children of God and heirs, in hope, of eternal life.

General Intercessions

Invitation to Prayer

In Christ, Emmanuel, the Word made flesh, we have beheld God's love for us; let us draw near to God in prayer, therefore, with joy and hope of all who trust in God's saving power.

For the church

For the holy church of God,
that we may be a sign of unity
and an instrument of God's peace,
let us pray to the Lord.

That the church may reflect God's love
      of the poor,
showing to all that God's reign is at hand,
let us pray to the Lord.

For the world

For the rulers and leaders of all nations,
that they reject violence
and together seek the ways of peace,
let us pray to the Lord.

For the peace of the whole world,
for stability of the holy churches of God,
and for the unity of all,
let us pray to the Lord.

For various needs

For the refugees and exiles in every land,
the foreigners and strangers in our midst,
and all separated from their families
      and homes,
let us pray to the Lord.

For those in positions of public trust,
that they may serve justice,
and promote the dignity and freedom
      of every person,
let us pray to the Lord.

For the local community

That the homeless ones in our town
      be welcomed as Christ
who has come to be with us,
let us pray to the Lord.

For the families and friends who gather
      in these days,
that Christ's peace reign in our hearts
      and homes,
let us pray to the Lord.

Attuned to the Sunday readings

For those who have not heard the good
      news of salvation,
those who have heard but have not
      believed,
and those who have forsaken their faith,
let us pray to the Lord.

For catechumens, candidates and inquirers

For the catechumens and candidates
      of the parish,
that they come to see Christ as the true
light of the world and welcome him
      into their lives,
let us pray to the Lord.

For the catechumens who seek the living
waters of baptism, for the candidate
      who will be called
to gather at the table of the Lord,
and for all their sponsors,
let us pray to the Lord.

For the dead

For the people of faith who have died
      in Christ,
that they share now in the glory
      of the resurrection,
let us pray to the Lord.

Concluding Prayers for the General Intercessions

CHRISTMAS:
God Most High,
your only Son embraced the weakness
      of flesh,
that we might have power to become
      your children;
your eternal Word chose a dwelling
      among us,
that we might live in your presence.

With grace upon grace, reveal in our lives
the share of his fullness we have all
      received;
and let us see the glory
which he has with you and the Holy Spirit
as God, for ever and ever.
— © ICEL

HOLY FAMILY:
God our Father,
we come into your house
filled with wonder at the extravagance
      of your love.
You sent your eternal Word among us—
one like us, yet our Redeemer,
the only-begotten Son, yet humble
      in obedience.

Teach us to ponder the mystery of his life
and his preaching,
that as your sons and daughters
we may find in you
the source and goal of every loyalty
        and love.
for ever and ever.
We ask this through your Son, our Lord Jesus
Christ who lives and reigns [with you in the
unity of the Holy Spirit,
one God] for ever and ever.
—© ICEL

MARY, MOTHER OF GOD:
Most high God,
you come near to us this Christmas season
in a child born of the woman Mary.
In the midst of darkness, she gave birth
        to the Light.
In the midst of silence, she brought forth
        the Word.

Grant that, like her,
we may ponder these things in our hearts
and recognize in her child the God
        who saves,
Jesus, your Son,
living and reigning [with you and
        the Holy Spirit,
one God,] for ever and ever.
—© ICEL

EPIPHANY:
We have seen the star of your glory
rising in splendor,
Lord God of the nations.
The radiance of your Word-made-flesh
pierces the darkness that covers the earth
and signals the dawn of justice and peace.

May his brightness illumine our lives
and beckon all nations to walk in your light.

We ask this through Emmanuel,
your Son, our Lord Jesus Christ,
who lives and reigns [with you and
        the Holy Spirit,
one God,] for ever and ever.
—© ICEL

BAPTISM OF THE LORD:
Open the heavens,
almighty Father,
and pour out your Spirit
upon your people gathered in prayer.

Renew the power of our baptismal cleansing
and fill us with zeal for good deeds.
Let us hear your voice once again,
that we may recognize in your beloved Son
our hope of inheriting eternal life.
We ask this through your Son our Lord
Jesus Christ who lives and reigns
        [with you in the unity of the Holy Spirit,
one God] for ever and ever.
—© ICEL

LITURGY OF THE EUCHARIST

Introduction to the Lord's Prayer

The Son of God took flesh among us as a child
that we might become in spirit and truth the
children of God; therefore with gratitude and
joy we pray:

Prayer for Peace

Lord Jesus Christ,
at whose holy birth the choirs of angels
        announced the glad tidings
        of peace to the world:
Look not on our sins, but on the faith
        of your church . . .

Invitation to Communion

This is the lamb of God, who takes away
        the sins of the world:
Emmanuel, God-with-us, born of Mary to be
the Savior of all nations. Happy are those who
are called to his supper.

CONCLUDING RITE

Dismissal of Eucharistic Ministers

Go forth in peace to the sick and homebound
of our community, bearing the word of life and
the Body of Christ, together with the assurance of our love and concern. Join their voices
to our hymn in praise of God's glory and in the
name of this community share God's peace
with them in the gift of Emmanuel.

Blessing

May the God of infinite goodness, who in the Word made flesh wedded earth to heaven and heaven to earth, fill your hearts with joy at the glad tidings of salvation and make you a light to those who long to behold the beauty of the Savior's face:
And may almighty God bless you . . .

Dismissal

As witnesses of God's glory and heralds of God's peace, go forth in joy and gladness to love and serve the Lord.

TEXTS FOR A CHRISTMAS VIGIL

These prayers may be used with the Christmas vigil outlined on page 35.

FOR USE AFTER READING I (Genesis):
O God,
in the human nature of your Son
you have given us the origin and fulfillment
    of our relationship with you.
Keep us faithful to this gift we
    have received,
for our every hope of salvation is in him,
who lives and reigns for ever and ever.

FOR USE AFTER READING II (1 Samuel):
Merciful God,
by the birth of your only-begotten Son
and by his death on the cross,
you have brought to completion the
    salvation of your people.
Grant us, your servants,
a firm faith in this wondrous plan of love,
that we may arrive at the fulfillment
    of your glorious promises
under the guidance and by the grace
    of Christ your Son,
who lives and reigns for ever and ever.

FOR USE WITH READING III (Isaiah):
Listen, O our Redeemer, to the supplication
of all who celebrate this joyful night.
To save us and bring us immortality,
you entered and renewed our
    human nature:
Bring us on the final day to your
    heavenly feast,
where you live and reign for ever and ever.

FOR USE WITH READING IV (Judges):
O God our Father,
In the mystery of your Son's birth
    among us,
you help us to understand your wondrous
    kindness
and your desire to save us.
Help us respond to such generosity
by living always as your children,
    doing good to all.
We ask this through Christ our Lord.

PROCLAMATION OF THE BIRTH OF CHRIST

The twenty-fifth day of December. In the five thousand and

ninety-ninth year of the creation of the world, from the time

when God in the beginning created the heavens and the earth;

the two thousand, nine hundred and fifty-seventh year after

the flood; the two thousand and fifteenth year from the birth of

Abraham; the one thousand, five hundred and tenth year

from Moses and the going forth of the people of Israel from

Egypt; the one thousand and thirty-second year from David's

being anointed king; in the sixty-fifth week according to the

prophecy of Daniel; in the one hundred and ninety-fourth

Olympiad; the seven hundred and fifty-second year from the

foundation of the city of Rome; the forty-second year of the

reign of Octavian Augustus; the whole world being at peace,
in the sixth age of the world, Jesus Christ, the eternal God,
and Son of the eternal Father, desiring to sanctify the world
by his most merciful coming, being conceived by the Holy
Spirit, and nine months having passed since his conception,
was born in Bethlehem of Judea of the Virgin Mary, being
made flesh. The Nativity of our Lord Jesus Christ
according to the flesh.

Suggestions for using the Christmas proclamation:

This proclamation, taken from the entry for December 25 in the ancient martyrology, could be sung at the beginning of the Midnight Mass. It should be done without explanation, with great simplicity and reverence in the silence and darkness as the assembly keeps vigil.

Acolytes, with lighted candles, might accompany the cantor to the ambo or another appropriate place in front of the assembly. The cantor may indicate with a gesture that the assembly is to stand; when all are standing, the proclamation begins. The tradition calls for the assembly to kneel after the words "having passed since his conception . . ." and to rise before "The Nativity of our Lord . . ." The cantor should stop at both times to allow this to take place. The acolytes and other ministers should know beforehand so that they can model for the assembly the kneeling and the rising.

When the proclamation is concluded, the entrance rites of Midnight Mass—which have truly begun with this chant—can continue with song.

PROCLAMATION OF THE DATE OF EASTER

Dear brothers and sisters, the glory of the Lord has

shone upon us, and shall ever be manifest among us, until

the day of his return. Through the rhythms of times and

seasons let us celebrate the mysteries of salvation.

Let us recall the year's culmination, the Easter Triduum

of the Lord: his crucifixion, his burial and his rising,

celebrated between the evening of the sixteenth of

April and the dawn of the nineteenth of April. Each

Easter, each Sunday the holy Church makes present

that great and saving deed by which Christ has forever

conquered sin and death.

From Easter come forth and are reckoned all the days we

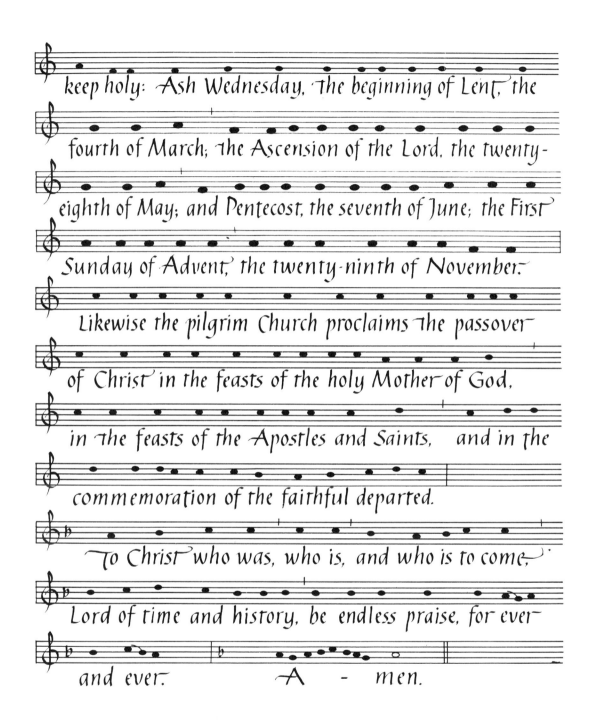

keep holy: Ash Wednesday, the beginning of Lent, the
fourth of March; the Ascension of the Lord, the twenty-
eighth of May; and Pentecost, the seventh of June; the First
Sunday of Advent, the twenty-ninth of November.
Likewise the pilgrim Church proclaims the passover
of Christ in the feasts of the holy Mother of God,
in the feasts of the Apostles and Saints, and in the
commemoration of the faithful departed.
To Christ who was, who is, and who is to come,
Lord of time and history, be endless praise, for ever
and ever. A - men.

Suggestions for using the Epiphany proclamation:

This proclamation, announcing the date of Easter and the various dates that depend on Easter, is chanted by a cantor after the gospel reading or homily on the solemnity of the Epiphany. The proclamation can be sung from the ambo with lights and incense as at the gospel. The line, "Each Easter, each Sunday, . . ." may sound like an error when chanted. The

Italian sacramentary reads: "Every Sunday, as in a weekly Easter, . . ." Cantors: take note of the key change in the final lines. These lines require great solemnity and proper timing.

Opening Prayer

God our Father,
in the Holy Family you have given us
    an example.
May the love that united Jesus, Mary,
    and Joseph
keep our families together in unity
    and peace.
We ask this through Christ our Lord.

Prayer over the Gifts

Holy God,
accept these offerings,
and grant that our families may
    live together
in your friendship and peace.
We ask this through Christ our Lord.

Prayer after Communion

Good and loving God,
you have fed us at your table;
help us now to follow the example
    of the Holy Family
that we may taste in our homes
    your joy and your peace.
We ask this through Christ our Lord.

TEXTS FOR THE ANOINTING OF THE SICK WITHIN MASS

Introduction/Reception of the Sick

The people who walked in darkness have seen a great light. As the angels sang glory to God and peace on earth, the Sun of Justice dawned with healing rays over a land shrouded in gloom. In these days of Christmas joy, we gather in the name of that child born for us of the Virgin Mary, Jesus, the Prince of Peace, Emmanuel: God with us. Let us ask him to be among us now as we celebrate his healing presence in the sacraments of anointing and eucharist.

Prayer after Anointing

To the ends of the earth, O God,
you have made known your saving power.
Embrace with health and wholeness
those whom we have anointed in the name
    of your Son.
Through him whom we acknowledge as
    the Word made flesh,
grant our brothers and sisters the comfort
    they seek
and that peace which is your will for
    all of us
through Christ our Lord.

WINTER ORDINARY TIME

*The word "ordinary" in Ordinary Time refers to the word "ordinal" or "counted."
The weeks of the year are given numbers so that the proper texts can be found
in the liturgical books. Ordinary Time is made up of the weeks
outside the seasons of Advent-Christmas and Lent-Triduum-Easter. Sunday after Sunday
during this time we hear the gospel proclaimed—this year it is the Gospel according
to Luke—and we respond by celebrating the eucharist. During this period of Ordinary
Time between Christmas and Lent, the gospel will provide us with several passages about
the beginning of Jesus' ministry and the impressive "Sermon on the Plain."*

Images of Ordinary Time

Ordinary Time is not very ordinary at all. Ordinary Time, the celebration of Sunday, is the identifying mark of the Christian community which comes together remembering that on this first day of the week the Lord of life was raised up and creation came at last to completion. Sunday as a day of play and worship is a sacrament of redeemed time. How we live Sunday proclaims to the world what we believe about redeemed time now and forever.

What happens in our churches every Sunday is the fruit of our week. What happens as the fruit of the week past is the beginning of the week to come. Sunday, like all sacraments, is simultaneously a point of arrival and departure for Christians on their way to the fullness of the kingdom. This is not ordinary at all. This is the fabric of Christian living. (*Saint Andrew Bible Missal,* p. 479)

ORDINARY Time really is not "ordinary" but "ordinal"—counted—time. It is simply the way the church organizes liturgical books, assigning each Sunday a number, counting each week one after the other. The term "Ordinary Time" is not meant to be significant by itself; it is not a season, nor should it be turned into a living part of liturgical spirituality the way Lent-Triduum-Eastertime and Advent-Christmastime should be. In other words, the only reason for knowing that it is the Seventeenth Sunday in Ordinary Time is to know where to turn in the lectionary and the sacramentary or, perhaps at home, in a missal to prepare for Sunday Mass.

Before the reforms of 20 years ago, these winter weeks carried the designation "after Epiphany." This was another way to name the Sundays. But that title had the effect of pulling Epiphany into the weeks of winter and away from Christmas. Thus, our current system has the benefit of clearly relating Christmas and Epiphany with each other. Similarly, the title "Sundays after Pentecost" and the extinguishing of the paschal candle at Ascension tended to separate Easter from Pentecost. Now the days of Eastertime are seen as the Fifty Days to celebrate the risen Jesus' gift of the Spirit.

■ FROM THE MOUNTAINTOP: No matter how Ordinary Time is explained, no matter how important Sunday is, the days right after Christmastime provide an abrupt change. The wonderful stories, lights, hymns, flowers and theological mysteries of Christmas are over. As Pius Parsch once expressed it, we have come down from the mountain to the plain. Our hearts ache as we must leave the snow-covered heights. One who has scaled the peaks remembers the experience, indeed is changed by it. Ordinary life will not be quite the same this year.

■ WINTER: While the liturgy has its rhythm, the climate has its own cycle, experienced in different ways in different regions. As the church lights trees and celebrates on the Lord's holy mountain, as we descend to the plain of Ordinary Time and even as ashes are spread on our faces, we often meet winter on the other side of the church door. Priests in Fairbanks and musicians in Miami may both talk about winter, but they surely refer to different sets of experiences. If there is anything in common, it is that the days are colder and darker now than they will be at the Assumption. They continue to lengthen ever so gradually, but in the North the cold and ice sometimes seem to have settled in forever. The further north we go, the more the assemblies tend to be clothed with multiple layers of protection—coats and all manner of gear that shield us from the elements and from so much more. As Robert Hovda pointed out 17 years ago:

> Most church buildings seem to have been planned without a thought about cloakrooms, accommodations for coats, hats, overshoes, umbrellas, etc. As a result we get congregations in which people are not only mentally and emotionally isolated from each other, but also physically and materially. If they aren't wearing coats, as if they were taking a breather during a walk in the park, then they are clutching them in their laps, as if determined to make the visit brief. To try to help a congregation in that condition to come to life in liturgy is an exercise in futility. Can you imagine inviting people to a party in your home and failing to take their coats and hats as they come in? (*There Are Different Ministries . . . ,* Robert Hovda, Washington DC: The Liturgical Conference, 1975)

■ THIS WINTER'S DISTINGUISHING CHARACTERISTICS: Our winter journey across this plain will be almost twice as long this year compared to 1991—51 days instead of 30. Such a long winter respite between the seasons comes about once every three years. We should relish this length, utilizing it to formulate all our plans for the Easter Triduum before Ash Wednesday, looking forward to all the benefits of a later Easter and Pentecost.

The week of prayer for Christian unity still is observed in many places, once again allowing these prayers to mark the earliest days of Ordinary Time. Two major national holidays—Martin Luther King, Jr., Day and Presidents Day—fall during these weeks, and one of our brightest feasts, the Presentation, falls on a Sunday this year.

■ SAINTS: We cannot enter any season without thinking of the saints present in the liturgy. Because Ordinary Time is not a season as such,

we do not have the pleasure and challenge of trying to celebrate the saints within the context of a particular season. The Conversion of Paul and the Chair of Peter form a natural pair as the only two saints' feasts of this period. Peter and Paul share the same day in late June, but here we have an opportunity to remember essential elements in the *cultus* of each individual. These feasts are joined by nine obligatory memorials and eleven optional ones.

■ THE GOSPEL OF LUKE is the most distinctive feature of Year C. It unfolds in semicontinuous readings mainly through Ordinary Time. To be fully equipped for their task, those who prepare the liturgy must become familiar with the year's evangelist and the sequence of scripture texts in this particular year.

Most scholars agree that the author of the third gospel was not an eyewitness to the events surrounding Jesus, but rather lived a little later, writing about 80 AD, after Mark and Matthew. This distance from his subject provides his central strength—he is able to relate the stories of Jesus to the growth of the early church. He was not a native Palestinian; he wrote this narrative for gentile converts to the new church. He was a well-educated person, perhaps a physician, and a sometime companion of Paul.

Tradition has consistently testified that the author was Luke from Antioch and contemporary biblical scholars see no reason to doubt this. He is mentioned several times in other books of the New Testament (Philemon 24, Colossians 4:14, 2 Timothy 4:11), but little else is known. He is said to have been martyred in Greece after living 84 years. His feast day, October 18, is not observed this year because it falls on a Sunday. The current texts for that day are fairly generic, praising God for choosing him to reveal the mystery of divine love for the poor, the mystery of Christ's tender compassion.

■ THE GOSPEL OF LUKE IN 1992: The portions read this year provide Catholic assemblies with a fairly complete recount of Luke's narrative. The basic outline of the proclamation for the Sundays and holy days of 1992 is:

- Prologue (1:1–4): Read on the first Sunday that we hear Luke in Ordinary Time, January 26.
- Infancy narrative (1:5—2:52): Large portions of this are read, naturally, during Advent and Christmas. Portions also are taken from here for the Presentation and the Assumption.

- Preparation for the public ministry (3:1—4:13): This brief section is read during Advent and Christmas, as well as on the First Sunday of Lent.

- Galilean ministry (4:14—9:50): This is read on most of the Sundays of winter Ordinary Time, on the Second Sunday of Lent and on the Solemnity of the Body and Blood of Christ.

- Journey to Jerusalem (9:51—19:27): This lengthy section provides most of the passages for the long weeks of summer and early fall.

- Jesus in Jerusalem (19:28—21:38): This intense narrative provides eschatological (end time) content for the First Sunday of Advent and for the two Sundays in November before Christ the King.

- Passion narrative (22:1—23:56a): This appears on Passion Sunday and a small selection is read on Christ the King.

- Resurrection narrative (23:56b—24:53): These passages find a home on Easter and the Ascension.

In other words, the arrangement of gospel excerpts over the Sundays does not follow a complicated formula. The birth and paschal sections appear in the seasons and the whole middle section is read, for the most part, chapter by chapter during Ordinary Time.

Luke also is read every year on the weekdays of autumn. The passages in September are from the earlier or Galilean phase. The selections in October and early November retell the journey to Jerusalem. Finally, the last days of the year are reserved for the eschatological message of the Jerusalem days.

■ SUNDAYS: The other elements of Ordinary Time pale in importance before Sunday as the key component of these weeks. All of us are obligated to continue immersing ourselves in our tradition, recognizing more and more the true nature of Sunday:

> Reverence for the Sabbath can be seen in every century of our history, often expressed as a *day of rest* theme influencing Sunday practices. . . . Even a cursory review of the seventeenth-century colonies in Virginia and Massachusetts would have to focus on their Christian sabbath laws. . . . Their Lord's Day practices and laws were quite rigorous, banning most forms of bodily activity. They saw no problem in transferring the most rigorous Jewish Sabbath strictures to their new Sabbath, Sunday. Their strong views were symptomatic of their broad differences with the ecclesiastical and civil powers in England. When they arrived in America, they formed a society whose laws and expectations resonated with strict Christian Sabbath-

keeping. The term *blue law* is an Americanism, signifying laws traceable to colonial New England that outlaw dancing, shows, sports and commerce on Sunday. While some Catholics may see parallels with their own *servile work* avoidance, the people of early New England could not even swim or walk (except to church) on the *Sabbatarian* Sunday.

> Catholics are not called to be extremist Sabbatarians, for there is another more important emphasis in our heritage. Even while the earliest Christians revered the Sabbath [on the seventh day of the week], the first day of the week became the day to celebrate the paschal mystery. All the evangelists agree that this was the day of the Lord's resurrection. Many of the post-resurrection appearances of Jesus were on the first day of the week. It was the day on which the gift of the Holy Spirit was bestowed [on Pentecost]. As Acts 20:7 tells us, early Christians gathered that day "for the breaking of the bread."

> From then until now the celebration of the paschal mystery took eucharistic form. From time to time, Sabbath influences have colored our observances, but these should not be seen as the central value of Sunday. It is not just a day of rest. It is a time to assemble for the liturgy. Any teaching which eschews *servile work* should do so only inasmuch as this frees us for the community assembly. An intimate brunch or a nap on the newspaper-strewn couch vie for place as the American Sunday. As pleasant as these may be, they do not, of course, amount to an ecclesial remembrance of the Lord Jesus. A Sabbath emphasis may have set the stage for some of this rest emphasis. One can almost hear the Catholics who draw on this strain of thought as they say, "I couldn't get to Mass. It's the only day I get to sleep late." (*Study Text 9. The Liturgical Year: Celebrating the Mystery of Christ and His Saints,* pp. 30–32)

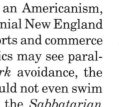

Preparing the Parish

ORDINARY or "counted" Time comprises over half of the year. During these months, we must be laying the groundwork for the parish's liturgical life: the discipline of keeping the day (with Morning, Evening and Night Prayer at home or in church); the discipline of keeping the week (especially in the rhythms of Fridays and Sundays); the discipline of keeping feast days (learning what it means to take time off to "play heaven"); the discipline of keeping a lifetime (turning to our ritual tradition at times of births and deaths, weddings and anniversaries, and all the many other occasions of joy and sorrow that mark our lives).

Ordinary Time allows liturgical planners to find the time to build up the liturgical ministries, to get the ball rolling for parish renovation and parish stewardship, to review and make adaptations in regular worship patterns. And it is not only liturgical personnel who can grow in respect for the calendar and make good use of Ordinary Time for their business. All parish ministers can be encouraged to schedule ongoing programs or special events such as fundraisers outside of the liturgical seasons.

Other business worth attending to is helping people better appreciate the communion cup or perhaps building up liturgical "etiquette"—such as the thorny problem of regular latecomers or early departures—or perhaps focusing every few weeks on one element of the rite, such as the sign of peace, or singing at worship, or anointings during Mass. Ordinary Time also lends itself to a parishwide discussion of Christian weddings and funerals—enormous topics that tend to generate enormous interest.

■ COMING IN FROM THE COLD: Parishes in southern California, the Southwest and Florida, as well as those in the mountain regions of the North, receive visitors every winter. They must be made welcome. The kind of hospitality that seasonal migrations of tourists call for demands a year-round education of the local community. Catholics, like all humans, must see hospitality as a central task. And all liturgical planners must review Sunday details to see if the assembly, ritual order, Mass schedule and music really draw visitors into a spirit of conscious and active participation. "Fast Masses" for the tourist crowds serve no one well.

■ LECTIONARY-BASED EDUCATION: Many religious educators now are basing catechetical and catechumenal sessions on the lectionary—a laudable practice. In Ordinary Time, however, this could become too didactic if leaders and discussion questions focus only on the scriptural passages in isolation. We are invited to see all the aspects of the liturgy, including the readings, in relationship with each other, with the season and with this assembly. When we reflect on the readings, we must reflect also on the experience of listening, of singing the psalm, of keeping awe-filled silence. We must discuss the homily and how it fed us. Gifted with this lectionary and the Roman rite in which it comes to life, we do not have a few themes to present. We have a liturgy to celebrate.

The Mass

INTRODUCTORY RITES

PEOPLE who prepare the liturgy must know their way around the options for selecting prayer texts—and familiarity with the sacramentary happens only through use. The norms can be found in the *General Instruction of the Roman Missal* (#313–16, #323) and in the helpful chart in appendix III of the *Ceremonial of Bishops.*

On saints' days in Ordinary Time, the prayers are from that saint's day but the readings are almost always from the seasonal progression. Only on rare and high-ranking days can the semicontinuous flow of scriptures be interrupted by other proper readings.

On regular weekdays of Ordinary Time (those without saints), any texts from the sacramentary can be selected—for example, from the previous Sunday's Mass, special needs and occasions, votive Masses or Masses of the Blessed Virgin Mary on Saturday. Once again, the readings are always from the seasonal list.

■ THE PENITENTIAL RITE should be brief and concise, with a simple introduction and clear invocations. The sacramentary texts A, B, C*i* and C*viii* seem right for this time of year, especially C*viii* on those Sundays when we see Jesus healing the sick and expelling demons. The Sunday option of blessing and sprinkling water may be considered, although many parishes reserve this rite for Christmastime and Eastertime.

■ GLORIA: The singing of the Gloria is sometimes reserved for holy days and other special occasions. At first, it may seem reasonable to recite the Gloria during Ordinary Time—but the Gloria is an ancient hymn in which the church, assembled in the Holy Spirit, praises and entreats the Father and the Lamb. Many sung versions of the Gloria are beautiful and simple. Again, it is perhaps best to continue with one version of a sung Gloria that becomes familiar (and sung well).

LITURGY OF THE WORD

■ SUNDAY READINGS: We have had 20 or more years to experience and to be formed in the pattern the framers of the lectionary gave us: a synoptic evangelist each year, read in a semicontinuous way; a selection from the Hebrew Scriptures paired with the gospel; a semicontinuous reading from one or another of the letters of the Christian Scriptures. This year, we have Luke as our guide. As is the case every winter, selections from 1 Corinthians will be proclaimed. Later, over the summer and fall Sundays, seven other New Testament letters will stand alongside Luke.

The 1981 introduction to the lectionary (#105–10) outlines early Ordinary Time in these words:

> On the Second Sunday in Ordinary Time the gospel continues to center on the manifestation of the Lord . . . through the traditional passage about the wedding feast at Cana.
>
> Beginning with the Third Sunday, there is a semicontinuous reading of the synoptic gospels. This reading is arranged in such a way that as the Lord's life and preaching unfold, the teaching proper to each of these gospels is presented.
>
> This distribution also provides a certain coordination between the meaning of each gospel and the progress of the liturgical year. Thus, after Epiphany the readings are on the beginning of the Lord's preaching, and they fit in well with Christ's baptism and the first events in which he manifests himself.

The selections from Luke beginning on January 26 describe the earliest phase of Jesus' ministry in Galilee. On two Sundays, we hear of his rejection by his relatives and neighbors but his acceptance by the first disciples. Then for several Sundays, the plan of Ordinary Time provides Luke's so-called "Sermon on the Plain." This is the first time in the 20 years since the current lectionary was formulated that a Year C winter has been long enough for us to hear all three excerpts from this important sermon. Here in winter we will assemble under the good news of Jesus' preaching and gathering disciples despite opposition. In the light of Epiphany, we see with amazing clarity the work of the Lamb of God.

■ SUNDAY RESPONSORIAL PSALM: Eight common psalms for Ordinary Time are listed in the lectionary at the end of #175. (Common psalm responses also are suggested at #174.) Music ministers may select just one of these eight psalms for the winter Sundays. This option provides for a frequent repetition by which the psalms can sink into people's consciousness and eventually go home to become "by heart" prayers. Because it is in harmony with the other scriptures for these weeks, and because it also is listed these weeks as a proper psalm, Psalm 103 is recommended for all these weeks. Settings include:

- Psalm 103, Richard Proulx, GIA, G-1921
- Psalm 103, Howard Hughes, *Psalms for All Seasons*, NPM Publications
- Psalm 103, "The Lord is kind and merciful," Marty Haugen, GIA, G-2664

■ WEEKDAY READINGS: When the scriptural flow is interrupted by one of the days with prescribed readings, those who prepare the liturgy should see if an important part of a narrative will be lost. The passage then can be transferred to a neighboring weekday. Other less-significant passages are dropped or all are combined in a way that does justice to the literary genre and to the integrity of the biblical book. This *Sourcebook* will suggest how to accomplish this during the weeks that it may be an issue.

Some memorials have "accommodated" readings that highlight a virtue or apostolate of the saint. These replace the semicontinuous lectionary only for a compelling pastoral reason—such as when the memorial is upgraded to a solemnity or feast for local celebrations or perhaps when the memorial is celebrated with particular vigor in your parish.

■ GENERAL INTERCESSIONS can be composed for use throughout blocks of Ordinary Time, with individual petitions changed as necessary, and a new set of petitions prepared every four to six weeks. One set can be used for all of winter's Ordinary-Time Sundays. Appendix I of the sacramentary has four sample sets for this time of year (#1–2, #9–10).

LITURGY OF THE EUCHARIST

We have nine approved eucharistic prayers in the United States. Three of them use seasonal prefaces, of which eight are for the Sundays in Ordinary Time and six for weekdays. Adrian Nocent, in volume 4 of *The Liturgical Year* (pp. 20–30), reviews the theology and history of each of the Sunday prefaces. As he puts it, they are short poems that seek to capture the reality of our daily lives and to lead us into the great hymn of praise sung eternally before God. The eucharistic prayer need not be changed every week. Rather, a particular one may be selected for use during a block of weeks within Ordinary Time. Occasionally, bits of noninclusive language appear in the prefaces. These will likely disappear in the revision of the sacramentary now being prepared for the mid-1990s.

■ ACCLAMATIONS: The eucharistic acclamations during this time should return to one of the "standard sets" of the parish. With publishers still offering new settings in every catalog and workshop, it is easy to assume that newer is better and that we do our people a disservice if we do not keep them abreast of the latest offerings. A few high-quality sets of responses, acclamations and litanies are all that is needed to let people know them well and sing them as prayer. If it is time to reconsider the quality and long-term effectiveness of your parish's settings, look for one that can be equally successful with or without a choir and additional instruments, and that everyone can look forward to singing again after it has been set aside for some time.

■ COMMUNION PROCESSIONAL: For the communion processional on these Sundays, consider "We have been told" by David Haas, the Taizé "Ubi Caritas" and Suzanne Toolan's setting of the Beatitudes that includes the brief and easily sung refrain "Blest, O blest indeed are you!" (GIA, G-2132).

CONCLUDING RITE

For these winter Sundays, the same prayer over the people or solemn blessing for Ordinary Time can be used every week. The *Book of Blessings,* in appendix II, reprints the solemn blessings found in the sacramentary and adds four more. Copy these four and add them to the others in the sacramentary until a new edition groups them all together.

As we consider the life of discipleship this season, a strong "sending-forth" song is in order. The two verses of "O God beyond all praising"

are just right, both in text and tune (Gustav Holst's "Thaxted"). You will find it in *Worship.*

MUSIC

Between the lavishness of Christmastime and the Lenten call to prayer, fasting and almsgiving, we journey through these Sundays of Ordinary Time. Mindful of the larger rhythm of the liturgical year, it is best to acknowledge this period as a time of less intensity, a time to do what we do well and simply and comfortably. How often have choirs heard, "If you sing so loudly in this section marked *piano,* you'll have nowhere to go when you get to the *forte* section!" The same principle applies here: Christmastime and Lent are able to maintain their distinctive characters only when there is some other way of doing things than that which we know as the norm. Service music should, therefore, be chosen from what is already in the parish's repertoire, perhaps returning to what was used the previous fall.

The scriptures of these Sundays are first centered on Christ revealed as God's Word, then turn to the call to discipleship and finally focus on the Sermon on the Plain. Some hymns that may be useful are: "Word of God, come down to earth" with its simple and lovely tune, "Liebster Jesu"; "God we praise you," whose well-crafted text is based on the Te Deum and paired in *Worship* with the rousing early American tune "Nettleton"; and Suzanne Toolan's "Two fishermen," worth knowing about for any celebration of discipleship and commitment.

Other Ritual Prayer and Sacraments

LITURGY OF THE HOURS

MORNING Prayer and Evening Prayer (and the other hours as well) are not treasures reserved for the big days and seasons. They form the rhythm of daily life.

■ STARTS WITH SUNDAY: Ancient customs and canons, recent councils and all contemporary liturgical books highlight Sunday Evening Prayer as the most important of the hours for all the faithful to celebrate. Evening Prayer is a part of what the whole church does on Sundays. As this most basic hour becomes more popular, local planners can begin adding vigil services on Saturday nights (perhaps at least on the biggest eves—of Christmas and Pentecost) and perhaps Sunday Morning Prayer as well.

Once Sunday's schedule begins to reflect the fullness appropriate to the Roman rite, those who prepare the liturgy can attend to the other important days, universal and local. Finally, daily hours can become the pattern of our ecclesial life. Not only is all of this the order of precedence based on liturgical tradition, it is a sensible "game plan" for gradually introducing the hours into the fabric of parish life.

■ VIGILS: Appendix I of the *Liturgy of the Hours* offers canticles and gospel references for expanding the Saturday night Office of Readings into an extended paschal vigil. It also gives similar texts for the eve of February 2 and for the commons if your titular solemnity or dedication anniversary occurs during these weeks.

BLESSINGS

■ CHRISTIAN UNITY: The days from January 18–25 are traditionally kept as times of intense prayer for ecumenical unity. The initial fervor of ecumenical efforts after Vatican II has given way to what would seem to be a quieter and longer era. Local churches still should feel compelled to pray for unity. In the *Book of Blessings,* the "Order for the Blessing of Ecumenical Groups" (#553–69) may be useful if your parish is joining other Christian communities for a service during this week. *Catholic Households Blessings and Prayers* offers two prayers for the same days.

■ RECEIVING BLESSED CANDLES: The rite in *Catholic Household Blessings and Prayers* for receiving blessed candles at home should not be overlooked. Because the Presentation and its blessing of candles falls on a Sunday this year, all communicants presumably would have candles to bring home. Given an opportunity to develop, this custom could become as powerful for the parish as bringing home blessed palms.

The Worship Environment

I N the North, winter means coatrooms. For many parishes, coatrooms are a wish that is listed with other renovation needs. In the meantime, perhaps an unused space can be turned into a coatroom (and be sure that leaving coats there and picking them up again can be carried out conveniently). Or set up and monitor coatracks in the vestibule. Yes, it looks a bit ugly, but it is hospitable. Or have everyone use another entry (perhaps one through the rectory or hall) and leave coats there. Or leave enough space in every pew to allow for a coat pile. No matter what solution works best, leave the heat on high enough for comfort, increase the number and training of the ushers and make inviting announcements about this.

While on the topic of winter, those who prepare the liturgy can cooperate with the janitorial staff in assisting with the whole church building—furnaces, entranceway mats, snow removal, etc. Care for the walkways and entrances is part of hospitality, and many folks will need to lend a hand. The dryness and cleanliness of floors, especially near the doors, must be attended to. Local regulations about salt and sand must be known and adhered to. Of course, the positive sides of winter can bless the parish. Consider ice sculptures on the parish lawn, the creation of "snow saints" or perhaps parish ice skating parties after Vespers. God is just as much a God of ice as a God of sun.

■ LITURGICAL VESTURE: Green is the color for Ordinary Time. There are many shades of green and many effective combinations of green with other colors. For example, a wintertime set of vesture, one that connotes the time of year can be worn.

■ GET TO KNOW YOUR BUILDING: We all have so much to learn, especially if we have been graced with a large or old building. This time between seasons lets us experience the sacred space unembellished, thus opening our eyes to the elements of fixed space, learning to appreciate its inherent dignity. When the season to decorate arrives, this appreciation will make us more sensitive to the space and perhaps less apt to obscure the sacred furnishings. In other words, we can learn to make the space work better from a liturgical point of view. We can inhabit every corner and feel its potential. We can define its special zones for rite and iconography.

Defining the ambo area, the altar area, the baptistry, the presider's chair and the Marian shrine generally is easy. Having them far enough apart so that they can "breathe" is sometimes more of a challenge. The work continues by experiencing each of these zones from various perspectives. Finally, we can see if any of our winter saints, the feasts of the Presentation of the Lord and the Conversion of Paul, the Chair of Peter or Jesus' ministry of preaching are depicted in any of our shrines, windows or statues. If so, then appropriate decorations—such as candles or a flowery wreath—can highlight them throughout this time or at least for the day.

Resources

ON ORDINARY TIME

SEVERAL of the general studies listed on page xix include sections on Ordinary Time. See especially Adam, Bishops' Committee on the Liturgy *Study Text 9,* Cobb, Martimort and Nocent.

ON THE GOSPEL OF LUKE

Many publishers offer books commenting on the lectionary passages. Those on Year C generally describe the Lucan narrative. Two of the most definitive commentaries on the gospel are:

Fitzmyer, Joseph A. *The Gospel According to Luke* (Anchor Bible Numbers 28 and 28A; New York: Doubleday, 1981 and 1985).

Karris, Robert J. "The Gospel According to Luke," *The New Jerome Biblical Commentary* (Englewood Cliffs: Prentice Hall, 1990), 675–721.

ON THE LORD'S DAY

Once again, the general studies on page xix should be consulted: Adam, Bishops' Committee on the Liturgy *Study Text 9;* Carroll and Halton; Martimort; Nocent.

Huck, Gabe. "Eucharist on Sunday," *Liturgy with Style and Grace* (Chicago: LTP, 1984), 72–73.

Kavanagh, Aidan. *On Liturgical Theology* (New York: Pueblo Publishing Company, 1984), 55–69.

Kollar, Nathan R. "Worshiping on the Lord's Day," *Liturgy* (Journal of the Liturgical Conference), vol. 6, no. 2, 15–21.

Marshall, Paul. "The Little Easter and the Great Sunday," *Liturgy,* (Journal of the Liturgical Conference), vol. 1, no. 2, 27–31.

Porter, H. Boone. *The Day of Light. The Biblical and Liturgical Meaning of Sunday* (London: SCM Press, 1960).

Rahner, Karl. "The Sunday Precept in Industrial Society," *Theological Investigations XIX.* (New York: Crossroads Press, 1983), 151–58.

——————. "Sunday, the Day of the Lord." *Theological Investigations VII* (New York: Herder and Herder, 1971), 205–10.

Rordorf, Willy. *Sunday. The History of the Day of Rest in the Earliest Centuries of the Christian Church* (Philadelphia: The Westminster Press, 1968).

Searle, Mark, ed. *Sunday Morning: A Time for Worship* (Collegeville: The Liturgical Press, 1982). Papers of the Tenth Annual Conference of the Notre Dame Center for Pastoral Liturgy, June 15–18, 1981.

Solberg, Winton U. *Redeem the Time: The Puritan Sabbath in Early America* (Cambridge: Harvard University Press, 1977).

January

MON 13
Lectionary #305   green
Weekday

Hilary, bishop and doctor, optional memorial/white. ▪ This fourth-century bishop of Poitiers, France, was enormously influential—building an enormous baptistry that still is standing, defending the doctrines of the church, writing the classic treatise on the Trinity and inspiring members of his church to live their faith to the fullest (he encouraged Martin of Tours to settle near Poitiers and start the first monastery in the West, one that still is active). The people of his see city keep his memory alive and every parish in the Western world would do well to do the same by observing his memorial.

The first reading at Mass will be from 1 or 2 Samuel through early February. They begin the course of readings set up for Year II in the weekday lectionary. The year begins with episodes in the lives of Samuel, Saul and David—the beginning of the royal dynasty of David. The historical narrative about kingship also is about the institution of prophetic leadership. In the first passages read this week, we hear of the birth and ministry of the prophet Samuel. Preachers may prepare by reviewing a commentary on these books (see Campbell, Antony F., and Flanagan, James W., "1–2 Samuel," *The New Jerome Biblical Commentary* [Englewood Cliffs: Prentice Hall, 1990], 145–59).

Last year, Year I, included more historical narrative than this year, which will be marked more by prophets and by New Testament letters. It is fitting that it begins with a narration about the first prophet for the whole of Israel, Samuel.

The gospels for the weekdays of Ordinary Time will be read from Mark through all these winter-time weeks. Because they are taken first from his earliest chapters, these gospels continue the manifestation themes emphasized over the final days of the Christmas season.

TUE 14
#306   green
Weekday

Because the sacramentary texts can be chosen freely on these non-seasonal weekdays, consider one of the Masses and Prayers for Various Needs and Occasions, 24. Beginning of the Civil Year.

WED 15
#307   green
Weekday

THU 16
#308   green
Weekday

FRI 17
#309   white
Anthony, abbot
MEMORIAL

One of the first "desert fathers" (early fourth century), Anthony lived in the wilderness after giving everything he owned to the poor. He was not the first Christian monk, but his influence, both during his life and afterward, was so great that he sometimes is called the founder of monasticism. The *Life of St. Anthony* by his friend, Athanasius, was widely distributed and became the classic handbook for ascetics. In his *Confessions,* Augustine of Hippo cites this book as being instrumental in his conversion. A selection from it appears in the Office of Readings today. As described by Anthony, the purpose of asceticism is not to destroy the body but to reestablish creation's original harmony.

Iconographic tradition represents Anthony with a *tau*-shaped cross, a bell, a pig and sometimes a book. The pig originated as a sign of the defeat of the devil, but in the twelfth century, it acquired new significance. The Hospital Brothers of St. Anthony were popular for their works of charity and also for taking good care of their swine. This latter virtue translated to their patron. Through such a fascinating history, Anthony became the patron of domestic animals during the late Middle Ages. The *Book of Blessings,* in chapter 25, provides an order for blessing animals. Today could become a customary day for people to bless their pets at home.

SAT 18
#310   green
Weekday

Blessed Virgin Mary, optional memorial/white. ▪ The Week of Prayer for Christian Unity begins today.

▪ MARY ON SATURDAYS: Issued in the United States in 1987, the little-known liturgical book, *Collection of Masses of the Blessed Virgin Mary,* provides us with 12 sets of presidential prayers and prefaces from a much larger Latin edition. Its introduction sketches the history of keeping Saturdays in Mary's honor. It suggests that on Saturdays of Ordinary Time not already devoted to a particular saint, a memorial of the Blessed Virgin Mary can serve as an introduction to the Lord's Day. As the weekly remembrance of the Lord's resurrection is prepared, she who watched by the tomb can be commemorated.

While the *Collection* includes scriptures for each Mass, its introduction (#41) calls on communities to discern carefully whether these would ever replace the weekday readings. It would seem that interruptions for such a purpose should be rare. The Marian readings are meant more for pilgrimages and special local festivals. Parishes dedicated to Mary without specifying her image or title may adopt one of these Mass titles as a favored one for use at solemn local gatherings.

■ SATURDAY IN UNITY WEEK: Diocesan ecumenical commissions and other sources (notably the Graymoor Friars) regularly circulate material for use during this Week of Prayer for Christian Unity. Communities can draw from the several sets of presidential prayers from the sacramentary, found under Masses and Prayers for Various Needs and Occasions, 13. "For Unity of Christians." The preface of Christian Unity (P76) also could be used. Intercessions every day this week can be for that unity for which we all should long. If today's gathering (or any gathering in Unity Week) includes children from the school or religious education program, see page 77 of LTP's *Leader's Manual of the Hymnal for Catholic Students* for prayer service ideas. For more general ecumenical gatherings, see page 59. For this Saturday, planners may turn to the *Collection of Masses of the Blessed Virgin Mary* and use the set entitled "Image and Mother of the Church" (Mass #25). These particular texts also are found in appendix X of the current sacramentary.

✸19 #67 green Second Sunday in Ordinary Time

After the intense liturgies of Advent and the festive celebrations of Christmastime, these winter Sundays should be marked by that "noble simplicity" for which the Roman rite is noted and for which the assembly will be grateful. See the notes beginning on page 56 about Mass at this time of year.

In Year C, Roman Catholics, and all those who use our lectionary, hear the gospel today about the marriage feast of Cana. It completes the triptych of magi, Baptism and Cana so foundational to Epiphany. This is the one year when it is quite clear that the framers of our lectionary wanted the transition from Christmastime to Ordinary Time to be marked by manifestation stories of all kinds.

■ CHRISTIAN UNITY: This Sunday falls in the middle of the week of prayer for Christian unity. At the least, a petition for this unity should be in the intercessions.

■ MARTIN LUTHER KING, JR.: This weekend the United States observes his birthday. Prepare well ahead of time by ordering the packet of materials for bulletin inserts and ecumenical prayer services (available also in Spanish and Vietnamese) distributed by the National Catholic Conference for Interracial Justice (NCCIJ), 1200 Varnum Street NE, Washington DC 20017; 202-529-6480. The prayer marking Martin Luther King, Jr., Day, found in *Catholic Household Blessings and Prayers* (p. 195), may be used to conclude the general intercessions.

M O N 20 #311 green Weekday

Fabian, pope and martyr, optional memorial/red. ■ *Sebastian, martyr, optional memorial/red.* ■ *Martin Luther King, Jr., Day.* ■ As happened last year, the memory of this great black American leader can be kept by Catholics in conjunction with commemorating an ancient martyr. The proper prayers for either saint, along with the Common of Martyrs, help us praise God for redeeming the blood of so many over all the centuries. The first reading of this weekday, placed here by coincidence, helps to appreciate the

witness of Fabian, Sebastian, Martin and all those who work for justice and equality. The Lord wants obedience. This does not mean groveling before a divine potentate; it means making a resolute commitment to be faithful to the Creator.

While Sebastian is the better known of today's two "optional" martyrs, principally because of the widespread images of his body pierced by arrows, communities selecting one of these memorials should not overlook Fabian every year. The early Christian biography found in his Office of Readings describes the courage Romans drew from his death. It is not a long stretch to conceive of black Americans and all people of good will drawing courage from today's national holiday.

■ THE WEEK AHEAD: The continuous series of scriptures will be interrupted on Saturday. Given the overall sequence and genre, there seems to be little need to combine these "lost" passages with other days this week. The brief gospel, though, may be appended to Friday's passage as a stark note about opposition to Jesus. His manifestation brought with it more than praise.

T U E 21 #312 red Agnes, virgin and martyr MEMORIAL

Reliable details about Agnes's life are few. She seems to have been martyred in Rome around the year 300. The great Christian leaders of the West during the next century praised her life and death: Jerome, Ambrose (quoted in today's Office of Readings), Emperor Constantine (who built a church over her grave), Damasus I (who decorated her tomb) and Augustine (who wrote about the two meanings of her name—*agna* or "lamb" in Latin and *agne* or "pure one" in Greek). The Latin translation occasioned a centuries-long tradition, continued until our own time, of blessing lambs at the Roman basilica of St. Agnes on this day. The wool from Agnes's lambs then is used to weave the palliums worn by archbishops and others of a metropolitan rank. This, like so many of our ancient customs, gives ritual expression to our communion with Rome.

WED 22 #313 green
Weekday

Vincent, deacon and martyr, optional memorial / red. ▪ Vincent, a Spanish deacon, was martyred around the same time as Agnes. His *cultus* spread as quickly as hers, and he was praised by such writers as Augustine, whose homily on Vincent appears in today's Office of Readings. Parishes can remember this early hero by combining his prayer texts with the weekday readings.

■ PRO-LIFE: Attempts to translate outrage at the Roe vs. Wade Supreme Court decision into a "pro-life" Mass on this day should be tempered. The martyr Vincent provides suitable liturgical texts and witness for entering into the eucharist this day. The weekday readings—about David and Goliath and about Jesus preserving life—should allow for a full and proper homily on the ancient heritage we share in standing against evil and death.

There is a danger when a group, perhaps gathered this day for a Mass on their way to a demonstration, uses the eucharist as a way to set themselves apart from other faithful members of their parish. The problem is not in listening to the readings and celebrating the martyr Vincent with pro-life concerns uppermost in one's mind. The improper manipulation of texts, the substitu-

tion of nonliturgical (albeit fervent) prayers, the use of hymns that fire up the crowd rather than praise God and the general attempt to shape a Mass to press home a point are the real concerns here. Any attempt to "ideologize" the sacraments and sacred space itself must be countered with sound, traditional liturgical sense.

THU 23 #314 green
Weekday

Especially because this is the only day in the Week of Prayer for Christian Unity without a memorial, the Mass for Christian Unity prayers (#13 in the Various Needs section) could be used.

FRI 24 #315 white
Francis de Sales, bishop and doctor
MEMORIAL

After celebrating several early Christian saints, we now meet a bishop and doctor of the church who ministered in the area around Geneva at the time of John Calvin. In his writing, Francis resisted the polemics of many of his contemporaries. He stood as a Catholic leader in a violent atmosphere, maintaining prudence and wisdom. The excerpt found in the Office of Readings (one of the gems in the Office) and the prayers proper to the memorial evoke the spirit of his pastoral care. One fine action for this week of Christian unity may be an ecumenical discussion of one of Francis's many works along with one of Calvin's.

SAT 25 #519 white
Conversion of Paul, apostle
FEAST

The week of prayer for unity was chosen so that it would end with this feast. Some saints have a secondary feast that usually is marked in local or religious order calendars, rather than in the universal calendar, to commemorate

the transfer or "translation" of the saint's remains from one place to another. This feast began as such a remembrance, but because the Latin *translatio* also can mean "conversion," later Romans may have decided it was in honor of that famous moment on the road to Damascus! The proper readings provide the narrative, and the proper prayers help bring us into the story. Pray for Christian unity and for those engaged in identifying their own conversion journeys. If the catechumens and candidates meet today, the story of Saul becoming Paul can inspire their discernment and conversion as Lent approaches.

This is one of the great feasts that fall on Saturdays during these months: Immaculate Conception, Holy Innocents, Conversion of Paul, Chair of Peter. If directors of religious education programs that meet on Saturday are looking for prayerful and inspiring ways to start or end the gatherings, these days could be observed with shared prayer, attentiveness to a story about the saint or an appropriate song.

26 #70 green
Third Sunday in Ordinary Time

A common flow in these winter Sundays may be planned using approaches such as those described on pages 56–58.

■ BLESSING LITURGICAL MINISTERS: Each parish can find the time most appropriate to prepare new ministers for the liturgy, to provide opportunities of renewal for current ministers and to bless or commission new and old. Parishes that do these things often follow one of four sequences:

▪ Preparation in the fall with blessings in early Advent, although this sequence tends to overload an already full time of year.

- Preparation in the fall with blessings on one of these wintertime Sundays. This sequence seems best suited to the parish and to its liturgy. This year, the manifestation and discipleship language of the scriptures on January 26 and February 9 suggests these dates.

- Preparation during the Easter season with blessings on Pentecost or on the prior Sunday. This model was espoused in many publications during the 1970s. It has caught on in many areas and has much to recommend it; however, great care must be taken not to transform Pentecost into a day that focuses just on the liturgical ministers.

- Preparation through the summer, with commissioning early in September or commissioning along with the religious education ministers on the day that has become in many areas "Catechetical Sunday." Although liturgically sound, this may focus too much on a school-year model of ecclesial life.

Each model has its adherents, and local traditions should be changed only with great caution. Yet these Sundays in late January and early February seem to provide the most suitable time for this blessing.

Of course, volunteers can function as ministers without such a blessing. Keep in mind that blessings are not ordinations or rites of empowerment. The term "blessing" has better connotations than "commissioning": We praise or "bless" God for the gifts of the Spirit. We ask for God's blessing on our ministers. Thus, the *Book of Blessings,* in chapters 61 and 62, provides orders for blessing readers, servers, sacristans, musicians and ushers. The term "commissioning" is used only in chapter 63, "Order for Commissioning Extraordinary Ministers of Holy Communion." Sources for this distinction can be found in the history of eucharistic ministers, which can be pursued by tracking down the footnotes of chapter 63.

Planners who wish to bless all the liturgical ministers at the same liturgy can add sections from chapters 61 and 63 of the *Book of Blessings* into the more inclusive chapter 62:

INTRODUCTORY RITES

- The greeting may be the one used on all the Sundays of this part of Ordinary Time or from the *Book of Blessings* (BB), #1836 or #1883.

- The introduction can draw from BB, #1858, adapted with phrases from BB, #1837 or #1884.

LITURGY OF THE WORD

- The homily, as described in BB, #1831 and #1852, will open the scriptures and reflect the blessing about to be celebrated.

- The ministers to be blessed are asked to come forward by name, by type of ministry or all at the same time. This presentation, depending on the guidelines of your diocese for the commissioning of ministers of holy communion, may include BB, #1875 and #1876.

- All stand. The ministers may be invited to kneel.

- The intercessions are introduced with the first paragraph of BB, #1853. Sung petitions can be drawn from BB, #1832, #1853 and #1879 and from those used on the Sundays of that time of year.

- The presider extends his hands over the ministers and concludes the intercessions with the prayer of blessing (BB, #1854, listing all categories of ministers and possibly adapting the prayer with phrases from BB, #1833, #1877 and #1878).

- The newly blessed ministers return to their seats.

CONCLUDING RITE

- Solemn blessing with invocations can be drawn from BB, #1845, #1869 and #1895, each concluded by a rousing amen.

MON 27 #317 green
Weekday

Angela Merici, virgin, optional memorial / white. • While some regions have shifted the dates, many dioceses observe this week as Catholic Schools Week. In 1992, three important educators form the sanctoral list—an educator of girls, one of boys, and the quintessential university professor.

Angela Merici established the Ursuline community, the first teaching order of women to be founded in the church. Her proper opening prayer and the common texts for teachers given as a cross-reference on this date admirably form the local church in an appropriate appreciation for education. The excerpt from Angela's *Spiritual Testament* given in the Office of Readings should inspire every teacher, ". . . be concerned about every one of your daughters. Bear them, so to speak, engraved upon your heart—not merely their names, but their conditions and states, whatever they may be."

TUE 28 #318 white
Thomas Aquinas, priest and doctor
MEMORIAL

One of the most famous doctors of the church may inspire intercessions for students, teachers and Catholic schools. With the readings of the weekday, the proper prayer and the seldom-used prayers from the common of doctors can be used.

W
E **29** #319 green
D **Weekday**

The oracle of Nathan in today's first reading forms one of the most important theological statements of the Hebrew Scriptures. Here the ground is laid for royal messianism in later Jewish and Christian discourse.

T
H **30** #320 green
U **Weekday**

F
R **31** #321 white
I **John Bosco, priest**
MEMORIAL

While Angela Merici is one of the most inspiring female educators, today we meet her equal for males. John was a spiritual son of Francis de Sales, and his Salesian communities minister throughout the world. The weekday readings and sanctoral prayers can be combined with general intercessions for youth.

February

S
A **1** #322 green
T **Weekday**

Blessed Virgin Mary, optional memorial/white. ▪ The fourth Mass in the *Collection of Masses of the Blessed Virgin Mary* may be appropriate today, especially if we see these Saturday memorials of Mary as preparing the assembly for the Sunday liturgy. Here the "Mother of God" title is inextricably linked to the actions of presentation and purification to be remembered tomorrow.

▪ BLACK HISTORY MONTH begins today. Communities wishing to mark this in the liturgy may do so in the intercessions and homilies. This observance, like so many others, expresses genuine human

dreams and sentiments, but the timing is difficult to mesh with the liturgy. The saints especially revered in black Catholic communities (for example, Peter Claver on September 9) would be good days for parishes to unpack the histories of black Americans. This same approach is perhaps the best one for relating any ethnic group to the church's tradition passed on to us through the liturgy.

✵**2** #524 white
Presentation of the Lord
FEAST

Having been to the mountain of the Lord for the great seasons of expectation and manifestation, and having spent a few weeks on the plain of ordinary weeks, we now have the gift of these weeks' brightest day. This year it falls on Sunday so that the entire parish can celebrate it.

▪ FROM THE MANGER TO JERUSALEM: This feast flows from the nativity narratives proclaimed several weeks ago and sets the stage for the paschal season beginning several weeks hence. The baby of Bethlehem is presented in Jerusalem, the site of sword and sacrifice, deliverance and glory. In the dark cold of winter, this day draws us to the core of salvation history. We are invited in by some of the most beautiful and memorable rites of the year.

▪ HISTORY: The power of the light of nations, the wonderment of the meetings with Simeon, Anna and us form the internal force of the

festival, giving birth to its rites and prayer texts and hymns for 1,600 years. Adolf Adam and others describe this evolution: In Jerusalem, the festival was reported at least as early as the year 386, soon developing a torchlight procession and the title of "Meeting" —the meeting of Jesus with Simeon and Anna. It was celebrated on February 14, the 40th day after Epiphany. A little later, the commemoration of this event began to be observed in Rome on February 2, the 40th day after the Nativity. The carrying of lights was seen here, too, at an early date, but it took on a penitential character (perhaps replacing a pagan procession of expiation). The name "Candlemas" or "Light Mass" naturally sprang up, so wonderful was the experience of this bright rite.

▪ GROUNDHOG DAY: Residents along the northeast corridor of the United States watch for Punxsutawney Phil to stick his head up from his burrow 90 miles from Pittsburgh. Local residents say that their custom goes back to the German *Lichtmesse* tales, which held that if an animal casts a shadow on February 2, there will be six more weeks of winter. But Phil is a stranger in the Midwest. There folks turn to a wild groundhog—untamed by a human name —in Sun Prairie, Wisconsin. No matter the mode of expression, the power of light and darkness holds sway over us. In its fleeting, annual moment in the world's media, this date marks a turning point from winter to spring, from Christmas to the Pasch.

▪ SUMMON THE ASSEMBLY: A feast of the Lord has a higher liturgical ranking than a Sunday in Ordinary Time, so we are able to celebrate this wondrous day with much larger congregations than usual this year. Given the rites with candles, a strong case can be made for encouraging as many parishioners as possible to modify their regular patterns of worship and to come on Saturday or Sunday evening. In some localities, this is also Boy Scout Sunday. If the parish includes scouting groups, perhaps they could be included in the planning as extra ushers to help with darkened steps or corners, or as discreet fire-extinguisher assistants. If the assembly will include large numbers of children, some of the ideas found in LTP's *Leader's Manual of the Hymnal for Catholic Students* (p. 78) may be useful.

■ HYMNODY: Consider the hymns specific to this feast from the *Liturgy of the Hours;* also fitting are "I want to walk as a child of the light" (*Worship* and *Hymnal for Catholic Students*) and "How brightly beams the morning star," which celebrate Christ as "sudden radiance" and "Lord and master," echoing the sacramentary texts for this day.

■ BLESSING OF CANDLES AND PROCESSION: The ritual action is described in the sacramentary and, more fully, in the *Ceremonial of Bishops.*

• All gather (with unlighted candles) in a chapel or some other place outside the hall of the eucharistic celebration. Ushers can assist the assembly; the presider and other ministers (vested for Mass) go there for the opening.

  Church architects, diocesan building commissions and church construction committees would benefit greatly by coming to liturgy on this day (and several others during the year) to reflect on the spatial requirements of the rubrics. We need large entranceways. In most parts of North America, these ritual gatherings cannot occur outdoors. The gathering space is not just for coffee, as important as that may be. The

space is necessary for the orthodox celebration of the Roman rite.

If weather or lack of spaces prevents the gathering in a separate space, adaptations are in order. Look at the "solemn procession" option described in the sacramentary and find a way to fill your worship place with candlelight. The procession should be a genuine action of the assembly—not just two people moving from the ambo to the altar. Perhaps the leaders and as many members of the assembly as possible could begin in the vestibule, in the baptistry area or by a Marian shrine.

• The candles are lit and a song (such as the canticle printed in the sacramentary) is sung.

• The sign of the cross is made and the liturgical greeting is given. These brief gestures are for all liturgies. Although unspecified in the sacramentary, they are called for in the *Ceremonial.*

• The invitation to the service can use the suggested text in the sacramentary, to be spoken (or chanted) by deacon or presider.

• The blessing over the candles is prayed (candles have been lit earlier and are held by every member of the assembly). The text itself announces the action: The candles are for carrying.

• The candles are sprinkled with water in silence.

• Incense is placed in the censer.

• An acclamation (found in the sacramentary) announces the procession and is spoken by the deacon or presider.

• The procession moves to the site of the eucharist with all bearing lit candles and singing either the canticle in the sacramentary or a hymn. A simple chant setting by Richard Proulx of the sacramentary texts for the "Blessing of Candles and Procession" is found in *Worship.* Other possibilities include singing one of the hymns suggested previously as the candles are lit or a solo instrument playing (and perhaps improvising

around) the melody that will be sung in procession. Although the rite suggests a processional canticle or hymn and an entrance hymn for the Mass, two different pieces of music followed by a sung Gloria makes this rite unwieldy. The Canticle of Simeon *(Nunc dimittis)* can be used to unify this entire procession. The translation, "Lord, bid your servant go in peace," can be sung to the tune "Morning Song," as in *Worship,* or the more familiar melodies of "Land of rest" or "St. Anne" can be sung, adding interludes and repeating verses as needed after singing the hymn once. Another possibility would be to process to the church singing the Taizé *"Nunc dimittis"* as an *ostinato* accompanied by handbells and hand-held percussion and other portable instruments, adding the canticle's verses (see sacramentary) set to a compatible psalm tone and sung by the cantor as the procession enters the church. Those providing the musical leadership in the procession must know when to give a clear indication that the *ostinato* singing should stop for the cantor's verse, and then lead the singing of the *Nunc* as a refrain after each verse.

• As the procession enters the church, the processional music continues or an entrance hymn for the Mass is begun. The presider venerates (and incenses) the altar while the hymn continues.

• The Gloria is sung—a full menu of joyous music!

■ LITURGY OF THE WORD: While a common responsorial psalm is recommended for the other wintertime Sundays, the proper psalm for this day, Psalm 24, should be sung. It expresses the day's heritage, meaning and distinction from other surrounding Sundays. Medieval and even more ancient rubrics called for all candles to be relit for the proclamation of the gospel. (Or simply leave the candles lit until the end of the gospel. If you do this, perhaps a hymn or carol or a reprise of the Alleluia can be sung after the gospel so the extinguishing of the candles does not follow too closely the conclusion of the gospel.) For inspiration, homilists may study the homily found in the Office of Readings. It witnesses to and draws meaning from the ancient candlelight procession in Jerusalem.

■ LITURGY OF THE EUCHARIST: The candles may be lit again as the assembly stands for the eucharistic prayer. This, then, could be a real "candle Mass."

M O N **3** #323 green
Weekday

Blase, bishop and martyr, optional memorial/red. ▪ *Ansgar, bishop, optional memorial/white.* ▪ Many local churches around the world choose to use the optional memorial of St. Blase, bishop of Sebaste (Armenia) and martyr of the fourth century. The commemoration often includes the blessing of throats. The "Order for the Blessing of Throats on the Feast of St. Blase" (*Book of Blessings,* chapter 51) is the recommended form for this blessing. If the blessing is to be integrated into the weekday Mass, see part I of this Order of Blessing. The texts include an introduction for the beginning of Mass, intercessions and the blessing rite for the conclusion of the general intercessions. Note #1626, which makes provision for other adaptations.

The blessing also can be celebrated at its own service, a liturgy of the word concluding with the blessing. This service can be led by a priest, deacon or lay presider.

Although blessing throats is a fitting custom in the middle of the flu season, this custom should not cause this day to become more noteworthy than yesterday. In other words, celebrate the blessing of throats only if Candlemas has been celebrated with vigor.

Ansgar, the great Scandinavian missionary of the ninth century, often is ignored by local churches. His witness is worth remembering at daily Mass. Planners should not feel guilty picking his memorial over Blase, especially if the blessing of throats will take place at another prayer service.

T U E **4** #324 green
Weekday

W E D **5** #325 red
Agatha, virgin and martyr
MEMORIAL

The proper and common prayers of the saint should be used. Agatha enjoyed wide veneration in ancient times. As Pius Parsch surveyed the winter, he wrote:

> [Agatha] is the last of the four great virgin-martyrs of the Roman church whose names occur in the Canon and whose feasts are celebrated month by month during the winter. The four are Cecilia (November); Lucy (the "shining one," in December, heralding the light of Christmas); Agnes (the "pure," in January); and Agatha (the "good," in February). (*The Church's Year of Grace,* vol. I, p. 446)

T H U **6** #326 red
Paul Miki and companions, martyrs
MEMORIAL

Twenty-six Catholics, Japanese and European, religious and lay, were martyred at Nagasaki on February 5, 1597. The excerpt from the account of their martyrdom found in the Office of Readings, is quite moving. On his noblest pulpit, his cross, Paul Miki proclaimed himself a Japanese and a Jesuit. Others would be martyred at Nagasaki during the next century (see Lawrence Ruiz and companions on September 28). It seems that this beautiful city cannot be thought of without reference to death. The proper and common prayers of the saints should be used at Mass.

Meanwhile, the semicontinuous readings for weekdays have brought us through 1 and 2 Samuel up to today and the first passage from the early chapters of 1 Kings. This book builds on the books of Samuel, extending the history of Israel to the destruction of Jerusalem in 587 BC. For the rest of this week and through the next, we hear of fidelity and infidelity, filling in more of the story about how Israel came to be in exile.

F R I **7** #327 green
Weekday

In the midst of the narrative about the history of Israel, we find here a seemingly odd insert from Sirach. It is explained in the 1981 introduction to the lectionary: "The religious significance of the historical events is sometimes brought out by means of certain texts from the wisdom books that are placed as prologues or conclusions to a series of historical readings" (#110).

When there is a free choice of prayer texts, presiders and planners may want texts to reflect the penitential nature of Fridays. Readings, as always, should be from the weekday. Appropriate Masses for Fridays include:

▪ Votive Mass of the Holy Cross (from September 14); of the Precious Blood (rich texts, providing *mythos* for the reception from the cup); or of the Sacred Heart (Karl Rahner and Bernard Lonergan wrote extensively on this fascinating image and its resurgence a few decades ago).

▪ Mass for persecuted Christians (Masses and Prayers for Various Needs and Occasions, 15)

- Mass for those who suffer from famine (#28), for refugees and exiles (#29), for those unjustly deprived of liberty (#30) or for the sick (#32).

SAT 8 #328 green
Weekday

Jerome Emiliani, optional memorial/white. ▪ *Blessed Virgin Mary, optional memorial/white.* ▪ If the community wishes to celebrate Jerome's memorial, the proper and common prayers of the saint evoke the spirit of his life. In keeping with his witness in sixteenth-century Italy, include orphans and the poor in the intercessions.

9 #76 green
Fifth Sunday in Ordinary Time

The general notes about winter Ordinary Time on pages 56–58 suggest patterns for this Sunday.

▪ THEMES OR IMAGES? The scriptures are not to be manipulated into tidy themes or messages. Because the gospel employs certain organizing images that ebb and flow throughout its pages, a week-by-week reading of a particular gospel gives a cohesiveness of imagery to certain stretches of weeks. These weeks when we read of the call and commissioning of disciples or during the month of November when we read the warnings of the end time are two examples of this. That is why this *Sourcebook* repeatedly suggests that Sundays be prepared not individually but in blocks, taking advantage of the naturally occurring ebb and flow of scriptural imagery. The 1981 introduction to the lectionary offers an often-overlooked liturgical principle in a discussion about why the framers of the lectionary did not give each Sunday a "theme":

An organic harmony of themes designed to aid homiletic instruction . . . would be in conflict with the genuine concern of liturgical celebration. The liturgy is always the celebration of the mystery of Christ and makes use of the word of God on the basis of its own tradition, guided not by merely logical or extrinsic concerns but by the desire to proclaim the gospel and to lead those who believe to the fullness of the truth. (#68)

MON 10 #329 white
Scholastica, virgin
MEMORIAL

Scholastica and her brother, Benedict, by their very names, form an archetypal pair—kind of the primordial monks. The legends that have become a part of their memory do not enter into our liturgical books. Here she is regarded as an example of love and perfect joy. The excerpt from Gregory the Great found in the Office of Readings, expands on that characteristic of love. This is a day to pray for all cloistered men and women, for all members of the Benedictine family and for the holiness, learning and good liturgy for which they stand.

TUE 11 #330 green
Weekday

Our Lady of Lourdes, optional memorial/white. ▪ The event at Lourdes, a private revelation, has been integrated into the calendar because it points to Mary's title as the Immaculate Conception.

WED 12 #331 green
Weekday

THU 13 #332 green
Weekday

FRI 14 #333 white
Cyril, monk, and Methodius, bishop
MEMORIAL

The brothers held up for commemoration this day were important ninth-century liturgical reformers and translators who worked in the region that later became Czechoslovakia. Petitions for that region of eastern Europe, for liturgists and for translators are in order.

▪ VALENTINE'S DAY: Liturgists cannot avoid this facet of the day. Whatever it says about the culture, it continues to exist. And it says many good things. For one, the keeping of the 14th demonstrates that feast-keeping is not a lost art.

The only thing that we can say with certainty about Valentine is that someone by that name was buried on the Flaminian Way outside of Rome on February 14. He was, presumably, a priest, martyred about the year 270. A basilica was built in his memory, and devotion to him spread. When it spread to Terni (near Spoleto in Umbria), the townspeople there decided that he had been their bishop! Because all we know is his burial place, we can only speculate on his connection with love.

One theory is that the custom of choosing a "valentine" on this day is linked to an old belief that birds choose their mates on February 14. Another possibility lies in the ancient celebration in the East on this day, 40 days after Epiphany, of the feast of the "Meeting," what we in the West have come to call the Presentation.

In schools and religious education classes this day, the desire to write and exchange valentines can give rise to prayers and songs of love and unity. Even such informal and "aliturgical" assemblies should avoid didacticism and excess verbiage.

S A T 15 #334 green
Weekday

Blessed Virgin Mary, optional memorial/white.

16 #79 green
Sixth Sunday in Ordinary Time

As noted in the introduction to winter, this Sunday, along with the next two, provides the first opportunity ever for Catholic communities to hear all three excerpts from the "Sermon on the Plain" found in the current lectionary. Whenever, in the past 20 years, Year C drew toward this section of Luke, Ash Wednesday came too early to allow it.

These three Sundays provide us virtually the entire sermon, and most listeners will note that it sounds somewhat like the "Sermon on the Mount" in Matthew. That sermon is read at this same time of the year next year in Year A. The differences between them are important. Large portions of the sermons are the same, but Luke leaves out large segments that seem to pertain more to the Jewish audience of Matthew. Luke is writing for Gentile Christians. He also is writing for the smug and the rich. His version of the beatitudes, partly because they are less familiar than Matthew's, seem to cut into many hearers' hearts. This is powerful material and the homilist had better approach it with a humble "We are

being addressed here," not an imperious "You are being addressed here." Those who prepare the liturgy should read the entire sermon before choosing hymns and composing petitions.

M O N 17 #335 green
Weekday

Seven Founders of the Order of Servites, optional memorial/white. ▪ Seven men—some married, some widowed, some celibate—of the merchant class of Florence, sharing a devotion to the Blessed Virgin, joined together to devote themselves to a life of prayer and preaching.

Founders of religious orders are disproportionately represented on the roster of saints. Not every optional memorial of founders must be celebrated by every local church. The list of all the options selected by a parish in a given year should include as high a percentage as possible (given the limitations of the current calendar) of local saints, of saints with a powerful witness for the local church, of those whose way of life can, indeed, be imitated by the assembly.

From now until Lent, the first reading each weekday will be from a New Testament letter, with most of the passages coming from James. Thus begins a whole new tone for the liturgies of the word at daily Mass.

▪ PRESIDENTS DAY: The prayer found in *Catholic Household Blessings and Prayers* for this day (p. 196) can be used at home or as part of the general intercessions. Certainly, these holidays should move churches to remember all members of our society and all whose lives we touch on this planet.

▪ THE WEEK AHEAD: The feast on Saturday will take precedence over the weekday readings. Nothing in

them indicates that they should be united to Friday's passages.

T U E 18 #336 green
Weekday

W E D 19 #337 green
Weekday

T H U 20 #338 green
Weekday

F R I 21 #339 green
Weekday

Peter Damian, bishop and doctor, optional memorial/white. ▪ If you decide to celebrate this reformer from the turbulent decades that began this millennium, then see him as a model for approaching the final years of that same millennium. They are bound to be years as turbulent as his, demanding the same commitment to ongoing reforms in the church. Use the seldom-heard Common of Doctors with his proper opening prayer.

S A T 22 #535 white
Chair of Peter, apostle
FEAST

The title of this feast sounds unusual. Celebrated since the fourth century, this feast is a sign of the unity of the church—a Christian expression of the old Roman feast *Paternalia,* literally, "forefather's day." An interesting coincidence places it on the birthday of George Washington, the "father" of the United States. The chair of Peter, the *cathedra* of *ex cathedra* pronouncements, also can remind us of the *cathedra* in our local cathedral.

Intercessions today may include prayers for the pope, for parishioners of the Lateran basilica (where the Roman *cathedra* now is located) and for all bishops.

✺23 #82 green
Seventh Sunday in Ordinary Time

The patterns of ritual prayer for the wintertime Sundays should continue, as should our close attention to the "Sermon on the Plain."

Ordinary Time does not always go so far into February as this, and thus it can be noted that the saints' days are fewer. The church has deliberately kept all of the weeks usually associated with the paschal seasons as free as possible. The seriousness of the church's focus was reflected in the practice of having the last Sundays before Lent specially structured to let communities hone in on the upcoming penance and renewal. Even though the "Septuagesima" Sundays are gone, our planning should be more than strategic— where is the paschal candle, who will arrange the ashes, how many ushers will we need? Lent is a time that needs our total offering of heart and wallet, stomach and voice. In fasting and singing, in praying and almsgiving, we will keep the traditions of our ancestors alive.

M O N 24 #341 green
Weekday

T U E 25 #342 green
Weekday

W E D 26 #343 green
Weekday

T H U 27 #344 green
Weekday

F R I 28 #345 green
Weekday

S A T 29 #346 green
Weekday

Blessed Virgin Mary, optional memorial/white.

March

✺1 #85 green
Eighth Sunday in Ordinary Time

■ ANNOUNCEMENTS AND HANDOUTS: Masses on this last Sunday before Lent probably will include many announcements. If you are handing out many papers, booklets and Catholic Relief Services "rice bowls," consider providing them all in one convenient bag for each household.

Three items for distribution to individuals and families are available from Liturgy Training Publications: *An Introduction to Lent and Eastertime* is a 16-page booklet that describes what it means to keep these seasons with the church, with attention to prayer, fasting and almsgiving. *Keeping Lent, Triduum and Eastertime* is a pocket-size prayer book for all the days of these seasons. *Paschal Mission 1992* is a series of Sunday handouts that offer lively reflections on the scriptures and day-by-day calendars for seasonal activity. *Paschal Mission's* handouts begin this Sunday.

■ LENTEN COVENANT: Some parishes put together an attractively printed brochure, calling it their *Parish Lenten Covenant*. These brochures may have been handed out or mailed during the preceding weeks so that individuals can ponder and prepare the coming season. Or they can be the most important "action" item handed out today. Such "covenants" sometimes offer suggestions for communal and household prayer, fasting and almsgiving, with an eye toward ways that these disciplines can be embraced by individuals for the spiritual welfare of the whole parish.

The covenant also can include schedules of parish liturgies and devotions, brief explanations of some of the less-familiar rites (such as communal penance or the catechumenal rites), an overview of the often surprising canons regarding the lenten disciplines (introducing people to the spirit of these laws rather than the bareminimum regulations that most dioceses publish) and concrete ideas (with names and addresses) for almsgiving to local and global concerns.

In their covenant, some parishes ask all members to pledge toward common lenten disciplines, such as praying a daily mealtime grace, fasting, turning the TV off on the Fridays of the season (or every day), helping out at a community clean-up day or contributing to one or two specific charities. Any such common observances must be chosen with care and presented with enthusiasm and sensitivity, avoiding anything that would make them appear to be this year's gimmick. The time of filling out these covenants is at hand: They can be collected on Ash Wednesday or on the First Sunday of Lent.

■ CARNIVAL SUNDAY: This Sunday is not just "Reminder Sunday." It's Carnival Sunday! Today is the last Sunday for the Alleluia until Easter. Some communities (children and adults) have great fun saying good-bye to it with due pomp and fanfare. When it rings out again at the Easter Vigil, it truly will be the victory shout of a people born again of water and the Spirit. Parishes can have great

fun during and after the recessional hymn: While all sing alleluias or a hymn full of them, ministers and children carry out an enormous banner with the word "alleluia" on it (one of the few times words belong on a banner) or they "bury" the Alleluia—a medieval custom—by locking up the word in some type of "tomb" (one of the long-unused tabernacles in a shrine works well for this) or actually burying it in the ground. Everyone leaves singing the recessional and following the alleluia banner. They gather around for the burial and wonder where the years go! This ceremony has its own song: See the hymn "Alleluia, song of gladness," #413 in *Worship*. The words also fit the melody of "Tantum ergo."

■ PREPARING ASHES: Another custom that says "Lent's almost here" is the burning of last year's palms outdoors after the recessional. Everyone will have been asked over the last few Sundays to bring old palms on this day. A great hymn of joy can be sung during the fire, such as "All creatures of our God and King" with its verse about "Thou fire, so masterful and bright."

MON 2 #347 green
Weekday

TUE 3 #348 green
Weekday

Blessed Katherine Drexel, virgin, optional memorial/white. ▪ Beatified in 1988, Katherine lived from 1858 to 1955. A woman of considerable means, she founded a religious community to serve the needs of native and black Americans. Until liturgical texts for her memorial are more generally available, the Common of

Virgins can be used. While her religious community and those touched by her (within living memory) certainly will observe this day, all Americans should cling to and celebrate the few truly American days we have in the calendar.

■ MARDI GRAS: "Greasy Tuesday" is a day needed by all those who take lenten fasting seriously. Every culture adds its own gifts to the fun. At the very least, today's liturgy deserves some of the ceremony added to liturgies last weekend, especially the many alleluias. Today also is called "pancake day" for the animal-product ingredients of pancakes were "forbidden fruit" throughout Lent. They had to be eaten in the form of pancakes, crepes, doughnuts and crullers. Note to anyone responsible for parish fund-raisers: A pancake supper or doughnut fry today or this past weekend is a traditional fund-raiser *and* a traditional part of carnival.

The annual prelenten carnival is not just an excuse for a good time—although we need all the help we can get to drive the cold winter away. A Mardi Gras potluck supper on Shrove Tuesday with a crowning of the carnival queen and king, a parish play, dance, bonfire, pantomime, magic show—anything—helps the parish to begin Lent.

CONCLUDING PRAYERS FOR THE GENERAL INTERCESSIONS

SECOND SUNDAY IN ORDINARY TIME:
God of wonders,
in the hour of his crucifixion
you have revealed your glory
      in Jesus Christ
and summoned all humanity
to find communion in him.

Show to your people gathered on this day
the power of your Spirit to glorify
      and transform;
and in this eucharist
give us to taste the wine you have kept
for the age that is to come.
We ask this through your Son,
      our Lord Jesus Christ,
who lives and reigns [with you in the unity
of the Holy Spirit, one God] forever and ever.
—© ICEL

THIRD SUNDAY IN ORDINARY TIME:
Lord God,
whose compassion embraces all peoples,
whose law is wisdom, freedom, and joy
      for the poor:
fulfill in our midst your promise of favor,
that we may receive the gospel of salvation
      with faith
and, anointed by the Spirit, freely proclaim it.

Grant this through your Son,
      our Lord Jesus Christ,
who lives and reigns [with you in the unity
of the Holy Spirit, one God] forever and ever.
—© ICEL

FIFTH SUNDAY IN ORDINARY TIME:
God all-holy,
earth and heaven are full of your glory,
and even a glimpse of it is more than
      we can bear.

May we recognize your power
at work in your Son
and join the apostles and prophets
as heralds of your saving word.
We ask this through your Son,
      our Lord Jesus Christ,
who lives and reigns [with you in the unity
of the Holy Spirit, one God] forever and ever.
—© ICEL

SIXTH SUNDAY IN ORDINARY TIME:
O God,
who alone can satisfy our deepest hungers,
protect us from the lure of wealth
      and power;
bestir our hearts to seek first your kingdom,
that ours may be the security and joy
of those who place their trust in you.
We ask this through your Son,
      our Lord Jesus Christ,
who lives and reigns [with you in the unity
of the Holy Spirit, one God] forever and ever.
—© ICEL

SEVENTH SUNDAY IN ORDINARY TIME:
Most high God,
you are kind even to the ungrateful,
merciful even to the wicked.
A true and generous father are you.

Pour out your love on this
      assembled people.
Soften our hearts, broaden our souls,
that we may be done with judging
and learn your way of compassion.
We ask this through your Son,
      our Lord Jesus Christ,
who lives and reigns [with you in the unity
of the Holy Spirit, one God] forever and ever.
—© ICEL

LENT

*Lent remains, as it always has been, the church's preparation for Easter.
This preparation is both baptismal and penitential. Catechumens are selected
for Easter sacraments. Every member of the parish is invited to prepare
for the Easter renewal of baptism by entering into penance and renewal.
This preparation also is social. It is not enough for us to make private promises and
to endure individual deprivations. Our private disciplines of fasting, prayer and
almsgiving must be linked to the wonderful rites and parish programs of this season. We
are invited forward to the paschal Lamb as a church.*

Images of the Season

ENTERING a grade-school classroom with collages of lenten themes on the wall, wondering how to deepen lenten fasting beyond merely giving up candy, listening to preaching about the public nature of penance, joining groups for the journey (such as *From Ashes to Easter*), struggling to convince some pastors that "converts" should be part of a catechumenate—these diverse experiences of Lent are but some of the more obvious symptoms of a fundamental shift within the church. The bishops at Vatican II sounded the call for change:

> Lent is marked by two themes, the baptismal and the penitential. By recalling or preparing for baptism and by repentance, this season disposes the faithful, as they more diligently listen to the word of God and devote themselves to prayer, to celebrate the paschal mystery. The baptismal and penitential aspects of Lent are to be given greater prominence in both the liturgy and liturgical catechesis. Hence:
>
> a. More use is to be made of the baptismal features proper to the lenten liturgy; some of those from an earlier era are to be restored as may seem advisable.
>
> b. The same is to apply to the penitential elements. As regards catechesis, it is important to impress on the minds of the faithful not only the social consequences of sin but also the essence of the virtue of penance, namely, detestation of sin as

an offense against God; the role of the church in penitential practices is not to be neglected and the people are to be exhorted to pray for sinners.

> During Lent penance should be not only inward and individual, but also outward and social. The practice of penance should be fostered, however, in ways that are possible in our own times and in different regions and according to the circumstances of the faithful. (Vatican Council II, *Constitution on the Sacred Liturgy*, #109–10)

■ HISTORY: The bishops of Vatican II, of course, did not invent the baptismal and penitential aspects of Lent. Three practices took shape in various centers of Christianity, and during the fourth century in the West these practices came together to form Lent: First, a prepaschal fast grew to 40 days. Some ancient sources relate this number to the Hebrew Scriptures. Others link it to the days Jesus spent in the desert. Some churches began the 40 days of fasting at the commemoration of the Lord's baptism at Epiphany. Most regions eventually arranged the 40 days to culminate at Easter. Second, initiation structures developed in all churches. In the West, these typically included an extended catechumenate, final weeks of intense preparation and baptism at the Easter Vigil. Finally, many churches began reconciling penitents at the Pasch, making Lent the time for completing penance.

For centuries, paschal preparations involved intertwining patterns of catechumenate, penance and fasting. The faithful experienced these as concrete and, often, public actions rather than just as spiritual ideas: There were diets to be planned and exorcisms to be conducted. These activities unfolded on set dates so that the patterns and images could become part of people's lives, passed from generation to generation. Even a theologian as relatively late as Thomas Aquinas could not imagine how baptism made sense apart from the imagery and celebration of Easter.

Over the centuries, though, the catechumenate and public penitential systems withered. Preachers focused on individual works of deprivation and on private identification with the passion and cross of Christ. Many still spoke of preparing for Easter, but the communal framework was weak.

Scholars and activists in liturgical renewal movements before 1960 were aware of this history. Those who still were alive in 1963 rejoiced to hear Vatican II give prominence to Lent's baptismal and penitential aspects. Their joy was doubled by the clear call for these aspects to have their properly social or communal expression.

More than 25 years later, we know that this vision of Lent is easier to voice than to live. Our slow progress in implementing it indicates that we are in a generations-long renewal movement. We are living in one of the few periods of human history when clergy and parents have not known exactly what to tell the next generation, when an inevitable fascination with novelty has accompanied monumental reforms. The ecclesial spirit of Lent needs to be "owned" by people and passed from parents to children and to their children's children. We must keep sharing insights, refining approaches to catechesis, promoting the full and active participation so central to the reforms and collaborating on liturgies that lead us into our own identity as a people.

■ THE MEANING OF LENT: Several interrelated meanings or aspects of Lent are given to us by our tradition and our current rites:

▪ The great stories of creation and salvation history, retold at the Easter Vigil, are woven through the lenten lectionary.

▪ The passion and death of Jesus is a central focus of the paschal seasons of Lent, Triduum and Eastertime and a primary focus for all Christians' lives.

▪ Penance is an attitude, a virtue and a style of life—the way the baptized find renewal on the road to Easter.

▪ Baptism finds expression in the catechumens' preparation for it and the rest of the community's renewal of it.

▪ In the Northern hemisphere, spring is part of the lenten experience; that relationship has been extolled in every century. Carroll and Halton, in the anthology listed in the resources, quote early Christian leaders who saw Lent as thawing the ice of malicious hearts, a season when the very elements of earth are renewed (*Liturgical Practice in the Fathers,* pp. 277–84).

■ THE ACTIONS OF LENT: There are numerous images and metaphors to direct those who prepare and observe this season, but the images do not always suggest programs of action. Foundational to any lenten action is the threefold lenten discipline—announced in the gospel passage for Ash Wednesday and the scriptures the next three days—that is almost as old as the season itself: We pray ("Go to your room, close your door and pray to your Father in private."); we fast ("No one must see you are fasting but your Father."); we give alms ("Keep your deeds of mercy secret, and your Father who sees in secret will repay you.").

■ FORTY DAYS: Most people know that Lent is 40 days long, but they think that the 40 days are the six weeks plus the four days of the week of Ash Wednesday (which totals 46 days), minus six Sundays, which equals 40 days.

But Lent does not end on Holy Saturday; it ends on Holy Thursday evening. Lent brings us to the Triduum, not to Easter Sunday. It is important that the whole of the Triduum be celebrated in its internal unity—as a three-day season unto itself and not as the final three days of Lent. The span from Ash Wednesday until Holy Thursday is 44 days.

Because our early ancestors were fascinated by numbers, there was no end to their theories and calculations of 40 days (Tally, in Part III of *The Origins of the Liturgical Year,* takes readers through them). For those who need to be exact, the 40 days now are calculated thus:

From the time of the Fathers, as the sermons of St. Leo the Great mention, the 40 days of Lent were counted from the First Sunday of Lent until Holy Thursday. The Roman Missal and Breviary have kept this practice to the present time. (Commentary of the *General Norms for the Liturgical Year and Calendar,* 1969)

■ THE INTERNAL STRUCTURE OF THE SEASON: At least four phases in the season of Lent can be discerned:

1. *Ash Wednesday and the next three days:* These four days form a solemn prelude to the season. In some

regions of the world in early Christianity, this distinction was formulated thus: Ash Wednesday began the fasting, the Sunday began the "Forty Days." Over these days, the scriptures and other liturgical texts announce the major aspects of the observance and call all to enter in. The sense of Sunday as a "beginning" day is expressed in the placement of the rite of election and of the penitential procession on the First Sunday of Lent.

2. *The 28 days from the First Sunday until the Saturday of the Fourth Week* receive much of their direction from the flow of scripture readings and from penitential rites: penance services, the penitential rite ordinarily celebrated on the Second Sunday for candidates for reception into the full communion of the church, and the first two scrutiny rites for the elect. Only two feasts, St. Joseph and the Annunciation, break this purple pattern in 1992. The Fourth or "Laetare" Sunday brings its own nuance to this time.

3. *From the Fifth Sunday* on, attention becomes focused on the passion of Christ.

4. *The last days, called Holy Week,* are an intensification of the third phase of Lent. These days are given the highest liturgical precedence so the church will not be distracted from final preparations for the Triduum.

■ THE SAINTS IN LENT: In various reforms over the centuries, church authorities have cleared most sanctoral observances out of Lent. In addition to the solemnities of Mary and Joseph noted in the previous section, there are nine memorials in Lent this year. These days, which may otherwise be obligatory memorials, become optional during Lent. Those who prepare the liturgy or presiders may want to take an overall look at Lent and chart out which of these nine optional days will be observed. Though few in number, they should only be celebrated if they have a special relationship with the local church. When thus commemorated in Lent, the opening prayer for the memorial may be used at that point in the liturgy or as a conclusion to the intercessions; elements of the homily and petitions of the general intercessions can rise from the memorial. Otherwise, the celebration remains a lenten liturgy: The vesture is violet and all other lenten texts are used. (See *General Instruction of the Roman Missal,* #316a.)

Preparing the Parish

PREPARING the parish for Lent involves year-round attention to the discipline of fasting. We must recognize the irreplaceable part fasting plays in world religions and in our own. Our stomachs and life-styles must be involved in lenten planning and observance.

■ ALLOWING RITUAL LAMENTATION: The liturgical year has few occasions for genuine lamentation, for expressions of brokenness and pain, for decrying injustice and pleading for assistance, for the trembling and tears that often accompany repentance, forgiveness and healing—and for turning to the cross of Christ as a sign of salvation and forgiveness, as our hope of glory.

No gathering of Christians should be an occasion for despair or facile emotions, but at the same time the genuine sorrows of the community never should be masked with a smile button. Yet that so often happens to Lent and Advent, to funerals and to services of reconciliation. If, for example, we sing the great psalms of Lent, such as Psalm 51 ("A clean heart create for me, O God") or Psalm 137 ("By the streams of Babylon"), the musical arrangements we employ often tend to soften the words with overly "friendly" musical styles that make them sound like an advertiser's jingle.

When children and adults experience divorce, racism, AIDS, sexism, violence, addiction, war or natural disaster, they do not need to come to church only to be told "everything is OK, don't worry." They must be able to bring their real pain and lament to the community of the altar and the psalms.

If we take away the sugar coating, we will have to prepare an honest answer to the inevitable accusation that the lenten liturgy is not "upbeat," that it does not leave everyone with a smile, that it fails "to meet our needs" and offers little therapeutic escape from the realities of the world. Remember: Lent is serious. It is about struggle; it is about the nature and price of salvation. The scrutinies are public exorcisms! At the same time, liturgies are not podiums from which angry preachers or liturgists can list everyone else's sins and the woes of the world. Our laments must be expressed, neither ignored nor thrown at each other. This is an enormous challenge to pastoral leaders, liturgical planners and educators.

■ IMMERSION IN THE SCRIPTURES: This is certainly an appropriate time of year to foster the desire to read the Bible on a regular basis. Never forget to press the idea in bulletins, lenten home handouts, etc. Bible study groups, sessions of adult education and children's religious education can include curriculum components or biblical excerpts in tune with Lent rather than business-as-usual. To help make the most of the season, see the suggestions for educators in LTP's *Paschal Mission 1992* and also in the *Leader's Manual of the Hymnal for Catholic Students* (LTP/GIA).

■ DOMESTIC PRAYER: Preparations also involve equipping households with the tools and the encouragement they need to keep Lent. Many parishes produce collections of prayers, meditations and domestic rites to complement the more public events of the season. Such local publications can link domestic prayers of penitence to the days when communal penance is celebrated and make prayers for the elect, candidates and catechumens specific. Also, people can turn to *Catholic Household Blessings and Prayers.* It includes:

- Table prayers for days of fasting and almsgiving (p. 62) and for the weekdays of Lent (p. 76).

- An "Ash Wednesday Blessing of the Season and of a Place of Prayer" (p. 132).

- Blessings of lenten disciplines: fasting, almsgiving (p. 137).

- A "Passion Sunday placing of branches in the home" (p. 140).

- Prayers for St. Joseph Day (pp. 165 and 346).

- A renunciation of sin, a profession of faith and a renewal of baptismal vows (pp. 371 and 372) to prepare for the Easter Vigil.

The Mass

INTRODUCTORY RITES

WHILE the notes in this *Sourcebook* focus on the Sunday liturgies, see the *Leader's Manual of the Hymnal for Catholic Students* (pp. 81–92) for models of weekday liturgy with children. See also the set of presidential prayers for lenten Masses with children found on page 100 of this *Sourcebook.*

■ OPENING SONG: The gathering music should sound lenten in text, tune and performance style. The classic lenten chant, "Attende Domine," is a possibility here; there are several translations available, for example, "Draw near, O Lord, our God," found in the *People's Mass Book.* Another lenten melody that people should know is the chorale "Erhalt Uns Herr," which is coupled with two lenten texts in *Worship.* "Again we keep this solemn fast," a Peter Scagnelli translation of a text ascribed to Gregory the Great, is a wonderful example of hymnody that is formative and catechetical; it captures the essence of lenten spirituality and lends itself particularly well to Ash Wednesday. "The glory of these forty days" mirrors the biblical images of Lent, emphasizing the prophetic figures of Moses, Elijah, Daniel and John the Baptist. Although both of these texts are in long meter, avoid coupling them with a commonly known tune such as "Old One Hundredth." As important as familiarity is, providing a melody that conveys a lenten character is of much greater value.

■ THE PENITENTIAL RITE may be celebrated with the entire community—including the presider —kneeling as a sign of repentance. Such kneeling should not be too rushed or too brief. We must become accustomed to the use of this posture, in church and at home, as one of penitence. A time of silence is in order here for pondering and praising God's mercy. The invocations at C*iv* and C*v* in the sacramentary seem to have been written with Lent in mind. Other samples are on page 97.

One way to order these rites would be to sing the first three verses of "Again we keep this solemn fast," kneel for the penitential rite that consists of a chanted "Kyrie" (consider "Kyrie cum jubilo" in *Worship*) with or without tropes and conclude with the final two verses of the same hymn.

Another fine resource for enhancing the penitential rite during Lent is "Three Plainsong Kyries" with tropes from the sacramentary. It includes simple *a cappella* settings for cantor and congregation arranged by Richard Proulx (GIA, G-3162).

LITURGY OF THE WORD

■ SCRIPTURES OF THE SEASON: The introduction to the lectionary notes that the Hebrew Scriptures and salvation history are highlighted this season:

> [The Hebrew Scripture readings on lenten Sundays] are about the history of salvation, which is one of the themes proper to the catechesis of Lent. The series of texts for each year presents the main elements of salvation history from its beginning until the promise of the new covenant.
>
> The readings from the letters of the apostles have been selected to fit the gospel and the Old Testament readings and, to the extent possible, to provide a connection between them. (*Introduction to the Lectionary, #97*)

When interpreting the scriptures, we can be guided by the principles of "liturgical exegesis" expounded by Nocent (see the resources list). We approach these pericopes in their liturgical setting and in relationship to each other. For example, we hear or "receive" the account of the transfiguration of the Lord differently in Lent than we do on August 6. And we appreciate the lenten telling of the transfiguration somewhat differently in each of the lectionary years. In Year C, the story related in Genesis of God making covenant with Abram and the transfiguration of our own bodies promised in Paul's letter let us hear Luke's account with fresh ears.

■ YEAR A READINGS: The lectionary and all the pertinent liturgical books encourage the use of the Year A scriptures every year on the Third, Fourth and Fifth Sundays of Lent. This is mandatory in those Masses where the scrutinies are celebrated but it also is valuable for other parishes and worshiping assemblies.

Those who pass over this rubric in the lectionary and use Year C readings on March 22, 29 and April 5 have many reasons, variety and the avoidance of missalette users' confusion among them. Variety is important, indeed that

is why we have three years' worth of Sunday readings. It simply is not the only value. The year is marked by many days with consistent scriptures. The rich treasure of these strong readings, especially the gospels, on these three Sundays should not be missed. They are too central to our lenten history and to the unfolding of the rites.

As for the argument that only Year C is in the missalette, one or two of these responses is appropriate: Change to a participation book/hymnal that provides all the legitimate options; leave the missalettes out of the pews these three Sundays; give pocket lectionaries or hand missals to parishioners who are hearing impaired; or write to the missalette publisher and ask that future years' editions contain the readings for both Year A and the current year for these weeks.

■ PSALM: Let the one psalm that will be used throughout Lent establish itself as the assembly's common prayer and the "sound of the season." Psalms 51, 91 and 130 are the seasonal responsorial psalms. Psalm 51 is assigned to Ash Wednesday and it appears three times in the lenten weekday lectionary. Its presence in so many other places in the liturgy (for example, every Friday at Morning Prayer) seems to call for this choice. Every Catholic should learn at least one setting of this psalm.

• The Marty Haugen refrain, "Be merciful, O Lord" (GIA, G-2664) is effectively used with the verses of Psalm 51 chanted to Meinrad Tone 6.

• Rawn Harbor offers a fine alternative refrain in *Lead Me, Guide Me* (GIA). Verses are chanted to a tone also found in this hymnal.

• The ICEL antiphon, "Have mercy, tender God, forget that we defied you," has been set by Robert Kreutz and Marty Haugen; both are found in *Psalms for All Seasons* (NPM), coupled with a plaintive tone for the verses.

■ GOSPEL ACCLAMATION: The alleluia is excluded completely, even for solemnities or ritual Masses that happen to fall in Lent. No hymn with it. No acclamation with it. No antiphon with it. No alleluias. Period.

■ HOMILY: See Austin Fleming's magnificent article, "What Kind of Lenten Homilies Does the Catechumenate Want?" in *Parish Catechumenate: Pastors, Presiders, Preachers* (LTP, 1988).

■ DISMISSAL OF THE CATECHUMENS AND THE ELECT: All year long, the catechumens are to be dismissed each Sunday after the homily. In Lent, they are joined by those of their number who have become the elect. The RCIA provides two texts for dismissing catechumens (#67) that make the spirit of the dismissal clear. Other words may be used, but any dismissal should convey concern and affection. A lenten seasonal formula is proposed on page 97 of this *Sourcebook*. If the catechumens (and elect) are being dismissed to continue reflection on the scriptures, the dismissal can commend them to their catechists.

Alternative forms of the dismissal are given in the adult initiation rite for particular moments in Lent: #116A is a formula for the First Sunday if catechumens are being sent to the cathedral; #136A provides a well-worded sentence on the paschal mystery to conclude the rite of election (if this is celebrated at your parish) or perhaps to be used for the dismissal on the Second Sunday, for it looks forward to the first scrutiny (which is celebrated on the Third Sunday). For the scrutinies, a similar choice of formularies for the dismissal is printed with each rite.

This ritual exclusion of the catechumens can be an incentive to the personal conversion of the faithful: "Why can I stay when they can't? What's so special about being in this community?" This ritual exclusion also can have effects —positive and negative—on catechumens and the elect who, like all of us, are challenged to grow but must be accepted and respected for who they are: "Why can't I stay and they can? What's so special about this community?" These concerns must be handled with prudence and vision.

■ PROFESSION OF FAITH: The profession of faith is called for on Sundays, on March 19 and on March 25. Some of the rites with the elect, such as the scrutinies, note that it is to be sung or said after the general intercessions. This order is present in many of the rituals integrated into the eucharistic assembly, reflecting a more ancient—some liturgical historians say more correct—ritual sequence by ending the liturgy of the word with the great profession of faith.

■ GENERAL INTERCESSIONS: The intercessions can take on a seasonal cast. See the examples on pages 97–98. Appendix I of the sacramentary also has two sample forms for the season. The presence of the elect throughout each diocese calls for every parish, even those without elect, to pray for them.

The rites of initiation during Lent change the conclusion of the liturgy of the word. On the First Sunday (at either the rite of sending or the rite of election), on the Second Sunday (at the penitential rite for the candidates for reception into the church) and then on the Third, Fourth and Fifth Sundays (at the scrutinies of the elect), the dismissal of the catechumens and the elect is followed by the general intercessions and then the creed.

Notice that there are two different kinds of intercessions—those for the elect and the general intercessions—close together in the liturgy. Keeping them distinct is important. The intercessions for the elect may be chanted with a sung "Lord have mercy" or "Kyrie" response. David Haas's Kyrie from "Mass of Light" (*Gather*, GIA) is effectively sung unaccompanied. The assembly then may use a familiar format for the general intercessions after the dismissal of the catechumens and elect.

The rubrics say that the general intercessions and the creed can be omitted on these Sundays "for pastoral reasons." If this is done, the rubrics allow the prayers for the church and the world to be added to the prayers for the elect. This option does violence to the tradition of keeping these intercessions as "prayers of the faithful." It makes sense only in parishes where the dismissal is omitted and the faithful are joined by catechumens for the eucharist— which does even more violence to the sacramental economy.

LITURGY OF THE EUCHARIST

■ EUCHARISTIC PRAYER TEXTS: Lenten Preface IV is prescribed for all fast days, presumably because of the Latin phrase *corporali ieiunio*— literally, "bodily fasting"—which becomes "lenten observance" in the English version. While a literal description may be too narrow to describe all the lenten disciplines, "observance" is too general. Perhaps we may say:

> Through our lenten observance,
> *our prayer, fasting and almsgiving,*
> you correct our faults
> and raise our minds to you.

Excluding the preface for the Chrism Mass, there are 12 lenten prefaces in the sacramentary (P8–P18). Many of them are poetic, several refer to the scriptures of particular days and some are more pertinent to late Lent. Two other

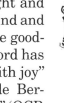

prefaces are used on feasts: Joseph on March 19 and the Annunciation on March 25. Read through all of them and also the two eucharistic prayers for reconciliation. Note also the special inserts available in the sacramentary (for the elect in Eucharistic Prayer I at Masses with scrutinies; for the deceased in Eucharistic Prayers II and III). Consider what words and images will nurture a sense of the season in your community. Then for the whole season choose one eucharistic prayer with many different prefaces, or one prayer with just a few prefaces, or two different prayers—one for weekdays and one for Sundays.

■ EUCHARISTIC PRAYER ACCLAMATIONS should lend unity to this season. They also can unite the seasons that lead to and flow from the great Triduum celebration. For instance, if the Sanctus from the Latin chant Mass XVIII is sung during Lent and coupled with one of the Danish Mass memorial acclamations and Amen (in the complementary tonality of F Major), then during the Easter season and through Pentecost, the memorial acclamation and Amen can remain the same even if the Holy changes to "A Community Mass" (Proulx, *Worship*) or "People's Mass" (Vermulst, *People's Mass Book*).

■ COMMUNION RITE: The third introduction to the Lord's Prayer in the sacramentary seems particularly appropriate for Lent. Another sample (as well as texts for "seasonalizing" the peace prayer, the introduction to communion and the sending forth of eucharistic ministers) is on page 100.

The communion procession provides an opportunity to sing the appointed psalms for the Sundays of Lent when a common psalm is sung consistently during the Liturgy of the Word. Some of these are probably in your parish's repertoire. If the readings of Year A are used, the appointed psalm for the Third Sunday is Psalm 95 with the refrain, "If today you hear his voice, harden not your hearts." Psalm 23 is assigned to the Fourth Sunday; try using the Gelineau antiphon, "My shepherd is the Lord," alternating with verses of "The king of love my Shepherd is" to the gentle melody of "St. Columba." Marty Haugen's setting of this psalm, "Shepherd me O God," with the paschal character of its antiphon, is much more successful as a communion processional than as a responsorial psalm.

Proper psalm antiphons for the Sundays of Year C include "Be with me, Lord, when I am in trouble" (Psalm 91), "The Lord is my light and my salvation" (Psalm 27), "The Lord is kind and merciful" (Psalm 103), "Taste and see the goodness of the Lord" (Psalm 34) and "The Lord has done great things for us; we are filled with joy" (Psalm 126). Other fine choices include Bernadette Farrell's "Unless a grain of wheat" (OCP, #7115) and "Now we remain" by David Haas (*Gather,* GIA), which is particularly appropriate for Passion Sunday and Triduum.

CONCLUDING RITE

The same solemn blessing may be used every day of the season—for example, the solemn blessing for Lent printed in the *Book of Blessings* at #2047.5. Put a copy of it in the sacramentary. If you decide to use the shorter style of the prayer over the people, see #6 for use throughout Lent.

MUSIC

Bernadette Farrell's "Praise to you, O Christ, our Savior" (OCP, #7126) lends itself both in text and musical character to use through the entire season.

"I heard the voice of Jesus say" already may be familiar in your parish from use in Ordinary Time; its use of water and light imagery makes it particularly useful in conjunction with the scrutiny rites.

"Lift high the cross" is a powerful song of victory, mission and conversion; both text and tune ("Crucifer") are strong and captivating. Augsburg publishes an arrangement by Donald Busarow (#11-1890) that offers an optional four-part choir setting of the verses, descant and a choice of 12 verses.

A useful collection for this season is David Haas's *Who Calls You By Name: Music for Christian Initiation* (GIA). This book provides music for the parish's celebration of Lent with the elect and provides litanies, acclamations and psalms as well as songs. A pastoral sense is evident throughout: The lenten gospel acclamation provides a verse for each of the Sundays of Year A; the pieces provided for the celebration of the scrutinies utilize the same melody for the assembly's refrain while matching the text to the gospel images of each Sunday; and reprintable music for the assembly is included.

Other Ritual Prayer and Sacraments

LITURGY OF THE HOURS

LENT provides another opportunity to introduce the community to Sunday Evening Prayer and, possibly, to daily Morning and Evening Prayer as well. People usually are more inclined to attend and participate and then to make these liturgies part of the joyful discipline of each day.

The patristic readings in each day's Office of Readings are fine substitutes for the brief pieces of scripture found in Evening Prayer.

■ VIGILS: The possibilities of Saturday night vigils can be explored for this season. For each Sunday eve, appendix I of the *Liturgy of the Hours* provides canticles and gospels to be added to the Office of Readings to produce an extended vigil. The gospels listed there are particularly evocative of Lent. Texts also are included for the Solemnity of St. Joseph and the Annunciation (especially fitting for communities that bear one of these titles).

COMMUNAL PENANCE

Most parishes schedule penance services during this season. For resources in planning an order of service, see the two lenten services in appendix II of the *Rite of Penance*. For parish schools and catechetical programs for children, see GIA/LTP's *Leader's Manual of the Hymnal for Catholic Students* (p. 87).

Lent may be the best time to mark the anniversary of Columbus's voyage and the beginning of evangelization in the Americas. See page xiii for reflections on this commemoration and for an outline of a penitential service.

COMMUNAL ANOINTING OF THE SICK

While the ritual Mass texts for anointing are forbidden on the Sundays of Lent, on March 19 and March 25, the rite can be celebrated at Mass even on those days. Sickness knows no season, and the lenten prayer texts plunge the anointing of the sick deep into the paschal mystery. Provision is made for one of the ritual readings to be substituted for a lenten scripture passage. The passages of the ritual Mass from Isaiah 52, from Romans 8 and from Colossians are particularly appropriate to Lent. See page 101 for lenten texts for the reception of the sick and for the prayer after anointing.

FUNERALS

Funerals may not take place at Mass on the Sundays of Lent. On weekdays, one may consider the day's scriptures as options because they are so rich in the imagery of the paschal mystery. The common psalm sung at all other Masses also may be used. If the day's scriptures are deemed appropriate, a selection from the funeral readings may be added, such as Job or Lamentations, one of the Passion narratives, or the two parts of the raising of Lazarus linked together as on the Fifth Sunday of Lent, Year A.

MARRIAGES

Even though the Roman rite has left the door open for marriages to occur in Lent, we are enjoined by the rite to explain to couples why, because of the nature of Lent, that door is best left shut. Liturgical committees, pastoral ministers and then the couples who will be preparing for marriage must accommodate the notice that lenten weddings must take account of the season (*Rite of Marriage*, #11; see also the *Ceremonial of Bishops*, #604). This "taking account" includes the same ban on flowers and instrumental music as at every other lenten liturgy.

STATIONS OF THE CROSS

Friday evening stations of the cross is a hallowed tradition in this country. Think about reviewing or revitalizing your community's experience of it. While venerable and fitting indeed, the "Stabat Mater" is not mandatory at stations. Consider using one of the readily available translations of "Vexilla regis," a powerful hymn celebrating the triumph of the cross. Remember, too, that the procession is central to this devotion. If at all possible, everyone should walk to each station with the cross, candle and incense bearers and the leader. For further texts, see the "Order for the Blessing of Stations of the Cross," chapter 42 in the *Book of Blessings*.

BAPTISMS AND CONFIRMATIONS

The Vatican has emphasized the inappropriateness of baptism and confirmation during Lent. See the *Circular Letter Concerning the Preparation and Celebration of the Easter Feasts, #27.* Like the development of a pastorally sensitive policy against lenten weddings, a parish policy that would defer baptisms and confirmations from Lent to the Easter season can capitalize on the inherent beauty and appropriateness of April and May to these sacraments.

The Worship Environment

THE often-ignored rubric printed in the sacramentary after the Mass texts for the Saturday of the Fourth Week remind us of a central tradition in lenten decorating. As previous generations of sacristans knew, this is the time for austerity, simplification and stripping of the worship environment. Most of the art and statuary can be removed or covered. A unified approach to stripping the space may help restore a unity to the room as a sacred space. The stripped-down worship environment allows us to focus on what is most important: the assembly, the penitents, the elect and the candidates.

■ NO FLOWERS: The Roman rite is specific about flowers this season—none are allowed. The only exceptions are March 19, 25 and 29. This includes a stripped-down sanctuary and nave for weddings and funerals.

■ NO CROSS: No cross? Lent is not an extended meditation on the passion. Just as we are waiting for the water and the light of the Paschal Triduum, so, too, we await the cross. That is a reason why it has long been traditional to veil or remove the cross throughout Lent: In ancient times, the cross, gilded and bejeweled as a sign of victory, would be veiled during penitential seasons. In medieval times, the entire sanctuary was hidden behind the "lenten veil" or "rood screen." This practice was continued in many places until the last century. Like giving up the alleluia during Lent only to sing it with gusto at Easter, one of the purposes of the lenten veiling

was the joyful restoration of the cross and images during the Triduum.

■ NO WATER: Many parishes that do not baptize during Lent seal the baptismal font, draining it (and all holy water fonts), covering it, making it unavailable. If you do this, pay attention to the style of your font; sometimes simply leaving it dry makes it look like someone forgot to put water in it. (And filling it with sand can make it look like a lobby ashtray.) If your font has a permanent lid, perhaps it can be bound in cords or simply veiled. Lent's ashes can be kept in a clay vessel nearby, a *memento mori,* a reminder of death.

■ NO OILS: One further element of stripping: The ambry should have the holy oils—or at least the chrism, oil of gladness—removed. These will be replaced with new oil at the first liturgy of the Triduum (see page 112).

■ ART IN LENT: Once the church is stripped, art and a few restrained decorations still have a place. Inspiration for bulletins or participation booklet graphics, for artifacts and book covers is best drawn from that early Christian era when Lent was still a time for catechumenate and penitents, when the privatized focus on the cross had not begun. Christian art prior to 800 AD shows Lent to be what we now once more know it to be—baptismal, penitential and communal in nature. Most of the local churches even used the same scriptural passages as those now in place. Few clip-art books or other contemporary resources utilizing late-medieval or baroque images help us visualize Lent as we now have it.

Communities may consult area residents who have studied early Christian art or get *Clip Art of the Christian World: Christian Art from Its Origins to the Fifteenth Century* (New York: Pueblo Publishing Co., 1990). See also the fuller work from which this was derived: *Art of the Christian World, AD 200–1500: A Handbook of Styles and Forms* (New York: Rizzoli International Publications, 1982). Here one will find several composite pieces, depicting the death or resurrection of Jesus framed by images from the very gospels now read in Lent and Eastertime. Some of these pieces were designed as ivory diptychs or covers for the Book of the Elect.

While returning our art to the same scriptural and liturgical sources it had in the first centuries, one must avoid too quick an adaptation of these emphases into spiritual dioramas.

When we hear about the woman at the well, the man born blind and the raising of Lazarus, there is a temptation to devise symbols of water, light and life in the worship environment. That is much the same as thinking—mistakenly—that liturgy needs a "theme" that can be captured in a word. For example, it would be wrong to add a sprinkling rite to Lent to capitalize on the word "water," or to fill the church with candles because the gospel mentions "light," or to hang butterflies to drive home the word "life."

If not in "lenten display" areas, then where can this art go? See the following notes on *catechumenon,* alms box, book of the elect, entranceway, outdoors and other buildings. Also lift the level of booklet and bulletin art by portraying the real Lent experienced in today's liturgy.

■ CATECHUMENON is the term used by architectural historians to designate spaces that may have been the rooms to which catechumens were dismissed, the rooms through which they passed to the baptistry on Easter. Where is yours? Give it special attention this season. Let everyone in the parish know which room is reserved for the elect and the catechumens.

■ ALMS BOX: If the parish has pledged its alms to a particular charity, a large vessel for collecting that money could be placed prominently in church—perhaps in the entranceway or at the side of the nave.

■ BOOK OF THE ELECT: The cathedral should place the diocese's Book of the Elect in a place befitting its importance. Visitors should be able to turn the pages and see the signatures of those to be initiated, for whom they are praying. In a similar vein, all parishes with elect or with candidates for full communion should have some place in the church where members can see pictures or at least the names of the local sisters and brothers preparing for the sacraments. Infants and their parents looking forward to infant baptism, children preparing for first eucharist during Eastertime and candidates for confirmation may be represented in photographs or names as well. Such a place may be the regular bulletin board, but it also could be a table or wallhanging situated elsewhere. Because these additional names will not appear in the richly bound Book of the Elect, their arrangement may be enhanced by an icon depicting one of the traditional lenten gospels.

■ ENTRANCEWAY: The gathering for any penitential procession on the First Sunday of Lent and for the blessing of palms requires another large space where all can at least stand. In most parts of the United States, the weather is not right for this to be an outdoor plaza. Similar concerns arise at infant baptism, funerals, weddings and the acceptance of catechumens all year. If such a place is available, be sure that it is ready for these lenten gatherings, outfitted in shades of purple, cleared of the saints' images that grace many vestibules.

■ OUTDOORS AND OTHER BUILDINGS: Advertise the season to the neighborhood. An arrangement of strips of fabrics in a monochromatic array of purples, perhaps, hung outside the church building, would be a simple way to announce that this community is preparing for the Pasch. And other buildings should not be overlooked. Lent is not just for an hour each day or each Sunday. The other places the parish calls its own also should contribute to the season. Parish centers, rectories, schools and shelters can and should be decorated with images of the lenten gospels or paschal invitations (the Easter Vigil must be called to every last person's attention), with austere arrangements of purple or enthroned Bibles. A procession of Easter bunnies decorating the windows of the school as people walk past in the procession of palms creates a jarring clash of symbols. This kind of seasonal attention will take negotiation among the adults, but the children will not mind drawing eggs and bunnies during the Easter octave.

■ LITURGICAL VESTURE is customarily purple, but different from the vesture of Advent. Some argue that royal purple (a deep, bloody purple) is especially appropriate as the color of the *vexilla regis,* the banner of the king who "reigns from the tree." Others argue that traditional lenten vesture was a somber blue-violet, almost black. Both traditions charge us to avoid a gaudy purple. Also avoid appliquéd lenten "symbols"; Lent is not a six-week-long Passiontide. Plainness and simplicity are as important as color.

On Laetare Sunday, rose may be worn. This color is a dusky "old rose," not a hot pink. White vestments will be worn for March 19 and 25, and for funerals if you do not use purple for these. The other color vestments will almost never be worn during Lent.

Resources

THE following bibliography is useful for Lent, Triduum and Eastertime. These seasons are truly part of a single season—the paschal season—and should be discussed and prepared together.

HISTORICAL BACKGROUND

Most of the general studies listed on pages xvi–xxii give extensive treatment to these seasons, which are at the heart of the liturgical year. See especially Adam, Bishops' Committee on the Liturgy *Study Text 9,* Carroll and Halton, Cobb, Martimort, Nocent, Parsch and Tally. Some special books on this paschal time:

Davies, J. Gordon. *Holy Week: A Short History* (Richmond VA: John Knox Press, 1963).

Hamman, Adalbert, ed. *The Paschal Mystery* (New York: Alba House, 1969). An excellent collection of early Christian writings on the Easter Triduum translated from Greek and Latin sources and with helpful annotations. The topical index will help homilists pursue various aspects of the season.

Stevenson, Kenneth. *Jerusalem Revisited: The Liturgical Meaning of Holy Week* (Washington DC: The Pastoral Press, 1988).

LITURGICAL/PREACHING HELP

Baker, J. Robert, Evelyn Kaehler and Peter Mazar, eds. *A Lent Sourcebook: The Forty Days.* (Chicago: LTP, 1991). A two-volume treasury of the prayers, scriptures, hymn texts, prose and poetry of the season with an order for daily prayer.

Congregation for Divine Worship. "Circular Letter Concerning the Preparation and Celebration of the Easter Feasts," (Washington DC: USCC). Issued by the Vatican in 1988, it is an excellent compendium of liturgical principles applicable in these weeks.

Hopko, Thomas. *The Lenten Spring.* (Crestwood NY: St. Vladimir's Seminary Press, 1983). Hopko offers a wealth of observations on the lenten themes and disciplines, written from the Ortho-dox tradition and oriented toward their liturgical observances, but providing helpful material for any observance of the season.

Huck, Gabe. *The Three Days: Parish Prayer in the Paschal Triduum* (Chicago: LTP, 1981).

Huck, Gabe, and Mary Ann Simcoe, eds. *A Triduum Sourcebook.* (Chicago: LTP, 1983).

Huck, Gabe, Gail Ramshaw and Gordon Lathrop. *An Easter Sourcebook: The Fifty Days.* (Chicago: LTP, 1988).

Irwin, Kevin W. *Lent: A Guide to the Eucharist and Hours.* (New York: Pueblo Publishing Co., 1986).

_____. *Easter: A Guide to the Eucharist and Hours.* (Collegeville: The Liturgical Press, 1991).

Lawrence, Emeric, OSB. *Believe the Good News.* (Collegeville: The Liturgical Press, 1982).

_____. *Risen and Still with You.* (Collegeville: The Liturgical Press, 1985).

Liturgy: Journal of the Liturgical Conference, vol. 3, no. 1. Entitled "Easter's Fifty Days," this issue is filled with historical information, model celebrations, Easter-in-the-home ideas and much more. May be obtained by writing to: The Liturgical Conference, 1017 12th Street NW, Washington DC 20005.

Merton, Thomas. *Seasons of Celebration.* (New York: Farrar, Straus and Giroux, 1983), 113–24 (Ash Wednesday), 125–43 (Christian self-denial), 144–57 (Eastertime).

Schmemann, Alexander. *Great Lent: Journey to Pascha.* (Crestwood NY: St. Vladimir's Seminary Press, 1974). A classic: Do not start Lent without it! Orthodox calendar and liturgy are reference points, but universally applicable meditations on fasting, discipline, celebration and Lent as pilgrimage are needed.

Simcoe, Mary Ann, ed. *Parish Path through Lent and Eastertime,* second edition. (Chicago: LTP, 1985).

Wilde, James A., ed. *Parish Catechumenate: Pastors, Presiders, Preachers* (Chicago: LTP, 1988).

March

WED **4** Lectionary #220   violet
Ash Wednesday

Day of fast and abstinence. ▪ As soon as we get up this day, we should know it is Lent. Breakfast, if it happens at all, can be different. Morning prayers, no matter how brief, can sound the cry of repentance. *Catholic Household Blessings and Prayers* (p. 132) provides an "Ash Wednesday Blessing of the Season and of a Place of Prayer." This and other lenten offerings in that book are good examples of domestic customs that benefit from renewal.

▪ DAY OF PUBLIC CATHOLICISM: Workers in areas with a Catholic presence will see folks with "dirty faces" walking around the office or filling the streets at lunch hour. This is just about the only day when Catholics stand out, when conversations at the photocopier may naturally turn to religion, to Catholic traditions, to the meaning of Lent.

▪ DAY OF ASHES: The ashes used today come from the palm branches blessed the preceding year on Palm Sunday. The old gives way to the new. Some parishes make a ritual of burning palms during a carnival fire yesterday or last weekend. Including the burning of palms as a part of today's liturgy, however, is not our tradition. Fire is not the symbol today; dead ashes are.

The wearing of ashes is a pre-Christian religious gesture witnessed to in Judith 9:11, Daniel 9:3, Jonah 3:6. Jesus was familiar with the practice (Matthew 11:21) and the early church made it a sign of public penance. Ashes were sprinkled on penitents' heads. Around the year 1000, ashes came to be used by all the faithful. In 1091, Pope Urban II recommended the custom to all churches in communion with Rome.

The rubrics call for foreheads to be signed with ashes, and tradition suggests that this be done in the form of a cross. We thus renew our "branding" with the sign placed there at the beginning and so often since—at infant baptism, at acceptance into the catechumenate, at confirmation, at every gospel proclamation.

▪ DISTRIBUTION OF ASHES OUT- SIDE THE PARISH MASS: The rubric printed at the end of the day's texts in the sacramentary notes the possibility of ashes being distributed at a service outside Mass. A full order for the blessing and distribution of ashes is available in the *Book of Blessings* (chapter 52). This celebration can be in the church or with a gathering of the sick (such as at a nursing home). When this service is led by a member of the laity, the ashes are blessed earlier. When a liturgy is scheduled with children, review the resources in the *Leader's Manual of the Hymnal for Catholic Students* (p. 81).

▪ ENVIRONMENT FOR WORSHIP: The church should be prepared for Lent during the days since last Sunday. Sacristans should consider ways to treat the ashes with the dignity and austerity they deserve. For example, old funeral candles may be placed around a high pedestal, which may hold a large earthen bowl containing the ashes. A purple-covered table or

pedestal may be set in the center of the assembly or near the font; a place by the entrance may be suitable if all can turn and face there for the blessing and if all can come there for the signing. If this latter option is chosen, the ashes may remain there for the season, or at least until Sunday. (These suggestions favor pedestals instead of tables because the furniture should neither compete with nor imitate the altar table.) In any event, ashes should not be placed on the altar or ambo, nor should they be just one more prop kept on the credence table.

▪ INTRODUCTORY RITES: The gathering rite today is sober and simple —no penitential rite on Ash Wednesday, no Gloria throughout Lent—announcing that we are about serious business.

▪ BLESSING AND GIVING OF ASHES: No formal introduction is provided in the sacramentary for this rite, but presiders may use the brief words found in the *Book of Blessings* (#1663), followed by the invitation to prayer found in the sacramentary.

The music for the distribution of ashes should be chosen to accompany a procession of all those gathered, without requiring a hymnal or worship aid. Hymns generally are not good choices here. Two Lucien Deiss pieces (World Library, *People's Mass Book*) would accompany this action well: "My soul is longing for your peace" (Psalm 131) and "Grant to us, O Lord," based on Ezekiel and Jeremiah. The refrain of "Give us, Lord, a new heart" by Bernadette Farrell (OCP, #7104) is quite lovely and easily coupled with the verses of any psalm that speaks of trust and conversion (such as Psalms 25, 62 and 130) chanted to Tone 14 by Joseph Smith, found in the *Lead Me, Guide Me* hymnal.

The processional singing would best continue until after the ministers wash their hands. This necessary hand washing then would be "covered" by the last verses of that psalm. The action of singing, processing and receiving ashes will be followed by the first praying of the season's intercessions.

■ LITURGY OF THE EUCHARIST: In addition to the suggested preface for this day (Lent IV), consider Lent III, which speaks of self-denial as a form of expressing thanks and of the social dimension of Lent.

THU 5   #221   violet
Thursday after Ash Wednesday

These days before the First Sunday of Lent are a more recent addition to Lent. They are the prelude days, the days before we start counting to 40. They get us warmed up for the great penitential procession and the Rite of Election on Sunday. The prayer texts and scriptures of these days review many of the "themes" of Lent, setting out our Catholic agenda for the next month and a half. The lenten book by Irwin listed in the seasonal resources on page 85 provides extensive coverage of each day's texts.

FRI 6   #222   violet
Friday after Ash Wednesday

Day of abstinence. ▪ Every Friday is a day of penance, but the Fridays of Lent claim special status as days of abstinence. Penitential practices are mirrored in the liturgical texts of all Fridays, for example, the presence of Psalm 51 at Morning Prayer and at the eucharist.

Some Protestant churches observe today as "World Day of Prayer." Planners of any ecumenical service should see if this event can express some of the motifs and traditions of the lenten season. Even if certain ministers prefer to avoid the term "Lent," Catholic planners should see if the service can present a more penitential or baptismal tone than if it were held during January's Week of Prayer for Christian Unity.

SAT 7   #223   violet
Saturday after Ash Wednesday

Perpetua and Felicity, martyrs, optional memorial. ▪ Martyred at Carthage in 203, these women are mentioned in Eucharistic Prayer I. It would seem especially appropriate to include at least a commemoration of martyrs in the fabric of Lent—either these women or Stanislaus (April 11) or both. As noted on page 77, these brief invocations of a saint's memory are part of what is otherwise a fully lenten liturgy. Thus, violet vesture continues to be worn, not red.

✵ 8   #24   violet
First Sunday of Lent

According to traditional liturgical practice, this is the first day of Lent, the day we start counting to Holy Thursday, day 40. As such, it features a special penitential procession, the gospel about Jesus' 40-day fast in the desert and the Rite of Election.

■ PENITENTIAL PROCESSION: The *Circular Letter* on the Easter feasts (#23) suggests that the penitential procession envisioned in the *Ceremonial of Bishops* (#261) be held in all parishes this day. See page 101 for an outline. While it is a new practice for most areas of the United States, its tradition is ancient. Again, the architectural question arises—do you have an adequate gathering place outside the main worship space? Keep moving the question and its resolution to the tops of planners' lists.

■ THE MASS: The alternative opening prayer suits today's scriptures. ("Human beings" would be more inclusive than "man"; "them" and "they" would be more inclusive than "him" and "he.") The seasonal introduction (on page 78) includes ideas for the texts of this day and for every other lenten Sunday.

■ RITE OF SENDING OR RITE OF ELECTION: If your diocese celebrates a rite of election at the cathedral, you probably will use the rite of sending the catechumens for election. The texts for catechumens (adults and children) begin at #111 of the RCIA. The order for parishes with baptized candidates for reception into full communion but without catechumens begins at #438 of the RCIA. The rite to use if a parish is blessed with both appears at #536.

In any event, the catechumens and candidates should not go to the cathedral alone. Their sponsors and the catechumenal team will accompany them, of course. But this is one of those days (the Chrism Mass is another) when every pastor can encourage the parish membership to go to the cathedral—limited only by the size of that building and by any consequent restrictions appearing on the invitation.

M
O
N
9 #225 violet
Lenten Weekday

Frances of Rome, religious, optional memorial. ▪ Orders of women religious may include this medieval heroine in their lenten sanctoral list. Like Elizabeth Ann Seton, Frances was a wife and mother before founding a religious community.

Utilizing an approach quite different from that used for weekdays in other seasons, the framers of the current lectionary selected passages for the gospel and for the first reading because of their relationship with each other. That is seen on this first regular weekday of the 40 days with a call to social responsibility. Lent is not a private enterprise.

T
U
E
10 #226 violet
Lenten Weekday

W
E
D
11 #227 violet
Lenten Weekday

Both readings invite us into the story of Jonah. Unfortunately, this powerful story appears only this one day in all of Lent-Triduum-Easter. In the earliest centuries of our church, Jonah was central to lenten liturgies, to art for the paschal season and to the curriculum for the catechumenate. The entire story, from the first call of Jonah to his brooding under the gourd plant, can be seen in countless illuminated liturgical books and on many mosaic pavements. The most extensive of these, in Aquileia (northeast Italy), graces the floor of what modern scholars consider to be a fourth-century *catechumenon*. That place for the meeting of catechumens could hold well over a thousand people. Jonah can form a central part of our private reading and meditation as Lent evolves.

T
H
U
12 #228 violet
Lenten Weekday

The first reading at Mass is from Esther, the only time it is read publicly from our weekday and Sunday lectionary. This book chronicles the events celebrated on the Jewish holiday of Purim. You may make this book your spiritual reading before Purim, which falls next Thursday.

F
R
I
13 #229 violet
Lenten Weekday

Day of abstinence.

S
A
T
14 #230 violet
Lenten Weekday

☀ **15** #27 violet
Second Sunday of Lent

The transfiguration of the Lord is celebrated on August 6 in both Roman and Orthodox traditions. The Lutherans celebrate this feast on the Sunday preceding Lent, recognizing that this gospel event is an epiphany that turns our eyes toward Jerusalem, the cross and resurrection. That is the function of our hearing the transfiguration story today: It turns our gaze toward the mountain of Calvary. In this context, the transfiguration story calls to mind the shining robes and candles of baptism.

▪ MASS: The preface for the Second Sunday of Lent (not to be confused with the preface titled Lent II) echoes today's gospel. Rather than approaching the transfiguration as a general theme, homilists may review the commentaries on Luke's distinct approach to it. They also may be inspired by Leo the Great's homily in the Office of Readings. To appreciate the special way the transfiguration can be interpreted in Lent, one may look at the differences between the liturgical texts for this day and those for August 6.

▪ PENITENTIAL RITE FOR THE CANDIDATES: The RCIA (#459 ff.) includes a "penitential rite" (similar to the scrutinies) for Catholics who are baptized but uncatechized and for those joining the Catholic church from other Christian communions. This may be celebrated today.

M
O
N
16 #231 violet
Lenten Weekday

In this week's scriptures, reflections on compassion and penitential approaches to life alternate with predictions of Jesus' passion and death. Predictions about the cross draw us to recognize the inevitability of the cross for all disciples. The texts selected for liturgical prayer throughout this season carry us closer to the Jerusalem of Daniel and of Jesus.

▪ THE WEEK AHEAD: The solemnity of St. Joseph will impede Thursday's readings this year. Because each day's readings together form an independent unit and are not in any linear sequence from day to day, the "lost" passages need not be added to an adjoining weekday.

T
U
E
17 #232 violet
Lenten Weekday

Patrick, bishop, optional memorial. ▪ In many parts of the United States, parades and green clothing prevail. If St. Patrick is your parish's title, then it is your own solemnity and is celebrated in white vestments, with readings from the Common of Pastors (Missionaries). As an example of how such titular and patronal festivals can be related to the particular season, see lectionary #722.2 for a lenten reading this day.

Catholics can find much fruit in relating Bishop Patrick to Lent. His *Confessions* are fine lenten reading (a portion is in the Office of Readings for his memorial). The famous shamrock was a teaching device for the catechumens preparing to be baptized at Easter in the name of the Trinity. The legend of Patrick's chasing the snakes out of Ireland is an image of Christ, who in his death and resurrection routed the powers of hell. Green became the ritual color associated with penitents returning to the church at Easter, much as white is associated with the newly baptized. It is even claimed that Patrick kindled (and "christened") the Celtic May Day bonfire as part of the *lucernarium* ritual of the Easter Vigil.

WED 18 #233 violet
Lenten Weekday

Cyril of Jerusalem, bishop and doctor, optional memorial. ▪ Today's memorial can prod us to read Cyril's instructions, written for catechumens during the fourth century, a time that has been termed the "golden age" of the catechumenate's evolution.

THU 19 #543 white
Joseph, Husband of Mary
SOLEMNITY

The preface for the day sensitively ponders Joseph's life: "He is that just man, that wise and loyal servant, whom you placed at the head of your family. With a husband's love he cherished Mary, the virgin Mother of God. With fatherly care he watched over Jesus Christ your Son, conceived by the power of the Holy Spirit."

▪ LITURGY: The lenten set of acclamations can continue today, with no alleluia. A hymn or two about St. Joseph would be helpful, along with the singing of the Gloria and perhaps the creed. *Worship* offers a fine and useful hymn in "By all your saints still striving;" the hymn tune "Theodulph" is familiar as "All glory, laud and honor," the hymn of entrance for Passion Sunday, and alternate verses are offered for feasts of the saints throughout the year, including Joseph. G. W. Williams's thoughtful text, "Come now, and praise the humble saint," deserves consideration for this day. You will find it in *Worship,* coupled with the well-known and singable American melody, "Land of rest." Flowers are allowed in the church on this weekday (and on the Annunciation). If there is a statue of the saint in the church, this is the most obvious place for the flowers. Parishes named after Joseph, as well as religious communities under his patronage, may consider

holding a vigil service on the eve, using the texts and outline found in appendix I of the *Liturgy of the Hours.*

▪ ST. JOSEPH'S TABLES: Because St. Joseph's Day always falls during Lent, this splendid custom is meant to combine the three lenten disciplines in a single event: prayer, fasting and almsgiving. Prayers and songs—both for Joseph and for Lent—are customary. The table features meatless dishes. A collection is made for the poor, not to pay for the food. An "Order for the Blessing of St. Joseph's Table" is found in chapter 53 of the *Book of Blessings.* Its texts (including an optional litany of St. Joseph) weave together the themes of service to the poor and fidelity to the paschal mystery in a format usable in every parish. His litany also is found in *Catholic Household Blessings and Prayers* (p. 346), and a domestic prayer in his honor is found in the same volume on page 165.

▪ PURIM: This day is also Purim, a festival of liberation for our Jewish neighbors. It celebrates the events in the book of Esther.

FRI 20 #235 violet
Lenten Weekday

Day of abstinence.

SAT 21 #236 violet
Lenten Weekday

As news reports and weather forecasts note the equinox, pray for good plantings and for a vibrant celebration of the Pasch, the "church's spring."

#28 (Year A) or #30 (Year C)
violet

✹22 Third Sunday of Lent

■ INTRODUCTORY RITES: The alternative opening prayer for today is somewhat wordy ("brothers and sisters" would be more inclusive than "brothers"). Notice the other opening prayer: How often prayer, fasting and almsgiving are echoed in the lenten texts! Clearly, something more intense is being referred to than once-a-week Friday abstinence.

■ LITURGY OF THE WORD: The seasonal notes given on page 79 review the two options for scriptures. The use of Year A readings is recommended.

■ FIRST SCRUTINY: The paragraph numbers refer to the *Rite of Christian Initiation of Adults.*

- Invitation to prayer (#152): The elect and their godparents gather before the presider and the assembly. Rather than asking them all to stand in the front of the assembly, consider placing them in the center aisle so that the faces of the elect can be seen. After the presider voices an invitation with very specific suggestions for prayer, the silence is to continue "for some time." This is important and needs careful preparation. The presider, too, is to enter into the silence and the prayer.

- Intercessions for the elect (#153): Godparents place their hands on the shoulders of the elect, and the intercessions begin. Note that these are prayers *for* the elect and not the usual general intercessions.

Musical and other suggestions are found on page 80.

- Exorcism (#154): A strong and important part of the rite, this consists of two prayers. Between the prayers, the presider places his hands on each of the elect in unhurried silence. The rite suggests that the exorcism be concluded with an appropriate psalm or song. The community may select one of the psalms suggested here and sing it at each of the scrutinies. Note that one of the suggested psalms is Psalm 51, a likely choice for a seasonal psalm during the liturgy of the word and thus familiar enough to be sung with real strength here.

- Dismissal (#155): A peculiarly worded optional text is provided in case the elect are, for some reason, not dismissed—an unfortunate option.

- After the scrutiny rite (#156): The profession of faith and the general intercessions should not be omitted. The earlier prayers over the elect serve a different purpose.

M O N 23 #238 violet Lenten Weekday

Turibius of Mogrovejo, bishop, optional memorial. ▪ Turibius was a bishop of Lima, Peru. Inclusion of this memorial can help parishes of North America recall their solidarity with South America.

■ THE WEEK AHEAD: Note that the lectionary (#237) offers a set of readings to be used some day this week by those parishes where the Year A set was not read on Sunday. The centrality of the gospel of the Samaritan woman to Lent is highlighted. For the same reason cited under last Monday's entry, there is no need to move the readings missed because the Annunciation takes precedence over Wednesday of the Third Week.

T U E 24 #239 violet Lenten Weekday

W E D 25 #545 white Annunciation of the Lord
SOLEMNITY

■ HISTORY: Many theories appear in scholarly circles on why this event is celebrated on this date. Some historians point to today's gospel, noting that Elizabeth was six months pregnant and then rehearsing the earliest Christians' calculations that the annunciation to Zechariah was on Yom Kippur, September 25. As noted in the introduction to the Christmas season (page 26), this would place the conception of Jesus on this date and the nativity on December 25. Other historians read the data and see prior concerns about marking the spring equinox. Still others cite ancient beliefs that Jesus died on this date and thus it was fitting that he was conceived on the same date.

In the liturgical calendars and lectionaries of earlier centuries, Annunciation observances can be found near Christmas—for example, on December 26 or on the Sunday before Christmas. Remembrances of the Annunciation remain in the Advent liturgy on the Sunday and weekdays just before Christmas.

■ MARYLAND: In this year commemorating the first landing of Christopher Columbus, with all that it implies for the retelling of our earliest Christian history in the Americas, it should be noted that March 25 is a state holiday in Maryland. Residents there commemorate the first landing of European settlers on this date in 1634. The feast, the name of the state and the exact date selected for landing are not linked by mere coincidence. Both Protestant and Catholic Christians stepped off those ships into a unique experiment in ecumenical collaboration. Although not without experiencing a certain amount of turmoil, this colony was one of the brighter spots amid the interreligious warfare that otherwise prevailed among the newcomers.

Neither is it a fluke that the first or primatial See in the United States was Baltimore. Catholics in the United States who want to come to terms with their own history must study Maryland. This may be the day for churches in that state to hold the penitential service outlined on page xiii. This may serve as an example for other states that observe days commemorating their beginnings. Such memorials, by their very nature, are linked to the Columbus commemoration and to the Native Americans who lived here long before.

■ FEAST OF THE LORD: For centuries, the Annunciation was thought of as a Marian feast, but the calendar reforms of 1969 returned the feast to its origins as a feast of the Lord. A similar shift was made on February 2. The exact designation is of limited importance, really just a reminder to keep the liturgy Christocentric. As shown in the hymns and intercessions of the *Liturgy of the Hours,* Marian hymns and references find their place this day. These are within an overall lenten context, treating this as a celebration of the beginning of redemption.

■ LITURGY: This is one of the two days each year when all are invited to genuflect during the profession of faith. However this was carried out at Christmas should be repeated on this weekday (and then repeated on these days every year): kneeling for the whole line that ends with the incarnation phrase or, genuflecting only for the phrase itself, introducing the creed with appropriate instructions. This is one of the three days in Lent when flowers are allowed in the church. They may best be placed by the Marian shrine or by an icon depicting the mystery.

T H U **26** #241   violet
Lenten Weekday

F R I **27** #242   violet
Lenten Weekday

Day of abstinence.

S A T **28** #243   violet
Lenten Weekday

#31 (Year A) or #33 (Year C)
violet or rose
✳ **29** **Fourth Sunday of Lent**

The lenten Sunday pattern should be used again this week and next —for the prayer texts, the music, the flow of the scrutinies, etc. Year A readings are recommended and should be used at least in parishes where the scrutiny rites are celebrated.

This is Laetare Sunday, with rose vestments and just a hint of spring flowers both possible. Such decisions should be part of an overall plan for the season. The first of the opening prayers is lovely, befitting this mid-Lent Sunday with its powerful image: "Let us hasten toward Easter." In the alternative opening prayer, "humanity" or even "us" would be more inclusive than "mankind."

M O N **30** #245   violet
Lenten Weekday

Today begins the semicontinuous proclamation of the gospel of John on weekdays, lasting until the Wednesday of Holy Week.

■ THE WEEK AHEAD: The lectionary (#244) provides another set of readings to be used one day this week by those parishes that yesterday presented the readings for Year C. Again the priority of these Johannine stories about the woman at the well, the man born blind and Lazarus is made evident.

T U E **31** #246   violet
Lenten Weekday

April

W E D **1** #247   violet
Lenten Weekday

T H U **2** #248   violet
Lenten Weekday

Francis of Paola, hermit, optional memorial. ■ Commentators such as Pius Parsch have noted that today's saint had as his favorite expression, "Out of love." Local churches that commemorate him can sing the refrain of this lenten weekday's psalm with special fervor. We do what we do because of all that the Lord has done out of love for us.

FRI **3** #249 violet
Lenten Weekday

Day of abstinence. ▪ Participation in the passion of Christ is evoked in our Friday abstinence. The letter of Athanasius in today's Office of Readings is an excellent invitation to the paschal feast.

SAT **4** #250 violet
Lenten Weekday

Isidore, bishop and doctor, optional memorial. ▪ This is the Isidore from seventh-century Spain. On May 15, the dioceses of the United States remember another Isidore from Spain, a twelfth-century farmer named after this great bishop. Hispanic communities would do well to observe both memorials, recalling the splendid heritage of Spanish-language Catholicism.

The rubric at the bottom of today's entry in the sacramentary can stimulate discussion before Lent begins regarding the covering or removal of all images and crosses. This rubric serves as a reminder that we have reached that part of Lent when the texts will press us in our liturgical actions to be more conscious of the passion of Christ.

✹ **5** #34 (Year A) or #36 (Year C) violet
**Fifth Sunday
of Lent**

The patterns continue from previous weeks of Lent (Year A readings are recommended), letting us become familiar with the listening, the acclaiming, the scrutinizing, the exorcising — bringing us more and more into the paschal rhythm.

▪ PASSION: Notice that the entrance antiphon and both opening prayers pick up on the shift of emphasis in Lent — we hear more now about the passion. While maintaining the core of your lenten repertoire, consider this an appropriate day to add one or two passion-oriented hymns, such as "O sacred head" or "What wondrous love." Don't miss the opportunity to repeat these hymns next Sunday and at Masses during this week.

▪ ANNOUNCEMENTS this week, while including all paschal celebration essentials, must focus on palm procession details. Where will the assembly convene next week? What must be said about bigger crowds and coming early for a better seat? How will details be worked out so that latecomers to the blessing and procession do not get all the seats when Mass begins?

MON **6** #252 violet
Lenten Weekday

The lectionary offers particularly rich fare today. The first reading, from Daniel, is the dramatic story of the innocent Susanna and her wicked and lustful accusers. It is far more nuanced in detail and symbolism than any courtroom series on television. The long form is far superior to the short, for the listener needs the first part of the story to appreciate Daniel's wise resolution. Yes, it will add a few minutes to the Mass, but rarely do we hear as memorable a story. Two gospels are given, both complementing the story of Susanna: the first one for those communities where the "A" gospel was read yesterday, the second for congregations that heard the "C" gospel.

▪ THE WEEK AHEAD: The optional readings (lectionary #251) should be presented some day this week in parishes that have not elected to proclaim the Year A readings on these three late-Lent Sundays. They should not be substituted for the powerful readings today.

TUE **7** #253 violet
Lenten Weekday

John Baptist de la Salle, priest, optional memorial. ▪ This hero of religious educators and founder of the Christian Brothers died on Good Friday. Observed in communities linked to his community, this commemoration encourages petitions for the young and for the ongoing education of the church.

WED **8** #254 violet
Lenten Weekday

THU **9** #255 violet
Lenten Weekday

FRI **10** #256 violet
Lenten Weekday

Day of abstinence.

SAT **11** #257 violet
Lenten Weekday

Stanislaus, bishop and martyr, optional memorial. ▪ The last of our lenten saints comes from eleventh-century Poland and is the patron of that country. Besides the optional memorial of Perpetua and Felicity on March 7, this is the only other opportunity in Lent to associate our weekday prayer with the witness of the martyrs.

✡ 12 #37–38 red
Passion (Palm) Sunday

The title given in English liturgical books is "Passion (Palm) Sunday." Those parentheses are a prosaic way of titling a day that has a rich history and significance. The Latin title, *Dominica in palmis de Passione Domini,* "the Lord's Day in palms of the Passion of the Lord," is more poetic and more precise.

HOLY WEEK

We enter the most solemn week of the year—the final, intense days of Lent and the great days of the Triduum. This will be followed by Easter week, when the Triduum flows into an octave of exuberant joy. This week called "holy" or "great" by our ancestors summons us to put aside all other activities in our parishes for a wholehearted observance of the Pasch. No other solemnity—not even the dedication anniversary of a parish—can be celebrated during these two weeks. We enter this time—with regrets about its imperfect celebration filed away for future work—awestruck before the treasure passed on to us. Our wonder can inform and inspire us, letting us know when to give our work a little extra effort and when to let go and not push toward an impossible level of completeness.

The Lord's Passion is not celebrated today as an event long ago

and far away, but as a living reality touching us and all who ever have lived and who ever will. Keeping this in mind, we can see how songs like "The palms," "The holy city" and "The old rugged cross" narrow our experience of today's celebration by fostering a distant, sentimental attitude of "I wish I would have been there;" they have no place in liturgy.

This week we are playing with historical events in a very particular way:

> This procession is not a historical reenactment of Jesus' entry into Jerusalem. It is a liturgical action opening the annual celebration of the Christian Passover. By this procession we profess our faith. We proclaim that by going to his death, Jesus inaugurated his return to the Father in glory. We keep the whole paschal journey before our eyes as each step is celebrated. (*Saint Andrew Bible Missal,* p. 266)

■ REMEMBER THIS RULE: No mimicry! Palm Sunday planning does not involve renting a donkey. Holy Thursday's evening Mass of the Lord's Supper is not celebrated in the context of a seder meal, nor is the washing of the feet necessarily restricted to 12 men. Good Friday's solemn liturgy is not turned into or overshadowed by a passion play. We celebrate the Roman rite so that we can be plunged into the Pasch. When we watch a play, we stimulate our minds or tickle our affections. If we meditate on the Jerusalem of Jesus' time, we expand our imaginations. But we do ritual—the Roman rite—to become the very presence that we celebrate.

If we alter the church's handed-on way of carrying out the rite, we can all too quickly marginalize the members of the parish. Instead of searching for novelty, we should be seeking the most traditional forms possible so that even visitors can participate fully. This does

not mean that traditional forms are to be celebrated without creativity, nor does it mean that we resist reforms in the ritual: The reforms of Holy Week in the 1950s, confirmed and enhanced after Vatican II, opened the internal logic—the authentic tradition of the sacramental life—for us to be immersed in once again.

THE COMMEMORATION OF THE LORD'S ENTRANCE INTO JERUSALEM

■ THE PALMS: Do not stint on your palm order. Try to acquire palms that are not stripped into smithereens (or if you do the stripping yourself, tear the fronds into sizable pieces). Invite a group of parishioners for a palm-stripping gathering the day before Palm Sunday. The emotional attachment of Catholics to this sacramental is marvelous, and pastors should do all that they can to encourage physical contact with the symbols of our prayer.

Decorate with fully open palm fronds so people can make some connection between the torn leaf in their hand and the actual plant. It is the date palm, native to the Mideast, that holds such intense religious significance for many Muslims, Christians and Jews, not the more readily available palmetto frond native to the American Southeast. Many palm retailers offer date palm fronds for sale; they are expensive, but a few can be purchased to honor the processional cross.

■ THE PROCESSION for Passion Sunday includes a large number of people moving—with bells ringing, trumpets blaring, everyone singing, palms waving—from the place where the palms were blessed to the space where the eucharist will be celebrated. Everyone who is not incapacitated by age or illness participates. People who feel that a real procession may stir up trouble because of its difficulty would do well to attend Orthodox Christian worship at Easter. Everyone happily joins in several processions; no one complains.

Rubrics restrict the procession to the principal Mass, not to restrict the parishioners' experience of this rite but to call for one grand liturgy for all parish members to join into—just as during the Triduum. This tells us that musical forces must be unified as well, a great gathering of the entire parish that may require unique Mass scheduling this day.

■ RITUAL OUTLINE: Quotes given here without reference are taken from the sacramentary. Others are from the *Ceremonial of Bishops* (CB).

- *Gathering:* All assemble in a place "distinct from the church to which the procession will move." Once again, the central actions of the Roman rite call for spaces beyond the main worship space.

- *Branches are distributed:* Palm branches are already in the hands of the assembly before the presider and other ministers arrive.

- *Red vesture:* The deacon and presider wear red Mass vestments, although the presider can wear a red cope.

- *Song:* As the presider and assisting ministers arrive, or after all are gathered, everyone sings the antiphon (Matthew 21:9) "or any other appropriate song." The "Hosanna to the Son of David" text recommended for this time is found in the Passion Sunday section of *Worship* set to chant mode VII adapted by Richard Proulx. Taizé (GIA) offers several "Hosanna" and "Benedictus" antiphons that would serve well as gathering and processional music. Also consider "O Christe Domine Jesu" from the same source.

- *Sign of the cross:* The presider leads all in the sign of the cross (CB, #266).

- *Greeting:* The presider gives the liturgical greeting (the one used on the other lenten Sundays).

- *Introduction:* If not using the introduction that is in the sacramentary, parish coordinators should prepare one with equal merit. This introduction also can be given by the deacon or by a concelebrant (CB, #266).

- *Blessing:* The presider voices the prayer of blessing with hands joined, with the first form in the sacramentary the preferred one.

- *Sprinkling:* The presider silently sprinkles the branches with water —which means everyone gets wet because the branches are being held by the people. Encourage everyone to hold their branches high. This may help people appreciate that the water is being sprinkled on the palms. In a large congregation, this action should take some time, with the presider walking among the people.

- *Preparation for the gospel:* The presider and the other ministers who have not carried branches from the beginning now take them (from a table or pedestal set up for the blessing—not from a cardboard box). Incense then is placed in the censer, and the deacon who is to proclaim the gospel is blessed. During these preparatory actions, a "suitable song" is sung (CB, #268). This is one of the few examples of a pre-gospel hymn in our tradition.

- *Gospel:* The deacon or a concelebrant or the presider (in that order of preference) proclaims Luke's gospel of the entry into Jerusalem.

- *Homily:* "A brief homily may be given."

- *Invitation to the procession:* The deacon (or presider) invites the assembly to join in the procession, using words such as those in the sacramentary (perhaps preceded by practical instructions given as briefly as possible).

- *Procession participants:* All carry palms unless they already are bearing a liturgical object such as thurible, cross, candle. The procession follows this order:
  - thurifer, with plenty of smoke billowing out of the censer
  - crossbearer, "with the cross suitably decorated with palm branches" (CB, #270), flanked by two candle bearers
  - deacon carrying the book of the gospels
  - lectors
  - concelebrants
  - presider and assistants
  - choir
  - assembly

- *Processional route:* The procession can move in a straight line toward the church, and on arrival it can encircle the church building, a powerful sign of yearning to enter into Jerusalem. Be sure that the thurifer and the crossbearer walk slowly enough to keep the procession in a line.

The route may necessitate the collaboration of the police. No group should presume permission to walk on public property without checking to see if a permit is needed. Traffic cannot be disrupted without the cooperation of civic authorities. Certain routes may require the suspension of parking along the curb. Many cities forbid assemblies in public parks without permits. Still others require permission for the use of audio systems outdoors (even on private property). These permits are not difficult to obtain—just the investment of someone's time for the harmony of the neighborhood.

Walk through the processional route beforehand, looking for possible trouble spots as you go. Will the banners and the cross fit through any tight places? Will the head of the procession—with the cross and its decoration colorfully prominent—be clearly visible? Are there places where part of the procession can bog down, where people can trip easily or become confused and take shortcuts?

- *Processional music:* "All glory, laud and honor" is a once-a-year text that everyone will come to associate with Passion Sunday if it is used consistently. Set to the tune "St. Theodulph," it is solid and easily sung in procession with leadership by the choir and portable instruments (drums, flutes, bells). A rhythmic and energetic reconstruction of the traditional chant (using the same text) by Richard Proulx is found in *Worship* and in octavo form (GIA, G-2915).

  If you prefer to sing different music for the outdoor procession and begin the hymn as the procession enters the church building, consider one of the alternatives mentioned in the "song" section of the ritual outline on page 94, or use the "Hosanna" antiphon from Howard Hughes's "Mass of the Divine Word" (GIA, G-2415 or *Worship*) with choir or cantor interjecting the "Blessed is he . . ." The tonality of the Hughes music is compatible with the rhythmic chant setting, but the "Hosanna" will have to be transposed to begin on B-flat if the "St. Theodulph" tune will follow.

- *Entrance into the church:* As the procession enters the church, the music continues. Additional responsory texts with the imagery of entrance are suggested in the sacramentary. The presider venerates the altar with a kiss and with incense, then changes from cope to chasuble if necessary.

- *Invitation to prayer:* After the ushers have helped all find places, the presider, standing at the chair, invites everyone to pray. (The formulas given for this invitation are quite good.) An extra measure of silence—to help participants quiet their hearts after the rousing procession—should follow.

- *Opening prayer:* The alternative opening prayer is difficult to comprehend; what does "estrangement might be dissolved" mean?

■ AT THE OTHER MASSES: Focusing the community's attention and the planners' energies on the principal celebration will mean, almost inevitably, a scaling down of the Commemoration of the Lord's Entrance into Jerusalem at the other liturgies on this day.

The "Solemn Entrance"—with the following adaptations—is a practical alternative for other Masses: The assembly is handed palms as they enter church, perhaps with the singing of one of the Taizé ostinatos beginning at least ten minutes before Mass is scheduled to start. At that time, the presider and other ministers "go to a suitable place in the church outside the sanctuary so that most of the people will be able to see the rite." The choir loft in an old building or a raised dais near the doors is a good place. In the same manner as in the principal Mass with the procession, the palm branches are blessed and the gospel of the triumphal entry is proclaimed, and then the ministers process through the assembly toward the altar while everyone sings a rousing hymn.

LITURGY OF THE WORD

■ READINGS: The "pastoral reasons" clause about omitting the first two readings should be invoked only with the utmost restraint. Those who come to the principal liturgy with its blessing of palms know that they are joining a substantial liturgy.

■ PSALM: The Howard Hughes setting of Psalm 22 in *Psalms for All Seasons* (NPM) is particularly powerful both in its music and in the imagery of the ICEL translation. A more haunting treatment of melody and harmony is found in the Christopher Willcock collection *Psalms for Feasts and Seasons* (Cooperative Ministries). "Psalm for Holy Week" by

Rawn Harbor in *Lead Me, Guide Me* (GIA) is also a worthy setting of the Psalm 22 antiphon; verses are set to a tone from Stanbrook Abbey, which is compatible in both tonality and mood.

■ THE PASSION ACCORDING TO LUKE is narrated without candles, incense, preliminary greeting or signing of the book. Note that this gospel may be read in parts, but need not be. The practice of the assembly reading "crowd" parts rarely works; it forces the community to keep their heads in their books. The scriptures are to be listened to, never read along with the lector.

As we learn from the Bach Passions, a hymn interpolated throughout the reading engages the assembly in active reflection on the Passion text. Either "O sacred head surrounded" or "My song is love unknown" would serve well. Choose carefully the places where the gospel will be interrupted and mark the text clearly.

After the verse about the death of the Lord, all kneel for a time of complete silence (*Ceremonial of Bishops*, #273).

■ HOMILY: Make the homily a strong bridge (but not necessarily a long one) between the procession and the scriptures and the work of these next days. It should serve as an invitation to keep Lent up to its last minutes on Holy Thursday and then to enter wholeheartedly into the observance of the Triduum. It is a call to give the time from Thursday night until Sunday over to fasting and vigiling and praying—three days like no other in the year.

Models for this style of preaching can be found in the patristic selections of the Office of Readings in the *Liturgy of the Hours*, especially the homily by St. Gregory Nazianzen in yesterday's office. Other patristic summonses

echo through the ages: Andrew of Crete in today's Office, the last paragraph of Melito of Sardis on Easter Monday and the second half of the letter by Athanasius on the Fifth Sunday of Lent.

Let the homily also perform the task of addressing the potential for the perpetuation of anti-Semitism in the passion account. If we truncate Luke's narrative to remove what may be interpreted as anti-Semitic statements, we risk losing the particular theological sense Luke brings. See the fine document on this question by the Bishops' Committee on the Liturgy, *God's Mercy Endures Forever,* #21–25.

■ DISMISSAL OF THE CATECHUMENS AND THE ELECT: One of the lenten dismissals continues to be used. Their reflections this week should be rich indeed!

■ PROFESSION OF FAITH AND GENERAL INTERCESSIONS follow in their regular lenten pattern. Ideas on expressing the image-world of Passion Sunday in intercessions can be found in Morning Prayer and Evening Prayer for this day. Those from the morning are particularly evocative.

LITURGY OF THE EUCHARIST

The lenten format for texts and music established weeks ago for the eucharistic prayer (with or without variable prefaces, such as today's brief one), for the communion rite and for the concluding rite continues today.

AT HOME

Catholic Household Blessings and Prayers (p. 140) contains a short rite for the "Placing of Branches in the Home." Introduce the parish to its many other blessings

and services of prayer for the coming Triduum and make this important book available for purchase. The steady, year-round work of fostering domestic prayer, folk customs and attention to the liturgy will bear fruit this week as no other.

M O N 13 #258 violet
Monday of Holy Week

Appendix I of the sacramentary provides a sample set of intercessions for these days (#7), but the general lenten ones also can be used. The preface titled, "Passion of the Lord II" (P18), is powerful enough and so specific to these days that it should be used these three days, even if another preface has been used consistently.

T U E 14 #259 violet
Tuesday of Holy Week

W E D 15 #260 violet
Wednesday of Holy Week

This day already was known as the "day of the betrayal" in 250 AD. Its denotation as "Spy Wednesday" has been forgotten in our own era, but today's gospel continues the tradition. The story of Judas figures prominently in the gospels proclaimed the last two days as well.

T H U 16 **Holy Thursday**

■ THE CHRISM MASS should draw representatives from every area of the diocese. The renewal of

priestly commitment in that liturgy is secondary to the blessing of oils and the consecration of the chrism—a celebration of the entire church gathered with the bishop. Many dioceses move the Mass to an earlier day during Lent. Whenever it is celebrated, consider using a van or bus to bring parish members to the cathedral. Their experience of the imagery of the olive oil, of ministries and of the gathered local church will add greatly to the richness of the Pasch. See page 112 regarding the rites for receiving the oils in the parishes.

■ MORNING AND AFTERNOON: Even though the Triduum does not begin until this evening, eucharistic celebrations, even for funerals, are not permitted. The reason is simple: The entire parish—even mourners, those who commute to work, schoolchildren, senior citizens and college students—is expected to gather tonight to begin the Christian Passover. This expectation, written into our rubrics, suggests that we take great pains to invite all the groups and communities and ages of the parish to attend all the liturgies of the Triduum.

■ SCHOOL ASSEMBLIES: Because Catholic schools often are in session this day, various practices have developed for their gathering this morning. The observance cannot be a Mass, but it can be a prayer service that is an extended prelude or "call to worship" for the Triduum. Students should be expected to attend the Triduum liturgies; encouraging attendance is a profound favor to young people because these liturgies will help form the students in the Catholic way of life. See the outline of ideas for this morning in the *Leader's Manual of the Hymnal for Catholic Students* (p. 90).

TEXTS FOR THE EUCHARISTIC ASSEMBLY

INTRODUCTORY RITES

Greeting

The grace and love of Jesus Christ, who calls us to conversion, be with you all.

Invitation to the Penitential Rite

WEEKS 1 TO 4:
As we begin this eucharist, let us heed the lenten call to conversion of heart and, by acknowledging our sins, seek reconciliation and communion with God and our neighbor.

WEEK 5 AND WEEKDAYS OF HOLY WEEK:
Acknowledging that we are all sinners cleansed by the blood of Christ, let us pardon one another from the depths of our hearts and ask pardon from God who is merciful and just.

Penitential Rite

The Confiteor (I confess) followed by a sung Kyrie is appropriate during the first four weeks of Lent.
Or:

FOCUSING ON INITIATION:
By water and the Holy Spirit, you have given us a new birth in your image: Lord, have mercy.

You have sent your Spirit to create a new heart within us: Christ, have mercy.

You called us to your supper to partake of your body and blood: Lord, have mercy.

FOCUSING ON RECONCILIATION:
You command us to forgive each other before we come to your altar: Lord, have mercy.

You asked your Father to forgive sinners as you hung upon the cross: Christ, have mercy.

You have entrusted your church with the ministry of reconciliation: Lord, have mercy.

LITURGY OF THE WORD

Dismissal of the Catechumens and the Elect

The Rite of Christian Initiation of Adults *provides proper texts of dismissal for the Rite of Sending, the Rite of Election, and the Scrutinies.*

AT OTHER EUCHARISTS:
My dear friends: with the assurance of our loving support this community sends you forth to reflect more deeply upon the word of God we have shared. May Christ who is the power and wisdom of God challenge you to be one with us in the disciplines of prayer, fasting and almsgiving, that you may be one with us at last in the paschal feast of the Lord's table.

General Intercessions

Invitation to prayer

In this, the acceptable time, the Lenten spring, the Lord invites us to be renewed in mind, purified in spirit, and more responsive to the needs of others. Let us ask God to accompany us on our journey to conversion, and to draw all the human family to the waters of life and the paschal feast.

For the church

For the church throughout the world,
that we turn from sin,
    and trust in the cross of Christ,
let us pray to the Lord.

For the church, all who have been baptized
    into Christ,
that we may hunger and thirst
    for what is right and just,
let us pray to the Lord.

For the world

For peace in the world,
that the arms race may end
and those in need may be lifted up,
let us pray to the Lord.

For the people of South Africa and all who
    are oppressed, that justice may come
    from their patience and suffering,
let us pray to the Lord.

For various needs

For the homeless people of this state,
that generous hearts and open hands
    may ease their burdens,
let us pray to the Lord.

For those who love us and those who hate us,
for those we have forgiven and those
    whom we cannot,
let us pray to the Lord.

For the local community

For the parish community,
that we be freed from all that binds our
    hearts and lives,
let us pray to the Lord.

For those among us with mental
    and physical burdens,
that their spirits may be strengthened,
let us pray to the Lord.

For all who remain faithful with Christ,
that they be renewed by the living word
    and the power of the Spirit,
let us pray to the Lord.

For the catechumens and the elect

For those called to the sacraments of new life,
that they be made worthy of praising God
    with the church,
let us pray to the Lord.

For the elect, called by name
    to the waters of life,
and for the Candidates, led by God
    into the fellowship of the church,
let us pray to the Lord.

For the dead

For those who have died in the hope
    of rising with Christ,
and for every just soul made perfect in faith,
let us pray to the Lord.

Concluding Prayers for the General Intercessions

FIRST SUNDAY OF LENT:
Lord our God,
you alone do we worship,
only your word gives life.

Sustain your Church on its lenten journey.
When we walk through the desert
    of temptation,
strengthen us to renounce the power of evil.
When our faith is tested by doubt,
illumine our hearts with Easter's
    bright promise.
We ask this through your Son, our Lord
    Jesus Christ,
who lives and reigns [with you in the unity
of the Holy Spirit, one God] forever and ever.
— *© ICEL*

SECOND SUNDAY OF LENT:
O God, glorious and faithful,
to those who seek you with a sincere heart
you reveal the beauty of your face.
Strengthen us to embrace in faith
the mystery of the cross,
and open our hearts to its
    transfiguring power;
that, clinging in love to your will for us,
we may walk the path of discipleship
as followers of your Son, Jesus Christ,
    our Lord
[who lives and reigns with you and
the Holy Spirit, one God,] for ever and ever.
— *Italian sacramentary*

THIRD SUNDAY OF LENT WHEN THE
READINGS OF YEAR A ARE PROCLAIMED:
O God, the fountain of life,
to a humanity parched with thirst
you offer the living water of grace
which springs up from the rock, our Savior
    Jesus Christ.

Grant your people the gift of the Spirit,
that we may learn to profess our faith
    with courage
and announce with joy the wonder
    of your love.

We ask this through our Lord Jesus Christ,
    your son
who lives and reigns [with you in the unity
of the Holy Spirit, one God,] for ever and ever.
— *Italian sacramentary*

THIRD SUNDAY OF LENT WHEN THE
READINGS OF YEAR C ARE PROCLAIMED:
Holy and merciful God,
your never leave your children forsaken
but constantly reveal to us your Name
and unfold for us the mystery and purpose
    of your will.

Break through the hardness
    of our minds and hearts;
that, with the simplicity and trust
    of children,
we may learn to embrace
    your commandments
as the way to fullness of life and love
and so come to bear the fruit of true
    and continuous conversion.
We ask this through your Son, our Lord
    Jesus Christ,
who lives and reigns [with you in the unity
of the Holy Spirit, one God] forever and ever.
—*Italian sacramentary*

FOURTH SUNDAY OF LENT WHEN THE
READINGS OF YEAR A ARE PROCLAIMED:
O God, the Father of light,
you look into the depths of our hearts.

Never permit us to be dominated by the
    powers of darkness
but open our eyes by the grace
    of your Spirit,
that we may be able to see him whom you
    have sent to illumine the world,
and may believe in him alone,
Jesus Christ, your Son and our Lord,
who lives and reigns [with you in the unity
of the Holy Spirit, one God,] for ever and ever.
—*Italian sacramentary*

FOURTH SUNDAY OF LENT WHEN THE
READINGS OF YEAR C ARE PROCLAIMED:
Compassionate God,
you reveal yourself to us
    as a forgiving Father,
slow to anger, rich in mercy,
welcoming with a loving embrace
sinners who return to you
    with repentant hearts.

To all of your sons and daughters
coming home to your mercy
    in this holy season,
extend that loving welcome,
and bestow the shining robe of salvation,
that they may feast with delight
and the paschal banquet of the Lamb,
your Son, Jesus Christ our Lord
who lives and reigns [with you and the
Holy Spirit, one God,] for ever and ever.
—*Italian sacramentary*

FIFTH SUNDAY OF LENT WHEN THE
READINGS OF YEAR A ARE PROCLAIMED:
Eternal Father,
whose glory is the human person fully alive,
we see your compassion revealed
    in the tears of Jesus
for Lazarus his friend.

Look today upon the distress
    of your church,
mourning and praying for her children
    dead in their sins.

By the power of your Spirit
    call them back to life.

We ask this through our Lord Jesus Christ,
    your Son
who lives and reigns [with you and the Holy
Spirit, one God,] for ever and ever.
—*Italian sacramentary*

FIFTH SUNDAY OF LENT WHEN THE
READINGS OF YEAR C ARE PROCLAIMED:
Loving God, bountiful in compassion,
in Christ you are making the whole
    creation new!
Before you we stand in the misery
    of our sinfulness,
awaiting the word by which we can
    be born again.
You have spoken that Word in Jesus,
the Son you sent not to condemn the world
    but to save it.
Forgive our every failing,
and in this lenten springtime of grace
let our hearts blossom anew
in a canticle of gratitude and joy.

We ask this through your Son, our Lord
 Jesus Christ,
who lives and reigns [with you in the unity
of the Holy Spirit, one God] forever and ever.
—*Italian sacramentary*

LITURGY OF THE EUCHARIST

Introduction to the Lord's Prayer

Let us come before the compassionate God
with hearts full of forgiveness toward others,
so that we may offer our prayer in the words
Jesus taught his disciples to pray:

Prayer for Peace

Lord Jesus Christ, through the paschal mystery of your death and resurrection you sea-
led the covenant of peace between heaven and
earth:
 Look not on our sins . . .

Invitation to Communion

This is the Lamb of God, who takes away the
sins of the world: our Passover sacrificed for
us, our peace and reconciliation. Happy are
those who are called to his supper.

CONCLUDING RITE

Dismissal of Eucharistic Ministers

Go forth in peace to the sick and homebound
members of our community, bearing the word
of life and the Body of Christ, together with
the assurance of our love and concern. May
these gifts strengthen our absent brothers
and sisters in their communion with us
through the pilgrimage of Lent to the paschal
feast of the kingdom.

Dismissal

As a people called to conversion on a journey
to new life, go in peace to love and serve the
Lord.

TEXTS FOR MASS WITH CHILDREN

Opening Prayer

God our Father,
help us to know Christ better,
and, because we are his baptized disciples,
let us be his witnesses every day
 of our lives.
We ask this through Christ our Lord.

Prayer over the Gifts

God our Creator,
let this bread and wine,
gifts of your love,
be for us the food and drink of salvation.
We ask this through Christ our Lord.

Prayer after Communion

O good God,
may the bread of heaven,
 which you have given us,
increase in us the desire to know you better,
and faithful to our baptismal promises,
to grow in faith, hope and love.
We ask this through Christ our Lord.

TEXTS FOR THE ANOINTING OF THE SICK WITHIN MASS

Introduction/Reception of the Sick

Though he was in the form of God, Christ emptied himself, becoming one of us, indeed the servant of all. It was our infirmities he bore, our sufferings he endured, becoming obedient for us even unto death, death on a cross. As we gather in this holy season of Lent to celebrate the sacraments of anointing and eucharist, let us recall that by baptism into Christ's death, we have become heirs with him to the glory of resurrection. Through this celebration may ours be a share in his redemptive suffering and risen glory.

Prayer after Anointing

God of the covenant,
in this, the acceptable time of your favor,
on this, the day of salvation,
you offer in Christ the healing power
    of your love
through the laying on of hands
and anointing with holy oil.
Immersed in Christ's life through baptism,
and now joined more closely to his passion,
may our brothers and sisters come
    to share fully
in the triumphant power of his resurrection,
who lives and reigns for ever and ever.

A PENITENTIAL PROCESSION FOR THE FIRST SUNDAY OF LENT

The *Circular Letter Concerning the Preparation and Celebration of the Easter Feasts* (January 1988) suggests that an appropriate way to mark the First Sunday of Lent with penitential solemnity would be to begin the liturgy with a procession during which the litany of the saints is chanted. Reference is made to #261 of the *Ceremonial of Bishops,* which describes how the procession is held.

- The community assembles in a place apart from the place where Mass will be celebrated.

- While a gathering song is sung, the presider and ministers go to that place.

- The presider (who may be vested in a cope) greets the assembly with the sign of the cross and then the seasonal liturgical greeting.

- The presider or a deacon or other minister offers a brief introduction, for example:

    We have come to the beginning of our lenten spring, the season to prepare the holy Passover that will bring our catechumens to the saving waters of rebirth, the Passover that will be, for those of us already initiated, a pilgrimage of conversion.

    Lent is a journey with the Lord who longs to draw us more closely to himself that he might speak to our hearts. Along the way we will be challenged to recognize Christ in the scriptures we read, in those we love and serve, and in those whom we so often neglect to love and

serve—for surely Christ is most specially present in them.

Therefore, let us begin the journey!

Our procession is in the spirit of the pilgrimage of the Israelites, our forebears in faith. We call upon the saints, our holy ancestors, who remind us that we do not journey alone.

Let us move forward in joy, keeping our eyes fixed on the goal of our lenten journey, which is Jerusalem, the holy city of God.

- The presider offers a collect: either that of the Holy Cross, September 14; or "For Forgiveness of Sins" in the back of the sacramentary (#40); or for the local church (under Masses and Prayers for Various Needs and Occasions); or from the prayers over the people in the sacramentary (especially #6).

- Incense is placed in the thurible, and the deacon announces: "Let us go forth in peace."

- The litany of the saints is sung as the procession moves to the church. Saints from the local parish's heritage should be added in their proper places, along with patrons of the diocese, place or parish.

- When the ministers reach the altar, the presider reverences it, kisses it and may incense it. The presider then goes to the chair (changing from cope to chasuble), and when the litany ends, chants the opening prayer of the Mass, omitting the penitential rite.

TRIDUUM

These are the most important days of the year in the life of our parish.
We meet each day to remember the events in Jerusalem—Jesus' resolute commitment
and the good news given to the first evangelists, the three women at the tomb,
"Why do you search for the living One among the dead?"
We meet at all hours to renew our own identity. We are the deer longing for running
streams, the exiles being brought back, the redeemed city,
the people risen with the living One.
We meet for the time that pulls us toward the Eighth Day, the day the Lord has made, the
New Jerusalem.

Images of the Season

THE Paschal Triduum is the three-day season, the days counted sunset to sunset, from Holy Thursday evening through Easter Sunday evening. During these days, we keep one festival, our Passover, our Easter. We come together with all the people of our parish—and in spirit with all Christians in every time and place. It is the Passover of the Lord!

Jerusalem is a key image or root metaphor associated with the Triduum, with forming and being formed by this great experience. The events that unfolded there and the geography of that city have shaped our faith and given rise to rituals that shape our spiritual perspectives.

On these three days that are to be experienced as one, we commemorate the Passover of Jesus in Jerusalem in a sacramental way, rendering that primal event present in our midst—an event that shapes us as the body of Christ. At the same time, in the same action, we stretch ourselves and we are pulled toward the New Jerusalem where all will be one. Notice, once again, here is the *hodie,* the church's "today" that is past, present and future rolled into one grand *now.*

■ HISTORY OF THE TRIDUUM: In his fine book *Jerusalem Revisited: The Liturgical Meaning of Holy Week* (Pastoral Press, 1988), Kenneth Stevenson notes:

It is the liturgy of Jerusalem that we are celebrating this week, partly the Jerusalem of the New Testament, partly the Jerusalem of the fourth-century pilgrims, and partly the spiritual Jerusalem of the mixed traditions of Christianity that made up the service books and the piety of the faithful in the Western churches. (p. 3)

In thus seeing three stages of historical development in the Pasch, Stevenson summarizes the current consensus of liturgical scholars:

Stage one: In the very earliest generations of Christians, the paschal event began to be commemorated in one intense night of vigil and initiation, a "Super Sunday."

Stage two: In Jerusalem, rites commemorating the historic moments of the paschal event developed around the actual sites at which they occurred. Various days and hours, generally based on the gospel accounts of the Passion and resurrection, were set aside for each site's specific rites. Then during the fourth century, the rites and their assignment to specific days spread throughout the West (thanks in large measure to pilgrims bringing home reports from Jerusalem), giving us Holy Week more or less as we know it today.

Stage three: The devolution of the rites and their transfer to odd times (most notably the celebration of the Easter Vigil moved to Saturday morning) went hand in hand with a proliferation of devotional practices that developed to compensate for this loss of liturgy. In an attempt to make the liturgy more dramatic and "meaningful," popular practices were added to the feast days set out in stage two: Tombs were built in churches; the faithful kept watch for hours before gardens of Gethsemane and the enthroned host (not falling asleep like the three apostles); donkeys or consecrated hosts (or both) led palm processions; fasting and watching became more important than the liturgy; stations of the cross drew bigger crowds than the Vigil; and the apostles came to be represented by feet washing of 12 males.

These devotions often lost touch with the gospel message and even lost touch with the gospel narrative—as in an overly romantic notion of what the Last Supper was. The *hodie* of Christian celebration became the "long ago and far away" of passion plays, of mimicry, of music and drama that catered to people's desire for an emotional rush.

■ HISTORY SHAPES OUR PRESENT EXPERIENCE: These three stages are represented in every parish today by three approaches to Holy Week (see Stevenson, pp. 9–12). Some members know and experience the paschal mystery through the ritual actions with light, word, water, chrism, bread and wine. They need a community with whom to celebrate, with whom to share a repertoire of symbolic actions, with whom to be church.

Others attend more to the historical allusions. They like to walk in procession carrying palm branches, but without a donkey. They venerate a cross, but see no need for a passion play. They, too, need a vibrant community with whom to celebrate.

Finally, many prefer drama. They are not so much interested in liturgical symbols and heritage as in a theatrical "high," a jolt of emotion as Christ comes to "me." They may or may not need a crowd for these experiences, but they usually are not aware of the communal nature of ecclesial life and ritual.

This generalization is not meant to imply that liturgy must be unemotional and unrelated to the shaping of human affections. Passion plays are not unliturgical because they evoke emotional responses but because they focus only on the past and because the emotions they tend to produce are too intense and individualized. The third group's desires are antithetical to liturgy. This is fundamental. Liturgy is a symbolic way for a church to act out its identity. It is not a drama to be watched. The incursion of drama into the liturgy threatens to burn the sacrament with its heat.

■ PLANNING THE TRIDUUM IN LIGHT OF THIS HISTORY: To these three stages in the development of the paschal liturgy we can add a new stage, happening in our own day, in the reform of the liturgy. This reform seeks a balance between the first two stages and some corrective to the emotional excesses of the recent past (third stage). But how does one balance the tendency to historicize the events of Jesus' death, burial and resurrection with the need to enter as a church into this paschal mystery? Leo the Great offered this ecclesial perspective rich with the "today" of the liturgy and of all sacramental action:

> The body that lies lifeless in the tomb is ours. The body that rose again on the third day is ours. The body that ascended above all the heights of heaven to the right hand of the Father's glory is ours. If then we walk in the way of his commandments, . . . we too are to rise to share his glory. (Office of Readings, Thursday of the Fourth Week of Lent)

The Triduum is about Jesus of Nazareth and about those who have "put on Christ." A recognition of this identification with Christ is overwhelming; it is so overpowering that it must be disciplined and channeled in community, in ritual and in symbol. Abbot Anthony Bloom has said that we have to pass beyond surface emotions and their momentary expressions to reach genuine Christian feeling. Ritual prayer, using established communal forms of approaching the *mysterium tremendum,* lets one be vulnerable and open to the mystery, not merely enthusiastic for it.

During the fourth century, Gregory of Nyssa visited Jerusalem and wrote of his disillusionment (see Carroll and Halton, pp. 220–21). What advantage is there in going to the holy sites themselves? None, he says, for the Lord seems more present back in Nyssa than in the sinful city of Jerusalem. The Easter mysteries are not captured by reconstructing Jerusalem. They take shape when a local church, in Nyssa or New York or Natchez or Nome, gathers in purity of love and spirit—far in time and scenery from Palestine of 30 AD, but really quite near, because Easter is here and now.

Preparing the Parish

EVERY group affiliated with the parish should be visited during the previous months with a warm invitation to Triduum participation. The list of expectations often given to the confirmation class and prospective "Ad Altare Dei" medal recipients should include this. Pastoral staff members, parish pastoral council members, the Knights of Columbus who use the parish hall for meetings, and the Legion of Mary all should place the Vigil and other Triduum events at the top of their annual calendars. This is not coercion. It is an honest statement about what constitutes the church and every community that is a part of the church.

Exhortations alone, of course, are not enough. The task of summoning the assembly includes other components. The scheduling of services should take into account local conditions. The specifications regarding the times of the liturgy during the Triduum are numerous — the liturgy of the hours at the proper times, Holy Thursday evening Mass, Good Friday celebration between noon and 9:00 PM (although customarily at 3:00 PM), the Easter Vigil sometime from Saturday nightfall through Sunday dawn — but within these parameters great creativity can be exercised. Plan a parish supper so that workers can come directly to church on Holy Thursday. Schedule the Easter Vigil at an hour early enough to ensure that households will come in great numbers, but late enough so that it really is night. Celebrate Paschal Vespers on Easter Sunday at a time when most people will not be sitting down to dinner.

■ THE PASCHAL FAST: Most Catholics know that Good Friday is a day of fast and abstinence, but few recognize what makes this distinct from other such days: This is a fast of anticipation. And it is to be extended, as far as possible, into Holy Saturday and up to the Vigil. It is "a way of coming to the joys of the Sunday of the resurrection with uplifted and welcoming heart" (Vatican Council II, *Constitution on the Sacred Liturgy,* #110). This tradition must be part of every parish's catechesis for all ages. It bespeaks the approach we take to these days, putting our homes and schedules and stomachs at the service of the great events that we celebrate.

While a complete fast is ideal, it is not possible for many people. Parish suppers in the spirit of the paschal fast are popular ways to encourage some type of fasting during the Triduum. "Fasting meals" may be scheduled on Holy Thursday evening and served buffet-style so people can take turns in eucharistic adoration; on Good Friday between the celebration of the passion and Night Prayer; and early on Holy Saturday evening, perhaps connected to Evening Prayer.

■ DOMESTIC PRAYER: *Catholic Household Blessings and Prayers* contains ten pages of advice and prayer texts for observing the Triduum in Catholic homes (pp. 143–52). These materials include meditations on the various days, an antiphon to echo through the days, suggestions for private prayer before the blessed sacrament on Holy Thursday night, texts of the baptismal renewal and a blessing of Easter foods.

■ HOMEBOUND PARISHIONERS can receive a blessed palm branch from their regular eucharistic minister or another parishioner early in Holy Week. The prayer for placing branches in the home from *Catholic Household Blessings and Prayers* is appropriate for such visits. With these visits, too, may come discussions of the parish's desire to pray for them at Easter. Communion visits after Holy Thursday's evening Mass and after the Vigil can be arranged. If these times are too late in the evening, then visits on Easter morning may be scheduled. Perhaps another parishioner or two could join in such visits to make the prayer more joyous. (Be sure to check this out with the homebound persons and those who care for them.)

Of equal importance is the presentation of their role in the Triduum — praying for the community, inspiring members with their patient endurance, sewing parish linens, helping with "telephone trees" in Triduum publicity. Invite them to light a candle at home Easter Eve and read the scriptures of the Vigil, or watch and pray with televised presentations of Triduum liturgies, or perhaps with a videotape of last year's parish liturgies.

Other Ritual Prayer and Sacraments

THE Triduum contains three main liturgies —Evening Mass of the Lord's Supper, Celebration of the Lord's Passion, and the Easter Vigil—and Masses on Easter morning still are many people's main celebration. But what should be on the schedule next? Planners and presiders possess finite energy. Parishioners will come to only so many events. What is most important after the big liturgies? The current liturgical books indicate that the next liturgies developed in a local parish should be the preparation rites for the elect on Holy Saturday and Evening Prayer on Easter Sunday afternoon, sometimes called Paschal or Baptismal Vespers.

■ LITURGY OF THE HOURS: Next, the other major hours—the combined Office of Readings and Morning Prayer on Good Friday and Holy Saturday (Tenebrae), and Easter Morning Prayer —so filled with paschal images, should be added to the parish schedule over a period of years. The other Hours and practices remain for later development: organized eucharistic adoration on Holy Thursday, Night Prayer on Thursday and Friday, Midday Prayer on each day and Evening Prayer on Saturday.

Other devotions and practices are on a lower level in our current economy of rites. Stations of the cross and other admirable devotions may find a proper place in the Triduum, but they should never compete with the full liturgy of the church on these holiest days. The liturgy of the hours is not reserved for monks. All Catholics should be able to drink from the riches of these days and hours.

EUCHARIST AND COMMUNION

Masses without a congregation are prohibited on Holy Thursday. Masses other than the Evening Mass of the Lord's Supper are greatly restricted. See the sacramentary's notes for this day and consult diocesan norms. On Holy Thursday and Good Friday, communion cannot be distributed outside the liturgy except to the sick. On Holy Saturday, communion can be given only as viaticum. Masses are not celebrated on either Good Friday or Holy Saturday.

FUNERALS

When someone dies during Holy Week, it may not be possible to delay the funeral until Easter Monday. If a funeral liturgy outside of Mass is scheduled for Holy Thursday morning or during the Triduum, the parish's care for the mourners can be expressed in these ways:

- #179 of the rite allows for the funeral rites to take place at sites other than the church.

- During the Triduum, the rite that begins at #183 in the *Order of Christian Funerals* must be used, and readings consonant with the day should be selected, using a few of the readings from the day's liturgies. The mourners know that it is Good Friday or Holy Saturday. These texts of the day help them experience the consolation of the death and rising of Christ.

- A eucharist should be scheduled for the bereaved during the Easter octave.

- Pastoral workers should help mourners appreciate the importance of the Easter Vigil. No wake should compete with it. Perhaps those who grieve may choose to pray in vigil for the deceased by coming to at least part of the Easter liturgies.

ANOINTING OF THE SICK

The sick and dying may not be aware of what day the anointing takes place. One of the day's readings and prayers relating to the Triduum may help the sick and those standing with them find strength in the paschal mystery.

PENANCE

Communal penance services violate the liturgical dynamics of the Triduum and should not be celebrated these days. Many pastoral ministers think that celebrations of individual reconciliation should be completed before sunset on Holy Thursday as well. Surely, penance was what Lent was for.

SEDERS

During the Triduum, a Jewish seder takes us from the rites of the Triduum, our Passover celebration. Because the Jewish Passover often begins as it does this year on the same weekend as the Christian Pasch, Catholics invited to Jewish homes for the seder should weigh the invitation carefully. Will it prevent participation in the parish's liturgies? Will the feasting compromise the paschal fast? Perhaps one of the evenings during the Easter octave would be more fitting for joint celebration. We should, of course, pray in union with Jews as we each keep the Passover.

The Worship Environment

T HE days and weeks before the Triduum offer pastors, liturgical committees and sacristans a once-a-year opportunity to draw on parishioners' awareness that "spring cleaning" is in order. Long before the season begins, a number of days should be set aside on the parish calendar for cleaning and arranging. Volunteer opportunity lists or a "Wall of Opportunity" with the dozens of tasks and sign-up space arrayed on posters should be available by mid-March. Such approaches let the community claim their building and its environs.

The bulk of this activity should take place the day before Palm Sunday and days or evenings early in Holy Week. Only last-minute tasks should be left for Holy Saturday morning, but these should be thought through and assignments made earlier in Holy Week, freeing coordinators and pastors for other work.

■ VESSELS AND ARTIFACTS FOR THE TRIDUUM: A careful review of liturgical outlines should help sacristans prepare a list of needed items, from towels for the foot washing to congregational candles to flowers or Easter eggs for all. This process can be assisted by cross-checking the list with a review of the sacramentary for these days and especially the "requisites" lists provided for each day in the *Ceremonial of Bishops* (#299, #315, #336).

■ VESTURE FOR THE TRIDUUM: The evening Mass on Thursday calls for white vestments. These should be as plain as possible, not the festive Easter vestments that should be seen for the first time at the Vigil.

Red is the color for Good Friday, without ornament (certainly without Pentecost symbols). The sacramentary calls for red Mass vestments —chasuble for the presider, dalmatic for the deacon. Red copes could be worn by the lectors

for the passion. Each parish will have to decide based on the best available vesture.

Violet is the color for Holy Saturday's liturgy of the hours or for the preparatory rites. On this simplest of days, perhaps only albs, the vesture common to all ministers, may be worn.

The vesture to be worn throughout the Fifty Days of Easter should be worn for the first time on Easter Eve. To add solemnity, consider vesting the cantors and lectors, especially the person who will sing the Exsultet, in albs—maybe even in copes. Albs are simply baptismal garments. They should be ready for all the neophytes this night.

■ LITURGICAL BOOKS should be worthy of the holy mysteries they serve, beautiful reminders of the presence of the word of God. The sacramentary, perhaps suitably covered by local artisans, is to be held by the assisting ministers— no flimsy missalette should be juggled by those attempting to draw the assembly into the sacred mysteries. The lectionary and any Book of the Gospels should tell even the youngest participant that this is important. (See the 1981 introduction to the lectionary, #35–37.)

For the Triduum, three other books must be considered. First, the book or scroll from which the Exsultet is sung should be beautiful. Second, most parishes will need to create a book for use by leaders of the liturgy of the hours. The variety of adaptations and the importance of locally selected music demand a tailor-made presider's book. A nicely covered looseleaf binder may suffice, but a beautifully bound book pressed into this new service usually is better. Removable tape and photocopiers allow for all the texts to be placed without damaging the book. A third book may be a locally arranged leaders' book for the Vigil—for presider, music director and anyone who needs the complete outline of this complicated liturgy. This book would include the appropriate texts from the sacramentary and the initiation rites, music and marginal notes to remind pastors and music directors of previously agreed on actions and signals.

■ DECORATIONS OVER THE THREE DAYS: The sacramentary and other official liturgical documentation should guide sacristans through these days.

▪ *Thursday evening (before Mass):* "The tabernacle should be entirely empty." That implies that the veil is removed, the vigil light is removed, the doors are left open. That rubric, as well as the norms of the sacramentary for Lent, imply that the entire church is stripped and cleaned—without candles or cloths or any unnecessary furniture (see page 83 in the lenten introduction). This is not "iconoclasm" born of a distaste for sacred images, for we Catholics are not given to Puritanism. It is, rather, a bareness brought about by the discipline of giving undivided attention to the ritual actions and giving rise to a hunger for splendor, a longing for things to be whole again.

- *Thursday evening (for the end of Mass):* The place for the transfer of the eucharist is described as "a chapel suitably decorated" and "conducive to prayer and meditation" (*Circular Letter,* #49). What is "suitably decorated"? Remember that it is Good Friday eve; think about the reception of the oils and about the possibility of using small olive trees or branches. Candles always are appropriate; they seem to beckon us to the eschaton. Save the lilies for Saturday night.

- *Thursday evening (after Mass):* Crosses are to be removed from the church or veiled. It also is customary to remove holy water from the fonts to await the Easter water. The removal of water or crosses, however, is a logical part of the church cleaning earlier in Lent or before Ash Wednesday. There should be little to strip from the church tonight except the altar cloth and the furniture used in the washing of the feet. Anything not part of the building itself (credence tables, kneelers, etc.) should be removed. The few items needed for the celebration tomorrow can be brought in for the service and then taken away. Although there is no ceremony for removing the altar cloth, strip the altar with great reverence and dignity. This simple action was for years a sign of our entering into the paschal fast. It took place while singing Psalm 22. The psalm still may be prayed by those performing this ministry.

- *Thursday midnight:* All candles, except for the candle near the tabernacle, are extinguished at the conclusion of eucharistic adoration or night prayer (whichever comes later). All other decorations are taken from the eucharistic chapel before the first hour of prayer on Friday.

- *Friday (before the Celebration of the Lord's Passion):* Only those items of furniture needed for the rite are set out. Candles are to be ready near the cross for its solemn entrance, and an altar cloth is kept to the side for later use. All else is bare.

- *Friday (for communion rite):* At the conclusion of the rite, any remaining eucharist is brought to a separate, private place to be kept for viaticum. This must not be the eucharistic chapel, for the reservation is not provided for visitation or private prayer.

- *Friday (after the Celebration):* The altar and sanctuary once more are completely stripped except for a shrine of the holy cross. The cross (which was carried in during the celebration) is placed with lighted candles in a place conducive both to quiet prayer and to reverencing the cross with a touch or kiss. The *Circular Letter* (#71) suggests the now-empty eucharistic chapel. If the cross is a stationary one—for example, the one suspended over the sanctuary—then candles (and perhaps a spotlight) now grace it.

- *Saturday in general:* The church should be decorated as late as possible so that it is bare for most of the liturgy of the hours, preparatory rites or any other assembly. The enshrined cross remains in its place of honor with or without lighted candles.

- *Saturday morning:* The *Circular Letter* (#74) suggests that an image or two may be introduced into the space for the whole day.

  The image of Christ crucified or lying in the tomb, or the descent into hell, which mystery Holy Saturday recalls, as also an image of the sorrowful Virgin Mary, can be placed in the church for the veneration of the faithful.

- *Saturday night (Vigil):* The *Ceremonial of Bishops* (#48) contains an interesting note reminding many old-time sacristans of hectic Vigils long ago: The rubrics ban the use of flowers from "Ash Wednesday until the Gloria at the Easter Vigil." For centuries, a reverent procession of flower bearers and veil removers (recall the rubrics regarding the removal of veils from the statues) took place at the Gloria. The possibility for this activity still exists.

■ RITES FORM ARCHITECTURE: Good ritual celebrations demand appropriate spaces, and the liturgies of the Triduum point the way in several important areas. This is not the time of the year for pastors and liturgical planners to worry about renovation plans, but it is the perfect time to jot down notes about what would have enhanced and facilitated the prayer of the assembly.

- *Thursday:* The place of reposition is the eucharistic chapel if this is separate from the main worship space. A parish that uses a side altar for the tabernacle faces a difficult challenge at times like this. It probably should set up another room for reservation. And then it should add this to the list of renovation topics. The liturgy of the church does not countenance the reservation of the eucharist in the same room in which it is celebrated.

- *Thursday (and later days):* When the elect and catechumens are dismissed before the general intercessions, they go to the *catechumenon* (see page 84)—a space apart from the baptized in fact but not in spirit.

- *Friday:* The size and location of the cross that will grace the worship space is related directly to the veneration on this day. A suspended cross must be attached in such a way that the assembly can touch or kiss it—no substitute cross should be brought in for this moment, especially if the regular cross is hanging overhead. The Roman Rite's preference for the church's regular cross to be a processional cross—not a permanently fixed cross —rises in part from this rite and its centrality in linking the parish to its cross.

- *Saturday night (and other days):* Because every household should come to the Vigil, a child-care facility will be needed. This is not peripheral to good liturgy. For 20 years, the *Rite of Baptism for Children* (#14) has called for an auxiliary room where children and infants should be taken until the time of baptism. The possible presence of infants to be baptized at the Vigil lends further strength to this Triduum exigency. (Of course, restroom facilities should be nearby.)

- *Saturday night (Fire):* The Service of Light effects particular architectural and landscaping demands. Renovation plans must consider the full observance of this liturgy, with all gathered in a place separate from the main space.

- *Saturday night (Water):* An immersion font is called for. The National Statutes for the Catechumenate, approved by the United States Conference of Bishops in 1986, tells us that immersion is the preferred mode of baptism (statute #17). Baptism by immersion—our worldwide ancient tradition—is now a national priority. Immersion does not necessarily mean full submersion. The "immersion baptism" mosaics of many early baptistries show people standing in water, usually up to their knees, with water being poured over their heads, so that the water runs over their bodies as a "robe of glory."

  Liturgical design committees continue to argue over the best place for the font, but it certainly is not right next to the other sacred furnishings. If you are constructing a font for this occasion, be aware that front and center is not always best. Allow this sacred action to unfold in its own area of the church, one that would allow for processions both to and from the site.

April

Lectionary #40   white
16 Holy Thursday
THU

ENTERING THE TRIDUUM

"We should glory in the cross of our Lord Jesus Christ, for he is our salvation, our life and our resurrection; through him we are saved and made free." Thus the tone of entry into the Triduum is set by the antiphon of the introductory rites. The other aspects that we associate with this evening —remembering the Last Supper and the roots of both the eucharist and its ministries, recalling the betrayal by Judas and the agony in the garden, portraying the love of Jesus through the washing of the feet—have a place only within this context. They must never take precedence over the drawing of the entire parish into the mystery of the Pasch. An understanding of Holy Thursday as a threshold experience can guide those who prepare the liturgy in selecting texts, music and ceremonial details.

INTRODUCTORY RITES

■ THE OPENING HYMN: If the entrance antiphon in the sacramentary is not used, this song should keep with the imagery of that antiphon. An ancient text by Venantius Fortunatis that is most appropriate to begin this celebration is "Sing, my tongue, the song of triumph." It is most effectively sung to the Mode III chant ("Pange lingua"), but can be found in *Worship* coupled with "Picardy," and also fits "Lauda anima." Using the same melody for this text to begin and the "Pange lingua" text at the transfer of the eucharist helps knit the many rituals of this evening into one unified celebration. Other possible music for gathering includes "Lift high the cross" and "Praise to you, O Christ our Savior" (Farrell, OCP, #7126).

■ ORDER FOR THE RECEPTION OF THE HOLY OILS: The custom of receiving the oils on this night has an ancient heritage, and many parishes have renewed the practice. In 1989, the Vatican confirmed the decision of U.S. bishops to include this in future editions of the sacramentary.

The reception of the oils can be incorporated into the Mass of the Lord's Supper with ministers carrying the vessels of blessed oil during the entrance procession. They place the vessels on a table or on pedestals near the altar and then honor the altar and the oils with incense. After the greeting, the presider says a few brief words about the oils and about their significance in the life of the local faith community. The oils then are carried reverently to the place where they are reserved in the ambry or by the font.

With such a simple gesture, we signify at yet another level that we are entering into the Triduum, the central moment of which will involve this sacred chrism. Allusions to other ministries come with these oils and are appropriate to this rite. These words, to be used after the sign of the cross and the greeting, are to be adapted as needed:

Oil of the Sick:
This oil of the sick has been blessed by our bishop for the healing of body, mind and soul. May the sick, who are anointed with it, experience the compassion of Christ and his saving love.

Oil of Catechumens:
This oil of catechumens has been blessed by our bishop for the anointing of those preparing for baptism. Through this anointing they are strengthened by Christ to resist the power of Satan and reject evil in all its forms, as they prepare for the saving waters of baptism.

Holy Chrism:
This holy chrism, a mixture of olive oil and perfume, has been consecrated by our bishop and the priests of our diocese. It will be used to anoint infants after baptism, those who are to be confirmed, bishops and priests at their ordination and altars and churches at the time of their dedication.

■ GLORIA: This is an occasion for a familiar "Ordinary Time" Gloria, rather than a lengthy, festive setting or one associated with the Christmas season. Consider John Lee's simple setting (GIA, *Worship*); it is arranged with handbell accompaniment by Richard Proulx in *Tintinnabulum,* also from GIA.

The tradition calls for church bells to be rung during tonight's Gloria, alerting the whole town that something big is beginning, and then the bells are silent until the Easter Vigil. The parish shares its most important moments with its neighbors. This rubric about bells during the Gloria is for churches with bells on the lawn or in the tower. Ringing little bells inside the church is not exactly a substitute. Custodians of these little bell sets can hand the collection over to the music department. Bells are no longer ceremonial props. They are musical instruments and should be handled as such. Then, if bell-sounding inside the worship space is appropriate to the Gloria, the music minister can arrange it.

■ OPENING PRAYER: The opening prayer for Holy Thursday was written with little attention to the fullness of the paschal mystery. The opening prayer for Tuesday of Holy Week is more in spirit with this evening, as is the beautiful Opening Prayer A for the Votive Mass of the Holy Eucharist.

LITURGY OF THE WORD

■ CHILDREN'S LITURGY OF THE WORD: If the provision noted in the *Directory for Masses with Children* (#17) for a separate liturgy of the word for children has been utilized, these liturgies should be planned with great care for these holiest of days. As always, they are led by adults capable of facilitating prayer. This liturgy is not another catechetical class. And it certainly is more than child care (which should be offered separately for toddlers). If the children are sent forth from the assembly, they should be dismissed after the Introductory Rites, so that they have seats claimed and, more importantly, so that they know that they are part of a wider assembly. On this night, they should return to the assembly after the homily in time to see the washing of the feet.

■ THE READINGS are clearly about entering into the Triduum. The surrounding verses of the second reading, 1 Corinthians 6:23–26, set it in the context of a warning: Our eucharist can be a judgment against us; it is the judgment of the cross. The other two readings this night contain life and death ultimatums: The angel of death descends to execute judgment; a sacrifice is required to

guarantee protection. If we are unprepared to be servants to each other, then we can have no part with Jesus. The liturgy of Holy Thursday evening clearly places these warnings before us as it sweeps us into the Passover.

■ THE PSALM: Choose a fine, singable setting of Psalm 116, the psalm appointed in the lectionary. Two that use the lectionary refrain "Our blessing-cup is a communion in the blood of Christ" are Michael Joncas's syncopated and enjoyable offering (NALR, JO 07-JON-SM) and the lyrical setting by Marty Haugen (GIA, *Gather*). If a fine cantor will serve at this celebration, be sure to look at the Conley setting with the refrain "What return can I make to the Lord?" (GIA, G-2528) and the lovely refrain and challenging verses of Stephen Dean's "How can I repay the Lord" (OCP, #7119).

■ THE WASHING OF THE FEET: The homily should lead naturally into the washing of feet with no other words of introduction—indeed, the "mandatum" action is a kind of visual homily continuing the work of interpretation begun by the homilist. Make sure all chairs are set up ahead of time. Generous towels, sturdy washbasins, pitchers full of warm, scented water—all these can be brought from the sacristy with a broad gesture as the singing begins and the participants move to their places. This singing continues throughout the washing and during any follow-up washing of the hands of the ministers. It ends just in time for the intercessions.

The music of the mandatum must be selected carefully and performed to complement the ritual as it is carried out in each parish. Although this action will look and feel different from community to

community, some constants remain. The entire assembly must be able to watch or participate in the foot-washing. A hymn, by its complexity of text, requires much attention; singing a hymn during the mandatum forces the assembly to choose between participating in the singing or participating in the ritual action. Some pieces that are responsorial and worth learning for this annual moment are Chrysoganus Waddell's "Jesus took a towel" (*Worship*, GIA), a remarkable and powerful piece; "Jesu, Jesu," #431 in *Worship*, a simple and lovely song from Ghana that speaks in concrete terms of our "mandatum" to serve as Jesus did; and the recitative setting of the "Mandatum Novum" of Taizé (GIA, G-2433).

■ DISMISSAL OF THE CATECHUMENS AND THE ELECT: The sending forth of the elect and of the catechumens follows the washing of feet. Tonight's dismissal is one of the challenges of the Triduum that will take some time for us to meet. The entire parish has gathered in mystery, and their catechists and the catechumenate coordinator will not want to be absent from the paschal assembly. Those who accompany the catechumens and the elect perhaps will learn yet another meaning of washing feet.

■ GENERAL INTERCESSIONS: For an example of how to word petitions in the light of the start of the Triduum, see the intercessions for today's Evening Prayer (a liturgy celebrated only by the homebound or by those who are otherwise unable to attend the evening Mass).

LITURGY OF THE EUCHARIST

■ PREPARATION RITES: This is the one celebration of the year when it is appropriate to bring forward something in addition to bread and wine during the preparation of the gifts: "gifts for the poor" says the sacramentary, "collected as the fruit of lenten penance" adds the *Circular Letter* (#52). Canned goods for a food bank, filled "rice bowls" for Catholic Relief Services or gifts for a parish's sister parish could be collected in this procession.

"Ubi caritas," the appointed song, is straight from the Reichenau Abbey of the year 800. No other preparation rite has a song assigned to it. Few hymns have as venerable a history. Do not let another Triduum planning season go by without looking at Richard Proulx's setting for unison choir/cantor and congregation, "God is love" (GIA, G-3010). The Taizé mantra "Ubi caritas" (*Worship,* GIA) establishes a calm, prayerful environment and lends itself to embellishment so that it can be sustained throughout the ritual. The well-known and worthy survivor from the 1960s, "Where charity and love prevail," is still another fine choice; you will find it with inclusive language in the *People's Mass Book* (World Library Publications).

■ EUCHARISTIC PRAYER: Preface of the Holy Eucharist I (P17) is called for, but other texts probably are more appropriate to the Triduum (for example, the Preface of the Sacred Heart or of the Triumph of the Cross). There are three special inserts for Eucharistic Prayer I.

Although Lent is over, it may be best to retain the acclamations used throughout that season, especially if these were understated and simple and certainly if they will be used during Eastertime as well. Save any new settings for the Vigil. If concelebrants are taking part, they must know the text of the eucharistic prayer and who will be responsible for offering

different parts of it well before Mass begins.

■ BREAKING OF THE BREAD: Every parish should use large bread loaves or hosts large enough to break for the community. The liturgical books and the tradition of our rite stress this over and over again. The breaking of the bread is an important part of the eucharistic action. It probably should not be a part of Good Friday's service. That will not be a eucharistic action—communion then is a simple distribution of eucharist consecrated this night. So the bread loaves or large hosts for tomorrow should be broken tonight.

■ THE COMMUNION PROCESSION: Psalm 34 is a happy choice for communion this night. Good, engaging settings include James Moore's "Taste and see" (GIA, G-2802), which begs for a cantor who can take some liberty with the wonderful gospel-style verses, and Stephen Dean's delightfully British "Taste and see" (OCP, #7114). David Haas has juxtaposed texts from Corinthians, 1 John and 2 Timothy in "Now we remain" (*Gather,* GIA); sing through this piece with the celebrations of Triduum in mind. "Love is his word" (*Worship,* GIA) gathers many of the images of this evening in a graceful musical setting by Robert Hutmacher ("Julinorma"), which is effective with cantor or choir singing the verses while the assembly responds, "Richer than gold is the love of my Lord, better than splendor and wealth."

■ DISMISSAL OF EUCHARISTIC MINISTERS: The *Circular Letter* contains a rubric (#53) that can find immediate implementation everywhere, linking homebound parishioners to the Triduum celebrations:

It is appropriate that the eucharist be borne directly from the altar by the deacons or acolytes or extraordinary ministers at the moment of communion, for the sick and infirm who must communicate at home, so that in this way they may be more closely united to the celebrating church.

■ AFTER COMMUNION: A large vessel with consecrated and broken bread for Good Friday's communion is placed on the altar. After a period of silence, the prayer after communion is chanted. There is no blessing, no dismissal, no announcements.

TRANSFER OF THE HOLY EUCHARIST

■ PURPOSE: This rite of transfer of the holy eucharist is just that, a transfer for reservation until Good Friday. It is not meant to be a devotional procession as on Corpus Christi. It is omitted if the Celebration of the Lord's Passion will not be kept in the same church tomorrow.

■ PREPARING FOR THE PROCESSION: Standing before the altar, the presider places incense in the thurible, kneels and honors the eucharist with incense. Meanwhile, the assisting ministers and all others kneel with lighted candles. The presider puts on the humeral veil, takes the vessel with the eucharist in it and covers the vessel with the ends of the veil—like the tabernacle veil with its image of the *shekinah,* the tent that God has pitched among us. At the same time, the ministers who will lead the procession gather in the correct order and prepare to leave on the assigned route. If the largest vessel available is not large enough to contain the hosts for Good Friday, a second vessel should be carried by a deacon or concelebrant also wearing a humeral veil. It is awkward, and therefore inappropriate, for two vessels to be carried by the same person.

■ PROCESSION: The presider carries the eucharist through the church to the place of reposition. The Roman tradition calls for the procession to be in this order and for all in it to be carrying lighted candles or torches: crossbearer, acolytes, deacons, concelebrants, two censer bearers, presider with the eucharist. Other ministers (for example, lectors and those eucharistic ministers who have not left to go to the sick) and other members of the congregation also can follow in procession, bearing lighted candles as well. The assembly follows this procession into the eucharistic chapel or into the area around it if there is room.

Both in text and melody, "Pange lingua/Sing my tongue" is a touchstone in Catholic ritual music. Verses can be sung in Latin or in English, or the two can be alternated. Customarily, the final two verses ("Tantum ergo sacramentum" and the doxology) are sung as the ciborium is placed in the repository.

■ CONCLUSION OF PROCESSION: Arriving at the place, the presider sets the vessel down in the tabernacle (leaving the door open) or just in front of it. He then removes the humeral veil, kneels and incenses the vessel with one of the thuribles. Then all sing the last two verses of the "Pange Lingua" ("Tantum ergo sacramentum"). The deacon places the eucharist in the repository (if the presider did not) and closes the door. A period of silent adoration follows.

A Taizé ostinato begun at this point can ease the formal ritual moment into a quiet mood of watchfulness. Appropiate choices include "Jesus, remember me," "Stay with me" and "Peace, I leave

you." A meditative choral motet also could serve this purpose.

EUCHARISTIC ADORATION

During the hours after the transfer of the eucharist, the faithful should be encouraged to continue in prayer within this "conducive" place. The *Circular Letter* (#56) calls for chapters 13–17 of John to be read as part of this time of prayer—a venerable monastic practice for this night. Many parishes encourage participation in this prayer by involving different groups in the vocal praying and in the singing—religious communities, prayer groups, Bible study groups or others. With a little coordination and division of time, the chapel can be filled for hours with communal prayer (although it should be communal and not the idiosyncratic devotions of any one particular group). See page 110 for notes on the environment of this adoration and on the stripping of the altar.

The rubrics call for the solemn adoration of the eucharist to end at midnight. They do not, however, forbid gathering in churches after midnight, nor do they encourage us to lock the church for the night. These three days exude a power that draws many to the building. In places where security issues are crucial, volunteers or custodians can be present in rotation. The open church can signify the importance of these days and can invite parishioners to keep their attention on ecclesial prayer and action.

NIGHT PRAYER

Many parishes begin a Triduum-long implementation of the liturgy of the hours by singing Night

Prayer together just before midnight. A Triduum antiphon is given in the *Liturgy of the Hours,* one that vies with the entrance antiphon tonight for our Triduum *leitmotiv* to resound and hum: "For our sake Christ was obedient, accepting even death."

F R I **17** #41   red
Good Friday

SCHEDULE

The day's schedule should be dictated by the time selected for the principal event, the Celebration of the Lord's Passion. Tradition calls for 3:00 PM, although rubrical norms (occasionally made specific by the diocese) allow for any time from noon until 9:00 PM. The bishop can give permission for the service to be repeated when the number of people trying to attend one service would not fit within the assembly space.

Once this service is set, the other hours of the liturgy can be scheduled, as many as possible: the Office of Readings and Morning Prayer combined as Tenebrae, Midday Prayer and Night Prayer. Evening Prayer is not celebrated publicly today.

Only after the liturgy of the hours is scheduled would other devotions be considered. In other words, the stations of the cross should not detract from Morning Prayer. Fasting lunches or suppers should be set to facilitate parishioners' presence at proximate liturgies.

AT HOME

This day, just as the rest of the Triduum, must be different at home, on the sidewalks and in the car. Today, and tomorrow until the Vigil, this means an extensive fast from work, entertainment and food, an intentional abstinence from meat and desserts— all in anticipation (not penitence) as we and the elect prepare for the great night.

OFFICE OF READINGS AND MORNING PRAYER

Over the centuries preceding Vatican II, Tenebrae was the paschal title for the Office of Readings ("Vigils") combined with Morning Prayer ("Lauds") during which candles were extinguished as morning came. Traditional readings, psalms and responsories for prayer during the predawn moments of Tenerae can be found in the Episcopal Church's *The Book of Occasional Services* (The Church Hymnal Corporation). The *Ceremonial of Bishops* (#296), the *Liturgy of the Hours* (#210) and the *Circular Letter* (#40, #62) call for something similar. Parishes should make a choice while more permanent rites for combining these hours are prepared: Use the Episcopalian book previously mentioned, celebrate the Office of Readings as in the *Liturgy of the Hours,* celebrate Morning Prayer as in the *Liturgy of the Hours* or combine these two Catholic liturgies using the *General Instruction of the Liturgy of the Hours* (#99) for structural guidance. This last option would follow an outline something like this:

- Proper antiphon (from Good Friday Office of Readings [OR]) and invitatory psalm (from Ordinary)
- Hymn (see suggestions listed under Morning Prayer [MP])

- Proper antiphons and psalms: Psalms 2, 22 and 38 (OR)
- Proper verse (OR)
- Hebrews 9:11–28, with its proper responsory (OR)
- Reading from St. John Chrysostom with its responsory (OR)
- Proper antiphons and psalms: Psalms 51 and 147, with the canticle from Habakkuk sung between them (MP)
- Isaiah 52:13–15 (MP)
- Proper antiphon (MP; same as at Night Prayer on Thursday)
- Proper antiphon (MP) and canticle of Zechariah (from Ordinary)
- Proper intercessions (MP) and Lord's Prayer
- Prayer (MP)
- Blessing and dismissal (from Ordinary)

CATECHETICAL ASSEMBLY FOR CHILDREN

■ TODAY'S SCHOOL OF FAITH: Most children are out of school on Good Friday. If they are not, then the religious demands of this day are such that Catholic parents should do what Jewish parents do with their children on Yom Kippur: Free them for both home and public worship.

■ CHILDREN IN THE TRIDUUM: As always, those who prepare the liturgy must consider the presence of children and their entrance into the great prayer of the church. Child care for the youngest ones should be provided, at least for the main celebrations on these Triduum days. Ways to involve preschool and older children should be planned carefully. Options include:

- The celebration of Midday Prayer (or stations of the cross) with some of the musical repertoire taught to the children during religious

education classes and in the parochial school, but avoiding the "for kids only" ambience

- A separate liturgy of the word for small children during the Celebration of the Lord's Passion (ensuring that it is a liturgy, not a class)
- References to the faith life of children as part of the homily
- Participation of the children in preparing the church building for the Triduum
- A catechetical assembly for all children of the parish on the morning of Good Friday and the morning of Holy Saturday

■ CATECHETICAL ASSEMBLIES: One powerful way to assist the conscious and active participation of young people in the liturgies may be to hold catechetical assemblies of all parish youth on Good Friday and Holy Saturday mornings. Parents will appreciate the attempt to draw their children into the great mystery of faith. Children will enjoy the gatherings if the assemblies are planned well. Such events may involve all youth from preschool through grade six or so. They would gather each day for an hour-long event organized more or less as a celebration of the word. What distinguishes this from being a "children's liturgy" competing with the principal liturgy is that it must clearly point to the parish assembly—a kind of rehearsal and preparation to enable children to participate fully in the principal liturgies.

On Good Friday morning, such an assembly may include:

- Music that opens the experience of the passion and the cross and that also will be used at the Celebration of the Lord's Passion
- A reading or two from the day's liturgy of the hours, using images with which children can identify

- Instructions, given by one or more of the parish leaders, that introduce the liturgy that they will enter later in the day, helping everyone enter its image-world. Instructions may be given in smaller groups by age level.

- Rehearsal and gracious explanations for the solemn actions that they will perform with the adults later on. Such rehearsals are like a preparatory act of prayer.

- Some preparation of the physical requirements of the principal liturgy: For example, the children can see the stripped-down church and reflect on it, or help to prepare a resting place for the cross, or get the cross out of storage and bring it to the place from which it will be carried in solemn entrance.

- Praying some of the general intercessions chosen from the Celebration of the Lord's Passion.

MIDDAY PRAYER

Good Friday noon triggers a reaction in many Christians. They feel drawn to church. Presuming that the Celebration of the Lord's Passion is at 3:00 PM or later, this would be a great opportunity to add this hour of the church's prayer to the parish's life. The order is simpler than Morning Prayer. It can be extended to allow for more silence and reflection on this most holy Friday. A passion-oriented hymn follows the regular words of introduction. A psalm antiphon referring to noontime follows. The assigned psalms bring participants into ancient traditions of this day: Psalms 40, 54 and 88 all help us identify with the Lord on the cross. A powerful passage from Isaiah is followed by the proper antiphon that the community of Taizé has made popular in its music: "Jesus, remember me." A simple prayer concludes the service. If a longer service is desired, this format can be expanded with readings from the patristic selections in the Office of Readings in Holy Week, with a homily or with very long periods of silence between the psalms.

CELEBRATION OF THE LORD'S PASSION

Introductory Rites

■ SILENCE: A silent gathering without the usual processions (cross, candles, incense) signals the continuation of the Triduum liturgy. A stark silence serves this moment best; avoid the temptation to cover the discomfort of it with a solo instrument, choral motet or timpani pulse. Any musical meditation on the stations of the cross or the seven last words, for example, should have ended well before this service.

■ FALLING PROSTRATE: As the service begins, the presider and assisting ministers reverence the bare altar and then fully prostrate themselves. Ordinarily, everyone else kneels in silence. If the physical arrangement of the room allows (admittedly a rare thing), anyone in the assembly can join in the prostration. Kneeling is only a substitute for this profound gesture. Prostrate or kneeling, then, all pray silently as the sacramentary suggests "for a while," that is, long enough to let the banging of kneelers and the clearing of throats yield to an intense silence, then longer as this silence turns to true communion. The time for this silent posture to begin and end may be signaled by a sound, such as a knocking on wood (perhaps using the old "clappers" that replaced bells this day).

■ OPENING PRAYER: Going to the chair, the presider neither greets the people nor invites them with the traditional "Let us pray." Instead, with hands outstretched (according to the *Ceremonial for Bishops*), the presider simply offers the prayer and sits down for the liturgy of the word. The second, longer alternative prayer is more traditional. ("Humanity" would be more inclusive than "manhood.")

Liturgy of the Word

■ LITURGY OF THE WORD FOR CHILDREN: If the children are regularly invited to their own liturgy of the word, and if they are truly liturgies (not classes), then this may occur today as well. The children should be present for the prostration and opening prayer, helping them to see that they are a part of a broader assembly and that this is a serious gathering indeed. If they do not return for the general intercessions this day, then their presiders should be sure that their own intercessions are fuller and more inclusive than on other days. If they are returning after the intercessions, and if their numbers allow, they may enter into procession with the cross, going barefoot, kneeling in the aisle at each of the three invocations. This obviously would require some preparations in their liturgy of the word and in any prior catechetical assembly. These instructions should be given as an extended meditation or homily on the cross and our relationship to it, not just as a strategic rehearsal.

■ THE PSALM: The psalm will be the first music of this gathering. Musical instruments can be remarkably powerful during this celebration by their absence or sparing use. Choose music that is sung easily and well understood without extensive accompaniment; chant would serve well. Consider using the setting of Psalm 22 that was used for Passion Sunday. The setting by Howard Hughes is particularly striking in its simplicity.

■ THE PASSION: The singing of the passion by three strong singers should be given priority over any other means of proclamation. The rubrics in the sacramentary permit the nonordained to sing it. This is performed in an austere manner, without incense and candles, and without the greeting of the people and the signing of the book. After the verse about the death of the Lord, all kneel and a brief silence is observed.

The assembly again may interpolate the verses of a hymn within the proclamation of the passion; this hymn should respect the unique character of the Johannine account. "O sacred head surrounded" should give way today to "Take up your cross," a hope-filled text that works nicely with the tune "Erhalt uns Herr." Other good choices are "Sing, my tongue, the song of triumph," paired with the haunting "Picardy" tune in *Worship* and "The regal dark mysterious cross" ("Vexilla Regis"), a common meter text found in the *Hymnal for the Hours* (GIA).

Several missalettes involve the congregation in the reading of the passion with a "crowd" part. The proclamation of the scriptures is never to be a read-along. Communities that use such missalettes would do well to invite the congregation to relinquish the "crowd" lines, put down the missalettes and listen to the word as it is proclaimed.

■ HOMILY: The proclamation of the passion and the homily that follows it should be prepared in the spirit of these comments from the U.S. episcopal conference:

> Because of the tragic history of the "Christ-killer" charge as providing a rallying cry for anti-Semites over the centuries, a strong and

careful homiletic stance is necessary to combat its lingering effects today. . . . The message of the liturgy in proclaiming the passion narratives in full is to enable the assembly to see vividly the love of Christ for each person, despite their sins, a love that even death could not vanquish. . . . To the extent that Christians over the centuries made Jews the scapegoat for Christ's death, they drew themselves away from the paschal mystery. For it is only in dying to one's sins that one can hope to rise to new life. (*God's Mercy Endures Forever,* #21–22)

■ DISMISSAL OF THE ELECT AND THE CATECHUMENS: The rubrics do not mention it, but this is one logical place for this dismissal. According to our tradition, the elect and the catechumens should not be present for the general intercessions, which are the prayers of the baptized faithful. They may leave with a catechist (perhaps a different person than was dismissed with them last night) to continue their reflection on the passion. They then may return to the assembly space after the liturgy to venerate the cross and offer prayer.

■ GENERAL INTERCESSIONS: Several styles are possible; use the one that will best encourage the participation of the community.

- The deacon (or another minister) at the ambo introduces each petition and then invites everyone to kneel in silent prayer. After some silence, the presider stands at the chair and everyone else rises as well. Then the presider sings the prayer, and the assembly seals it with a sung Amen. Then the next petition and kneeling follow. Pacing is all-important for there is a tendency to rush.

- A second possibility features the assembly kneeling throughout all of these introductions, silent periods and prayers.

- A third eliminates all kneeling, with everyone standing in silence between the introductions and the prayers.

- In the fourth and preferable option, each invitation is followed by silence. Then the assembly joins in singing an acclamation of petition (for example, a Kyrie). As the acclamation is completed, the presider voices the prayer.

Veneration of the Cross

■ THE CROSS: Venerating the cross that is used all year long in the worship space lends meaning to the wood all year. Whether the principal cross is suspended and stationary or a processional cross, that is the one to use.

To expedite the veneration, some parishes add two or three crosses. But what does that say about the significance of the grand procession of all the people to *the* parish cross, with the chanting, the kneeling? A large cross will allow two lines of people to process simultaneously, as ushers graciously direct the flow of worshipers. The alternative—an extremely poor alternative—is the presider inviting the people to venerate the one cross by holding it up for them to worship from their places in silence.

■ SHOWING THE CROSS: The two options given in the sacramentary are an "uncovering" and a "bringing in." The "uncovering" form is necessary if the cross for this liturgical space is suspended or otherwise stationary. Even here, architects or interior designers should have planned for lowering it for this rite. Note carefully what the rubrics say: The veiled cross is not carried in and unveiled in stages along the way. Rather, the gradual unveiling occurs entirely in one place.

Just as the processional cross is the preferred form for the parish's one cross, so, too, the "bringing-in" form today is the preferred format. The presider or deacon moves through the assembly with the cross, making three stops: at the entrance to the worship space, in the middle of the assembly, in front of the assembly. This movement is patterned after the bringing in of the paschal candle, a nonverbal link between Good Friday and the Easter Vigil. Other ministers can surround the cross-bearer with bowls of incense and candles, like a gospel procession. The cross is not carried over the shoulder (like a picture of Jesus ascending Calvary); it is carried the way one holds a processional cross. At the three stations, the cross must be hoisted as high as possible and held steadily, a feat that is possible if rehearsed well. After the final station, assistants should come to help hold the cross, and the candles and incense can be placed nearby.

■ VENERATING THE CROSS: Some parishes make sure that the cross always is held by people during the veneration, and some parishes simply lay it flat on a large carpet or on a bed of flowers. The cross should not be propped up on furniture, much less on the altar.

For the veneration, the assembly comes forward to reverence the cross. There is a simple genuflection "or another sign of reverence, . . . for example, kissing the cross." Local custom in many places is both a genuflection (or prostration) and a kiss. It is best not to explain to the assembly how to venerate the cross; that reduces the intense mystery of the rite to a set of prosaic instructions. (We would not think of informing loved ones how to embrace one another.) Let the first

people who venerate the cross do so with broad, authentic gestures, enabling those who come after to feel free to worship the holy wood with affection.

A beautiful, powerful gesture on this day is for all ministers—indeed, all the people—to come to the cross barefoot or in stocking feet. While it is not mentioned in the sacramentary, it is called for in the *Ceremonial of Bishops* (#322). That rubrical book calls for the presider to leave his chasuble and shoes at the chair. They should be taken off before the entrance of the cross, so that the procession flows into the veneration. This tradition, observed by many monastic orders and mentioned by ancient writers catches on quickly—if the presider and other assisting ministers handle it with grace. Announce it in the participation booklet or in a brief verbal invitation. If the presider is seen taking his shoes off while others in the sanctuary do the same, the assembly will feel comfortable removing their shoes.

■ MUSIC FOR THE VENERATION: When selecting music for the veneration of the cross, keep in mind that during each of the Triduum gatherings we celebrate the full paschal mystery; on this night, we believers display the cross not in grief and despair but as a trophy and triumphant symbol of life and hope. Our primary means of expressing this attitude is music. One way to establish this mood is an invitation to come and adore sung by the cantor near the cross followed by a strong proclamation of praise such as "Agios, o Theos/ Holy is God" composed by Howard Hughes (in *Praise God in Song,* GIA, G-2270).

This procession will take time and cannot be rushed; prepare plenty of music; vary the styles and musical forces (mix congregational singing with pieces sung by

the choir; using cantor or soloist in either case will add further interest). Begin and end with music that involves the assembly. "Sing, my tongue, the song of triumph" is appropriate, with its final two verses addressed to "faithful cross" and "tree of glory"; the "Picardy" melody found in *Worship* is well suited, particularly if used last evening. Taizé offers several wonderful ostinati for this purpose: "Crucem tuam," "Adoramus te, Domine I" and "Jesus, remember me" are all strong choices. "Jesus, remember me" can be used to weave a common thread through the Triduum gatherings, providing a transition into quiet watchfulness after the Transfer of the Eucharist on Thursday, during the veneration or at the end of the service tonight, and calling us to gather for the service of light tomorrow.

If you have not used the Taizé-style ostinati in your parish or community because you suspect that limited music resources will not sustain this form, be assured that this blissfully simple and evocative music is used with great success "as is" in the Taizé community; its beauty is in its flexibility and adaptability to different situations and musical forces. Although various instruments, choral (or congregational) harmonies and cantor verses do add another dimension to the singing and praying these mantras, you will find them just as authentic when performed simply.

Two extraordinary pieces of music for the veneration of the cross bear investigating: "By the blood with which we marked the wooden lintels," composed by Joseph Gelineau, is found in the hymnal *Cantate Domino* (Oxford University Press). The translation by Fred Pratt Green of a Didier Rimaud text employs our finest Catholic tradition of piling one image or type on another. For wonderful images of our tradition put in a fresh light, see "The tree of life," an Eric Routley paraphrase of a text by Imre Pecsely Kiraly (copyrighted by Hinshaw Music). The meter is compatible with the familiar passion tune "Herzliebster Jesu," and a fine original tune is provided by K. Lee Scott (Morning Star Music, MSM-50-3000). This setting for choir and congregation provides a congregation page that may be reproduced if quantity copies are purchased for the choir.

Choral arrangements of hymns appropriate to Good Friday's liturgy abound, and the power of spirituals for this ritual should not be overlooked.

Holy Communion

■ COMMUNION: See the rubrics in the sacramentary regarding the simple transfer of the eucharist to the altar as the cloth is being placed there. The candles carried with the cross are arranged by the altar. The communion music from last night may be repeated tonight; David Haas's "Now we remain" (*Gather*, GIA) is especially appropriate. Softly singing "Jesus remember me" or one of the other Taizé mantras suggested for veneration or to close last evening may help to ensure this "silence."

■ AFTER COMMUNION: The eucharist remaining (for Holy Saturday viaticum) is carried without ceremony by an assisting minister to a suitable place outside the church.

■ PRAYER OVER THE PEOPLE: Without the traditional greeting, the presider extends hands toward the assembly and offers this prayer. There is no dismissal.

■ SILENCE: Catholics recognize the time immediately after a liturgy as an occasion for socializing. Today all are urged to keep silence for the benefit of those remaining in vigil, keeping the paschal fast in speech as well as food. Mention this in the bulletin and in the worship aid, but the best teacher is the example of the ministers as they take their places before the cross in quiet prayer. Perhaps such "silence" can be ensured by the soft singing of a Taizé ostinato, perhaps the same one sung last evening, while those who must leave make their departure. Dimming the lights (except for the exits), with a spotlight focused on the cross, can further encourage quietness.

NIGHT PRAYER

This liturgy, perhaps after a parish supper in the spirit of the paschal fast, includes the same proper antiphon as last night and this morning: Christ was obedient unto death.

S A T **18** violet **Holy Saturday**

CATECHETICAL ASSEMBLY FOR CHILDREN

See the introduction to this concept under Good Friday on page 116. Today's catechetical session may include any of these items:

- The participation of the children in the preparation of the elect,

especially if children of catechetical age will be prepared

- The participation of the children in any of the liturgies of the *Liturgy of the Hours* that follow; if the children will be present in large numbers, those who plan the session could select psalms and prayers that facilitate the children's entrance into this.
- The painting of Easter eggs to be distributed to all after the Vigil
- Hearing (and dramatizing) scriptures from the Vigil
- Preparing the worship space for the great night

These activities are meant to prepare the children for the Vigil and should presume their participation in it. One great task of this day is the teaching of silence; silence and children ordinarily are not partners, but on this day a deliberate silence is woven through all our efforts.

PREPARATION RITES FOR INITIATION

■ PREPARATION RITES FOR THE ELECT: The *Rite of Christian Initiation of Adults* (starting at #185) calls for preparation rites on Holy Saturday: song and greeting, reading the word of God and homily, and celebrating certain rites ("giving back" the creed and/or the rite of *ephphetha*).

These rites can be scheduled on their own, with the full participation of parish members encouraged. They also could be part of one of the liturgies described below from the *Liturgy of the Hours*. In this case, the preparation actions would follow the proper psalmody and scripture reading.

Notice that the anointing with the oil of catechumens is no longer part of these preparation rites. The current edition of the rite prescribes this anointing—as a repeatable rite—for the period of the catechumenate.

■ RITE OF RECEPTION OF CHILDREN: If infants will be baptized at the Vigil, #28 of the *Rite of Baptism of Children* calls for a preparatory rite with the infants, their parents, the sponsors and parish members. Except when in danger of death, infants should not be baptized in Lent. Easter is the traditional time for baptizing them. To be true to our liturgical values, we must consider these points: We do not want to prolong the Vigil unduly, but it is the time for all manner of initiatory practice; we want the babies' families at the Vigil, just like we want everyone there; unless they will go to two Easter Masses, they will skip the Vigil if we celebrate the infant baptisms on Easter Sunday morning; infant baptisms can be celebrated on the Sundays of Eastertime, of course.

Given all of this, a preparatory rite for all those involved with the infants to be baptized on Holy Saturday may be necessary. It would involve at least the rite of receiving the children (at the door), the prayer of exorcism and the anointing with the oil of catechumens. This may be celebrated before a "fasting lunch" or in conjunction with one of the hours of the liturgy.

■ COMBINED PREPARATION RITE: A service combining this reception of infants with the Preparation of the Elect is possible, uniting in one assembly the prayers and intense expectation of many elect and parents, sponsors and catechists.

- Gathering hymn with the entire assembly at the entranceway

- Rite of receiving the infants (with texts and action of signing from the *Rite of Baptism for Children* [RBC], #35–41)

- Procession of all, with an appropriate refrain or a well-known hymn sung by all, to the place where they will be seated

- Psalms and scripture of the appropriate hour of day *or* the proclamation of one or two of the scriptures listed in the Preparation of the Elect (*Rite of Christian Initiation of Adults* [RCIA], #179–80, #194, #198)

- Homily

- Preparation rites for the infants: prayer of exorcism (RBC, #49) and, possibly, the anointing with the oil of catechumens (RBC, #50)

- Preparation rites for the elect (adults and children of catechetical age): one or more of the rites listed in the introduction to the Preparation of the Elect (RCIA, #185.2)—the presentation of the Lord's Prayer (#180 ff.), the recitation of the Creed (#195 ff.), or the *ephphetha* (#199)

- Singing of a hymn (see suggestions in the *Liturgy of the Hours* printed at the start of Holy Week) or of the gospel canticle (if this is part of Morning Prayer or Evening Prayer)

- Prayer of Blessing (RCIA, #204)

- Dismissal (RCIA, #205)

OFFICE OF READINGS AND MORNING PRAYER

The public celebration of the Office of Readings before Morning Prayer is strongly recommended today. What a beautiful patristic reading that Office features! Suggested outlines for this service (sometimes called "Tenebrae") are given in this book under the entries for Good Friday.

Many parishes combine some or all of Morning Prayer with the Preparation Rites for the Elect or with the Rite of Reception of Children (before infant baptism) on this day. Notes regarding such a service are given under the previous section on "Preparation Rites."

If many parishioners will gather for a final session of cleaning and preparing the environment, they may be encouraged to join in this Morning Prayer before they begin their tasks.

MIDDAY PRAYER

As noted previously, the preparation rites for infants or for the adult elect (or a combined rite) could be celebrated at Midday Prayer. This also may be an apt time to gather the children for a special assembly preparing them for the Vigil. This liturgy also may mark the end of the cleaning time or precede a fasting meal. In any event, the texts of this hour plunge all into the image-world of hell and the traditional reflections of this day on the phrase of the Apostles' Creed now translated, "He descended to the dead" rather than the confusing phrase "descended into hell."

By midday, some churches with old-world roots are filled with people looking for the blessing of Easter food. But today is not a day for blessing foods. This is a holdover from the days when the Easter Vigil was held on Saturday morning. Restore this beautiful custom to its proper liturgical place and hold the blessing of food after the prayer after communion during the Easter Masses, especially the Vigil. See chapter 54 of the *Book of Blessings*.

EVENING PRAYER

Depending on the time of the Vigil, this hour may be best for the preparatory rites for the elect. It also may be the best prayer hour to link to a fasting meal. If the

Vigil is very late or just before dawn, those in the habit of coming to church at an early evening hour for Mass may appreciate the scheduling of Evening Prayer at that time.

18–19 Easter Vigil
#42 white

THIS MOST HOLY NIGHT

We should solemnize with all devotion the celebration of such an important night, because on this night the world was redeemed. On this day, death was vanquished and life became victorious. Today the captives of the world are set free. Rightly, then, this night is called the Lord's Vigil, because it is celebrated most devoutly throughout the whole world in honor of his resurrection. . . . There are as many individual prayers on this holy day as there are individual desires; as many lights on this holy night of the Lord's resurrection as the gifts of blessing which he poured down. (Chromatius of Aquileia, fourth-century sermon. [See Hamman in the resources list on p. 85.])

The sacramentary rubrics say of the Easter Vigil: "It should not begin before nightfall." That does not mean twilight; it means after dark. The sacramentary continues: ". . . it should end before daybreak." This is not the same time every year. Last year most time zones were in standard time. This year, Easter falls after most time zones have changed to daylight savings time and night is one hour later. The Vigil can be held before dawn. This should be given serious consideration.

The night is made holy by the presence of every parish member. If there is not enough space for everyone who wants to come, consider the options:

- Celebrate the Vigil in a larger space, such as a school auditorium or a civic center. This option involves a tremendous amount of work, the parish's sacred furnishings may not be included and the configuration and ambiance of most auditoriums do not fit the liturgical actions — but at least everyone is present.

- Celebrate the Vigil in a tent. One large enough for 1,500 to 2,000 people is not difficult to rent with enough notice, but it may be more expensive than using an interior space. A tent also may be difficult to accommodate to the liturgy. If the tent is near the church building, the procession before initiation could bring the elect into the church's baptistry.

- Begin the Vigil after nightfall and then hold another Easter Mass at midnight or before dawn. Both of these times are naturally appealing. This second Mass does not repeat the Vigil, but it uses the liturgy of the word of the Vigil and the other texts of that Mass, and it includes the renewal of baptismal promises. Creativity is needed: Candles around the church and in everyone's hands can be lit from the paschal candle, which is already lit while the worshipers arrive. Breakfast can follow a dawn Mass.

THE SERVICE OF LIGHT

A fire is kindled. The Latin word for this fire is *rogus,* "bonfire." This means a real fire, outdoors, one that gives off heat and brilliant flame. A bonfire can be built on a lawn with no harm if a thick tarp is put down and then about ten inches of sand laid over it — a good job for the scouts! A large trough made for watering livestock also can be used to contain the wood, as long as sand or cinder blocks are placed underneath as insulation.

Everyone should meet in the place where the fire will be lighted. The worse the weather, short of a downpour, the more the assembly will welcome a cheerful fire. So often we try to protect people from their own best interests. In churches with a tradition of outdoor ceremonies, it is often the oldest and feeblest who are most eager to take part.

If decisions are made to limit the number of people by the fire, or if parishioners insist on going inside on a chilly night, be sure that all who want to be at the fire are so encouraged. Be sure, too, that sufficient seats are saved indoors for those who are at the fire. It may be good to assemble everyone in the church first and then process to the fire. Then the ushers could close off access to the seats vacated by those who processed with the ministers. This may help fulfill both the desire of earlycomers to get front seats and the need for the elect to sit with their families near them.

For safety's sake, remember that a bonfire can become dangerous on a windy night. Flames from the burning of dried evergreens can swirl 30 feet or more, even without wind. The fire department or fire marshal's office may have to be consulted. Many communities have regulations about fires, even if set up on private property. Public safety and pollution controls need not be seen as antiliturgical, but if the civic administrators are unwilling to cooperate, options are possible. Mount a campaign to get an exemption — giving members of the parish who are lawyers and politicians a good way to prepare for the Triduum. Or do what the liturgy calls for in a reasonable, safe way and cite the freedom of religious expression and the rubrics if you are questioned. Or construct the fire in a way that meets local codes.

No responsible pastor would allow civic (or even religious) officials to strip away one of the central instruments of this service of light: the lighted candle in every person's hand. Of course, ushers should be alert, with full knowledge about how to snuff out a fire using a thick blanket. One should be kept on hand along with fire extinguishers.

■ THE BLESSING OF THE FIRE AND THE LIGHTING OF THE CANDLE: The rubrics (and good liturgical sense) specify that the paschal candle must be made of wax, must never be artificial (this also outlaws liquid wax in a plastic cylinder), must be renewed each year and must be sufficiently large in size. No matter what certain manufacturers and suppliers of church goods claim, only real wax candles fulfill the liturgy's requirements.

An acolyte carries the unlit candle to the fire. The censer bearer carries the censer with unlit charcoal. No cross or other candles are carried. The presider leads all in the sign of the cross (*Ceremonial of Bishops*, #339) and gives one of the liturgical greetings. Then he or a deacon or a concelebrant gives the "instruction," using what is in the sacramentary or similar words.

After the blessing of the fire, the paschal candle is prepared and lit. (Unfortunately, many parishes forgo the symbolic decoration of the paschal candle.) A tight bundle of thin wooden sticks attached to a pole will transfer the flame from the fire to the candle better than a wax taper, which will melt near a bonfire.

■ PROCESSION: The censer is supposed to be prepared by the lighting of coals from the fire and the addition of incense at this point. It takes time, however, for the coals to burn before they are ready to receive incense. Instead, charcoal can be tucked into the flames after the fire is first lit and then removed at the appropriate time with long-handled tongs.

The deacon carries the candle (held high, the sacramentary says), preceded only by the censer bearer and followed immediately by the presider. They lead the procession into church. Everyone's candles should be lit early in this procession. The one who will chant the Exsultet—perhaps wearing a cope—carries a fine book or scroll with the text and music. If the deacon will sing this proclamation, an assisting minister becomes the "scroll bearer."

If the fire is built some distance from the church, consider constructing a beautiful glass windguard for the candle. The people's candles can be lit before the procession if you also provide windguards for these. Paper cones are available; Orthodox church-goods stores offer pretty red plastic windguards designed to be placed on the substantial candles they use in their processions.

The "Light of Christ, thanks be to God" acclamation becomes the processional song, but it can be augmented by fuller acclamations in honor of Christ. Because it is from this ritual that we derive any other evening service of light or *lucernarium,* one recommendation is to intersperse the verses of the classic evening hymn "O radiant light" *("Phos hilaron")* set to the chant melody "Jesu, dulcis memoria" between these brief acclamations. The coordination of movement, music and ministers cannot be left to chance. Be sure, for example, that the pitch

for the acclamation is clear and matches the key of the hymn; if each acclamation or hymn verse will be sung at a higher pitch, carefully prepare and rehearse the transitions.

■ PREPARATION FOR THE PROCLAMATION: The candle is honored with incense when it is placed in its stand; this stand is customarily near the ambo where the Exsultet is sung. The censer bearer stands nearby with a swinging censer, or a bowl of lighted charcoals and incense carried in the procession is placed by the candle. If a deacon sings the Exsultet, he asks for and receives a blessing, which is a proper text for this moment but nevertheless is said in a low voice.

■ THE EASTER PROCLAMATION: Despite the suggestion in the sacramentary, do not turn on the electric lights until after the Exsultet is sung. (Several lights can remain dimmed until the Gloria.) Once a year we are privileged to experience this proclamation, one of the most beautiful vestiges of solo repertoire that has survived the nearly 2,000-year history of Christian music. Like the presidential prayers, it is solo music, sung by the deacon, cantor or presider. It comes from the tradition of the cantor/deacon office of hundreds of years ago. For the sake of all gathered, the person selected to chant the Exsultet should be a confident singer, able to bring this glorious text to life with musicality and clear diction. "Exsultet" by Robert Batastini (GIA, G-2351) is a smooth working of the English text to the traditional chant melody for single cantor. Christopher Walker offers a setting for cantor and SATB choir in which the assembly enters for the concluding Amens (St. Thomas More, OCP, #7175). The beautiful integrity of the text for cantor and successfully incorporates the assembly in brief opening and closing sections. The piece is extended by interpolated chorales for SATB choir that may be omitted easily.

LITURGY OF THE WORD

The proclamation of the word in a prolonged fashion is the foundation of any vigil service. On this "mother of vigils," the church meditates on all the wonderful things God has done from the beginning. This is the night of creation, of liberation, of resurrection. Solid catechesis and liturgical practice can help prepare the community for this evening's lengthy proclamation of the scriptures. The introduction to the liturgy of the word found in the sacramentary may be helpful in recalling this catechesis.

■ CHILDREN AND THE LITURGY OF THE WORD: The whole church—including the children, and the parents of babies—should be here tonight. Child care should be available throughout, but the toddlers who are able to appreciate the service of light should be at the fire. They can be brought to the nursery before the liturgy of the word. If the children are celebrating their own liturgies of the word this Triduum, they should return to the main assembly space for the first singing of the alleluia and the gospel.

■ NUMBER OF READINGS: LTP's *A Triduum Sourcebook* contains tables of all the traditional readings for the Easter Vigil, should you choose to add to the nine readings in the lectionary.

■ PSALMODY: The psalms of this night are as ancient and as stirring as the readings. They should be respected as integral to the proclamation of the word. Do not deprive your parish of these songs of Israel and of the church by considering the time between the readings as interludes between the scripture or as an opportunity for an Easter "festival of lessons and carols." While it is good to draw on the parish's repertoire of familiar psalm settings (remember this night and its psalms when planning the rest of the year), there is certainly room and good reason to use a few melodies that are unique to this celebration each year. Psalm 136 (the grand *hallel*) is a classic in its Gelineau setting (GIA, *24 Psalms and a Canticle*, G-1424). The first three verses can be used after the creation account, adding tambourines to the remaining verses after Exodus.

■ GLORIA: The position of the Gloria in this liturgy is a remnant from the time when the readings from the Hebrew Scriptures comprised "the Vigil," which was then followed by baptism (or at least the blessing of water) and then by "the Mass of Easter," which began with the Gloria. Parishes are advised to find ways to live within the present order if at all possible. This ensures continuity from year to year. If earlier experiments have led to a parish tradition placing the Gloria elsewhere, be sure the ritual outline is comprehensible enough to convince new worship coordinators, musicians and pastors.

According to the sacramentary, the candles on or near the altar are lit during the hymn (and if all the lights in the church were not put on after the Exsultet, the rest may be turned on now). Church bells (that means exterior bells) are rung now—announcing the good news to all within the area.

See page 110 about the possibility of decorating the worship place at this point (and not earlier.)!

■ GOSPEL ACCLAMATION: Liturgical decrees carefully spell out the alleluia choreography. It can begin with an old custom:

> The deacon or the reader goes to the bishop [presbyter] and says to him, "[Most] Reverend Father, I bring you a message of great joy, the message of 'Alleluia.'" (*Ceremonial of Bishops*, #352)

This may suggest a link with the alleluia banner "buried" before Lent. A deacon or reader should "exhume" it after the reading from Romans and then announce the alleluia, adapting the words quoted previously, to the person (presider or cantor) who will intone the alleluia.

The presider, having just received the message of alleluia, intones it three times, each time at a little higher pitch (assisted, if necessary, by the cantor). In the same key as the presider, all repeat the alleluia each time. The cantor then sings the verses of Psalm 118. All sing the same alleluia after each verse.

The gospel acclamation must be carefully selected and orchestrated around the elaborateness of the procession. Processions are meant to be seen by all—with movement, incensations, banners, candles, gospel book held high. We do not serve this ritual well if we ask people to bury their heads in a hymnal or pamphlet. Choose something well crafted and easily sung, and repeat it with the addition of choir, bells, brass, organ; welcome the alleluia back into our worship with everything you can muster.

The cantor or choir should intone the Easter alleluia (chant mode VII) while the procession comes together and incense is placed on the coals; this should be followed immediately with a vibrant singing of the "Celtic Alleluia" (*Gather,* GIA or OCP, #7106) with handbells, if possible. Transpose the chant so that it hovers around the pitch "A," and note the similarities in contour with the "Celtic Alleluia." "Alleluia X" from Taizé wears well even through much repetition. Two settings that can begin quietly and build throughout the procession to the proclamation of the gospel are Robert Hutmacher's "Gospel Processional" (GIA, G-2450) (with options for chorus, organ and brass) and Howard Hughes's "Gospel Processional (GIA, G-2505). The alleluia sung at the Vigil may be the one heard throughout the Fifty Days, or it may be reserved for this procession and perhaps the end of this Mass and Sunday Evening Prayer on Pentecost.

■ THE GOSPEL PROCESSION: Tonight's gospel demands a long procession. The deacon, carrying the book, and censer bearers (but no candle bearers) can process around the assembly while all the verses of Psalm 118 are sung. Those who prepare the liturgy may ask Jewish or Orthodox Christian neighbors how they carry the Torah or the Book of the Gospels in festive processions and how they offer the book to the assembly to be kissed or touched with affection.

INITIATION AT THE VIGIL

What the sacramentary refers to as the "Liturgy of Baptism" will take one of several forms, depending on the parish situation.

- *Parishes with elect to be baptized and candidates to be received into the full communion of the Catholic Church:* This outline is followed in the commentary that follows and in the *Rite of Christian Initiation of Adults* (RCIA), appendix I, 4.

Some of these parishes also may decide to baptize infants at the same assembly.

- *Parishes with elect to be baptized but without candidates for reception into full communion:* Follow Part I of the RCIA and use the elements commented on in the following section. But these elements are arranged in a different order. See the note on page 127. Some of these parishes also may decide to baptize infants at the same Vigil.

- *Parishes with only infants to be baptized and with candidates for full communion:* Use the same outline as listed previously for parishes with both elect and candidates.

- *Parishes with only infants to be baptized and with no candidates to be received into full communion:* Follow the rubric at #28 of the *Rite of Baptism of Children.*

- *Parishes without baptisms but with candidates to be received into full communion:* Use RCIA, Part II, 5, after the renewal of baptismal promises prescribed in the sacramentary.

- *If no one is to be baptized or received,* follow the order given in the sacramentary. The renewal of baptismal promises may be enhanced with some of the following elements.

INITIATION: CELEBRATION OF BAPTISM

■ PRESENTATION: The RCIA outlines three methods for the presentation of those to be baptized. This presentation always happens in relationship to the procession to the baptistry (#219 or #568). Almost every parish can use Form B well, regardless of the placement of the font. The summoning of the elect (and infants), their godparents and the infants' parents should be performed solemnly and slowly, calling their

names loudly and adding no additional words.

■ PROCESSION TO THE BAPTISTRY: Those who are to be baptized process to the baptistry, following the paschal candle, which is carried by an acolyte. The elect, the parents of any infants and the godparents are followed by the deacon, the presider and the assisting ministers. If the baptistry is outside the main assembly area, others can process as well. This procession not only is an image of the Israelites being led by the pillar of fire through the water to the promised land, it also moves the candle from the ambo to the font in a gracious manner. This procession should take as long a route as possible through the church to the baptismal font.

■ LITANY OF THE SAINTS: The litany of the saints is the processional song for this action. Prepare the cantor to sing it with the pacing appropriate to its form: many invocations moving rapidly into intercessions. As noted in RCIA, #221 (and #570), and in the sacramentary at #41, the following names should be added to the litany: the titular of the church (if it is a saint), patron saints of the area (diocese, city), the patrons of those to be baptized and the patrons of those to be received into the church. Such inclusions help make this the prayer of the people gathered as the church.

The list of those to be added is checked against the martyrology (we await the reformed martyrology some year soon) or in a thorough collection like *Butler's Lives of the Saints.* Of course, names of the saints have a seemingly endless number of language variations. The names are organized according to their type and inserted in the litany with the others of that type. The "types" include: titles of Mary; the angels; prophets nd ancestors of the faith, including John the Baptist and Joseph; apostles and disciples of Christ mentioned in the gospels and Acts; martyrs; bishops and doctors; priests and religious; holy women and men (see appendix II of *The Roman Calendar: Text and Commentary,* USCC, 1976).

■ INVITATION TO PRAYER: If Form B (of RCIA, #219 or #568) was used, this invitatory (RCIA, #220 or #569) comes after all are at the font and the litany has ended.

■ BLESSING OF WATER: This prayer of blessing can include repeated sung acclamations, even alleluias. The rubric that calls for plunging the candle into the font (once or three times) should not be overlooked. This is a great example of archetypal symbol language that needs no explanation. If the font is visible from the assembly area, sight lines should be maintained. Make sure that those in the font area do not crowd too close to the font.

■ THE PROFESSION OF FAITH: Liturgical scholars remind us that the profession of faith is the heart of baptism, the immediate prelude to the water bath. Follow the rite closely—and, unless there are hundreds of elect, ignore the options given "if there are a great many to be baptized." The elect are asked to renounce sin as a group or individually. The questions of the profession of faith are asked of each individual, who then is baptized immediately. Parents and godparents of any infants to be baptized are then addressed and questioned as in the *Rite of Baptism of Children,* #58, #60–61.

■ BAPTISM: As each person rises from the waters of baptism, an acclamation is sung by the assembly. You can leave the assembly free to watch the ritual *and* sing

an acclamation by using the call and response form; the cantor sings a line and the assembly repeats it. Suggestions include: "You have put on Christ" by Howard Hughes (GIA, G-2283); "Rejoice, you newly baptized" by Hutchings (*ICEL Resource Collection,* GIA, G-2514) or any rousing alleluia, perhaps repeating tonight's gospel acclamation as a brief shout of praise.

■ EXPLANATORY RITES: If there are infants, they are anointed with chrism after the prayer (RCIA, #228 or #577 or RBC, #62).

The newly baptized (infants and adults) then are dressed in their baptismal garments. Godparents should assist them in drying off as they emerge from the font and in robing (in a side room) while other professions of faith and baptisms proceed. The words at the robing (RCIA, #229 or #578) can be omitted or said in private by their godparents as the newly baptized are dressed.

The most important of these explanatory rites is described in RCIA, #230 or #579. The presider and godparents pass the light to the neophytes. Plain smallest-size paschal candles, with candle followers, make good baptismal candles.

Those parishes with baptisms but without receptions into full communion should skip the next three sections of commentary and first read the section entitled, "Initiation: Rites after Baptism when There Are No Receptions."

INITIATION: RENEWAL OF BAPTISMAL PROMISES

The RCIA presumes that the baptismal promises are spoken from the font and that the water comes from the font. If the font is in a separate place, the renewal will

follow a procession back to the assembly area. The candidates for reception join in the renewal—which is placed here (RCIA, #580 ff.) so that their reception flows from it.

All stand and the assisting ministers pass light from the paschal candle to the assembly. The neophytes share the flame from their candles. Presiders must practice asking the baptismal questions, paying attention to their tone and emphases. When the last question has been posed, water is drawn from the font (if it has not already been brought from the font). During the sprinkling or signing, parents and godparents of any newly baptized infants bring them back to their places in the assembly.

■ SPRINKLING: The act of sprinkling should be as full as possible. People should feel the water. This may mean that assisting ministers sprinkle the side aisles while the presider takes time with one section of the assembly.

■ SIGNING: In place of a sprinkling, everyone in the assembly may be invited to come to the font (if it is somewhere in the worship space) or to bowls filled with water drawn from the font. The people may approach the font or bowls in lines from all sides; there they sign themselves or others with the water.

■ MUSIC FOR THE SPRINKLING OR SIGNING: The music of the sprinkling (or signing) should remain consistent throughout the Sundays of Eastertime, expanding the symbolic action with participation of the head (text), heart (music) and body (the act of singing and listening). Whether or not you already have used it, the O'Carroll/Walker "Celtic Alleluia" (St. Thomas More/OCP) suits this ritual well both in its infectious, folksy (in the best sense) melody and in the text that echoes the Exsultet and scripture of the Easter season.

If you own handbells, do not overlook Robert Batastini's setting of the Isaiah canticle "You will draw water" (GIA, G-2443) for cantor and assembly (if you will use this on all the Sundays of Easter, plan to sing the refrain in canon). With bells as the only accompaniment, this piece has clarity and "sparkle" and can set the sprinkling rite apart by this refreshing contrast. The Taizé "There is one Lord" can be effective, particularly with the overlaid cantor verses, and, because of its flexible musical form, it can be concluded gracefully as the ritual ends. Bernadette Farrell's "Give us, Lord, a new heart" (OCP, #7104) works well also. A more challenging refrain that is worth learning for use throughout the season is Richard Hillert's "Lord Jesus, from your wounded side" from "Festival Liturgy" (GIA, G-2649) also found in *Worship*.

INITIATION: CELEBRATION OF RECEPTION

■ PROCESSION: If the font is in a separate building, the procession will have unfolded before the renewal. If the neophytes and the ministers are in the main church building, they now return in procession to the front of the main worship space. Following the paschal candle, neophytes carry their lit baptismal candles.

The RCIA, #584, suggests a hymn at this time. The *Ceremonial of Bishops* (#366) suggests "You have put on Christ." Another appropriate text is "Baptized in water" by Michael Saward, coupled in *Worship* with the familiar Gaelic melody "Bunessan." The Taizé ostinato "Beati in domo

domini" is another good choice, particularly for its flexibility if the procession will not be lengthy.

■ ACT OF RECEPTION: The rite of reception (RCIA, #584 ff.) is brief, but it demands solemnity and deliberateness. The neophytes and their godparents should be nearby, but not blocking the assembly's relationship to this act. Those being received and their sponsors should stand in such a way that the congregation can see their faces.

INITIATION: CELEBRATION OF CONFIRMATION

If both neophytes and newly received are present to be confirmed, the introduction given at RCIA, #589, is used. Confirmation is the same for both the newly baptized and those received into the church. They are not anointed in any particular order. A Taizé ostinato, such as "Veni, Sancte Spiritus" or "Confitemini Domino," can be sung throughout the laying on of hands, prayer and chrismation; the song may continue to be sung quietly (or hummed) during the prayer. Another effective piece to use in this way is Christopher Walker's "Veni, Sancte Spiritus" (St. Thomas More/OCP, #7116). The refrain repeats the text several times and is graceful and easily singable; omit the overlaid cantor verses for this occasion, unless the number to be confirmed is large.

After all are signed with chrism, they take their places in the assembly. The neophytes continue to wear their robes throughout the Vigil.

INITIATION: RITES AFTER BAPTISM WHEN THERE ARE NO RECEPTIONS

When there are baptisms but no receptions, the grand procession back from the font to the front of the assembly area takes place after the explanatory rites (RCIA, #231). Confirmation (#233 ff.) takes place next, using the musical suggestions highlighted previously. Then the renewal of baptismal promises (#237 ff.) invites the signing or sprinkling of all, as already described. During that signing or sprinkling, the neophytes can return to their places in the assembly.

INITIATION: GENERAL INTERCESSIONS

This entire ensemble of rites, given the umbrella-like title of "Liturgy of Baptism" in the sacramentary, brings neophytes "for the first time" to one of the central tasks of the church: to lift up the needs of the world and the church to God constantly. Surely these intercessions will neither be omitted nor simply spoken. The form and musical response for the general intercessions should be established here and remain consistent throughout Eastertime. Look to the Kyries of Taizé, which are intended to be sung with movement and energy, or to Ronald Krisman's "Gracious Lord, hear us, we pray," found in *Worship*.

If there are newly received Catholics, a few petitions can be drawn from the RCIA, #496. The petitions in the *Liturgy of the Hours* for Easter Sunday and during the octave provide clues on how to bring the Easter experience into a framework of petition. Worthy of special mention tonight are all those who are to be initiated in the parish—confirmation candidates, catechumens, babies who will baptized, children preparing for first eucharist.

LITURGY OF THE EUCHARIST

This is the moment when many who prepare the liturgy feel tremendous relief. We are doing something we know how to do without constant reference to notes pasted into a booklet! Yet how important this is, the central act of this gathering.

■ PREPARATION RITES: This is the perfect time for the choir to show its artistry. Preparing the altar deserves attention: Up until now, the altar may have been completely stripped, bare since Holy Thursday. The placing of the cloths on the altar, and of candles and flowers nearby, will require choreography, but it is a gracious action that speaks of our moving now from fasting into feasting. The neophytes bring up the bread and wine for the eucharistic banquet in which they will share for the first time.

■ EUCHARISTIC PRAYER: Preface of Easter I is used with the words, "on this Easter night." Eucharistic Prayer I contains two or three inserts:

- "Remember . . ." from the ritual Mass of baptism if there were baptisms (paste the godparents' names into the sacramentary).

- "In union . . ." from the Vigil Mass (and printed with the prayer in most editions of the sacramentary).

- "Father, accept . . ." from the ritual Mass if there were baptisms or from the Vigil and the pages of the prayer itself if there were no baptisms (the two versions of this insert start the same but the initiation text is richer).

Intercessory inserts for the newly baptized are used in Eucharistic Prayers II and III. These inserts will be found in the back of the sacramentary under the title "Ritual Masses, Christian Initiation, Baptism."

■ COMMUNION RITE: The RCIA notes that: "Before saying 'This is the Lamb of God,' the presider may briefly remind the neophytes of the preeminence of the eucharist, which is the climax of their initiation and the center of the whole Christian life" (#243). A similar note appears at #594 for the newly received.

For the communion procession, Tom Parker's "Praise the Lord, my soul" (GIA, *Gather* or G-2395) is full of baptismal imagery and provides appealing musical material for choir, cantors and assembly. In light of the presence of the newly initiated at the Lord's table, settings of Psalm 34 with the refrain "Taste and see the goodness of the Lord" are fitting; so is "I received the living God" in *Worship,* also found in a striking choral setting (one step higher than the hymnal version) by Richard Proulx (GIA, G-3071). The moving Taizé antiphon "Eat this bread" (GIA, G-2840) has become a favorite in many communities; its verses recall scriptural images of Eucharist.

CONCLUDING RITE

The dismissal of the Vigil, with its double alleluia, could be sung to the Gregorian melody. Note that it is sung at least every day of the octave, which includes next Sunday, and then again on Pentecost. In the Episcopal Church, this dismissal is sung throughout the Fifty Days. Some Roman parishes have begun doing the same.

THE BLESSING OF FOOD AND FOOD FOR ALL

While discouraging the blessing of foods earlier on Holy Saturday, chapter 54 of the *Book of Blessings* provides texts and outlines for tonight's blessing of food for the first meal of Easter. See the discussion of this custom beginning on page 130.

If you distribute Easter eggs or hold a parish Easter breakfast this night, include these foods in the blessing. Such a breakfast is not just a "reception" for the neophytes, although there should be plenty of hugging for them. It is a splendid outpouring of Easter for every parish member.

Be sure Easter water is available for people to take home tonight and tomorrow. Easter eggs (and fresh flowers) may be given to all as they leave or as they circulate at the breakfast. The eggs may have been colored at the catechetical assembly of children earlier or prepared and now distributed by the candidates to be confirmed during Easter's Fifty Days.

19 #43   white
Easter Sunday

MORNING PRAYER

Perhaps dawn will see many gathering at the front door of church to intone Psalm 95, the invitatory psalm that, by tradition, belongs to the beginning of the church's prayer every day. Lights may be kindled again from the paschal candle (which has been left burning brightly all night), and all may sing the glorious psalms and antiphons of Easter Morning Prayer.

This hour of the liturgy is the church's "sunrise service" every day. It reveals strong possibilities for Easter dawn ecumenical services. In areas where such events are popular, Catholics and all liturgical Christians can invite others into their way of greeting the risen Christ, the Sun of righteousness.

A "sunrise service" may take place in the church or outdoors on the parish grounds. Meeting at a lake or hill or east-facing beach is tremendously appealing, but no matter where the setting, sunrise gatherings should begin well before the sunrise, while it is still quite dark, not just at 6:00 AM every year. The experience of seeing the sun come up is a powerful draw, and the early hour bonds participants together. Of course, if many parishioners find the energy to participate in such a service, perhaps consideration should be given to scheduling the Vigil itself near the end of the night period.

MORNING MASS

In his book *Liturgies of the Future,* Anscar Chupungco highlights three elements "that can be elaborated to enhance the solemnity of the liturgy [of Easter Sunday]." The sequence, the special gospel selections and the post-renewal sprinkling rite "can effectively bring into focus the two principal objects of Easter Sunday anamnesis, namely, baptism and the apparitions of the risen Christ" (p. 183).

■ INTRODUCTORY RITES: The renewal of baptismal promises and sprinkling take place after the homily, so water is not used at the

opening rites. A penitential rite with joyous acclamations using form C*v* or C*vi* would be appropriate. In the alternative opening prayer, "those" would be more inclusive than "men."

■ LITURGY OF THE WORD: The 50 days of readings from the Acts of the Apostles begin. The seasonal psalm and the seasonal gospel acclamation for Eastertime begin today. Any sung alleluia can be used as a psalm response during Eastertime.

After the reading of one of the New Testament letters about living out the paschal mystery, the sequence is sung. It is one of the most classic of chant melodies and should not be omitted. Many settings are available.

The sequence prepares the way for a gospel acclamation in scale with the day and the crowds—with plenty of incense, a gospel book worthy of public viewing and a procession with it to the ambo near the Easter candle. Then the gospel is proclaimed—from Luke or from John.

■ RENEWAL OF BAPTISMAL PROMISES: The sprinkling action today, as last night, may involve several buckets and sprinklers, or perhaps, instead of the sprinkling, process the entire congregation to the font for a ritual signing with the Easter water (see the notes on the Vigil). Buckets or bowls should be filled from the font at this time, then poured back afterward for all to see how valuable this water is.

For many, this day's Mass is the only contact with the church since Christmas. No one—not bulletin writers, preachers or announcement makers—may poke fun at twice-a-year Catholics. Even calling attention to them likely will be interpreted as an insult. Let

ears that rarely hear sacred stories be intrigued by today's message of reconciliation, forgiveness, peace, the invitation to believe. Model the homily after John Chrysostom's Easter words: "And you who did not fast, come and rejoice as well!" Let hearts that may be restless find rest in the risen Lord visible in the midst of the assembly.

Veteran musicians, liturgists and pastors reach a point in their passage through the years where they recognize that fine holiday celebrations will not change the patterns of worship for some people. But this never gives any member of the faithful an excuse to be anything less than gracious to these "visitors" who often make more demands than the "regulars." By all means, swallow any cynicism and do what you can to invite everyone, visitors and regulars alike, to return to the parish gatherings of Eastertime, to its Sundays, its feasts, its special liturgies and its special events.

■ LITURGY OF THE EUCHARIST: If Eucharistic Prayer I is used, include the proper inserts. Preface of Easter I is prescribed.

■ CONCLUDING RITE: Today has a proper solemn blessing. As on Christmas, the seasonal greetings and statements of appreciation must not perpetuate a sense that "the priests and the parish staff thank you for how you helped them at Mass." Nor should any show of appreciation, make it sound as if we have just performed a stage production.

■ HOSPITALITY: A custom that is not so expensive as one may think, and one greatly appreciated, is to give every worshiper (not just the children or women) a spring flower as they leave Mass last night or today. Easter eggs also can be given to all. Even parishes that frequently gather after Mass around coffee and doughnuts tend to postpone these get-togethers on great feasts. The crowds, the rush, the demands of family all can become excuses to let hospitality slip. After-worship camaraderie today can take on several customary guises: hot-cross buns and eggnog after Mass (not as expensive as may be imagined—especially if a generous parishioner is also a baker), an egg hunt for adults and children alike, a visit from the Easter bunny in the parking lot as folks are leaving, a parish breakfast on this happy day that breaks the paschal fast.

THE BLESSING OF FOODS AND EASTER DINNER

Blessing Easter food is not simply a quaint ethnic custom; it is a tradition for all Christians. Make it a part of the parish's liturgical life: Throughout Lent remind people to bring baskets of food as well as children's Easter baskets to any Mass on Easter Sunday, including the Vigil. Tables may be set up to receive the baskets. Ushers should be informed so they can direct folks to place their food on these tables, especially at the Easter Vigil when people arrive in the dark. Alternatively, household members can keep the foods with them in their places, ready to raise them up for the blessing prayer.

The brief prayer of the "Order of the Blessing of Food for the First Meal of Easter" should be used from the *Book of Blessings*. This blessing can take place after the prayer after communion (#1723) or at the start of post-Mass refreshments.

MIDDAY PRAYER

The blessing of food can serve as the conclusion to Midday Prayer. This may be welcome by those who were at the Vigil but not at morning Mass, who wish to observe the entire Triduum ritually.

This blessing also can be a service on its own (*Book of Blessings,* #1707–19). This latter option works best when the parish holds a festive Easter dinner—for homeless or elderly people, for those who may otherwise eat alone, for those who prefer to eat their meal and sing their songs in a community bigger than the domestic one. The 20 or so minutes for this prayer and for Easter carol singing would be just the right length of time and would be appreciated by all.

AFTERNOON MASS

Who else can possibly be left to come to Mass? Such is the question every year in parishes that regularly hold Sunday afternoon Masses, and every year some people come. The ministers may be at their wits' ends, but this may be the only paschal experience for many in the congregation.

Those who prepare the liturgy should arrange for musicians and other ministers for this Mass—perhaps those who would have been at the Vigil but have a lighter schedule in the morning. The lectionary suggests a special gospel for this evening, and its content may direct the choice of hymnody. Because these worshipers may be less involved in ecclesial traditions, the most familiar acclamations should be selected.

PASCHAL VESPERS

Easter Evening Prayer closes the Triduum. This is one of the principal Triduum liturgies, yet often it receives short shrift. Many parishioners may be looking for something to do in the spirit of the holiday, an Easter outing, another opportunity to offer praise. As one family exclaimed as it gathered for Paschal Vespers: "We're here for another dose of Easter!"

Catechists should be convinced of the power of this event, convincing the elect, the candidates and their sponsors to mark their crowded calendars and to participate. This is an appropriate way for the parish community and its neophytes to revel in the afterglow of the Vigil. Great liturgy needs "unpacking"—just eavesdrop on people leaving a fine liturgy—and here the church has developed a way to "unpack" the previous night.

The liturgical books and their commentaries (the *Circular Letter,* #98; the *Ceremonial of Bishops,* #371; and the *Liturgy of the Hours,* #213) advocate the restoration of "Baptismal Vespers" to complete the Triduum. If you have not yet implemented this, perhaps this is the season to do so. It requires a well-celebrated and well-attended Triduum before it, but a vibrant celebration of the Triduum without it seems incomplete.

Anscar Chupungco in *Liturgies of the Future* devotes much attention to this celebration and its history (pp. 175–84). It is a stational liturgy, meaning that all move from one location or "station" in the church complex to another. In early Christian and medieval Rome, the Christians, at their cathedral, went in procession from one building to the next, from the eucharistic space to the baptismal space to the chrismation space. "The stational Vespers of Easter Sunday thus can be regarded as a ritual recalling, an *anamnesis in situ,* of the paschal sacraments of baptism, confirmation and eucharist" (p. 179).

This outline is suggested:

- The paschal candle has been kept burning all day. All gather nearby, with booklet and taper.

- Service of light (found, for example, in GIA's *Worship*) begins. All candles of the assembly and of the church are lit from the paschal candle. No electric lights are turned on, to emphasize the gathering shadows of evening.

- Opening dialogue

- Hymn praising Easter light, sung by all. The traditional hymn, "At the Lamb's High Feast," is found with two tunes in *Worship.* "Salzburg" is the more well known, but if most of the folks who attend Paschal Vespers are music readers and/or adventurous souls, consider the strong and festive "Sonne der gerechtigkeit."

- Thanksgiving for light, sung by the cantor. Easter texts are available in GIA's *Praise God in Song.*

- The assembly's candles can be extinguished and any necessary lights turned on for the psalmody. The appointed psalms have wonderful antiphons.

- During the New Testament canticle from Revelation, a congregational alleluia should be repeated often; cantors sing the verses. This is the music to accompany a procession of all to the font. The shortest route does not have to be taken. All follow the incense bearer, a minister bearing the paschal candle and the presider.

- Depending on the size and location of the baptistry, all remain there until after the baptismal commemoration or until the end of the service.

- Hebrews 10:12–14, or the gospel about the Emmaus experience (Lectionary #47, at the end of the Easter pericopes), or a patristic selection from the Easter octave may be read.

- A homily revels in the Easter symbols around us.

- Silence

- Responsorial song or the proper responsory listed at Easter Sunday Evening Prayer

- Prayer over the blessed Easter water (adapted from RCIA, #222D or #222E; or from option C of the sacramentary's sprinkling rite)

- All approach the font and sign themselves and each other. Those unable to reach high enough or stoop low enough can be helped by those nearby. Meanwhile, all sing an antiphon such as the one from the blessing of water at the Vigil.

- The Magnificat is sung with its proper antiphon as all are honored with incense.

- Intercessions can be drawn from the *Liturgy of the Hours.*

- Lord's Prayer

- Prayer of Easter

- Solemn blessing of the day

- Dismissal with the traditional sung double alleluia

- Recessional hymn sung by all. "Come ye faithful, raise the strain" ("Gaudeamus pariter") would provide a rousing conclusion.

EASTERTIME

*The 50 days of Eastertime draw Christian communities into a rich
and colorful world of images. In the Acts of the Apostles, we glimpse the early church with
its resurrection faith and the Spirit's fire. In the book of Revelation, we envision
the New Jerusalem pulling us to itself.
During these days, we do not just commemorate the time
spent by the apostles in the upper room of Jerusalem nor do we just throw a birthday party
for the church. These are the days during which we come to know in a most intense way
that we are Jerusalem. We are church. The images of Eastertime plunge us into the mystery
of Jesus' Spirit, and there we discover that we are the body of Christ!*

Images of the Season

The 50 days from Easter Sunday to Pentecost are celebrated in joyful exultation as one feast day, or better, as one "Great Sunday" (Athanasius). These above all others are the days for the singing of the Alleluia. The Sundays of this season rank as the paschal Sundays, and after Easter Sunday itself, are called the Second, Third, Fourth, Fifth, Sixth and Seventh Sundays of Easter. The period of 50 sacred days ends on Pentecost. (*General Norms for the Liturgical Year and Calendar, #22–23*)

THESE weeks have carried many names over the centuries: "Great Sunday" and the "Fifty Days" (or "Pentecost") have been the most prominent among them. In the churches that keep the season, this is a time of great rejoicing, of singing the alleluia, of decorating with lilies and spring flowers and of listening to the Acts of the Apostles. The Roman Rite's liturgical books call us to recover other elements of the festival, including celebrations of confirmation and first communion during this season, more frequent use of the sprinkling of baptismal water, keeping the paschal candle lit through Ascension to Pentecost, paying more attention to postbaptismal reflections and celebrations (mystagogy), and using lectionary selections fitting the "spirit of joyous faith and sure hope proper to this season" (1981 introduction to the lectionary, #100).

The liturgical reforms of these days have begun their generations-long process of shaping our faith. Yet, back home, the Fifty Days still do not create the same impact on our daily lives as do the Forty Days of Lent. The loss of appreciation for this season is particularly widespread in the United States. Many other Western nations still observe Easter Monday, the Ascension and Pentecost with civic holidays, picnics, festivals and pilgrimages to hilltops. Perhaps this is a by-product of being assimilated into an avowedly interreligious and often areligious nation. Whatever the reasons, church leaders have not always helped to promote the observance of the season; some have introduced extraneous devotions or terminated the season on some other day than Pentecost. A clear understanding of the season's origins, goals and structure is in order.

■ OUR JEWISH HERITAGE: Our Jewish neighbors celebrate a Pentecost festival 50 days after Passover. Its origins and images have shaped all 50 days of the Christian Pentecost.

The "feast of harvest" of the ancient Hebrews also was known as "Shabuoth" or "Weeks." It represented a period of seven weeks (a "week of weeks") plus one day, kept from Passover. The days from Passover to the fiftieth day were sacred. "Pentecost" day itself was the solemn conclusion of the period. (See the varied histories of the liturgy on the resources list, especially Tally, pp. 57–66.) The feast marked the end of the barley harvest, and its ritual customs included special food offerings or "firstfruits." By the time of the first Christians, this festival also had become a remembrance of the giving of the Law on Mount Sinai. (Two classical studies of Jewish festivals are Theodor Gaster's *Festivals of the Jewish Year: A Modern Interpretation and Guide* [New York: Morrow Quill Paperbacks, 1978] and the three-volume work by Eliyahu Kitov, *The Book of Our Heritage* [New York: Feldheim Publishers, 1978].)

This festival developed certain customs over the millennia, some of them influenced by the Christian observances of Pentecost: readings from Ruth, interpretations of the Sinai event that said that God had spoken in a multitude of tongues, the singing of poetry resembling the Book of Revelation and the use of roses and greens to decorate the *bema* (ambo) and the Torah.

Jewish teaching always has insisted that the feasts are not mere recollections. All generations fled from Egypt. All were present at Mount Sinai. All have the promise of sure strength to withstand enemies. All look forward to next year in Jerusalem. Thus the festival of harvest and Law continues to put observant Jews in touch with their very identity as God's creation, as the People of the covenant.

■ OUR CHRISTIAN HERITAGE: "[Pentecost indicates] the season of seven weeks that separated the agricultural feasts of 'Unleavened Bread' and 'Firstfruits.' The experience of Exodus and Sinai gave to these primitive feasts the significance of Passover and Covenant, and to the weeks between the flavor of Lamb and Law, prefigurations of Christ and the Spirit" (Carroll and Halton, p. 295, commenting on a text of Augustine). Images of Christ as paschal Lamb and as firstfruits are the earliest Easter images, spoken of by St. Paul and flowing from these festivals.

By the second century, all Christian communities seem to have included this 50-day period of rejoicing on their festal calendars. The customs and images associated with the days were as much related to Exodus and Sinai as they were to the empty tomb and upper room. The Spirit came on the very day of the Law. It was an octave of Sundays, an "Eighth Day," signifying time beyond the seven days and an experience of Paradise. Ruth and Revelation were proclaimed. Roses and greens decorated the ambo and the scriptures.

Within a few more centuries, however, the unitive nature of these Fifty Days began to lose some of its force. The resurrection, the post-resurrection appearances, the ascension, the waiting in the upper room and the descent of the Holy Spirit all came to be honored successively. In the process of evolution, Pentecost's focus became separated from that of Easter. The union of the death and resurrection of Christ with the outpouring of the Spirit was not denied or completely forgotten, but the community's memory of this unity faded. In popular understanding, Easter and Pentecost became two separate days rather than the two names for the same 50-day period. Still remaining is a popular misconception that paschal baptism into Christ is not enough. Cults spring up telling the faithful baptized that they must "get the Spirit" to be saved. The recent liturgical reforms once more have positioned these two aspects of the saving mystery in seasonal relationship with each other: *Pentecost is Easter.*

■ EASTERTIME IS BOTH EASTER AND PENTECOST: In his masterful work, *The Church's Year of Grace,* Pius Parsch wrote at great length about the two poles of this season (vol. III, pp. 205–6):

> At Easter, Christ, the divine Sun, rose in splendor; it is high noon at Pentecost and he sheds upon his vineyard the bright, warm rays that redden and ripen. Another comparison: At Easter the garden of the church is abloom with beautiful blossoms—Christians newly baptized and confirmed. By Pentecost these blossoms have developed and have matured into fruit, and now hang heavily upon the trees. The Gardener who tends the trees is our Savior Jesus Christ; the sun that ripens the fruit is the Holy Ghost. And a third comparison: At Easter we were born anew as children of God. Like infants we sought our Mother's nourishing milk, the holy eucharist; carefree and happy we grew up in our Father's house. As we became older, Mother Church warned us that the happy time of childhood would pass. She taught us that we were strangers and pilgrims on this earth, that we must suffer and be patient. Now at Pentecost we have come of age.

The metaphors may seem outdated, but the same kind of thoughts can delight us as we prepare the journey from Lamb to firstfruits.

■ EASTER MEANS US: With our Jewish sisters and brothers, we know that our feasts are not just historical recollections. We came from the tomb with Jesus. We received the Spirit. Easter is the neophytes, the newly baptized among us. Easter is the newly confirmed and those who are brought to the table to make their first eucharist. For all who gather in joyous assembly and turn to the Acts of the Apostles, Easter, in all its Fifty Days, is the renewal or enfleshing of the apostolic experience.

■ EASTER MEANS INITIATION: The paschal season, with the Triduum at its source, is profoundly baptismal in its images and rites. The neophytes engage in postbaptismal reflection. Those who were baptized in previous years gather in remembrance of their own initiation. This is the principal time of the year for the confirmation of those baptized as infants. This is the season for the abundant use of water from the font at Sunday gatherings for eucharist.

■ EASTER MEANS THE EUCHARIST: The liturgical books remind us that this is the eucharistic season *par excellence*. Its Sundays are the privileged days for celebrations of first eucharist (*Circular Letter,* #103). See the texts for a "Mass for the Celebration of First Communion" on page 160. These days are also the time for catechesis on the precept (canon 920) concerning paschaltide communion, a time to discuss (or begin) communion from the cup and a premier time for renewed attention to bringing communion to homebound Catholics (*Circular Letter,* #104).

■ EASTER MEANS STILL MORE: Pierre Jounel (in the volume by Martimort in the list of resources) notes that the entrance and communion antiphons provide rich summaries of the basic themes that have evolved in the Eastertime liturgy. After the Easter octave, the entrance antiphons for each day of the week highlight particular motifs: Monday's antiphons say "Christ is risen"; Tuesday's refer to the triumph of the risen Lord at the end of time; Wednesday's are the "psalmody of the redeemed"; Thursday's are celebrations of the new exodus; Friday's, naturally enough, call to mind the saving blood of the risen Christ; Saturday's highlight new life in Jesus. During the week preceding Pentecost, the communion antiphons contain Jesus' promises of the Spirit, sharpening our preparation.

Another accessible resource for imbibing the spirit of Eastertime is found at #303–4 in the lectionary. The verses of the gospel acclamations listed there provide an evocative summary of the scriptures that our Western rites associate with the Fifty Days.

■ STRUCTURE OF THE SEASON: This season is composed of three phases, but these internal variations in rhythm never should eclipse its unity as the great Fifty Days.

- Octave: The first eight days lift us into the alleluia of the next 42 days. The tradition of postbaptismal formation during this time influenced the composition of liturgical texts and the selection of scriptural passages.

- The 31 middle days: The gospels of the Sundays give strong color to Eastertime. The first three Sundays of Easter relate postresurrection appearances. The Fourth Sunday always focuses on the powerful image of the Good Shepherd. The next three Sundays of the season draw from what has come to be known as the "farewell discourse" or "high-priestly prayer" in the gospel according to John. These paschal references and the overall appreciation of the Fifty Days' unity should not allow excess attention to May as "Mary's month." The paschal season can include references and hymns to Mary, but they must never dominate. See the notes at May 1 in the calendar section.

- The final days: Ascension Thursday marks a transition to the next nine days and then to Pentecost itself. Despite old memories, the season does not end here. Over the following nine days and then on Pentecost day itself, liturgical assemblies are invited into the most intense prayer for the Holy Spirit found all year. And Eastertime, the Fifty Days, end there. In previous times, Pentecost day had an octave and Catholics spoke in terms of making their Easter Duty by Trinity Sunday; there was some confusion about when Eastertime ended. No more: Eastertime ends with Pentecost Sunday.

■ EASTERTIME SAINTS: The time frame of this season can differ by up to a month each year, so the saints caught up in it each year change somewhat. No Marian day occurs during this season this year. The apostolic church is represented by Matthias, the one whose very election takes us to the upper room. Ten different martyrs establish a significant presence this year, leaving all who remember them in the paschal context a vivid sense of the resurrection's implications. Twelve other memorials, either obligatory or optional, offer planners the challenge of observing these memorials in the light of the paschal season.

Preparing the Parish

AT first, this season's meanings seem self-evident: Christ is risen! Alleluia! But even a review as brief as the one just at the beginning of this section indicates how much room there is for ongoing reflection and formation on the nature of this season. Few respond to lectures on the liturgical year. Education on the season is best conducted in indirect, pervasive and persuasive ways: carefully scheduling appropriate sacraments and parish socials on the right days, selecting hymns, holding parties for the neophytes, delivering well-crafted homilies, continuing the use of water and taking care that the liturgical decorations remain in place for all Fifty Days.

■ MYSTAGOGY FOR ALL: Eastertime is the season to channel energy and to learn mystery. The process is deceptively simple, beginning with questions prompted by the great spectacle of Easter Eve itself. The paschal liturgy often releases a great flood of whys and hows. Such questioning may provide the groundwork for the paschal seasons in years to come, the groundwork for the catechumenal adventure of others who now are inquirers in the faith. The mystagogical homilies of the Fathers, captured in the Office of Readings in the early days of Eastertime, show how to open the sacramental actions just experienced.

■ CATECHESIS IN CEMETERIES: Adults often are afraid of cemeteries; children learn the fears at an early age. Our Catholic tradition should hear none of this. A parish that has its church building set in the middle of a cemetery possesses both the ideal setting in which to have the funeral Mass and committal rites flow well and the best "vestibule" to the weekly paschal mystery—a burial ground. Because this is important, new parishes should consider taking on all the extra work implied in running an active cemetery.

Lacking such a setting, most parishes bury their dead at one of several nearby cemeteries. A gathering there on Memorial Day weekend, or any day during Eastertime, could use the rites described at November 2 (p. 200). Children may create rubbings or drawings of old graves. Families could walk together to their relatives' tombs,

telling stories of the deceased, perhaps bearing holy water from a parish gathering. In shared actions, prayer, silence and even presentations on local history, the participants come face to face with the "living One."

■ CATECHESIS BEFORE FIRST EUCHARIST: Some children who were baptized as infants may be preparing for communion during these Fifty Days. The final weeks of catechesis can be organized around the paschal mysteries just celebrated. Mystagogy is not only for adults. The children preparing for first eucharist should have been present at the Easter Vigil, and they may well meet sometime thereafter with any children of catechetical age who were initiated at the Vigil.

■ DOMESTIC PRAYER: The examples of domestic prayer given in *Catholic Household Blessings and Prayers* should inspire local leaders to provide similar samples to assist households during this season or, at the very least, to make the book itself available for purchase. Eight different sections beckon each household deeper into the prayer of Eastertime: the blessing at table (p. 84), the blessings of homes (p. 153), the blessing of children before confirmation (p. 230) or before first eucharist (p. 231), a blessing for Mother's Day (p. 197), intercessory prayers for Memorial Day (p. 198) and for the blessing of fields and gardens (p. 166), and a fine prayer for Pentecost day itself (p. 157).

The Mass

INTRODUCTORY RITES

THIS may be the season to replace the penitential rite on Sundays with the thanksgiving over the Easter water (Prayer C in the sacramentary or the example on page 156) and a generous sprinkling (or signing). This rite can use music drawn from the rich Easter and baptismal collections of our tradition. By selecting music that the congregation will sing well and then repeating it each Sunday, you may establish it as the "theme song" of Eastertime. The water, of course, should come from the baptismal water in the parish font.

- **PENITENTIAL RITE:** When a penitential rite is used, forms C*v*, C*vi* and C*vii* in the sacramentary are most appropriate. Also see the example on page 156.

The Gloria should be able to wear well and convey the spirit of this season over the next eight Sundays. Richard Proulx's "Gloria for Eastertime," based on the alleluia from "O filii et filiae," certainly does both and is available for cantor and congregation (GIA, G-3086) or two-part mixed/equal choir and congregation (GIA, G-3087), with optional trumpet fanfare and descant. Another well-crafted piece that involves the assembly in several acclamations throughout is Jones's vibrant "Glory to God" (St. Thomas More Centre/OCP, #7110).

- **OPENING PRAYERS:** Adrian Nocent, in volume 3 of his study on the liturgical year (p. 264 ff.), elaborates on the opening prayers of Eastertime and the great themes of these 50 days. See page 159 for suggested presidential prayer texts for Masses with children during the Easter season.

LITURGY OF THE WORD

- **ACTS OF THE APOSTLES:** The reading from Acts is an ancient way of keeping these days, of celebrating the flowering of Jesus' Spirit in the primitive Christian communities and of drawing our own church life into the paschal fire. This calls for far more than historical commentaries on the missionary journeys of Paul and the election of Matthias. The homilies and ancient commentaries collected in the season's Office of Readings show the way toward the truest paschal sense: The same God who acted then acts now. We are caught up in the same Spirit, the same imperatives for action.

- **REVELATION:** On six out of the eight Easter-time Sundays in Year C, we read from the Book of Revelation—with its images so similar to the ones heard in synagogues during these same weeks. These evocative texts distinguish this year's scriptures and lend a stronger "future" sense to the season. Every year we meet the Risen One. We hear from the "last discourse." We look at the primitive church. But on this one year out of three, we also see a huge crowd from every nation and race; a new Jerusalem; God wiping every tear from our eyes; the tree of life accessible to all. Emboldened by the good news of Mary Magdalene, enflamed by the Spirit, we look with sure hope to the future: "Worthy is the Lamb!"

- **THE DISCOURSE AT THE LAST SUPPER:** The chapters in John making up this powerful and wide-ranging discourse provide the gospel passages for the three Sundays before Pentecost Sunday and for most of the weekdays of these same three weeks.

- **THE PSALM:** Psalm 118 should be given the greatest weight when selecting an Eastertime psalm to use throughout the season. It is the psalm for the grand gospel acclamation at the Easter Vigil, the source for all the gospel acclamation verses for the octave weekdays and the proper psalm of Easter Sunday and its octave. Richard Proulx's setting of Psalm 118 is a classic, appropriately joyful in tone and easily embellished by canonic singing of the refrain and descant; the octavo edition offers parts for handbells, triangle and tambourine (GIA, G-1964). Also consider Marty Haugen's madrigal-like setting in *Psalms for the Church Year,* (GIA), which is effective with choir and cantor or cantor alone.

- **SEQUENCE:** As this season begins, and again as it ends, don't deprive your community of the Easter and Pentecost sequences—marvelous melodies which have evolved throughout their long history into various chant and metrical carol settings. Because these are once-a-year occurrences in the structure of the eucharist, it is easy to forget about their presence until it is too late to select and adequately prepare them in the midst of Triduum rehearsals. The Mode I chant setting of the "Victimae Paschali" text translated by Peter Scagnelli is available in *Worship* (#837); the same hymnal also offers a hymn based on the sequence, "Christ the Lord is risen today." A lively, rhythmic setting of the chant with congregational refrain is "Easter Sequence" (GIA, G-3088), arranged by Richard Proulx.

- **GOSPEL ACCLAMATION:** This is the season to bring out the community's most attractive and captivating alleluias. Again, the exuberant "Celtic Alleluia" (OCP, #7106) with Easter verses serves well, as does the more gently moving Robert Hutmacher "Gospel Processional" (GIA, G-2450). If you have brass available, look at the Biery arrangement of the Vulpius alleluia, "Gospel fanfare for Easter morning" (GIA, G-2719).

The familiar alleluia refrain from "O sons and daughters" is particularly appropriate for this season; see the arrangements by John Schiavone for Easter Sunday, the Ascension and Pentecost (GIA, G-2162) and Marty Haugen's "Easter Alleluia" (*Gather*, GIA), which provides verses for each of the Sunday gospels to the tune of the "O sons and daughters" verses. For fresh, interesting harmonic treatments of familiar gospel acclamations that may be used at any time, see Ed Nowak's "Five Alleluia Settings and a Lenten Acclamation" (GIA, G-3103).

■ HOMILY: The "presence and needs" of the neophytes are to be kept in mind during the preparation of homilies (cf. RCIA, #248). Postbaptismal formation should be undertaken in the context of the season's scriptures as proclaimed and preached in the parish this year. See "What Kind of Eastertime Homilies Does the Catechumenate Want?" by James Telthorst in *Parish Catechumenate: Pastors, Presiders, Preachers* (Chicago: LTP, 1988).

■ DISMISSAL OF CATECHUMENS: While we pray for and work toward the full incorporation of the neophytes into the life of the church, many communities also are blessed by the presence of catechumens who continue to prepare for paschal initiation—perhaps in 1993. Their dismissal and the continued dialogue with them is as important now as it will be next Lent.

■ GENERAL INTERCESSIONS should take on a seasonal cast—finding the images to express our dependence on God in the Easter metaphors of sheep and pasture, new life and fire. Form 8 in the appendix to the sacramentary is a model. It is not explicit enough, however, in praying for the neophytes. Other examples for the season begin on page 156.

If the parish follows a strong tradition of sung intercessory prayer, the Eastertime responses to the intercessions in the *Liturgy of the Hours* are fitting. Choose one and sing it for all of the Fifty Days. Some of the best are:

- "Victorious King, hear our prayer" (Easter Sunday, Evening Prayer II)

- "Send forth your Spirit and make the whole world new" (Pentecost, Evening Prayer I)

- "Lord, make the whole world new" (Pentecost, Morning Prayer)

LITURGY OF THE EUCHARIST

■ EUCHARISTIC PRAYER: Along with the unity of the season achieved by vesture, ritual patterns and musical acclamations, the choice of prayer texts is crucial. The Eucharistic Prayer for Masses with Children III provides three variable parts for this season. The words and the format with more frequent acclamations may make it a candidate for continual use in a parish with large numbers of children.

Five prefaces are designated for the Fifty Days, with two more added to the list during the last days (Ascension) and with one more possible for Pentecost. Choose just one or two to use, because a good text will continue—or just begin—to reach us with this repetition. Later in the prayer, inserts are provided for the octave, for the Ascension, for Pentecost (all in Prayer I) and for Masses at which infant baptisms may be celebrated (in Prayers I–IV).

This is the time to bring out your parish's most festive setting of the eucharistic acclamations. Two settings that work well in this springtime of the church year are "Festival Eucharist" by Richard Proulx (*Worship* or G-1960), which adapts well to Masses with choir or with cantor alone, and Paul Inwood's "Coventry Acclamations" (St. Thomas More Centre/OCP, #7117), which works best when a choir is available. Brass and percussion parts are available for both.

■ COMMUNION RITE: See page 159 for suggestions for texts that bring an Eastertime spirit to the communion rite. For the communion procession, the Joseph Gelineau setting of Psalm 136 (GIA, *24 Psalms and a Canticle,* G-1424) or the buoyant setting in *Psalms for All Seasons* (NPM) by Ronald Nelson would be wonderful processional music. The two Taizé ostinati, "Surrexit Christus" and "Christus Resurrexit" (GIA, *Music from Taizé,* Volume II, G-2778), employ segments of Psalm 118 sung by the cantor, answered by the assembly in short, singable acclamations. The stories of Jesus' appearances to the disciples are the inspiration for Bob Hurd's "In the breaking of the bread" (OCP, #8776), and Bernadette Farrell's "Bread of Life" (OCP, #7152) features an inviting antiphon and reinforces both the paschal images of life and death and the unity of those who approach the Lord's table.

CONCLUDING RITE

■ BLESSING: The sacramentary's section on solemn blessings contains several texts that may be used this season. Blessing 7 may be memorized by the presider and used throughout the Fifty Days or other texts may be selected on certain days—#6 on Easter Sunday, #8 on the Ascension, #9 on Pentecost.

■ DISMISSAL: While the deacon (or in the deacon's absence, the presider) can modify the "Go in peace" given in the sacramentary—and should do so in harmony with the season— these great Fifty Days follow their own custom: the addition of a double alleluia after the words of dismissal and after the assembly's response. Musical settings are suggested at the end of the section on the Easter Vigil in this book. This familiar and valuable custom is called for on every day of the Easter octave. An often overlooked rubric calls for its appearance again at the end of the Pentecost eucharist and at the very conclusion to the season—the last lines of Evening Prayer II on Pentecost. Other traditions suggest continuing the chant throughout all the Fifty Days.

MUSIC

Easter hymns are to be sung for all of the season, not just for Easter Sunday. Remember the power of tunes that are associated with this season; too often our vision of Easter hymnody does not include tunes such as "Gaudeamus pariter" or "Puer nobis" unless we were privileged to grow up in a parish with a good tradition of hymnody. Seeking out these classic tunes for the seasons and feasts of the church year and planting seeds for future generations of worshipers is a large part of our mission as liturgical leaders in today's church.

"O filii et filiae," mentioned earlier as the basis for gloria and gospel acclamation settings, is familiar as "O sons and daughters," which retells the Easter story (including Thomas's doubting), interrupted constantly by alleluias.

"Puer nobis" dances brightly as "That Easter day with joy was bright"; don't miss the opportunity to enhance its character with hand-drum and finger cymbals.

"Duke Street" is one of the most noble of the Easter melodies; coupled with the text "I know that my Redeemer lives," it is available in many

concertato settings (festive arrangements that heighten a hymn by various musical means including choral verses, instruments and interludes, while still involving the congregation in singing the familiar text and tune).

"Gaudeamus pariter" has never been more enjoyable than when it is coupled with John M. Neale's translation of a text taken from John of Damascus and Exodus 15. Who could resist singing of Israel being led through the Red Sea "with unmoistened foot"?

"Come, ye faithful, raise the strain" cleverly weaves springtime and resurrection images. And because the melody lines are in AABA form, there are only two lines of music to learn.

"Llanfair" is a particularly easy tune to learn for the same reason; it also is quite serviceable as an Easter hymn, "Christ the Lord is risen today," and as a hymn for Ascension, "Hail the day that sees him rise" (both are Charles Wesley texts). Even assemblies just beginning to sing hymns (as well as young children who struggle with too many words) can sing the alleluias at the end of each line.

"Noel nouvelet" is a sprightly French carol also associated with Christmas. Recalling that the "Christmas" word "noel" is a cry of "new birth," the marriage of this tune to the text "Now the green blade rises" with the recurring phrase, "Love is come again like wheat arising green," is a happy one.

Other Ritual Prayers and Sacraments

LITURGY OF THE HOURS

SATURDAY night resurrection vigils can become part of the parish's liturgical life. If we look back at the Easter Vigil and ask ourselves why the church was not bursting at the seams with attendance, perhaps one answer lies in the yearlong practice of the parish regarding vigils, especially the vigil of the resurrection that should be part of our keeping of every Lord's Day. In other words, the "Great Sunday" of the year can be even greater if all the Sundays of the year are kept well. Appendix I of this season's volume (II) of the *Liturgy of the Hours* includes special texts for vigils for each Eastertime Sunday and for the Ascension. See the notes at Pentecost on page 153 regarding special provisions for its preeminent vigil.

COMMUNAL ANOINTING OF THE SICK

When the sick are anointed or when a community gathers to share communion with homebound parishioners during Eastertime, the scriptural passages from the Acts of the Apostles listed in the rite are appropriate, as is the Johannine selection on the Good Shepherd. See page 160 for suggested seasonal adaptations for the introduction/reception of the sick and the prayer after anointing.

MARRIAGES

As in the celebrations of the anointing of the sick at Mass, one of the scriptures given in the marriage rite can be used on the Sundays of Eastertime, but all other texts of the day draw the celebration into the great Fifty Days. On Easter Sunday, on the Ascension and on Pentecost, no such substitution is permitted. The season should press couples and ministers to look at the passages from First John (lectionary #775.8, #775.9), Revelation (#775.10) and the latter parts of John (#778.8–778.10).

FUNERALS

The first days of the octave may be marked by eucharistic celebrations with the people who buried their loved ones during the Triduum. The scriptures of these days can serve well at these Masses, linking the bereaved to the paschal mystery in the most explicit of terms. The presidential prayers from Funeral Mass C were composed for the Easter season. Because the liturgy will not be concluded by a procession to the cemetery, this is a great opportunity for the parish to provide food and hospitality.

Funerals later in the season may draw from the readings of the day as well. Within the *Order of Christian Funerals,* the passages from Acts and Revelation and the gospel about Emmaus (Luke 24:13–35) stand out for their Eastertime resonance. Our tradition does not allow the celebration of funeral Masses on the Sundays of the season or on the Ascension.

OTHER RITES AND BLESSINGS

■ BLESSING OF HOMES: The document that in 1955 brought about the reformation of Holy Week included a strong call for the continuance of blessing homes in paschaltide. More recent documents and the *Book of Blessings* (chapter 50) have repeated the call and noted that such blessings should come after Easter Sunday, not before (and certainly not on Holy Saturday). If the blessing of homes is not a practice in your area, it may be placed on the wish list for this year or next. It involves a lot of work, but it does situate the pastoral visitation of homes in a seasonal context. Large parishes may choose to split the households and neighborhoods between a blessing at Epiphany and one during the great Fifty Days. All pastoral ministers can be involved. Indeed, the order of blessing provides alternatives for a lay minister. No matter how large the parish, this is never to be a quick "in and out" visit.

■ BLESSING OF GARDENS, FIELDS, ORCHARDS, FLOCKS, SEEDS: Catholic communities that are linked closely to the cycles of natural life find a wonderful treasury of blessings available to them during springtime. Rogation days were customarily celebrated on April 25 and on the three days just before the Ascension. They were times for fervent prayer for growth and fruitfulness. In the *Book of Blessings,* chapter 26 contains an order for the blessing of fields and flocks. Chapter 27 provides a blessing of seeds at planting time. These orders may be supplemented by resources in the sacramentary and lectionary: Masses and Prayers for Various Needs and Occasions, 26. For Productive Land (#851–55 in the lectionary). Other rural-life-oriented prayer materials, including *Rural Life Prayers, Blessings and Liturgies* (1988, Victoria M. Tufano, editor), are available from the National Catholic Rural Life Conference, 4625 N.W. Beaver Drive, Des Moines IA 50310.

■ MEMORIALS OF INITIATION: Our heritage and our liturgical books encourage the observance of each person's anniversary of baptism.

> On the anniversary of their baptism the neophytes should be brought together in order to give thanks to God, to share with one another their spiritual experiences, and to renew their commitment. (RCIA, #250)

This presumes that contact is kept with each year's neophytes, an embarrassing omission in too many communities. The principal anniversary of Easter baptism is each year's Easter. A person baptized in the Vigil of 1986, when asked, "When were you baptized?" probably will say "Easter." She or he may not even remember that Easter was March 30. So the renewal of baptismal promises at Easter is the principal way to observe the anniversary, even for those baptized on dates other than Easter.

Yet the intent of the RCIA directive previously quoted includes sharing beyond the confines of a liturgy. One option is a common anniversary gathering on some day early in the season—after evening prayer on the octave Sunday may be just right. The party also could be scheduled on the parish's titular solemnity if the title is an Eastertime saint such as Catherine of Siena, Pius V or Boniface.

The Worship Environment

The Fifty Days should look and feel like the great festival they are. Those who prepare the environment might consider these traditions.

■ THE FONT: Our tradition calls for using the water blessed at the Vigil throughout the season. Parishes with fonts in separate places sometimes display a large bowl of water somewhere near the front of the church. (Too often this looks like a punch bowl and not a sacred vessel.) It would be far more sensible to keep attention fixed on the font no matter where it is located. During the sprinkling rite, maintain some association with the font, even if that means drawing Easter water from it and then carrying this water into the assembly for the prayer of thanksgiving over the water.

■ PLACE FOR THE NEOPHYTES: The newly baptized and their godparents should occupy special places in the assembly throughout the Easter season. Perhaps special seats could be reserved for them near the candle and ambo.

■ SMELLING EASTER: Certain smells plunge people right into a season. Smell the lilies? It must be Easter. Smell the evergreens? Christmas. Ah, the roses! Our wedding anniversary. The

dressed turkey filling the kitchen air? You know what day it is! Many of the churches with whom we are in communion never have given up this appreciation for the olfactory. Parishes can respect this sensual dynamic and allow the memories to help frame certain seasons. For the Easter season, "gardenia" incense (available from Orthodox Church suppliers) is most traditional. For Pentecost, in Jewish and Christian festivals, the smell of roses has priority. Planners can chart out such a list for the whole year and then pass on this tradition. The selection process, of course, should not be arbitrary. Think of the liturgical seasons and the natural seasons, and consult Orthodox neighbors about their fixed traditions.

■ THE EASTER CANDLE should be purchased or commissioned before Christmas. Most Easter candles are too small for the buildings they illuminate, too short for the times they burn. The candle holder often is the limiting agent. Even if it is too late for this year, begin looking for a stand with the right scale and style for your building. It must be right for the Easter Vigil, for the Fifty Days in the main worship area and then for the rest of the year in the baptistry. Some places, faced with a huge worship space and a small baptistry area, use two different stands for the same candle.

The wax nails included with most paschal candles are just a colorful way to attach the grains of incense, which are the real symbols. The incense grains can be seen better and will be truer to their form if capable parishioners prepare the five insertions by attaching chunks of incense (tiny granules will not do) onto five large pins or by shaping the incense into a point sharp enough for insertion and adhesion.

When baptistries were in separate rooms, the candle was placed where everyone could see it during all of Eastertime; specifically, it was placed so that the gospel could be read by its light. Or, place the candle in the center of the assembly—the Risen One in our midst.

Wherever it is placed, it should be kept lit for every gathering this season. Also, it should be shining brightly even before people gather: Once the candle is lit on Easter Eve, it is never extinguished, at least publicly. Other candles can be lit from it, a gracious gesture at the beginning of any liturgy.

■ FLOWERS: In an interesting parallel, synagogues follow a long tradition of using lilies for their Fifty Days celebration. Three other traditions of the festival of "Weeks" may inspire Catholic decorators—not so that parishioners can be told that we are doing such and such because Jews do it, but because the ancient traditions capture some of the same ambience the Fifty Days should have for us. Texts highlight the apple tree with its beautiful blossoms (the tree is said to bear fruit 50 days after it blossoms); branches, boughs and greens are placed about the *bema* (ambo); and Torah scrolls are decorated with roses.

Those who prepare the liturgy should consider the entire worship space throughout the period from the Gloria of the Easter Vigil through Pentecost Sunday. Even if certain flowers will need to be replaced during the Fifty Days, the overall plan should be consistent.

■ OTHER DECORATIONS: If the worship space will be decorated with banners that employ Eastertime images, they should not duplicate the imagery already present in the worship environment, such as water, candle, font, cup, book. It would be better to illustrate the paschal stories: the creation, Jonah, the Exodus, the giving of the Law at Sinai, Daniel in the lions' den, the three youths in the fiery furnace, Esther and Mordechai. Any of this large-scale decoration should direct attention to—and not draw attention from—the altar, ambo, chair, font, paschal candle and cross. Keep most of it out of the vicinity of the altar; use decoration to grace the assembly's space. Portals, walls, interior floors and exterior sidewalks and walkways are too often ignored as potential places for art that unifies the people and place.

Outdoors, the whole world should know of our joy with springtime wreaths on the church doors, banners and bunting merrily waving. A chalk drawing of the Exodus or of the Jonah story on the front plaza will not soon be forgotten.

■ VESTURE: There should not be one set of vesture for Easter Sunday and then other white fare for the rest of the season. Let the clothing itself say that these days are one unit of time and celebration. The red days provide exceptions: apostle Matthias, numerous martyrs and, of course, Pentecost. This red vesture may be unique to Eastertime, not the more somber vesture of the passion.

Ideally, whatever fabrics and trim patterns were chosen for vesture, altar cloths and book covers for the previous Sundays of Eastertime can be reflected in the Pentecost vesture. Only the colors of these fabrics would change, thereby establishing a strong connection.

April

MON 20 #261 white **Easter Monday** SOLEMNITY

■ EASTER OCTAVE: The most venerable of the traditions of Easter week is the daily gathering of the newly baptized in their baptismal robes for mystagogical preaching and eucharist. Godparents are to be there, too. That implies the gathering of a parish assembly on each of these eight days. While such a tradition may not be possible in many parishes, alternatives may be considered: a gathering of the neophytes with those baptized on previous Easters, evening eucharists with extended mystagogical sharing or neighborhood suppers with the neophytes of each section of the parish.

Even parishes without neophytes should consider ways to enter into the intense prayer of rejoicing. Like the disciples on the road to Emmaus, all of us are called to declare, "Were not our hearts burning inside us?" We need opportunities to savor the experience, to retell the stories of how this local church passed through the Triduum. Liturgical planners and volunteers, at least, should gather to swap stories, make notes for next year's Easter planning, sing Easter carols and treat each other to Easter foods.

For Morning Prayer and Evening Prayer, the same psalms, canticles and antiphons are used from Easter Sunday all through the week—an extraordinary departure from the usual variety and a noble attempt to let us all internalize the songs of Easter.

■ THIS DAY IN THE LITURGY: The scriptures for this day indicate the direction that they will take throughout the week. The first reading from Acts begins a semicontinuous reading of that early Christian document. The gospels this week recount the appearances of the risen Lord. The gospel acclamation verse will repeat the refrain of Easter's *Liturgy of the Hours* all week, "This is the day the Lord has made; let us rejoice and be glad."

The patristic reading in the Office of Readings is as fine an invitation to this season as one might hope for: Melito of Sardis calls from the second century, inviting us to the paschal Lamb.

TUE 21 #262 white **Easter Tuesday** SOLEMNITY

Once more we meet the protoevangelist, Mary Magdalene. The apostles are remembered as the prime evangelizers in the primitive church—witness Peter in today's Acts. But the role of women as the first evangelists cannot be eclipsed. The gospels consistently place the women, particularly Mary Magdalene, as the first ones at the tomb, as the first to see the risen Lord and as the first to carry the news back to the disciples.

WED 22 #263 white **Easter Wednesday** SOLEMNITY

Many still observe Earth Day, which is meant to be a consciousness raiser for environmental issues. The work that must be done is enormous, and liturgical planners make a profound contribution. The full observance of the paschal season—from the creation story at the Easter Vigil through the Revelation visions of our earth recast—engenders respect for all living things.

THU 23 #264 white **Easter Thursday** SOLEMNITY

The second reading from the Office of Readings today provides a model for mystagogy and homilies. It speaks directly to the neophytes and to all of us: "You were led into the font. . . ."

FRI 24 #265 white **Easter Friday** SOLEMNITY

The Jerusalem Catecheses in the Office of Readings continue to tell us how to interpret the Pasch— "We were transformed into the likeness of the Son of God."

Despite ongoing secularization, this Friday is a favorite day for "Easter hikes" or pilgrimages in certain sections of Europe. Residents walk for hours, with banners flying and hymns filling the air, to devotional shrines and traditional assembly places. Church communities in the United States would do well to collaborate with each other, allowing their diverse congregations to converge into a bright and joyous throng for at least one day of the Fifty. The diocesan assembly with the neophytes may be one such occasion.

SAT 25 #266 white **Easter Saturday** SOLEMNITY

Today the Jerusalem Catecheses let us find deeper appreciation for the eucharist: It is the Easter sacrament, the fullness of initiation. This day's intercessions may well include prayers for our Orthodox neighbors, who begin their celebration of Easter tonight.

☼26 #46 white
Second Sunday of Easter

Orthodox Pascha. ▪ Pray in union with all the Eastern Christians who have just been up all night, keeping the most holy night this week. In many parts of the world, this Sunday is the traditional day for children to receive their first communion.

▪ TITLES FOR THIS DAY: This Sunday was called, in the former calendar, the *Dominica in albis,* literally, "Sunday in whites." The neophytes wore their baptismal garments for the whole of what some Eastern churches call "Bright Week," laying them aside after Vespers today.

Another of the old designations for this day, "Low Sunday," often left us with the wrong impression. The words "high" and "low" meant beginning and end (of the octave), not big and little. What is most important about today is that everything of the exuberance and majesty of Easter Sunday is also part of this Eastertime Sunday—and of all the Easter days until Pentecost. Many parishes with strong ethnic traditions observe this "second Easter Sunday" as a day for a parish potluck supper where folks bring ethnic specialties—a type of parishwide Easter breakfast.

▪ LECTIONARY: The gospel on this Octave Sunday is the same every year. The repetition shows the level of importance that our tradition assigns this story. The first two readings are different each year, coloring each year's reception of the Thomas story. When carrying these passages to the homiletic preparation desk, bring the passage from Augustine in today's Office of Readings, too. The bishop of Hippo gives a marvelous mystagogy on this octave day.

▪ INTERCESSIONS: While reviewing the petitions and format outlined on page 156, planners for this Sunday should consider adding petitions that unite Catholic congregations with Jews everywhere. In these days after Passover, and especially on this week's Holocaust Memorial Day, they and we should remember the unspeakable tragedies of half a century ago. Christians can pray for the victims and their survivors, for vigilance against indifference and for common fidelity to our loving God.

27 #267 white
Easter Weekday

Now that we have moved from the octave days into the central section of Eastertime, the semicontinuous readings from Acts are joined by a similarly progressive unfolding of John's gospel.

▪ THE WEEK AHEAD: If local communities have decided to keep the optional memorial of Joseph the Worker with its special readings, then this *cursus* of Acts and John will be interrupted. The Acts passages for Wednesday through Friday tell the story of the apostles' trial before the Sanhedrin. Without Friday's passage, the congregation would not hear the testimony of Gamaliel and the resolution of the story. The Friday selection can be appended to Thursday's reading.

28 #268 white
Easter Weekday

Peter Chanel, priest and martyr, optional memorial/red. ▪ This is the first saint we meet in Easter this year. He stands in a glorious tradition of paschal recollections of the blood of the Lamb.

One of the first Marists, Peter was martyred on Futuna (now an overseas territory of France between Fiji and Samoa) in 1841. His proper opening prayer is a fine example of keeping a saint's memory in Eastertime. The specificity of the references is rare, for Easter can vary by as much as a month either way. Only a few saints' days are perpetually within Easter. Up until the most recent calendar reforms, his feast was kept liturgically only in Australia, New Zealand and in Marist communities. His inclusion now in the universal calendar is one of the clearest examples of the Vatican striving to include saints from all the regions of the world.

▪ MARTYRS IN EASTER: For centuries, the "Commons" Masses for the various types of saints have included "Masses in the Easter Season" for martyrs (as well as for Mary). This was a deliberate attempt by our ancestors in liturgical work to show the intimate relationship between the Lamb and the martyrs.

Ten martyrs appear in Easter this year, some of them as optional memorials. Observance of many of these days, especially Peter Chanel and Charles Lwanga (June 3), brings their special paschal witness to Africa and Oceania of the last century. The good news went to the farthest corners of the world through all the centuries.

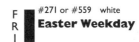

**W
E 29** #269   white
D **Catherine of Siena,
virgin and doctor**
MEMORIAL

This fourteenth-century mystic and recently declared doctor of the church lived an extraordinary life. She wrote extensively about the cross, negotiated secular and ecclesiastical treaties, encouraged the pope to move from Avignon to Rome and turned people away from an anti-pope. When declaring her a doctor, Pope Paul VI termed her "the mystic of Christ's Mystical Body." He also noted how she encouraged internal reforms that were basic to any external ones (see the *Documents on the Liturgy,* #3963–65).

■ OFFICE OF READINGS: The Easter message of Catherine is well evoked in the excerpt included in her Office of Readings. In the seasonal texts for today, the second reading of the Office of Readings is well worth the time of all liturgical planners. This gem of an Easter sermon by Leo the Great speaks of how "God took our human nature into so close a union with himself" and of how "all that the Son of God did and taught for the world's reconciliation is not for us simply a matter of past history." It also highlights the union of all the baptized with the martyrs of paschaltide.

**T
H 30** #270   white
U **Easter Weekday**

Pius V, pope, optional memorial / white. ▪ This observance recommends itself because Pius was the pope who implemented the decisions of the Council of Trent, publishing a Roman Catechism, the Breviary and the Missal used for 400 years until 1970. Our Eastertime saints must be real people who performed real work for our

resurrection faith to be concrete. (It also helps to know that our ritual books do not just fall out of the sky.)

■ HOLOCAUST MEMORIAL DAY: Today is Yom Hashoah, the Day of the Destruction. On the Jewish calendar, this occurs 12 days after Passover. Certainly the intercessions today should include prayers for the victims and their survivors. Catechists can find material for their curriculum planning in LTP's *When Catholics Speak about Jews.* See also LTP's *Prayers of Jews and Christians Together* and *From Desolation to Hope: An Interreligious Holocaust Memorial Service.*

If the parish has made any efforts to restore ember days, then this might be one that is kept each year. Within the Fifty Days of Eastertime there would be something broken — a fast day, a mourning day, a day for renunciation of evil. In the midst of Easter it would have to raise up every question the Holocaust itself raises.

> Reflection upon the *Shoah* shows us to what terrible consequences the lack of faith in God and a contempt for humanity created in his image can lead. There is no doubt that the sufferings endured by the Jews . . . are today a warning, a witness and a silent cry before all peoples and all nations . . . and also for the Catholic Church a motive of sincere sorrow, especially when one thinks of the indifference and sometimes resentment which, in particular historical circumstances, have divided Jews and Christians. (Pope John Paul II, 1987 letter to the president of the National Conference of Catholic Bishops, reprinted in the *Newsletter of the Bishops' Committee on the Liturgy.*)

May

F #271 or #559   white
R
I **Easter Weekday**

Joseph the Worker, optional memorial / white. ▪ May Day celebrations originated many centuries ago and became linked to the medieval custom of dedicating the month of May to Mary. Her *cultus* was seen as a proper antidote to old Celtic, Roman and German springtime rites. Many nations have seen May Day become better known as Labor Day over the past century. Customs from both titles endure. For example, while workers march in the avenues and effectively close Paris every year, one can go into any metro station or provincial back road and buy lilies of the valley to wear.

■ ST. JOSEPH: Pope Pius XII, in 1955, declared this a day in honor of Joseph the Worker. This now has been reduced to the level of an optional memorial and, unless the parish's title or religious community links it to Joseph, it would seem better to move the proper texts to our own Labor Day in September.

■ FRIDAY IN EASTERTIME: As will also be the case on some other Eastertime Fridays, the patristic reading in the Office of Readings is a fine meditation on the tree of life. It shows how the images of every Friday can be unfolded in an Easter style.

■ MARY, QUEEN OF APOSTLES: May, for many people, still signals a time of greater intensity for devotion to Mary. The liturgy neither encourages nor discourages this designation, but such *cultus* should never eclipse the paschal nature of all Fifty Days.

In the worship environment, even the desire of some faithful to highlight a statue of Mary during this month may compromise the season's visual unity. If the Marian shrine is to be highlighted, it should be done for all 50 days.

Devotional gatherings such as May processions and May crownings should not take place on the Ascension (or on Pentecost when this falls in May). On other days, participants should be led into an Eastertime praise of Mary: praying the "Regina caeli" instead of the Angelus, singing Easter carols (such as "Be joyful, Mary, heavenly queen") and remembering the witness of Mary praying with the apostles before Pentecost. This last image is really the most traditional way to enter into the *cultus* of Mary in the Fifty Days: invoking her as an instrument of the Spirit's fire. While votive Masses generally are restricted to Marian shrines in Eastertime, prayer texts for other devotions can be drawn from the Mass of "Queen of the Apostles" in the *Collection of Masses of the Blessed Virgin Mary*.

SAT 2 #272 white
Athanasius, bishop and doctor
MEMORIAL

His name means "the deathless one," and it was Athanasius who first called the Fifty Days of Easter, "The Great Sunday." Athanasius is an *alter Christus,* another Christ, whose very name speaks to us of Easter. The prayers are proper to the saint, but the readings are of the season.

☼3 #49 white
Third Sunday of Easter

See pages 138–41 regarding Eastertime ritual patterns, which by now should be familiar to the congregation. Today's gospel is another account of a postresurrection appearance, allowing homiletic reflections to build on last week's experience.

The passage from Justin in the Office of Readings provides a fascinating account of Sunday eucharist in his second-century community. Reread it whenever you wonder if all the effort put into Sunday is worth it!

MON 4 #273 white
Easter Weekday

The semicontinuous proclamation of Acts brings us to the martyrdom of Stephen. The first readings today and for the next few days let us add his witness to the martyrs who followed him and whose memory is kept during the Easter season. The resurrection and paschal faith produce far more than lilies. They issue forth in blood and sacrifice.

TUE 5 #274 white
Easter Weekday

WED 6 #275 white
Easter Weekday

THU 7 #276 white
Easter Weekday

FRI 8 #277 white
Easter Weekday

The antiphons given today in the sacramentary for the introductory rites and for communion are the kind of brief lines that can be learned "by heart" to repeat over and over on Fridays, especially during Eastertime. The sermon by Ephrem in the Office of Readings should inspire any homilist on any Friday.

SAT 9 #278 white
Easter Weekday

☼10 #52 white
Fourth Sunday of Easter

■ THE GOOD SHEPHERD: Before the reforms of 20 years ago, "Good Shepherd Sunday" was celebrated one week earlier. Now the presence of shepherd-centered readings and prayers makes this halfway point in the season a time for entering deeply into this central paschal image. The *Liturgy of the Hours,* the presidential prayers and the scriptures all help us appreciate that the Good Shepherd image is not a romantic one. This is the shepherd who lays down his life. Faced with contemporary wolves and hirelings, we, too, must find life only in the Good Shepherd.

■ SACRAMENTS IN EASTERTIME: This Fourth Sunday of Easter would be fitting as the parish's annual first communion day. Both confirmation and first eucharist deserve celebrations on Eastertime Sundays.

■ MOTHER'S DAY: An intercession can be included today for all people who are examples of a mother's love. Three sample intercessions are found in the *Book of Blessings*, #1727. The prayer over the people for the conclusion of Mass today from the *Book of Blessings*, #1728, seems just right as a recognition of this day's cultural power and as a "liturgical" view of motherhood. *Catholic Household Blessings and Prayers* (p. 197) provides a similar prayer for use at home.

M O N 11 #279 white
Easter Weekday

Today's gospel continues the focus on the Good Shepherd.

■ THE WEEK AHEAD: The seasonal progression will be interrupted by Matthias's feast on Thursday. The superseded texts can be added to Wednesday or Friday, but their omission will provide no difficulty in understanding the narrative of Acts and the preaching of Jesus in John.

T U E 12 #280 white
Easter Weekday

Nereus and Achilleus, martyrs, optional memorial / red. ■ *Pancras, martyr, optional memorial / red.* ■ Parishes may well observe one of these optional memorials, linking Easter to the Roman persecutions of the first centuries. Parsch (vol. III, p. 286) and others pass down the traditional identification of Pancras (Pancratius) with fidelity to oaths. The origins of this rest in the mists of history, but we are sure that the "station" or place where the pope celebrated Mass on the Second Sunday of Easter was at the sixth-century basilica dedicated to Pancras. There the neophytes were exhorted to remain faithful to their baptismal promises.

W E D 13 #281 white
Easter Weekday

T H U 14 #564 red
Matthias, apostle
FEAST

Matthias's election was part of the disciples' prayer and action immediately before Pentecost. John Chrysostom comments on it in the Office of Readings. It is a fine feast—and a great coincidence—for these days when we are united with Mary and the apostles in prayer.

F R I 15 #283 white
Easter Weekday

Isidore, optional memorial / white. ■ His memorial was added to the U.S. calendar by the request of the National Catholic Rural Life Conference. This twelfth-century Spanish farmer (and patron of Madrid) should be observed especially by those communities in rural areas and those affirming their Hispanic roots.

S A T 16 #284 white
Easter Weekday

☀ 17 #55 white
Fifth Sunday of Easter

We hear Christ's commandment of love. It is not the love of MTV, nor the love expressed on greeting cards. It is the love of enduring despite tension, of keeping the commandments, of laying down one's life. Our Easter alleluias are born from pain and endurance, trusting in the indwelling of Jesus' Spirit.

This gospel selection marks the first of three Sundays when the gospel reading is from the "farewell discourse" in John. The Eastertime ritual patterns continue and should be familiar to all by now. As the homilist interprets the gospel's discourse in the context of these liturgical experiences, some deeper appreciation of this section of John is in order.

Two of the more important commentaries are found on pages 581–782 in Raymond Brown's *The Gospel According to John (XIII–XXI)* Anchor Bible 29A (Garden City NY: Doubleday, 1970) and on pages 972–79 in Pheme Perkins's "The Gospel According to John" in *The New Jerome Biblical Commentary* (Englewood Cliffs NJ: Prentice Hall, 1990). They show how the "Last Discourse" exemplifies the literary practice of attributing farewell speeches to great heroes. They also indicate that this discourse is really a collection of several that later were combined by John. Because of this, there is no apparent connection of the content from Sunday to Sunday nor on the weekdays these weeks.

Brown gives an important reminder about the homilist's task of interpretation and inspiration:

> The Last Discourse is best understood when it is the subject of prayerful meditation; and scientific analysis does not really do justice to this work of genius. Just as a great painting loses its beauty when the individual parts are studied under a microscope, so the necessary discussion of the composition and division of the Last Discourse may tend to mar the overall realization that one is dealing with a masterpiece. (p. 582)

MON 18 #285 white
Easter Weekday

John I, pope and martyr, optional memorial / red. ▪ If the local community has been observing the various martyrs' days in Easter, then this sixth-century pope will offer his own witness of standing up to civil rulers.

TUE 19 #286 white
Easter Weekday

WED 20 #287 white
Easter Weekday

Bernardine of Siena, priest, optional memorial / white. ▪ This saint was famous for his advocacy of devotion to the holy name of Jesus (see the proper opening prayer) and for his popularizing of decorated "IHS" (Jesus) standards. He knew the power of signs!

THU 21 #288 white
Easter Weekday

FRI 22 #289 white
Easter Weekday

SAT 23 #290 white
Easter Weekday

✸ 24 #58 white
Sixth Sunday of Easter

Eastertime patterns continue and are joined by powerful scriptures: The Council of Jerusalem is described, the new Jerusalem and the Lamb are praised and the gospel leads us into the image of the Spirit.

Gabe Huck presents homiletic ideas on these readings in LTP's *When Catholics Speak about Jews,* pages 60–61. Preaching during these weeks of Eastertime is sometimes made more difficult by homilists' expectations that they must explain the Council of Jerusalem or tell their listeners the varied meanings of the new Jerusalem and Lamb. The late Orthodox liturgist Alexander Schmemann reminded us that the homily is not supposed to be about the Good News. The homily is supposed to be the Good News. We Christians are not dispensers of information but announcers of news hot with the fire of the Spirit, the fire of true evangelization.

MON 25 #291 white
Easter Weekday

Venerable Bede, priest and doctor, optional memorial / white. ▪ *Gregory VII, pope, optional memorial / white.* ▪ *Mary Magdalene de Pazzi, virgin, optional memorial / white.* ▪ This day provides complicated choices for liturgical planners.

▪ EASTERTIME SAINTS: Religious orders of women and, of course, all Carmelites, probably will observe Mary Magdalene de Pazzi. The other two options have strong reasons commending their selection—the English historian and doctor (the only one of our language) or one of the greatest reformers and popes. The choice will be difficult—consider celebrating them in alternating years.

▪ MEMORIAL DAY: This year in the United States these optional memorials may be passed over in favor of prayer texts bringing Memorial Day into the rite. This national holiday has been turned by some into All Souls' Day in spring. In fact, it often gets far more attention than All Souls as a day to remember the dead—an enormous loss within our tradition. Memorial Day was born after the Civil War in a spirit that connected remembering those who died in the war to the desperate need to forgive and to rebuild. Many families in this country mourn their war dead; they need to forgive and to rebuild what war has destroyed. We seem to have forgotten so much of our history, including the origins—and the necessity—of Memorial Day.

The scriptures of the weekday in Ordinary Time confront the Memorial Day congregation with promises of hardship and with the sure hope of the Paraclete. Whenever Memorial Day falls in Eastertime, the prayers should be from the paschal weekday—certainly these images will help us relate our prayers for the dead to the Lamb and Spirit.

Chapter 57 of the *Book of Blessings* provides a suitable set of prayers for visiting a cemetery. This can be done as a congregation, going in procession to a nearby cemetery after the prayer after communion (cf. #1739). See page 200 of this *Sourcebook* for fuller notes on this order. A more domestic-scale service can be found in *Catholic Household Blessings and Prayers* (pp. 178, 280).

▪ PLANNING THE CALENDAR: The local decision to use seasonal texts with prayers for the dead instead of observing one of the saints is a good example of how weekday presiders and those who prepare the liturgy should look ahead at the liturgical calendar. A common outline can be shared in the parish, noting the optional memorials and the civic observances that are selected. Then those parishioners who pray the liturgy of the hours and do spiritual reading can link these practices to the memorial celebrated by the parish.

■ PRAYERS FOR THE FIELDS AND GARDENS: These three days before the Ascension were once designated as Rogation Days. See page 142 regarding blessings appropriate to these days.

T
U 26 #292 white
E **Philip Neri, priest**
MEMORIAL

All biographies of this saint, a great reformer of religious life in Rome, stress his humor and joy. It is a sign of his Easter appropriateness that the prayers that would have been used, had this been simply the Tuesday of the Sixth Week, stress the joy of youth. As it is, his proper prayers provide explicit linkage between this cheerful saint and the fire of the Holy Spirit.

W
E 27 #293 white
D **Easter Weekday**

Augustine of Canterbury, bishop, optional memorial/white. ■ The apostle of England should be commemorated by parishes with strong links to that land. The sermon of St. Leo found in the seasonal weekday's Office of Readings offers a fine review of the days between resurrection and ascension.

T
H 28 #59 white
U **Ascension**
SOLEMNITY

[Ascension] is a day that unfolds the promise that Jesus will return. . . . [On this day] we do not observe a departure. We celebrate a presence. Thus this day in the 50-day sweep of Easter is a peculiarly opportune time for relishing our hope and our status. . . . We should approach this day with open hearts. We do not gather at the eucharist to have the Ascension explained or to memorize exegetical points. We come to be inspired, to offer praise, to proclaim the Risen One who never leaves us. (*Saint Andrew Bible Missal,* p. 446)

This Eastertime day is so central that Masses for funerals, weddings and anointings cannot be celebrated today. The celebration should follow the same patterns established for all of Eastertime, with the few exceptions noted below.

■ INTRODUCTORY RITES: A strong opening hymn such as "Hail the day that sees him rise" ("Llanfair") or "A hymn of glory let us sing" ("Lass un erfreuen") would serve admirably as an introduction to the liturgy. Notice how the proper prayer texts speak not of absence but of the mystery of our presence alongside the Lord Jesus in the peaceable kingdom.

■ LITURGY OF THE WORD: The responsorial psalm for today is one of the most powerful in the psalter and is a fine exception to the use of a seasonal psalm—or it may become the seasonal psalm every year for the days from the Ascension to the Saturday before Pentecost. For this once-a-year use, choose one setting of Psalm 47 that is worthy of the solemnity and that you will want to use again each year. Richard Proulx's setting fits these criteria (*Worship,* third edition, lectionary accompaniment/cantor book, GIA). Other recommended settings include Hal Hopson's offering in *Psalms for All Seasons* (NPM), "Sing out your praise to God," and Christopher Willcock's Psalm 47, "God mounts his throne," in *Psalms for Feasts and Seasons* (Cooperative Ministries).

■ LITURGY OF THE EUCHARIST: The first of the Ascension prefaces is the richer one and may provide a bulletin summary (the week before) of what the feast is all about. There is a special insert for Eucharistic Prayer I. See also the solemn blessing for this feast (#8 in the sacramentary).

■ THE PASCHAL CANDLE remains in the prominent place it has occupied. It continues to be lighted for all the days of "Pentecost" until and including Pentecost Day itself. In former times, a ritual associated with Ascension Day was the extinguishing of the paschal candle after the gospel. The cathedral in Milan is equipped with a special wire and pulley that allows the paschal candle to ascend to the incredibly high ceiling during the proclamation. Other places trivialize such customs by releasing balloons to "symbolize" the Ascension. All such customs now are shunned by the Roman rite, for the candle remains in place and the season carries on.

F
R 29 #295 white
I **Easter Weekday**

Eastertime is coming to completion with a grand review of its images—the neophytes (opening prayer), the ascension (especially in Leo's sermon in the Office of Readings) and the descent of the Spirit.

S
A 30 #296 white
T **Easter Weekday**

☀ 31 #62 white
Seventh Sunday of Easter

We are a community rejoicing in the exaltation of our risen Lord. Everything should be moving toward next Sunday's culmination of the paschal season in the glorious celebration of Pentecost.

This Sunday, the music can facilitate our looking ahead to Pentecost; the familiar Eastertime patterns should remain largely the same, perhaps with a new gathering song and psalm (repeat Psalm 47 from Ascension). Consider "Alleluia, sing to Jesus" with its reference to the Ascension and Christ's promise to remain with us or "Come down, O Love divine" to the gracious Ralph Vaughan Williams melody, "Down Ampney."

June

M O N ▌ #297 red
Justin, martyr
MEMORIAL

This early martyr is known for his writings describing the liturgies of the second century. The opening prayer helps relate this memorial to the paschal realities of the cross and the resurrection.

▪ THE WEEK AHEAD: This is not only a week of intense prayer in union with Mary and the apostles in the upper room, it is a week when the three obligatory observances of martyrs recall the blood of the Lamb. The martyrs earlier

in this year's Eastertime were all optional observances. Justin, Charles Lwanga and Boniface witness to the resurrection and to the Spirit from three very different eras. Our devotion to their memory is itself a powerful link to the upper room.

T U E 2 #298 White
Easter Weekday

Marcellinus and Peter, martyrs, optional memorial/red. ▪ If these lesser-known martyrs are omitted, Justin gives ample representation to the early Christian era.

W E D 3 #299 red
Charles Lwanga and companions, martyrs
MEMORIAL

These saints, martyred in Uganda a century ago, are commemorated with presidential prayers that resonate well today—calling all to respond to Pentecost's fire.

T H U 4 #300 white
Easter Weekday

F R I 5 #301 red
Boniface, bishop and martyr
MEMORIAL

A celebration of Germany's apostle and patron may include intercessions for the people of that great and changing land. The opening prayer and the priority of "martyr" over "bishop" as a category of saints suggest that the common of martyrs be used.

S A T 6 #302 white
Easter Weekday

Norbert, bishop, optional memorial/white. ▪ Patron of Bohemia, leading reformer in the changes initially undertaken by Gregory VII (remembered two weeks ago) and founder of the Premonstratensians, Norbert can be part of

Pentecost eve. Remembering some aspects of his life may give rise to intercessions for Bohemia and for all of Czechoslovakia.

Whether the seasonal Mass prayers are used or not, the opening prayer should become today's oft-said petition: "Let the love we have celebrated in this Easter season be put into practice in our daily lives."

☀ 7 #63–64 red
Pentecost
SOLEMNITY

IMAGES

This is a great day—far more than a commemoration of a historic event in first-century Jerusalem, far more than a birthday party for the church. It is a day for being Jerusalem, being church; for praising the Sun of justice, the Gardener, the Mother. It is a day for letting our human affections be shaped by the experience of completing Easter in full voice and heart. The church's tradition and the liturgical books always have recognized the importance of this festival. Thus, most other rites are forbidden this day: funeral Masses and ritual Masses of anointing and the marriage Mass texts.

▪ DAY OF NEOPHYTES: Pentecost became the day for the initiation of those who were sick or otherwise unable to be initiated at Easter. This heritage and the general Eastertime ambience of baptism continue to find expression in carefully prepared liturgies of Pentecost:

- The neophytes are to be honored (in the homily and the worship folder and in postliturgy hospitality) and prayed for (in the intercessions). They dress in their robes of white and sit for the last time in their special places.

- Catechumens are to be prayed for and dismissed with eloquent words about their own preparation for the Easter mysteries.

- Those who were received into full communion should not be neglected, with intercessions and homiletic references and special seating giving expression to their role during this parish's Eastertime.

- The young people who were confirmed over recent weeks also should be mentioned explicitly in our prayers—and expected to be there with us, perhaps dressed for the liturgy in the white robes that they wore at confirmation.

- The young people who celebrated their first communion during the Fifty Days may be dressed again in their white clothes, always a marvelous reminder of baptism.

- Babies baptized at Easter and throughout the past year can be in their christening gowns, accompanied by their parents, siblings and godparents.

- Finally, there may be infants to be baptized this day and first communion may be celebrated with children whose parents chose to do this outside the principal parish celebration of first communion.

■ DAY OF MINISTRIES: Some resource books and ministerial training programs have suggested Pentecost as the day for commissioning new ministers of the church. See page 63 regarding other possible (and better) dates and ritual ways to approach what should be a blessing rite instead of a "commissioning." If Pentecost has become the day for this blessing in your local community, you may want to review other options; however, changes should be made with

great care and at slow speed. Local traditions are important and usually spawn a whole network of preparatory sessions, catechetical allusions and domestic customs. They should not be changed without timely, long-term and pastorally sensitive groundwork.

EVENING PRAYER I

The Pentecost festival begins on Saturday evening. The traditional hymn "Veni Creator" can be the "ushering in" of this holy day. Even if your parish observes few celebrations of the liturgy of the hours, this great day may suggest a fuller schedule.

SATURDAY NIGHT MASS

Masses celebrated Saturday afternoon or evening use the Vigil of Pentecost texts (#63 in the lectionary). A fuller vigil celebration of the eucharist is recommended by our ancient tradition and by recent documents from the Vatican. This will not work as a substitute for the regular 5:00 PM Saturday Mass. Any such extended Vigil with eucharist should be held at a later hour.

PENTECOST VIGIL

In Jewish tradition, Pentecost is observed by a vigil in remembrance of the night-watch Israel kept at the foot of Mount Sinai before receiving the Law "in fire and wind." The tradition of the church is also to keep vigil for Pentecost, in the manner of the Easter Vigil, with a lengthy liturgy of the word (the heart of any vigil keeping) and the liturgy of the eucharist when the vigiling is complete.

An outline and texts for the Pentecost Vigil are found beginning on page 161. A prerequisite for the

Pentecost Vigil would be the raising of parish consciousness and enthusiasm for the importance of Pentecost, making sure the festival is kept not just at Mass but throughout the day, from Saturday vigiling to Sunday morning eucharist to an afternoon picnic and Sunday Evening Prayer. What is being spoken about here is not one more liturgical service added to the parish's docket of worship —with the high hopes that maybe a hundred people may show up. What a resurrection vigil is, what the observance of Pentecost is, involves a parish whose consciousness of the countercultural demands of its liturgical life has been raised mightily. And this is something that can happen over years, not just in extra-special parishes with extra-special people but in ordinary communities of ordinary people, especially where parish leadership has remained faithful to year-by-year tradition and where religious education, the parish school, the various ministries of the parish all regard the liturgy as the source and summit of their life together.

MORNING PRAYER

A review of the other major festivals may help encourage you to plan Morning Prayer. Did parishioners appreciate Morning Prayer on Christmas Day? Did they come on Easter morning? If so, then this day deserves a full celebration of this hour with the households who are sincerely attempting to make the whole day holy. As on the other great mornings of the year, this may be followed or preceded by a shared breakfast.

MASS DURING THE DAY

Some parishes schedule one principal liturgy on Pentecost and ask everyone to attend it. Because the day marks such a high point of the year for Christians and because it is about being many yet one, it is an ideal Sunday to cancel as many Masses as possible so that the entire parish can come together at one Mass—the same principle that leads us to hold a single Celebration of the Lord's Passion or a single Easter Vigil. This also would be the same pattern for titular solemnities and dedication anniversaries.

The day's importance and the desire to assemble together may mean moving outdoors to a field or to a lot behind the church or to a large rental tent (a tent for 1,500 people is not so expensive as you may guess, and its rental may be a worthwhile expense). In some parishes, this can mean combining ethnic and language communities, "choir music" and "contemporary music" communities—all types of communities. Choose neutral times and involve everybody, not in competition but in a well-planned joint effort. Friendly persuasion may be necessary. The liturgy must be celebrated well, with good singing and a carefully prepared homily. This cooperation can teach us much about the advantages of liturgy in a "full house."

■ INTRODUCTORY RITES: The patterns for ritual order used throughout the Fifty Days should not be forgotten this day. The sprinkling rite should be carried out well, as on previous Sundays. Perhaps the beautiful alternative opening prayer from the Vigil Mass could be used at all Masses. The alternative prayer for the Mass during the day sounds a bit like a pop song from the 1960s: "horizons of our minds"!

If infant baptisms are part of the Mass, note #29 of that rite: The introductory rites take place at the door of the church or at the rear of the assembly, with a sung Gloria or opening hymn accompanying the processional that occurs between receiving the children and the opening prayer. In this case, the sprinkling rite would best be delayed and included right after the baptisms. This can take place while the babies are dried and while all sing a hymn or acclamation for all the initiation God has brought these Fifty Days.

■ LITURGY OF THE WORD: Psalm 104 is appointed for this last day of Eastertime, a spectacular psalm indeed. For this day, nothing equals the drama of Alexander Peloquin's "Lord, send out your Spirit" (GIA, G-1662). The driving rhythm and cantor's consistent ascending whole-tone patterns add to the energy and excitement. The choir parts also support the effect. A more lyrical setting is Robert Edward Smith's "Lord, send out your Spirit" in the GIA cantor/congregation series (G-2122).

■ THE SEQUENCE SHOULD BE SUNG: Reciting it makes no more sense and has no more impact than speaking alleluias. Preference should be given to the chant called the "golden sequence," which may be performed effectively by alternating between choir and cantors. Peter Scagnelli's translation, found in *Worship* (#857), is good; because of its division into lines of 777.777, it is best used with the melody provided. The Anthony Petti translation, found in *Hymnal for the Hours* as "Holy Spirit, God of Light," is divided 77.77.77, which makes finding a compatible hymn tune easier; "Dix" is one familiar tune in this meter. The "Veni, Sancte Spiritus" of Taizé

can be effective with cantor verses in the various languages provided in *Music from Taizé* volume I (GIA, G-2433). The Christopher Walker setting, "Veni Sancte Spiritus" (St. Thomas More Centre/OCP, #7116), is melodically more interesting and attractive, easily learned and effective with or without the overlaid cantor verses.

■ LITURGY OF THE EUCHARIST: There is a proper preface for today as well as an insert for Eucharistic Prayer I. These should be taken into account when choosing the eucharistic prayer for the day or for the whole season. The acclamations of the Fifty Days should be repeated, perhaps this time with more instruments and with more harmonies.

■ CONCLUDING RITE: A proper solemn blessing is given in the sacramentary. Notice that the dismissal includes the double alleluia, which implies continuing this song with a recessional rich in our Easter word of praise.

■ HYMNODY: A metrical setting of the "Veni creator spiritus" chant by Richard Wojcik is coupled with the John W. Grant translation in "O Holy Spirit, by whose breath" in *Worship* (#475). This can be effective with the choir interpolating the Latin chant verses. "Veni, creator spiritus" is translated with poetic grace by Ralph Wright in the *Hymnal for the Hours* (GIA); couple it with the traditional chant or to an 88.88 meter tune, such as "Puer nobis." Another fine and challenging text is "Spirit of God within me" by Timothy Dudley-Smith. It is paired with a Randolph Currie tune in *Worship* and also is available in a flowing musical setting by Michael Joncas in octavo form (GIA, G-2831). If your parish learned the merry carol tune "Sonne der gerechtigkeit" during the earlier

Sundays of Eastertime, this will serve you well again with the text "Hail this joyful day's return." A lively Gonja folk song is provided by Hope Publishing Company in "Spirit Friend" (*Gather* and *Lead Me, Guide Me,* both GIA).

MIDDAY PRAYER AND DOMESTIC PRAYER

While some places schedule public celebrations of Midday Prayer, the prayer at the middle of the day also may be observed at home. Prayers for home use are found in *Catholic Household Blessings and Prayers* (p. 157). The outline for Eastertime table prayer still is pertinent for today (p. 84).

PARISH PICNIC

Many parishes practice the great custom of holding a Pentecost picnic—in fact, in many places in Europe, "to make a Pentecost" means eating *al fresco,* like the disciples spilling into the streets. If you are fostering a new custom, consider the options—breakfast together after the principal eucharist (if it is early), dinner together after the principal eucharist (if it is at noon), before Evening Prayer, after Evening Prayer (if you live in a warm climate). One of the original Jewish titles for Pentecost is *Yom ha-Bikkurim,* the day of firstfruits. The picnic can include some firstfruits in the form of rhubarb pie or strawberry shortcake.

EVENING PRAYER II

This marks the end of Eastertime and deserves attention. It ends with the double-alleluia dismissal and is followed by the transfer of the Easter candle to the font. If the candle has been in the midst of the assembly or by the ambo, and the distance to the baptistry is substantial enough, this end-of-the-season transfer can be a fine way to end the liturgy. After the dismissal, the best and longest Easter hymn (or the alleluia from the Easter Vigil gospel) is sung as all follow the candle to the font. As the candle is placed there, the music continues and all come to the font and sign themselves with the saving waters.

INTRODUCTORY RITES

Greeting

The God of life, who broke the bonds of death and raised Jesus from the tomb, be with you all.

Rite of Sprinkling Holy Water

Dear brothers and sisters: let us implore the blessing of God that this rite of sprinkling may revive in us the grace of baptism through which we have been immersed in the redeeming death of the Lord, that we might rise also to the glory of new life.

O God Most High,
from the Lamb sacrificed for us
   upon the cross
you have made spring up for us
   fountains of living water:

R. Alleluia.

O Christ,
you have renewed the
   youthfulness of the church
in the cleansing of water
   with the word of life: R.

O Spirit,
you have brought us up
from the waters of baptism
as the firstfruits of a
   new humanity: R.

Almighty God,
who in the sacred signs
   of our faith,
renew the wonders of creation
   and redemption,
bless this water
and grant that all who have
   been born again in baptism
may be heralds and witnesses
   of the paschal mystery,
which is forever renewed
   in your church.
We ask this through Christ our
   Lord. Amen.

—*from the Italian and Spanish sacramentaries*

Penitential Rite

For weekday Masses or Sunday Masses when resources would not permit the sprinkling rite to be done well.

Christ, risen from the dead, shines upon us, the people he redeemed with his own blood. Coming together at his call to celebrate the paschal feast, let us die to our sins and rise with him to newness of life.

Lord Jesus, you are the faithful witness, the firstborn from the dead: Lord, have mercy.

You have loved us and have washed away our sins in your blood, Christ have mercy.

You have joined us to your death through baptism to make us one with you in resurrection: Lord, have mercy.

LITURGY OF THE WORD

Dismissal of the Catechumens

My dear friends: with the assurance of our loving support, this community sends you forth to reflect more deeply upon the word of God we have shared. May Christ who is risen from the dead, and who shines with special radiance among us in this Easter's newly-baptized, fill you with joyful hope and steadfast perseverance, so that in the beauty of an Easter yet to come, you, too, may at last be one with us in the paschal feast of the Lord's table.

General Intercessions

Invitation to Prayer

By the resurrection of Christ, God has given us a new birth unto a living hope. Let our Easter prayer embrace the needs of all the human family, as we offer it through Christ who intercedes for us at the Father's right hand.

For the church

For all who believe in the risen Lord,
that our unity and humble service
proclaim Christ to the world,
let us pray to the Lord.

For the holy church throughout the world,
given new life by the death and resurrection
    of Christ,
let us pray to the Lord.

For the world

That the risen Christ lead us from violence
and show us the way to peace,
let us pray to the Lord.

For our enemies and those
    who wish us harm,
and for all whom we have injured
    or offended,
let us pray to the Lord.

For various needs

For seasonable weather,
an abundance of the fruits of the earth,
and the well being of all who work
    with the land,
let us pray to the Lord.

For those among us who are sick,
that their health be restored
and they be joined with us in prayer,
let us pray to the Lord.

For the local community

For all who gather here,
that the risen Christ sustain us
in faith, in hope and in love,
let us pray to the Lord.

For all candidates for public office,
that they speak with honesty
    and serve the common good,
let us pray to the Lord.

Attuned to the Sunday readings

For all who seek healing in their lives
    and hearts,
that in Christ's name they be raised
    to new life,
let us pray to the Lord.

For catechumens, candidates, inquirers, elect

For the newly baptized into Christ,
and for those received into the fellowship
    of the church,
that the spirit of God now strengthen them
    in faith,
let us pray to the Lord.

For the catechumens of the church,
and all who search for faith,
that the risen Lord may lead them to new life,
let us pray to the Lord.

For the dead

For all who have died in Christ,
that they be raised with him into
    the splendor of new life,
let us pray to the Lord.

Concluding prayer

EASTER DAY:
Fill your church, O God of glory,
with the power flowing
    from Christ's resurrection,
that we may be present
in the midst of the world
    your Son redeemed
as the beginnings of a renewed humanity
risen to new life with Christ,
who lives and reigns for ever and ever.
—*Italian sacramentary*

EASTER AFTERNOON/EVENING:
O God, worker of wonders,
you made this day for joy and gladness.

Let the risen Lord abide with us
    this evening,
opening the Scriptures to us
and breaking bread in our midst.

Set our hearts aflame, and open our eyes,
that we may see in his sufferings
all that the prophets spoke,
and recognize him at this table
as the Christ, now entered into his glory,
living and reigning forever and ever.
— © *ICEL*

SECOND SUNDAY OF EASTER:
God of life,
ground of our faith,
with Jesus you have raised us up
in the waters of baptism
and given us life that endures.

Day by day refine our faith,
and remove every trace of unbelief,
that we may confess Jesus
    as our Lord and God,
and share more fully in his risen life.

We ask this through your Son,
    our Lord Jesus Christ,
who lives and reigns [with you in the unity
of the Holy Spirit, one God] forever and ever.
— © ICEL

THIRD SUNDAY OF EASTER:
Glorious God,
your risen Son showed himself
to the disciples,
by prospering their labor
and providing their meal.

Reveal him in this assembly
as the Savior you have exalted,
that, confessing him as Lord,
we may find strength to serve
and courage to witness.
We ask this through your Son,
    our Lord Jesus Christ,
who lives and reigns [with you in the unity
of the Holy Spirit, one God] forever and ever.

FOURTH SUNDAY OF EASTER:
Safe in your hand,
Father,
is the flock
your Son shepherds:
ransomed for eternal life,
never shall they perish.
Count us, we pray, among those
who hear his voice,
who know and follow him:
the Lord Jesus, one with you,
[in the unity of the Holy Spirit, one]
God for ever and ever.
— © ICEL

FIFTH SUNDAY OF EASTER:
We behold your glory,
O God,
in the love shown by your Son,
lifted up on the cross
and exalted on high.
Be glorified anew
in the love we have for one another
as disciples of the risen Lord Jesus,
who lives and reigns [with you,
in the unity of the Holy Spirit, one God,]
for ever and ever.
— © ICEL

SIXTH SUNDAY OF EASTER:
Great and loving Father,
your bequest to us in Jesus
is that peace which the world cannot give;
your abiding gift
is the Paraclete Spirit he promised.

Quiet our troubled hearts,
dispel our anxious fears,
that, confirmed in love
and faithful to your word,
we may be a dwelling place
fit for you and your Son,
who live and reign [in the unity of the
Holy Spirit, one God,] for ever and ever.
— © ICEL

ASCENSION:
*[In some countries, this solemnity replaces
the Seventh Sunday of Easter.]*

God of majesty,
you brought the Messiah
through suffering to risen life,
and took him up to the glory of heaven.

Clothe us with the power
promised from on high,
and send us forth to the ends of the earth
as heralds of repentance
and witnesses of him
who lives and reigns [with you,
in the unity of the Holy Spirit, one
God,] for ever and ever.
— © ICEL

SEVENTH SUNDAY OF EASTER:
Righteous One,
your beloved Son prayed
that his disciples in every generation
be one as you and he are one.

Look upon this assembly
gathered in your name.
Fulfill the prayer of Jesus
and crown our celebration of this
    paschal season
with your Spirit's gift of unity and love.
We ask this through your Son,
    our Lord Jesus Christ,
who lives an reigns [with you in the unity
of the Holy Spirit, one God] forever and ever.
— © ICEL

LITURGY OF THE EUCHARIST

Introduction to the Lord's Prayer

We are called children of God, and by baptism that is indeed what we have become; and so we have the courage to pray:

Prayer for Peace

Lord Jesus Christ,
on the day of your glorious resurrection
you greeted your disciples
and offered them your gift of lasting peace:
    Look not on our sins . . .

Invitation to Communion

This is the Lamb of God, who takes away the sins of the world:
Christ our Passover who was sacrificed for us:
Happy are those who are called to his supper.

Dismissal of Eucharistic Ministers

Go forth in peace to the sick and homebound of our community, bearing the word of life and the Body of Christ, together with the assurance of our love and concern. By your presence and the holy gifts you share, remind them of the communion that is ours in the risen Lord whose paschal mystery has made us one Body and one Spirit, in the one baptism by which we have been born to new life.

CONCLUDING RITE

Blessing

The God of peace, who brought Jesus the great Shepherd back from the dead through the blood of the everlasting covenant,
make you perfect in every good work
and pleasing in his sight.
    And may almighty God bless you . . .

TEXTS FOR MASS WITH CHILDREN

Opening Prayer

Great and powerful God,
in these days of Easter
you have taught us how great and
    how beautiful
is your love for us:
Help us to journey with the risen Jesus
toward that joy which lasts forever.
We ask this through your Son,
    our Lord Jesus Christ,
who lives and reigns [with you in the unity
of the Holy Spirit, one God] forever and
ever.

Prayer over the Gifts

Holy God,
receive your church's gifts in this
    happy season.
You are the source of all our joy:
Help us always to be joyful in your Spirit.
We ask this through Christ our Lord.

Prayer after Communion

O good and loving God,
you have given us Jesus, the bread of life,
to be our food.
May we all work together
as we journey together with you
    to your house,
our heavenly home.
We ask this through Christ our Lord.

TEXTS FOR MASS IN CELEBRATION OF FIRST COMMUNION

Opening Prayer

Good and gracious God,
you have invited these children
to your table for the first time
that you may carry toward completion
their sharing in the life of your family,
      the church.
Help them always to live
in friendship and communion with Jesus,
as living members of his mystical body.
We ask this through your Son,
      our Lord Jesus Christ,
who lives and reigns [with you in the unity
of the Holy Spirit, one God] forever and ever.

Concluding Prayer of the General Intercessions

With a father's watchful care and
      a mother's tender love,
protect, O God, these children
you have called to be nourished
      with the bread of life.

Through the saving power
      of these mysteries
preserve them from evil
and make them generous witnesses
of the love of Christ
who is Lord for ever and ever.

Prayer over the Gifts

O God, in this celebration
we share in the sacrifice of Christ
who lovingly offered himself for the life
      of the world.
May these children, our first communicants,
grow in their knowledge of Christ
and their living experience of his love,
who lives and reigns for ever
      and ever.

Prayer after Communion

Lord God,
the bread of life and the cup of salvation
are the sign and source of that eternal
      youthfulness
that belongs to those who welcome
      your kingdom
with the openness and trust of children.
May these first communicants always
      serve you
with loving hearts and joyful spirits.
We ask this through Christ our Lord.

—Translated and adapted from the Ambrosian sacramentary, Messale ambrosiano festivo *(Milano: Marietti, 1983)*

TEXTS FOR THE ANOINTING OF THE SICK WITHIN MASS

Introduction/Reception of the Sick

In the joy of the Easter season, the church celebrates the Lord's passover from death to life, his conquering of sin and death. With the Prophet Hosea and the Apostle Paul, God's people sing: O death, where is your victory? O death, where is your sting? Gathered to celebrate the sacraments of anointing and eucharist, may we, who in baptism died with Christ to share his resurrection, rejoice in the triumph of the Lord and claim for ourselves a share in his victory and new life.

Prayer after Anointing

In the surpassing glory of Christ's
      resurrection,
you have filled your church, Lord God,
      with new hope.
Touch with your healing power
those on whom we have laid our hands
      in Christ's name.
Transform with your saving grace
those we have anointed with holy oil.
Surrounded by the love and concern
of all who have been baptized into Christ,
may our brothers and sisters experience
the victory of the cross
and the triumph of new life.
We ask this through Christ our Lord.

A VIGIL SERVICE FOR PENTECOST EVE

If Mass begins in the usual way, after the Kyrie the priest offers the prayer "God our Father . . . ," which is the alternative opening prayer of the Pentecost Vigil Mass.

The liturgy of the word is expanded this night. The presider instructs the assembly in these or similar words:

Dear brothers and sisters: We gather this holy night, following the example of the apostles and disciples who, with Mary, the Mother of Jesus, persevered in prayer, awaiting the Spirit promised by the Lord. Let us listen now with quiet hearts to the word of God. Let us contemplate how much God has done for us, and let us pray that the Holy Spirit, whom the Father sent upon those first believers, will bring God's work to perfection throughout the world.

All the "first readings" from the Vigil Mass in the lectionary are proclaimed in the following order:

Reading I

Reading

Genesis 11:1–9

"It was called Babel for there the speech of the whole world was put to confusion."

Psalm

Psalm 32:10–15

Prayer

Grant, we pray you, almighty God,
that your church may always be
    that holy people
gathered together by the unity
of the Father and of the Son and
    of the Holy Spirit,
so that it may manifest
    to all the world
the mystery of your unity
    and holiness
and itself come to the perfection
    of your love.
We ask this through Christ our Lord.

Reading II

Reading

Exodus 19:3–8, 16–20

"The Lord descended on Mount Sinai in the sight of all the people."

Psalm

Canticle of Daniel 3:52–56

Or:

Psalm 18:8–11

Prayer

O God, who in smoke and fire
    upon Mount Sinai
gave the old law to Moses,
and who this day revealed the
    new covenant
in the fire of the Spirit:
grant, we pray, that kindled
    by that same Spirit
which you wondrously poured
    forth upon your apostles,
and gathered from among all
    peoples to be the new Israel,
we may receive with joy
    the eternal commandment
    of your love.
We ask this through Christ our Lord.

Reading III

Reading

Ezekiel 37:1–14

"Dry bones, I will send spirit into you and you will live."

Psalm

Psalm 106:2–9

Prayer

Let your people ever exult, O God,
renewed in youthfulness of soul
    by your Holy Spirit:
that we who now rejoice to have
    restored to us
the glory that is ours as your
    adopted children,
may look forward in sure and
    certain hope
to that great day of resurrection
    and reward.
We ask this through Christ our Lord.

Reading IV

Reading

Joel 3:1–5

"I will pour out my Spirit upon my servants and handmaids."

Psalm

Psalm 103:1–2a, 24 and 35c, 27–28, 29bc–30

Prayer

Graciously fulfill, O Lord,
the promise you have made
    in our regard:
that your Holy Spirit,
    when the Spirit comes to us,
may make us witnesses
    before all the world
to the gospel of our Lord
    Jesus Christ,
who lives and reigns with you
    forever and ever.

Gloria

Opening prayer

Taken from either the first or alternative opening prayers for the Pentecost Mass during the Day in the sacramentary. After the opening prayer, the liturgy of the word continues with the reading from Romans and the gospel, and Mass continues in the usual way.

Dismissal

In dismissing the people, the deacon or the presider adds the double alleluia to the invitation as do the people to their response.

IF EVENING PRAYER IMMEDIATELY PRECEDES THE VIGIL

The celebration begins either with the introductory verse, "O God, come to my assistance," and the hymn, "Veni, Creator Spiritus," or with the entrance antiphon from the Pentecost Vigil Mass. The presider greets the people, omitting the penitential rite (cf. General Instruction on the Liturgy of the Hours, #94 and #96).

Evening Prayer may begin with a lucernarium, *the thanksgiving for light, except that the paschal candle would already be lit as everyone gathers.*

The psalmody of Evening Prayer follows up to, but not including the short reading. After the psalmody, the presider offers the prayer "God our Father . . . ," which is the alternative opening prayer of the Pentecost Vigil Mass. The vigil then continues with the introduction and readings above.

A Vigil that has combined Evening Prayer with the Vigil Mass ends in this way: After communion the Magnificat is sung with its antiphon from Evening Prayer, "Come, Holy Spirit." Then the prayer after communion is offered and the concluding rite takes place as usual.

SUMMER AND FALL
ORDINARY TIME

*Until October, the selections from the Gospel of Luke describe Jesus' journey to Jerusalem
and his teachings along the way. The geography of ancient Palestine is less central to
this travel account than the teachings about the "way" of discipleship.
This "map of life" unfolds in 1992 as the people of the United States prepare for elections
and as those of many nations remember Christopher Columbus. Just as Jesus resolutely
faced Jerusalem, the city of his and our fate, we, too, must be resolute about the tasks
of justice and reconciliation in our own cities and towns. Here we celebrate
the New Jerusalem, which pulls us to its own beauty.*

Images of Ordinary Time

THE days right after Pentecost are an abrupt surprise. With some regret, we leave the heights awash in bright Eastertime flowers. These plainer days, the Ordinary Time of summer and autumn, comprise almost half of 1992. They are more fully described beginning on page 171.

■ THE GOSPEL OF LUKE, read progressively from the ninth to the twenty-first chapters, makes this year different from the previous two. On two Sundays this year—Trinity and All Saints—we hear from Matthew. On two other Sundays—the Body and Blood of Christ and Christ the King—we hear from other sections of Luke. This means that for 20 Sundays we are in the midst of Luke's narrative. We will follow step by step as Luke describes Jesus' journey on the road to Jerusalem and his arrival there for the final foreboding days.

The numbered Sundays after the solemnities of the Trinity and of the Body and Blood of Christ bring attentive congregations to the start of Jesus' journey: "As the time approached when Jesus was to be taken from the world, he firmly resolved to proceed toward Jerusalem." This journey will provide the framework for the assembly's weekly listening until November.

The last time that we heard the Lukan story, in 1989, we had several Sundays to enter into Ordinary Time before those fateful words. In 1995, the resolute embarkation will be similarly less dramatic.

Each year's passage through its synoptic gospel is colored by the accompanying scriptures, psalms and prayers. For example, on August 2 this year, we will hear from the Book of Ecclesiastes—its first appearance on a Sunday since 1986. This is because the Transfiguration feast sometimes falls on a Sunday and the same coincidence means that Qoheleth will not be heard from again until 1998. This is not overly important, hardly worth mentioning except that it does point out the lectionary's sparse coverage of some Hebrew Scriptures and the unique way in which each year is given to us. Planners and homilists should take a long view of the whole of Ordinary Time, charting out musical selections, special rites and educational outlines that will complement the lectionary of a given year.

To assist long-term planning, this annual *Sourcebook* has divided the weeks of summer and fall into "blocks" of Sundays, keeping to the actual structure of the given evangelist. While these were never set arbitrarily, their placement is not prescribed by the lectionary. They seem to be appropriately sized blocks for the consistent use of certain psalms, hymns and liturgical texts. They have been set with an eye to the gospel, but some parishes may prefer blocks arranged according to other realities of the assembly—perhaps a block during summer when tourists abound and a block with different music after Labor Day, or a block for each of the prolonged passages through the New Testament letters or even a block for each side of a dedication festival. What is important is that texts become known over blocks of weeks, not that Ordinary Time is magically sliced into sections for all places and all years.

■ NATIONAL ELECTIONS: Those who live in the 50 states cannot but be affected by the primaries just completed, by the Democratic and Republican conventions of the summer, by the election campaigns of the fall and by Election Day itself in November.

Even if the candidates attack each other rather than address the issues, the people must review civic priorities. Americans who live outside the 50 states—in Puerto Rico, in the various territories, in the District of Columbia—even if their representation and power remain constitutionally limited by those who live in the states, must use the energies flowing from the debates and the election to frame their vision of society. Even if they reside there without documentation or citizenship, they must participate in the shaping of the public agenda.

When they gather for the eucharist, for any other sacrament or for Morning or Evening Prayer, American Catholics bring the concerns and hopes generated by this every-fourth-year examination of national values and priorities. These evaluations and energies shape the consciousness of assemblies; liturgical actions should, in turn, shape the affections of the faithful. Sundays and seasons, and the actions by which we Catholics mark them, open the hearts of our congregations not only to be residents of the given nations but also to be citizens of God's reign. As Americans approach the elections of November, they should be intensely conscious of the image-world fostered by November's liturgies:

> We have our citizenship in heaven; it is from there that we eagerly await the coming of our savior, the Lord Jesus Christ. (Philippians 3:20, read this past Lent on the Second Sunday and on the Friday three days after the elections. It is also one of the choices for the Masses for the Dead.).

Some or all of these suggestions can be used in the states and territories, especially during Ordinary Time and as local communities confront debates, conventions and elections:

- Sets of prayers for the eucharist are given in Masses and Prayers for Various Needs and Occasions, II. Civil Needs. The six sets (#17–22) include a variety of opening prayers for the nation, the president and others in public office. These can be used with the prayers over the gifts and the prayers after communion from Masses for "Progress of Peoples" or "Peace and Justice." All of these can be used on those weekdays of Ordinary Time that are not assigned memorials. The weekday readings are kept as always.

- The prayers listed for Independence Day (under July 4 in the "Proper of Saints" and in appendix X.6) also are entitled, "Other Civic Observances." All but one of these prayers transcend the specific language of national anniversary and can be used on Ordinary Time weekdays as communities lift their concerns to God.

- The *Book of Blessings,* #1965, contains an adaptation of the prayer used by Archbishop John Carroll at the inauguration of George Washington in 1789 (also in the *Shorter Book of Blessings;* an abbreviated form appears in *Catholic Household Blessings and Prayers,* p. 196). The prayer, with any of its optional middle paragraphs, provides a fine conclusion to intercessions or an invocation for a civic event. In paragraph E, the word "citizens" could be changed to "residents."

- Intercessions drawing on the images of these suggested prayers may be prepared throughout Ordinary Time.

- Homilists and planners may do well to spend one of their meetings this summer praying all of these texts, listing their acclamations and petitions, discussing their import for this particular community and allowing themselves to become imbued with the spirit of this liturgical collection.

■ SUMMER: Nature's seasons and the liturgy follow different calendars, but the two are inhabited by the same folks. We should not superimpose summer's themes and cultural imperatives on the Roman rite. Nor can we expect our liturgical celebrations to exhaust the summertime possibilities in a parish. Each has its role. Each has influenced the other for centuries. Each is to be understood on its own terms.

We can look to summer and see some of the affections and attitudes worshipers bring to the liturgy. Summer's leisure has spawned an amazing complex of national, state and local festivals. Although some of them are the crafty products of tourism offices, many others express deep human desires and have been around for a very long time. The people of Scandinavia, for example, stay awake throughout the bright days and bright nights around June 21. Their neighborhoods become intergenerational festivals, and the nightclubs include senior citizens and babies in strollers among their patrons. The late-night scene in many of our own city neighborhoods includes people sitting on porches, visiting with friends.

In a marvelous collection of children's art, Betty Nickerson wrote:

> All over the world people work best and feel best in summer temperatures between 65 and 75 degrees. Food is more plentiful, and the specter of death visits less often in summer than any other season of the year. . . . Summer is the time most often chosen for migration to new places and emigration to distant countries. . . . Even in cities, families are more likely to move in summer. By accident or design, many older nations and most younger ones have chosen the summer of the year to celebrate nationhood. . . . Since summer is the easiest and most pleasant time to travel, people gather together, see new sights and exchange goods and gossip. Summer has long been the favorite time for fairs and fetes. (*Celebrate the Sun* [Philadelphia: J. B. Lippincott, 1969], 48)

If a community's titular solemnity or dedication festival falls in the summer—what luck! These churches just have to tap into the enormous desire for fun that every community possesses.

■ AUTUMN: The cadences of summer give way to school and to work. Once again, the liturgy follows its own path—not unrelated to fall, but to be understood on its own terms. The evangelist Luke continues describing the journey to Jerusalem. The sanctoral calendar and many local calendars turn to dedication festivals. The eschatological tone becomes more serious in later fall. The saints and souls of past and future animate the church.

The days become shorter and shorter, colder and colder. The harvest, in progress or completed, is a primary reality in many areas. For many, autumn is a time for plunging into new worlds and new circles of human contact. Parish groups search for new members and start up their programming. Through it all, we continue to grow in the paschal mystery, shaped by eternal realities as we careen through time.

■ THE SAINTS IN SUMMER AND AUTUMN: Because calendar reforms over the centuries have tried to keep saints' days away from the seasons of Incarnation and Pasch, these Ordinary Time weeks are quite rich in saints. Five of the festivals ranked among the greatest in our tradition

fall on weekdays this year: Birth of John the Baptist, Sacred Heart, Peter and Paul, Assumption and All Souls. There are almost a dozen other major feasts of the Lord, of angels and of saints. Looking at the other obligatory and optional observances, a given parish may observe as many as 100 other memorials or as few as 40. This is one of the most praiseworthy features of the current calendar. Parishes everywhere follow the scores of days on the universal calendar. Nations add several more that relate to their histories and emotions. Then each local community adds those optional days it selects and those local days that define them (see the last section of this book regarding these local days).

■ COMPLETING THE CALENDAR: Besides the flow of Sundays and liturgical feasts, these are the months for many local observances and for much of the business that goes into making parishes work. Here is a partial list of events that probably find their best homes on Sundays in Ordinary Time:

- Two Sundays for accepting new catechumens (p. 189)
- One or more Sundays for the anointing of the sick at a Sunday eucharist
- Eucharistic devotion outside Mass (notably June 21 this year)
- Local days: Titular solemnity (p. 216), dedication anniversary solemnity (p. 213), feast of the diocesan patron (p. 219), feast of the anniversary of the dedication of the cathedral (p. 220)
- Blessings of married couples, perhaps in the early summer (p. 168)
- Blessings for ministries: catechists (p. 192), liturgical ministers (p. 63)
- Blessings for new parishioners (p. 185)
- Blessings for students and teachers (p. 189).

The Mass

SEE page 56 for a fuller description of the Mass in Ordinary Time. Other notes appear in the calendar section that follows, highlighting selections that can be made for each "block" of Sundays.

■ THE STRUCTURE OF LUKE AT SUNDAY MASS: Four "blocks" of Sundays can be set apart, based on the internal structure of Luke's gospel between the late spring solemnities (Trinity and the Body and Blood) and Christ the King:

- BLOCK ONE: Sunday 13 (June 28) to Sunday 20 (August 16): "Journey to Jerusalem, Part I." This is "for the most part a literary compilation of sayings of Jesus, pronouncement-stories and a few miracle-stories, all set in the framework of the journey to Jerusalem" (Fitzmyer, p. 825 in the *Anchor Bible* volumes for Luke; see the resources list). This long section of Luke continues through all the Sundays until November. It has been divided here into three blocks in the way most scripture commentators have divided it—three subsections, each beginning with an explicit reference to the resolute Jesus headed to Jerusalem.

  Thus this section starts with the first reference to the journey, and parishes spend eight Sundays listening to the stories that Luke has attached to this reference. Lessons about discipleship are combined with direct warnings about the opposition that one may expect. The assembly may lose track of the travelogue, but the geography is less important than the teachings about the "way" to life. The middle four Sundays of the block feature the letter to the Colossians. These beautiful passages— hymns, really—offer a counterpoint of praise to Luke's sober narrative. Several ideas for liturgical texts that enhance our listening to this portion of the gospel are noted at June 28 beginning on page 176.

- BLOCK TWO: Sunday 21 (August 23) to Sunday 27 (October 4): "Journey to Jerusalem, Part II." With another explicit reference to the journey, congregations move into another seven Sundays learning about the "way." The first Sunday's verses about the kingdom, with entry or not, set a tone for the rest of the block. Premonitions about the death of Jesus and the opposition to be expected by his disciples seem to be more numerous. Liturgical texts that enhance our celebrating this kingdom are suggested at August 23 on page 187.

  During the Year of Luke, with this block related so closely to those on either side of it, we see the limited role these "block" divisions should have. They are meant as simple demarcation points for utilizing particular common psalms and hymnody over several weeks.

- BLOCK THREE: Sunday 28 (October 11) to Sunday 30 (October 25): "Journey to Jerusalem, Part III." The third major reference to the city of Jerusalem carries us into the last subsection of the journey narrative. During this brief block in October, Jesus' sayings are received in tandem with proclamations from 2 Timothy. These pericopes are something of a final exhortation from Paul to Timothy, placing the teachings about kingdom and discipleship, about Jerusalem and the "way"

in the framework of the early church and its pastoral responsibility. The entry for October 11 on page 194 contains listings for liturgical elements to help these gospel passages become our eucharist.

- BLOCK FOUR: All Saints (Sunday, November 1) to the Solemnity of Christ the King (November 22): "Jesus in Jerusalem." As is always the case in November, the weeks of Ordinary Time draw to a close with more attention to the "last things." The new Jerusalem is seen in contrast to the earthly city and its rejection of the Lord. All Saints falls on a Sunday this year, and its images of fullness set the stage for the rest of the month. See November 1 (p. 197) for specific ideas about more eschatologically-oriented liturgical texts.

Other Ritual Prayer

BLESSINGS

THE course of ecclesial life over these months presents opportunities for communities to praise God and to pray over individual members. The *Book of Blessings* contains several chapters that can become part of a community's gatherings during the summer and autumn months. Many of these blessings will be noted in the calendar section on days that seem fitting occasions for celebrating them. Parishes should spend time with this book, noting blessings that are suitable for the community and planning the most appropriate date for each.

■ ORDERS FOR THE BLESSING OF A MARRIED COUPLE, found in chapter 1 of the *Book of Blessings,* seem far more appropriate than an annual "renewal of vows" on a Sunday near Valentine's Day (called World Marriage Day in certain regions), or on the feast of the Holy Family or on some day when the lectionary happens to mention love. Expecting all couples to be ready to renew their marriage vows on a given day tends to trivialize these sacred promises.

This does not mean, however, that the parish should not celebrate wedding anniversaries. The sacramentary carries seldom-used presidential prayers for these events. It may be time for many parishes to find ways to expand this ritual possibility, to lift the anniversary rituals from occasional events celebrated only for those couples who are friends or relatives of a priest to regular parish celebrations held for the benefit of all married couples.

The parish community can make wedding anniversaries part of their Sunday assembly as long as the integration is handled with sensitivity. The texts of the day would be used, or some of the lectionary and sacramentary texts for "Marriage (anniversary)" may be interpolated with them. One creative approach is to schedule this rite during one or more of the Masses on Trinity Sunday, partially transforming this "idea festival" into a fleshly appreciation of triune love in our midst.

SCHOOL ASSEMBLIES

These ordinary months provide two extraordinary times for the young members of our parishes: Schools close. Schools open. For the closing of school and for graduations, see page 97 of LTP's *Leader's Manual of the Hymnal for Catholic Students.* For the opening of the school year, see page 53 of the book. Chapter 5 in the *Book of Blessings* includes an order of blessing for students and teachers perfect for a Mass on the first day back in a parish school. This also can be used as part of Sunday Mass as a blessing for all students in the parish.

This nonseasonal time of the liturgical year may provide an opportunity to bring children into the church building for a tour of different areas, for a trip through the parish's history or for fostering familiarity with the symbols and furniture that serve them and the entire community. The tour should be more than verbal: Take time to sing pertinent hymns in varied places, to look at parish treasures and to peer into forgotten corners. Prayers from the anniversary of the dedication of a church may be useful. When teachers search for field trips for those end-of-the-year days, one good destination is just across the parking lot.

The Worship Environment

UNLIKE the seasons before and after, Ordinary Time does not have specific, seasonal requirements. We have an opportunity to focus on year-round issues. A few of the long-term issues that may be addressed over these long months are:

■ FLOWERS: Ordinary Time gives us a chance to think about our methods of floral decoration. Do bridal parties and funerals regularly bring flowers to the worship space? Is guidance given to them regarding appropriate placement, the seasonal moods, the inappropriateness of artificial flowers, an avoidance of spray-painted cardboard containers and other contraptions, and the scale of space? A printed sheet of guidelines may help, or a parishioner could be delegated to contact all funeral directors, florists and engaged couples, or a policy can be established that flowers for special occasions will be placed in a particular shrine that can accept a wide range of shapes and colors.

Lacking a comprehensive modern guide to the liturgical use of flowers, one may turn to the outdated but still reliable book by J. B. O'Connell, *Church Building and Furnishing: The Church's Way* (Notre Dame IN: University of Notre Dame Press, 1955). His four pages on flowers (201–4) are a masterful summary of our tradition and a cogent guide for our practice. O'Connell notes that flowers were used to adorn the tombs of martyrs and the *confessio,* where the body of a saint was enshrined. As early as the fourth century, flowers were used in the church and around (but not on) the altar. Foliage or garlands were hung on the walls, on columns, on doors, on the ambo and on the canopy over the altar.

Other practices evolved over the years: Flowers and sweet-smelling herbs were scattered on the floor (sometimes with dramatic touches, such as rose petals dropped during the Pentecost sequence); flowers and branches were strewn before the path of a bishop entering his diocese or in the street before the Corpus Christi procession; petals or blossoms were spread all around the place where the washing of the feet took place on Holy Thursday. O'Connell's review of history concludes with words given to the pastors of the diocese of Rome in 1932: "Artificial flowers (of whatever material—cloth, bronze, brass, earthenware) are forbidden. They must be removed at once from churches and oratories, and from altars, and they may not be placed there for any reason whatsoever."

The current liturgical books ban altar flowers during Lent and at funerals, calling for "moderation" in Advent (*Ceremonial of Bishops,* #48, #236, #252, #824). In other words, flowers (like instrumental music) are seen as expressions of a festivity from which we prescind in the penitential season and in celebrations of the dead. The *Order of Christian Funerals* used in the dioceses of the United States softens the application of these norms at funerals: "Fresh flowers, used in moderation, can enhance the setting of the funeral rites" (#38).

Moving from a historical review to an examination of the scene in his own decade, O'Connell's words still apply:

> When an altar is continually cluttered up with flower vases, flowers cease to adorn and lose their symbolic value as a mark of special joy and festivity. They introduce on the altar accessories (such as stands for vases and flowerpots) that often hide its beauty and spoil its lines and proportions, and sometimes overshadow the liturgical furnishings. Often the use of plants . . . impedes ceremonial movements in the sanctuary. To turn the altar— the awesome stone of sacrifice—into a stand for flower vases betrays an ignorance of liturgical principles and traditional correct usage, and sometimes results in a vulgar and costly display. (p. 203)

Sacristans and those who prepare the liturgy can ask parishioners to sign up to provide flowers according to seasonal guidelines regarding scale and location. When establishing the flower budget, the coming year's needs and the places that may be graced with flowers (other than the altar area, such as the baptistry, tombs, columns, doors, vestibule) must be taken into consideration.

■ SAINTS AND SHRINES: A good introduction to the practice and benefit of using images in churches can be found in the brief introduction to chapter 36 of the *Book of Blessings* ("Order for the Blessing of Images for Public Veneration by the Faithful").

A review of the images in a parish church will help all planners, catechists and homilists to inhabit their home liturgical space and to use its resources for rite and for education. Images shape people's affections, and it is wise to know the images and the sacred furnishings that surround and shape us as a church. This review may include making a list of the images found, some research into their origins and a study of the symbols accompanying each image. Art historians are, of course, irreplaceable assets in a community. If they are ready to help, but need some information on the saints and on our heritage of artistic symbols, refer them to such basic works as Parsch (see the resources list) and *Butler's Lives of the Saints.* This is a great assignment for young parishioners in upper grades of parish schools or for those doing field assignments for their public high schools. Parishes located near institutions of higher learning should not hesitate about calling their art departments for help. They may see this as an opportunity for students to do field-work.

After such an inventory, the next step may be a review of the placement of the images. As the *General Instruction of the Roman Missal* states, "There is a need to situate [images] in such a way that they do not distract the people's attention away from the celebration" (#278).

June

MON 8 Lectionary #359   green
Weekday

■ SCRIPTURES: Back to Ordinary Time! Down from the summits of Easter, we resume the semicontinuous reading of the weekday gospels and Hebrew Scriptures. Monday of Week 10, Year II, marks a turning point in the Ordinary Time lectionary. The gospel of Matthew is opened for the first time, starting at chapter 5. While Luke's telling of the "Sermon on the Plain" fell on the Sundays just before Lent, Matthew's longer version, the "Sermon on the Mount," will unfold on these first days after paschaltide.

After weeks with the Acts of the Apostles, we return to the Hebrew Scriptures and 1 Kings. Opening to chapters 17–19 all this week, we remember Elijah. The story begins with him confronting both King Ahab and the idolatrous worship of Baal, the god of storms.

■ PRAYERS: On these Ordinary Time weekdays, prayers from the sacramentary can be taken from the previous Sunday or from almost any other section. They should not be taken from those for Pentecost Sunday; that festival yesterday completed Eastertime.

The use of votive Masses on days without a sanctoral observance has a long tradition. The Tridentine Missal even codified these traditions, assigning certain Masses to particular days of the week. The reforms of a few decades ago left us with 15 votive Masses without restricting these prayers to particular days. The readings of these votive Masses are to be used rarely, if ever; the lectionary for the weekdays is to be followed. Special attention to the cross on Fridays and to Mary on Saturdays is still appropriate,

and these references permeate the various liturgical books.

■ THE WEEK AHEAD: The story of Elijah will be interrupted by the proper reading for Barnabas's memorial on Thursday. The passage to be skipped does finish the account of the drought and King Ahab, but the dramatic contest recounted on Wednesday also serves as Yahweh's response. There does not seem to be a need to combine the readings.

TUE 9 #360   green
Weekday

Ephrem, deacon and doctor, optional memorial / white. ▪ The first saint we meet in Ordinary Time this year is the only entry on the universal Roman calendar from the ancient churches of Mesopotamia. That region between the great Euphrates and Tigris rivers, where civilization as we know it is said to have begun, was and still is central to the world's heritage and hopes. The garden of Eden, the flood and the exile were here. The sites of Nineveh and Babylon can be visited along with hundreds of early Christian churches. The political boundaries have shifted over the centuries, and the region is now in Kuwait, Iraq, northern Syria and southern Turkey. The city of Ephrem's birth (Nisibis) and the city where he founded a theological school (Edessa) are both in southern Turkey now, but "Ephrem the Syrian" represents the ancient cultures of the other Mesopotamian countries as well.

The passage by him in the memorial's Office of Readings, as well as the several other passages by him included in the *Liturgy of the Hours,* express the range and beauty of his thoughts. Including his memorial on the local parish's

calendar allows the local church to be linked more explicitly to Mesopotamia and its ancient heritage —a priority when many Americans see that region just as a turbulent desert.

WED 10 #361   green
Weekday

THU 11 #580 or 362   red
Barnabas
MEMORIAL

An early apostle of Christ in Cyprus, Jerusalem and Antioch, Barnabas's liturgical texts include one of the few times we see him in the scriptures (first reading). The gospel can be from the saint's day (#580) or from the weekday in Ordinary Time (#362). The selection in the Office of Readings by Chromatius of Aquileia is a wonderful commentary on apostleship and on the gospel (Matthew 5:13– 16) that was read on Tuesday.

FRI 12 #363   green
Weekday

The selections from Ambrose in the Office of Readings for today and tomorrow provide an excellent commentary on the pleasure and value of singing psalms. They might be used for a reading at this week's choir rehearsal.

SAT 13 #364   white
Anthony of Padua, priest and doctor
MEMORIAL

A man of irony! One of the earliest Franciscans in Italy, Anthony started out as a Portuguese Augustinian. A doctor of the church and theologian, he is invoked most often for help in finding lost objects. Buried and honored by tremendous numbers of pilgrims in Padua, his initial intention was to preach the gospel in Morocco. A strong man of great will, he often is pictured in overly sentimental poses with a sweet baby Jesus in his arms. A quick review of church graffiti, votive candle stands and "ex voto" titles reveal him to be just about the most popular saint in Western Christianity (second only, perhaps, to another paradox, Theresa of Lisieux). The common of doctors texts best complement the proper opening prayer.

⊙ **14** #167 white
Trinity Sunday
SOLEMNITY

Having spent over 93 days in feasts related to the history of salvation, we now meet "idea feasts" this Sunday and next. Celebrating these rather cerebral feasts is best done through familiar trinitarian or eucharistic hymns. "The feast is only a feast if we follow the lead of the assigned scriptures and acclaim a God of love, not dissect an arcane theological treatise" (*Study Text 9*, p. 60). Today's feast provides the occasion for remembering the centrality of the Trinity in every act of liturgy.

The selection of music and the church's decorations should not convey a sense that Eastertime has been extended by two more weeks. The church's decorations should look simpler now than on Pentecost, and the white vestments should be noticeably different from Eastertime's vesture.

■ INTRODUCTORY RITES: To differentiate the blocks of time, today's Mass probably should not include the sprinkling rite if it has been used each week in the Easter season. The proper prayers for this

day are found after all the Ordinary Time Sundays. Use a Gloria different from that of Eastertime.

■ LITURGY OF THE WORD: While the gospel is taken from the "Last Discourse," its similarity to the gospels on the last Sundays of Easter should not prompt homilists to continue Eastertime, at least no more than in the general ways that every Sunday is linked to the "Great Sunday." The specific season and solemnity on which a particular gospel is proclaimed should color its reception and interpretation. See page 168 for suggestions regarding a blessing of married couples at the conclusion of the liturgy of the word.

15 #365 green
Weekday

The first readings on Monday and Tuesday of this eleventh week tell the story of vineyard owner Naboth and his neighbor King Ahab. Congregations, already cued to Ahab's faults by last week's readings, can find here a dramatic story of sin and penitence. Within the framework of 1 and 2 Kings, it is a key episode explaining the decadence that led ultimately to exile.

The early Christian readings in the Office of Readings all week are from Cyprian, the bishop of Carthage who was martyred in 258. Beginning with the segment that would have been read if yesterday had been the Eleventh Sunday, the seven passages provide a marvelous commentary on the Lord's Prayer—a fine topic for homilies anytime.

16 #366 green
Weekday

17 #367 green
Weekday

With the flash of a fiery chariot, today's first reading completes the story of Elijah told over the last week and a half.

18 #368 green
Weekday

We find here one of the pieces of Wisdom literature inserted in the midst of a historical sequence from the books of Kings. As noted in the introduction to the lectionary (#110), this is meant to bring out the "religious significance" of the narrative, in this case the story of Elijah. It is also an example of how the same incident can be related differently in narrative and in wisdom literature.

The prayers for this day might be from the Eleventh Sunday or from other sections of the sacramentary.

19 #369 green
Weekday

Romuald, abbot, optional memorial/white. ▪ Today's saint died around 1027 after decades spent founding monasteries. As the year 2000 approaches, bookstore shelves are being filled with predictions, with commentaries on millenarianism and with New Age works that are as pagan as any of the ancient Gnostic works. In the liturgical calendar, three saints appear who were active in the year 1000: Romuald, Henry and Stephen of Hungary. Their biographies should be as available to parishioners as the tales of other tenth-century figures.

From another era 1800 years before Romuald, the first readings today and tomorrow give further evidence of the evils that led to the exile. Looking in on the crimes of ancient Judah, remembering the desire of so many to flee the secular world as 1000 approached, and witnessing our own apprehensions before a new millennium, we need the counterpoint of Saturday's gospel—do not worry about tomorrow!

S A T 20 #370 green
Weekday

Blessed Virgin Mary, optional memorial/white.

✴**21** #170 white
Body and Blood of Christ
SOLEMNITY

■ HISTORY: This feast's origins are found in the extraordinary (and sometimes extreme) focus in the later Middle Ages on the realistic physical presence of Christ in the eucharist. This is not the place for a long discussion about the history of doctrine on "real presence," but excellent resources do exist: See James Megivern's *Concomitance and Communion* (Fribourg, Switzerland: The University Press, 1963), available in theological libraries, and the more generally available *Cult and Controversy: The Worship of the Eucharist outside Mass* by Nathan Mitchell (New York: Pueblo Publishing Company, 1982).

By the time that this observance was passed down to us, it included a procession with the eucharist as its most distinctive feature. The reforms of the past decades have suppressed the feast of the Precious Blood and linked this mystery to this late spring festival, changing the day's name to "Body and Blood of Christ."

■ FATHER'S DAY: This holiday of "civil religion" should be observed by the church in much the same way as Mother's Day. The *Book of Blessing* (chapter 56) contains three suggested intercessions (some editions erroneously call these intercessions "introductory rites") and a simple blessing for

this day. Since this observance falls this year on the Body and Blood solemnity, parishes planning a eucharistic procession will have to adapt even these brief ideas. People's attention also can be called to the blessing in *Catholic Household Blessings and Prayers* (p. 198).

■ HYMNODY: Beautiful Latin hymns such as "Pange lingua" and "Adoro te devote" have their place today. Although musically challenging for some, they are drawn from the rich treasury of the chants of the church and are well worth the effort. English translations are available and could be used in alternation with the Latin verses. "Jesus, my Lord, my God, my all" ("Sweet Sacrament") is also appropriate for this celebration, as are Owen Alstott's "Gather us together" (OCP, #8725) and "You are our living bread" by Michael Joncas (NALR, *Glory and Praise Comprehensive Edition*). Any of these could be used during the eucharistic procession.

■ LITURGY OF THE WORD: The sequence, optional and difficult to set to familiar music, should be sung by all. We have few enough of this genre, and none so full in its language. Searching for a way that a congregation can sing this will be time well spent. The intercessions can be modeled on the intercessions found in Morning Prayer or Evening Prayer this day. They also should include the petitions listed under Father's Day in the *Book of Blessings,* #1732. If the parish normally blesses mothers and fathers at the concluding rites on their special days in May and June, and if a eucharistic procession is scheduled, the "prayer over the people" from the *Book of Blessings,* #1733 should be moved to the conclusion of the intercessions.

■ EUCHARISTIC PROCESSION: If the procession with the eucharist follows, the blessing and dismissal are omitted and the order found in *Holy Communion and Worship of the Eucharist outside Mass,* #101–8, is followed. Helpful notes can be found in the *Ceremonial of Bishops,* #387–94.

· As the distribution of communion ends, a monstrance is brought to the altar, and a host consecrated at this Mass is placed in it.

· The prayer after communion is said from the chair.

· Participating priests (of whatever number) may wear white copes (*Ceremonial of Bishops,* #390—part of a minor revival of the use of this vestment).

· The thurible is prepared, and the host is honored with incense as all kneel and begin singing eucharistic hymns.

· The presider puts on a humeral veil and takes up the monstrance as singing continues.

· The procession, accompanied by music, proceeds in this order: cross-bearer and acolytes with candles, ministers of the Mass (lectors, ministers of the eucharist), deacons or concelebrants, two thurifers with burning incense, the presider carrying the monstrance, and the members of the assembly. The rubrics specify that all the liturgical ministers are to carry lighted candles; certainly everyone else can too.

· Songs and prayers that are both well known and Christocentric should be planned for the entire procession time.

· The procession should move from one place or building to another: for example, to a neighboring parish, from church to parish hall via neighboring streets, or from the church to a cemetery chapel.

- Upon entering the destination, the presider places the monstrance on the altar, lays aside the humeral veil and performs an additional incensation. Meanwhile "Tantum ergo" (or something similar) is sung.

- A prayer from *Holy Communion and Worship of the Eucharist outside Mass* (#98) is said (Note that the dialogue about the bread from heaven is no longer in the rite).

- A blessing with the host is given.

- An acclamation or a hymn of praise is sung. (The "Divine Praises," recited for so many decades at this point, are now a series of acclamations. Singing is called for here, and any sung acclamation would be in place of these.)

- The deacon or other minister privately takes the host back to the chapel of reservation.

■ THE WEEK AHEAD: Two great solemnities—the birth of John the Baptist and the Sacred Heart—are before us during this twelfth week. These days, which always bring Catholics of the northern hemisphere into summer, will interrupt the sequence of readings from 2 Kings and Matthew. This seems to be a problem only with the 2 Kings passage to be missed on Friday. It could be combined with Thursday's passage so that the final days before the exile are set before the listeners, bringing to a close the narratives of the past few weeks.

M O N 22 #371 green Weekday

Paulinus of Nola, bishop, optional memorial / white. ▪ *John Fisher, bishop and martyr, and Thomas More, martyr, optional memorial / red.* ▪ The first reading continues, as it will throughout the week, the story of infidelity and crime, of God's people bringing about their exile.

Joined to the weekday readings, both Paulinus and the English

pair can inspire contemporary Catholics. Reflect on which memorial will assist your community or which links best with the local heritage—or alternate years between the two.

Paulinus, contemporary and correspondent with Augustine, Ambrose and Chromatius, left us a splendid body of literature. It is as deserving as Augustine's of our study. The martyrs Fisher and More are well known in American culture. More's daughter, Margaret Roper, passed on the letter that has been made part of the Office of Readings. It shows that the man is not just a civic "man for all seasons."

T U E 23 #372 green Weekday

W E D 24 #586–587 white Birth of John the Baptist SOLEMNITY

■ HISTORY OF THE DAY: This is an ancient feast, placed on this date because the annunciation to Zechariah was said to have taken place at Yom Kippur. The calculation of this pregnancy and birth have always been intimately related to the annunciation and nativity of the Lord. The placement of all these dates at the turn of the seasons was not arranged so that they could have solar symbolism, but once the dates became established at the equinox and solstice times, they became filled with images and meanings related to sun and climate. See the notes at Christmas, page 25, for more on this theory, which is gaining consensus among liturgical scholars. Others theorize that ancient beliefs and customs related to the summer and winter solstices caused our ancestors to structure the scriptures to have the births meet these dates.

■ LITURGY: The proper prayers might be adapted in a few places to read "birth" instead of "feast." The intercessions from Morning and Evening Prayer provide models of how to frame intercessions in the light of this solemnity. Several settings of the Canticle of Zachary can be found in resources for the liturgy of the hours, particularly *Praise God in Song* (GIA, G-2270). The three-verse setting coupled with "Ellacombe" in the *Hymnal for Catholic Students* is particularly lively and singable. The text, "The great forerunner of the morn," often coupled with the tune, "Winchester New," is also happily wedded to "Puer nobis."

Pastoral planners should try to schedule a gathering of the parish on the evening of the 23rd or 24th —or both if John is the local patron. If the eve is selected, the texts suggested in appendix I of the *Liturgy of the Hours* could help to shape an extended vigil. On the 24th itself, an evening gathering could use Evening Prayer II, perhaps adding a lengthier scripture reading or the passage from Augustine in the Office of Readings. Either liturgy, or the eucharist itself could, indeed should, be followed by summertime festivities. This might be one of the times when it is worth the effort to schedule the prayer in the parish yard or in some public place—near water, if possible.

T H U 25 #374 green Weekday

As noted at the beginning of this week, today's first reading should also include the verses normally read on Friday of the twelfth week. The attention they focus on exile might prompt planners to draw the day's prayers from the Masses and Prayers for Various Needs and Occasions, 29. For Refugees and Exiles.

F R I 26 #173 white
Sacred Heart
SOLEMNITY

"The day is not meant to be a detached viewing of a sentimentally colored portrayal of Jesus pointing at his large heart. The Mass texts point us beyond the relatively modern image to perennial love of God seen in Jesus" (*Study Text 9,* p. 60).

■ HISTORY OF THE FEAST: Long a favorite devotion of some mystics, liturgical celebrations under this title did not begin until a few centuries ago. As noted by Pierre Jounel (p. 106 in Martimort, see resources), many Mass formularies have circulated, and they show two currents of thought: thanksgiving for the inexhaustible riches of Christ (see the first opening prayer) and reparative contemplation of the pierced heart (the alternative opening prayer). These same emphases have marked First Friday traditions in many Catholic circles.

■ CELEBRATION OF THE EUCHARIST: The rich menu of scriptures associated with the feast ground these themes in primordial tradition. The prayer texts are found after all the Sundays in Ordinary Time, right after the Body and Blood texts used last Sunday. As is often the case, Morning and Evening Prayer provide good examples of expressing a feast through intercessions.

■ INTERRELATED IMAGES: In Year C, the scripture readings and psalm highlight the image of God as the ever-loving shepherd. These same attributes were, of course, attributed to Jesus. While the main celebration of the Good Shepherd each year is the Fourth Sunday of Easter, occasional days like this appear, reminding us of this central image. So the Sacred Heart is associated here with the more ancient image of shepherd.

The solemnity of this title or image should encourage planners and all who observe the feast to examine the role of images in leading us to the "prototypes" they represent. See chapter 36, Part I of the *Book of Blessings* ("Order for the Blessing of an Image of Our Lord Jesus Christ") for background on this. See especially its prayer at #1272 where the relationship of image and faith is expressed. Its words about the heart of Jesus provide an excellent overview of this solemnity:

> We search the deepest reaches
> of his heart,
> and our own hearts burn with that
> fire of the Spirit
> which he spread in order to renew
> the face of the earth.

The Sacred Heart is not placed before us to encourage our passivity and private comfort. It is a day to enflame us with enthusiasm for the same good news spread by the apostles at Pentecost.

■ FURTHER CELEBRATIONS: The *Liturgy of the Hours* (appendix I) suggests ways to have a vigil service, particularly important in parishes and in religious communities that have this as their titular solemnity.

S A T 27 #376 or #573 green
Weekday

Cyril of Alexandria, bishop and doctor, optional memorial / white. ▪ *Immaculate Heart of Mary, optional memorial / white.* ▪ *Blessed Virgin Mary, optional memorial / white.* ▪ The last of the memorial options should not be used this year. If a Marian celebration is desired or if the parish is dedicated to the Sacred Heart, the Immaculate Heart texts should be used. The selection of Immaculate Heart brings with it a proper gospel at #573 and the freedom to choose a first reading from the Marian commons. The *Liturgy of the Hours* texts for the memorial are located right after May 31, with sacramentary texts similarly placed at the beginning of June. See Anscar Chupungco's *Liturgies of the Future* (p. 210) for a fascinating description of the political history of this memorial.

The opening prayer and the *Liturgy of the Hours* for the first-mentioned memorial express the tradition that Cyril was instrumental in furthering devotion to Mary. The choice of his memorial allows the local church to honor one of the few "doctors" and to hear the scriptures of the weekday —Lamentations—responding to the events narrated over the previous days. We have all too few opportunities for expressing our lamentations in liturgy, for bringing the real pains we endure to liturgical expression. The proper psalm for this day is an extraordinary opportunity for the singing out of these genuinely human emotions.

☀28 **Thirteenth Sunday in Ordinary Time**

#100   Green

Today we begin the first of four "blocks" in Ordinary Time. For an overview of Luke and these divisions, see page 167.

Sundays 13–20 (June 28–August 16): Journey to Jerusalem, Part 1.

■ LUKE: The gospels for these weeks form what is "for the most part a literary compilation of sayings of Jesus, pronouncement stories, and a few miracle stories, all set in the framework of the journey to Jerusalem" (Fitzmyer, p. 825 in the *Anchor Bible* volumes for Luke; see the resources list). This long section of Luke will continue through all the Sundays until November. It has been divided here into three blocks in the way most scriptural commentators have divided it—three subsections, each beginning with an explicit reference to the resolute Jesus headed to Jerusalem.

This section starts with the first reference to the journey. Parishes spend eight Sundays listening to the stories Luke has connected with this reference. Lessons about discipleship are combined with direct warnings about the opposition one might expect. The assembly might lose track of the travelogue, but the geography is less important than the teachings about the "way" to life.

■ INTRODUCTORY RITES: For penitential rite invocations, look to the scriptures for phrases that capture the sense of what is going on, words that will sink in over the next few weeks. For example, form c_i can be used each week, with the scriptures of that Sunday lending a phrase to one or another of the three invocations

in that set. On this Thirteenth Sunday, the first or third invocation might be, "You freed us for liberty: Lord, have mercy." "You call us to Jerusalem" or "You call us to discipleship" could just as readily be used. The principle, as recommended in the *Sourcebook* each year, is this: Even if minor modifications are made week-by-week, stay with one set of texts for several weeks at a time.

Because it is so soon after Eastertime and we should stress the distinction of seasons, it might be best to pass over the option of the sprinkling rite during this block of weeks. Collects related to the scriptures are on page 205.

■ LITURGY OF THE WORD: Several psalms are listed as possibilities for common use at this time of year (see lectionary #175, at the end; note that early editions of the lectionary still have the designation "Season of the Year"). Pastoral liturgists and musicians have recognized the benefit of these common psalms for some time. Sung over several weeks, these psalms let the community's praise become internalized and thus more expressive. One psalm is suggested here for each block of Ordinary Time.

For this block, Psalm 63 or Psalm 95 is recommended. Both of these bring the motifs of journey and of longing to communal expression. The Gelineau setting of Psalm 63 with the Proulx antiphon, "My soul is thirsting for you, O Lord . . ." (GIA, *Gelineau Gradual*, G-2124) is a worthy setting favored by many assemblies. The simple and direct translation of this Psalm from the ICEL Liturgical Psalter Project ("God, my God, you I crave; . . .") enjoys a sturdy, singable antiphon and psalm tone by Marty Haugen (NPM, *Psalms for All Seasons*). Psalm 95, "If today you hear his

voice," is set by David Haas in *Psalms for the Church Year*, vol. I (GIA, G-2664); *Psalms for all Seasons* (NPM) contains the ICEL translation in an energetic ostinato setting with overlaid cantor verses composed by Christopher Willcock. Consider also David Clark Isele's setting in his collection *Psalms for the Church Year* (GIA, G-2262) with choral verses, or with verses chanted to a psalm tone as recommended in *Lead Me, Guide Me*, #533 (GIA).

Verses for the gospel acclamation are not usually assigned to specific Sundays in Ordinary Time. Planners may want to select one from lectionary #164 and use it throughout these weeks.

A well-worded set of intercessions should be repeated over these weeks. The use of such a set does not preclude the addition of weekly variants that express particular needs or relate to the day's scriptures. Many parishes will want to include petitions for children (samples in *Book of Blessings* [BB], #148), for parishioners who are moving (sample in BB, #1937), for the United States (on Sundays June 28 and July 5), for justice and equality and other values inherent in the electoral process (especially as the political conventions unfold), and for travelers (samples in BB, #629).

■ LITURGY OF THE EUCHARIST: Select one of the Sunday prefaces and combine it with Eucharistic Prayer I, II or III. Then stay with this choice for the entire block of weeks so that everyone will begin to feel its cadences and make it their own prayer action. If the aspect of Jesus' obedience, so central to the journey to Jerusalem, will be one of the elements emphasized during this year's movement through Luke, then the preface for Sundays in Ordinary Time VII (P 35) should be a candidate

J U N E

for this consistent use. The presence of Independence Day with its thoughts of justice and images of journey might suggest using the preface, "Independence Day and Other Civic Observances II" (P 83). While the title appears to be limiting, it is a fine preface for frequent usage. The reference to "all men" can be "all." Certainly the prayer should contain the same sung acclamations over the several weeks.

For the communion procession, consider using Marty Haugen's "Now in this banquet" (GIA, G-2918) with its Advent refrain "God of our journeys, daybreak to night; lead us to justice and light. Grant us compassion, strength for the day, wisdom to walk in your way." Michael Joncas's setting of Psalm 63 in *Psalms for All Seasons* (NPM), while too extended for use as a responsorial psalm, is a fitting communion processional.

■ CONCLUDING RITE: Pick one of the solemn blessings (remember that the appendix in the *Book of Blessings* supplements the sacramentary here), and make it your own for these two months.

■ HYMNODY: "Center of my life" (OCP, #7136) by Paul Inwood reinforces some of the gospel themes found during these Sundays. The strong and timely text by Frances W. Davis, "Let there be light," paired with David Hurd's "Sprague" in *Worship* (GIA), speaks of the challenge of discipleship in our day. The kingdom imagery of the gospels is carried through in "On our journey to the kingdom" by Tobias Colgan, OSB, (OCP, #9054). This same text appears with some variations in *Gather* (GIA), this time marching along to the early American tune "Holy manna." On some of the Sundays of this section, the call to discipleship can be

reinforced with a strong sending-forth hymn, such as "Lord, you give the great commission." This hymn concludes each stanza "With the Spirit's gifts empower us for the work of ministry." This text is most effective when coupled with the expansive tune "Abbot's Leigh," found in *Worship*.

■ THE SUNDAY BEFORE PETER AND PAUL: This is the Sunday frequently selected in coastal communities for the blessing of the fleet. See chapter 22 of the *Book of Blessings*). The presence of that solemnity on Monday means that Masses on Sunday night may be the vigil Masses for Peter and Paul (check diocesan norms).

■ THE WEEK AHEAD: The solemnity of Peter and Paul, the feast of Thomas, and Independence Day mean that on two or three days this week the weekday flow of scriptures will be interrupted. This is the week of Amos, and, while it is a shame to miss any of his strong words, their absence does not necessitate any adjustments to the surrounding days' scriptures. The same is true for this week's block of readings from Matthew.

#590–591   red

✸29 Peter and Paul, apostles
SOLEMNITY

The opening prayer of the Vigil Mass succinctly lauds this pair's invaluable contribution to Christianity by referring to them as "the apostles who strengthened the faith of the infant church."

■ HISTORY OF THE SOLEMNITY: This is the day when the church of Rome and all churches in communion with it celebrate their apostolic foundation. As noted by various commentators (for example, Adolf Adam, p. 236), three different liturgies were once celebrated on this day, second only to Easter in Rome. Peter was remembered in his basilica on the Vatican hill and Paul at his tomb on the road to Ostia; then everyone journeyed to a catacomb where the remains of both (or at least their heads) were kept during a persecution. This rich history of their *cultus* has left a treasury of texts from which the current texts were drawn.

Despite the logistical difficulties of getting from one part of Rome to another, the two apostles ever remained linked in celebration, iconography and preaching. Documents and artifacts from every century show their union as twin pillars, as complementary witnesses. Their different approaches led to serious confrontations (for example, at the Council of Jerusalem). Indeed, this day celebrates that at the very moment of its foundation, the church of Rome was marked more by its ability to love in the midst of tension than by its facility for living calmly in tranquil surroundings.

■ LITURGY: Just about all of the texts are proper to the day, with a once-a-year solemn blessing printed at the Day Mass (but also appropriate for the vigil). A solemnity has greater precedence than an Ordinary Time Sunday, so Masses on Sunday night may use the saints' texts: Local practice in your diocese will determine this. The appendix of the *Liturgy of the Hours* has texts for fashioning an extended vigil on Sunday night, and they should certainly be used by the many churches carrying the title of either or both of these apostles.

**T
U
E 30 #378 green
Weekday**

First Martyrs of the Church of Rome, optional memorial/red. ■ This optional day was added to the current calendar because many feasts of the earliest Roman martyrs were suppressed. Akin to All Saints' Day, and certainly in line with that festival's "All Martyrs" origins, this memorial offers the holy witnesses in Roman Catholicism's earliest days global praise. Just as the solemnity yesterday allowed us to remember our apostolic foundation, so today we remember our foundation and growth in the blood of martyrs. The second reading in the memorial's Office of Readings is an account from their own era of their witness to the gospel.

July

**W
E
D 1 #379 green
Weekday**

Blessed Junipero Serra, priest, optional memorial/white. ■ *Canada Day.* This is a new memorial proper to the dioceses of the United States. Like other days on the proper calendar of the nation, its attractiveness to local congregations will depend somewhat on geography and ethnic background. Catholics in California will find this an important (even if somewhat controversial) day. Parishioners in Maine may be unaware of the controversy about this beatified friar's dealings with Native Americans.

In every diocese of the United States, this still is a fine time to link the weekday scriptures to a part of our history, to the ambiguous trek of frail humans and to the message God speaks through them. Prayers for missionaries and for the descendants of the Native Americans of early California may be included in the intercessions. Proper presidential prayer texts are not in the latest sacramentary but may be available from the local diocesan liturgy office. If not, the Commons for Pastors (Missionaries) can be used. In the dioceses now in the region that was Junipero Serra's mission territory, this might be the most fitting day for the penitential service described on page xiii.

■ CANADA DAY: Prayers for the people of Canada are fitting for the general intercessions today. Parishes there have a special set of Mass texts and prayer services in their blessings book.

**T
H
U 2 #380 green
Weekday**

**F
R
I 3 #593 red
Thomas, apostle
FEAST**

Early Christian documents cite Thomas's presence and martyrdom in India. Prayers for the peoples of that land are appropriate today. Stories also circulated in the fifth century describing the transporting ("translation") of some of his relics to Edessa (in northern Mesopotamia) on July 3, 384. Medieval calendars of Western churches (used until 1969) placed his feast on December 21, but a desire to clear the week before Christmas led the Vatican to use this ancient translation day (celebrated by the Syriac and Malabar churches) as the new feast date for the Roman rite.

**S
A
T 4 #382 or as noted below green
Weekday**

Elizabeth of Portugal, optional memorial/white. ■ *Blessed Virgin Mary, optional memorial/white.* ■ *Independence Day (U.S.A.), optional proper Mass/white.* ■ The optional memorial for Mary should be saved for Saturdays that do not have other propers. The optional memorial of Elizabeth might be passed over in most U.S. parishes because the proper national texts, if used sensitively, can be expressive for parishes that gather this day.

■ INDEPENDENCE DAY IN THE SACRAMENTARY: Prayer texts for Mass may be taken from those listed under this date in the "Proper of Saints" pages in the sacramentary or from appendix X of the sacramentary—a choice of five opening prayers, four prayers over the gifts, five prayers after communion and a proper solemn blessing. Two prefaces are recommended there, but some parishes might want to use Eucharistic Prayer for Reconciliation II with its words about nations seeking the way of peace together.

■ INDEPENDENCE DAY IN THE LECTIONARY: The readings cited at both mentioned places in the sacramentary require a lot of page-turning in the lectionary to select appropriate passages. Most of them, however, are in #831–35 ("Peace and Justice"). This review of readings might serve as a mini-retreat guiding a group of parish members through a reflection on the biblical message to the people of God divided into different nations.

■ MUSIC: The music for today might include American hymns, but this is not an occasion to use patriotic or civic songs. Such music, while often stirring, tends to turn the liturgy toward a celebration of country over God. Even if they mention God or praise the "divine power," their melodies and associations seem unfit for the celebration of the eucharist. If one must be used, it only can go at the end of the Mass.

5 #103   green
Fourteenth Sunday in Ordinary Time

The patterns noted on pages 176–77 should be used again on this second Sunday of the block of Sundays. The principles already noted regarding inclusive prayer texts and national music apply with even greater vigor on this Saturday night and Sunday.

Americans must pray for their hemisphere—and with a particular set of memories in 1992. North Americans must pray for their continent—encouraged and saddened by the ambiguous history that we share. The regions colonized by the Spanish, the French, the British and the Russians must join in fervent prayer for the American natives who lived here

first and for all the immigrants who continue to come to Mexico, Canada and the United States. In the midst of these year-round prayers, this is the prime weekend for residents of the 50 states to pray most intensely for wholeness and reconciliation.

The genre and cadence of Catholic liturgical expression must be respected. We must not twist liturgy into a mere teaching device. On this particular Sunday, this would mean that the patterns begun last week for liturgical texts and music, the attention to the journey to Jerusalem and the regular decor of summer Ordinary Time are not to be replaced by a celebration of the American holiday. National concerns are to be adapted to proper liturgical forms.

■ PARISHIONERS WHO ARE LEAVING: As schools close, as many businesses' fiscal years end and as summer sets in, the "Order for the Blessing of a Departing Parishioner" (in chapter 67 of the *Book of Blessings*) may be of pastoral benefit. A petition for inclusion in the general intercessions is given. At #1938 there is a rubric about inviting the person or family forward, then a fine suggestion to use the solemn blessing designated Ordinary Time V.

6 #383   green
Weekday

Maria Goretti, virgin and martyr, optional memorial/red. ▪ The first readings for the weekdays in Year II feature more of the prophetic books than those of Year I. Today we meet Hosea, and selections from his book continue through the week. While scattered passages from Hosea are used occasionally through the year, this is the only week every two years when we read the book in a

semicontinuous way. The framers of the lectionary were careful to include passages from each of the major sections of the book. This strong-voiced prophet speaks through the millennia of a morality or life-style that is broadly social and deeply religious. The witness of the simple child Maria, martyred when she was 12, is another reminder that the quest for wholeness is eternal.

7 #384   green
Weekday

8 #385   green
Weekday

9 #386   green
Weekday

10 #387   green
Weekday

11 #388   white
Benedict, abbot
MEMORIAL

This day is given the rank of a feast in Europe (where he is patron) and of a solemnity in Benedictine monasteries. While his name is well known and while even secular historians recognize his role in Western civilization, today's memorial in the United States is a good example of a few principles of the Roman Catholic calendar. Even the great saints are not venerated with equal strength worldwide. Thus even a great man like Benedict rests happily with the ranking of "memorial," allowing the festival to rise up in communities dedicated to his name. Pray today for monastic communities.

☀12 #106 green
Fifteenth Sunday in Ordinary Time

See page 176 for suggestions regarding the pattern of liturgical prayer that might carry into these weeks when the Journey to Jerusalem is unfolding in the lectionary and in listeners' hearts.

■ CHRIST, IMAGE OF THE INVISIBLE GOD: This Sunday we hear the first of four evocative passages from the letter to the Colossians. This first selection is a primitive Christian hymn, incorporated by Paul into his letter. It is still sung in communities that celebrate daily Evening Prayer, especially on Wednesdays when it is regularly assigned as the New Testament canticle. Some parishes might decide to chant this reading today—always an option and most fitting when the pericope is itself a hymn. Celebrating the role of Christ in creation, the community finds refreshment along the road to Jerusalem.

The challenge presented to listeners by today's gospel should not motivate homilists and planners to turn the liturgy into a classroom on how "you out there in the congregation" should be good Samaritans. Nor can the liturgy be a sensitivity group to open us to the needs of others. This is the assembly that has gathered to sing, to praise, to give thanks. Of course the Teacher Jesus is present, but always through and in the action of a redeemed people. The teachings are "transmitted" (better, "appreciated") through the actions of the liturgy, through the interaction of the body of Christ. We do not interrupt these actions to scold or browbeat.

■ CHURCH, IMAGE OF THE INVISIBLE GOD: The readings from the early Christian era this week (in the Office of Readings) are from the treatise "On the Mysteries"

by the great fourth-century bishop of Milan, Ambrose. The principle that catechumens should not know all the ins and outs of rites, that the content of the sacraments is best left for postbaptismal catechesis, is repeated often these days by experts in the catechumenate and catechesis. Paragraph #245 of the *Rite of Christian Initiation of Adults* is the most definitive and current statement of this. Today's opening paragraph from Ambrose remains the classic articulation:

> Now the season reminds us that we must speak of the mysteries, setting forth the meaning of the sacraments. If we had thought fit to teach these things to those not yet initiated through baptism, we should be considered traitors rather than teachers. Then, too, the light of the mysteries is of itself more effective where people do not know what to expect than where some instruction has been given beforehand.

All of the Ambrosian passages this week stand as a marvelous link to Easter, as an inspiring example of how to open the mysteries and share moral principles with the baptized.

13 #389 green
Weekday

Henry, optional memorial/white.
■ This holy emperor is one of the three saints in the universal calendar from the years around 1000. With Romuald and Stephen of Hungary, this emperor remains an example of true millennial faith. They trusted in the Second Coming, not in false reports of it. Their *cultus* teaches us not only through instruction, but also through union with their memory at the altar and praise of their witness for their own era. Through these, we are drawn into the same mysteries as they were, and gradually

shaped in our own day into the eternal mysteries.

The first readings for the next five days are from Isaiah, all from the part of that canonical book that can be traced back to Isaiah himself. Isaiah can be appreciated quite differently here than in Advent. In the bright sun of summer, we can cherish his words as our Hebrew ancestors did, without too quickly affixing them to Christmas meanings. Hearing them in the order they appear in the book, rather than as scattered companion pieces to gospels, we can better appreciate the life of Isaiah.

14 #390 white
Blessed Kateri Tekakwitha, virgin
MEMORIAL

■ HER LIFE: This year, 1992, we should approach with great care this memorial of the young Mohawk woman who died at the age of 24 in 1680. Little is known of her life, but the few details point to the innocence which brought her the title "Lily of the Mohawks." Born in an area now part of New York, she was orphaned at an early age and disfigured by smallpox. Growing up with relatives near Montreal, she met Jesuit missionaries there and soon enrolled in a catechumenate. At the age of 20, after six months as a catechumen, she was baptized on Easter Sunday. This in itself serves as evidence that the catechumenate, while little known in the United States before Vatican II, survived, at least in part, in mission territories. As was the practice then, she received first communion almost two years later. Through all of this growth in the faith, her non-Christian relatives were, to put it mildly, not supportive. She seems to have made the Christian Mohawk community across the river from Montreal her family. There an older

Christian woman, Anastasia Tegonhatsihongo, acted as a sort of mystagogue, leading Kateri deeper into Christianity.

■ HER MEMORY IN LITURGY: Through the short but intense years of her catechumenate, approach to the altar and dedication to virginity, Kateri became an icon of a "sacramental person." All that we know of these four years are the records of her baptism, eucharist and death, and her preparations for them, made all the more earnest by her relatives' opposition. Her story seems mercifully free of the violence between nations and peoples that accompanied the movement of the Europeans to America. In her case, the French missionaries seem to have been sensitive to the native people, but the annals of all the Christian groups—French, Spanish and English—include many cases where this is not so. Without any apprehensions about forced conversions, we can use the beautiful opening prayer for her day, asking that all peoples of every tribe, nation and tongue sing hymns of God's greatness.

■ HER MEMORY IN QUEBEC: The memory of Kateri is most tangible in the Mohawk communities near Montreal. There, hospitals, churches and schools proudly bear her name. But the conflicts between Mohawks and the government of Quebec, between many Native American nations and their French-speaking neighbors, have turned the place of her sacramental initiation and early death into a battleground of cultures and even religions. The sins and shortcomings of previous generations are visited upon present citizens in the shadows of her shrines. Her feast in Canada is observed on April 17, and its coincidence this year with the Easter Triduum reminds one of

her Easter baptism. This regular remembrance of her in paschaltide keeps the terms clear: Only the Deathless One can bring about the reconciliation still needed by Kateri's own.

■ HER MEMORY IN 1992: The innocent "Lily" provides an opportunity for Catholics who keep her memory to celebrate a reconciliation service—a service of thanksgiving and reparation for all that has gone on in the name of "innocence" (see page xiii). If such a service is not possible this evening, then the weekday eucharist, at least, can be enhanced by petitions appropriate to this day: for the reconciliation of Canada, Quebec, and the United States with the many nations that existed here long before the European colonists created these boundaries; for the presence of spiritual guides like the Jesuits and Anastasia; for all who are ostracized by their communities; for all American Indian and Inuit tribes and their following of the gospel within the spirit of their cultures; for the assembly gathered and its growth in intercultural tolerance.

W E D 15 #391   white
Bonaventure, bishop and doctor
MEMORIAL

Bonaventure—a learned man—is remembered this year on the day when we read "what you have hidden from the learned and the clever you have revealed to the merest children" from Matthew's gospel. Homilists and intercession writers will have to sort through this seeming contradiction. The gospel should not support any anti-intellectual bias.

T H U 16 #392   green
Weekday

Our Lady of Mount Carmel, optional memorial/white. • This optional memorial will surely be celebrated by Carmelite communities, and it is a favorite day among several ethnic groups.

F R I 17 #393   green
Weekday

S A T 18 #394   green
Weekday

Blessed Virgin Mary, optional memorial/white. • Micah takes center stage for the next few weekdays, encouraging weekday congregations to become more familiar with him.

✷ 19 #109   green
Sixteenth Sunday in Ordinary Time

See pages 176–77 for suggestions for this block of Sundays.

■ BLESSING OF TRAVELERS: The summer season often provides an opportune moment for making use of chapter 9 of the *Book of Blessings,* the "Order for the Blessing of Travelers." Form I can be used at a special prayer service if a large parish group is leaving at the same time—a scout group on its way to a jamboree, for example. Form II can be used after the Sunday liturgy for those who will be leaving that week on vacation.

■ THE WEEK AHEAD: The progression through the prophets and the semicontinuous proclamation of Matthew will be interrupted twice this week, Wednesday and Saturday. Eliminating Wednesday's readings may present a problem. The first reading that would have been proclaimed if the memorial of Mary Magdalene were not celebrated then describes the call of Jeremiah. This reading's absence might hinder the full appreciation of the many passages from Jeremiah to follow over the next two weeks; its verses could be appended to the first reading on Thursday. The gospel on Wednesday would have been the parable of the sower. Here, too, its absence would be missed, since the Thursday and Friday gospels presume it has been heard. It should be read as part of a longer gospel on Thursday. Lengthy narratives encourage us to sing the psalm after the reading. We need music, not another "reading," to center our hearts and express our joy in the God of the prophets.

M O N **20** #395 green **Weekday**

T U E **21** #396 green **Weekday**

Lawrence of Brindisi, priest and doctor, optional memorial/white. • The biography of Lawrence in the liturgical books says that he was "an effective and forceful preacher." Pray that more leaders recognize this apostolic duty and devote more time to the rigors of preparation and interpretation. Catholics too often see the homily as an intrusion or as something easily omitted when the weather seems too hot.

W E D **22** #603 white **Mary Magdalene** MEMORIAL

Our tradition refers to her as *apostola apostolorum,* "apostle to the apostles," because she was the first to see the risen Jesus and the first to carry the good news of the resurrection back to the apostles.

Her apostolic role is contained in the passage proper to this memorial and is articulated in the day's prayers. It is unusual for memorials to have so many proper texts, even a verse for the gospel acclamation and special antiphons for all the psalms in the

Liturgy of the Hours. This indicates the importance of her memory and the greater festivity surrounding it in earlier traditions.

Mary Magdalene is not to be confused with the sinful woman described in Luke 7:36–50, nor is she the same person as Mary of Bethany, even though traditions have long existed that made such connections. Other legends have sprung up, even more fantastic and ungrounded, positing her as the wife of Jesus or as the mother of a French dynasty. She also has become one of the most revered figures in some "new age" circles, as writers and the curious trek to Vezelay and St. Maximin, the two French shrines claiming to have her remains. The attractiveness of devotion to her has not been founded just on her apostolic role. The association of Mary Magdalene with the prostitute has caught each era's imagination: The profane becomes holy. Such testimony to the vitality of her secular commemoration should inspire us to review ways that her liturgical commemoration might express the role of women as apostles and messengers of liberation.

T H U **23** #398 green **Weekday**

Bridget, religious, optional memorial/white. • Wife, mother, widow, founder of a religious community, mystic and reformer of the church, this patron saint of Sweden joins us as we begin the book of Jeremiah. Pray for prophetic imagination and holiness in her religious community, in Sweden and in a reformed church.

F R I **24** #399 green **Weekday**

S A T **25** #605 white **James, apostle** FEAST

James was the brother of John and one of the three closest men to Jesus. He is to be distinguished from the James commemorated on May 3 (about whom we know little). The gospel proclaimed on this feast tells of James the Great and his mother jostling for honor, but it also hints at his pending martyrdom. The proper prayers note that he was considered the first of the apostolic martyrs.

His *cultus* was tremendously popular in the Middle Ages; it seems almost everyone in Europe traveled in pilgrimage to his tomb in northwest Spain. These pilgrimage routes, the architectural forms developed along them and the cultural customs connected with them were principal factors in the shaping of Western Europe. Prayers may be voiced today for the hundreds of thousands who make pilgrimage on these routes every summer.

Pilgrims to the shrine of St. James wear a scallop shell—a symbol that traditionally guarantees them the hospitality of any village through which they pass. The seashell, with its baptismal allusions, thus is a symbol both for John the Baptist and for James —and for anyone coming home from a summertime trip to the beach! This is a grand day to review parish hospitality and to consider hospitality to a new breed of "pilgrims"—folks on vacation.

⊛26 #112 green **Seventeenth Sunday in Ordinary Time**

See pages 176–77 for prayer patterns for this block of Sundays in Ordinary Time.

The letter to the Colossians continues to lend counterpoint to the gospels. Today we come upon a short selection that Paul seems to have drawn from hymns or mystagogical catecheses. Each of the phrases carries its own power, right up to the ending, "nailing it to the cross." Such a short and powerful passage calls for great care. It may be chanted; it may also suggest a complementary hymn later in the liturgy.

The gospel on the Lord's Prayer may prompt homilists to turn to the patristic readings from Cyril in the Office of Readings for the eleventh week.

■ THE WEEK AHEAD: The memorial of Martha on Wednesday intervenes in the semicontinuous reading of Matthew. There does not, in this case, seem to be a need to recover the parable that will be lost. The strong words of Jeremiah throughout this week and next should prompt homilists to review the various commentaries on this prophet.

M O N 27 #401 green
Weekday

T U E 28 #402 green
Weekday

W E D 29 #403 and 607 white
Martha
MEMORIAL

The gospel readings proper to Martha's day take precedence over those of the weekday, but Jeremiah continues. We know very little about this sister of Mary of Bethany and Lazarus. Intercessions could include the need for hospitality, the need for welcoming Jesus and the need for working for his comfort in the poor, the homeless and the immigrant.

T H U 30 #404 green
Weekday

Peter Chrysologus, bishop and doctor, optional memorial/white. ■ The fine selection from this "preacher of [the] incarnate Word" (opening prayer) given in the Office of Readings may be filed away for use at Christmas.

F R I 31 #405 white
Ignatius of Loyola, priest
MEMORIAL

Pray for Jesuits and for all who use Ignatius's exercises in their search for God.

August

S A T 1 #406 white
Alphonsus Liguori, bishop and doctor
MEMORIAL

We meet another founder of a post-Reformation religious order. His preaching frequently centered on the eucharist (see the prayer after communion). While the readings of the weekday should be used, the proper reading cited at #610 in the lectionary (for use where this day is a feast or solemnity) is a useful meditation for those trying to appreciate the manner in which tradition remembers Alphonsus.

☀ 2 #115 green
Eighteenth Sunday in Ordinary Time

See pages 176–77 for suggestions on linking this day to the other Sundays of this block.

This Sunday marks one of the very rare appearances of the book of Ecclesiastes in the Catholic liturgy. This is the only Sunday in the three-year cycle when it appears, and it will be read on a few weekdays later this fall. The short passage includes some of the most remembered portions of the brief

book—the only other part people seem to know was made famous in the song "Turn, turn, turn." While it might be unusual in most communities to have the homily focus only on the first reading, this passage may be worth it. The need to come to terms with "vanity" and uselessness knows no end. Behind the question found in today's gospel, "What does it profit one to gain the world and lose one's soul?" lies the question "What profit comes to anyone for all the toil and anxiety?"

■ THE WEEK AHEAD: The feast of the Transfiguration takes precedence over the weekday readings from Jeremiah and Matthew. The important chapter with Peter's confession of faith may be appended to Friday's reading.

M O N 3 #407 green
Weekday

T U E 4 #408 white
John Vianney, priest
MEMORIAL

John was from the same diocese and decades as Peter Chanel (see April 28), and they represent the contrasting religious trends of the early nineteenth century. Peter was an intellectual, a seminary professor; John barely made it through the basic course of studies. Peter enthusiastically embraced one of the new religious communities springing up in post-Revolution France; John exemplified the traditional parish priest, wedded to his village. Peter went off to the foreign missions; John never went far from his birth place, ministering within his own culture in the styles traditional to it.

Few diocesan priests are celebrated in the Roman Calendar—not because they have been less holy, but because religious orders have had better systems for promoting the causes of their holy ones. On this day prayers for all diocesan priests are in order. Their cultural and liturgical tasks are somewhat different now than in John's time, but we pray for their "zeal and concern" (opening prayer).

WED 5 #409 green
Weekday

Dedication of St. Mary Major, optional memorial/white. ▪ Every parish should keep its own church's anniversary of dedication as a solemnity (see page 213) and the anniversary of the dedication of the local cathedral as a parish feast. In addition, all of the churches in the Roman rite remember the dedication anniversaries of the four major church buildings in Rome. The formative nature of these days should call for their annual celebration (even though most are optional memorials). Besides St. Mary Major, these "mother churches" are St. John Lateran (the cathedral of Rome, a feast on November 9), St. Peter (remembered on November 18), and St. Paul (remembered together with St. Peter). These five days, linking us to four Roman buildings, to our diocese and to the local gathering place, form a separate stratum in the listing of saints' days.

While the texts of this optional memorial are generally from the commons of Mary, some of the texts for the "Common of the Dedication of a Church" (2. Anniversary of Dedication, B. Outside the Dedicated Church) might serve as a reminder that the character of this Marian day is its link to a place. These texts help us to become aware of the awesome power of sacred space in the development of our identity.

THU 6 #614 white
Transfiguration of the Lord
FEAST

▪ HISTORY: An ancient tradition held that the transfiguration took place 40 days before the crucifixion. Because the cross is celebrated on September 14, this feast was placed 40 days earlier. Other stories explain the date by references to dedication anniversaries on Mount Tabor (see Jounel in Martimort, *The Church at Prayer,* vol. IV, for more).

August 6 has had a peculiar history with regard to war. In 1457, the pope put this already ancient festival into the Roman calendar in gratitude for a victory over the Turks near Belgrade on August 6. The anniversary of the bombing of Hiroshima in our own century is changing the observance again.

▪ EMBER DAYS: Two ember days that deserve to be part of the rhythm of the year are August 6 and August 9. *Catholic Household Blessings and Prayers* (p. 186) describes the concept of ember days and gives a prayer appropriate for domestic use and for the assembly's intercessions.

▪ LITURGY: The parish's main celebration—a Mass or Evening Prayer joined to an "ember day supper"—may take place in the evening. It is a celebration of all that we are meant to be for each other and all that we are meant to become in the Lord. The account from Luke, repeating the gospel

from the Second Sunday of Lent, is heard in a different way today. The feast's focus, the time of year and the accompanying readings and chants let us see this gospel and the whole feast day as celebrating that "heavenly vision that will give us a share in his radiance, renew our spiritual nature and transform us into his own likeness" (Office of Readings). The proper prayers also highlight our share in the brightness.

FRI 7 #411 green
Weekday

Sixtus II, pope and martyr, and companions, martyrs, optional memorial/red. ▪ *Cajetan, priest, optional memorial/white.* ▪ The first reading today is the one appearance of the book of Nahum in the entire lectionary. It is a short book and its main purpose is well expressed in this pastiche of verses—the triumph of God's people over Nineveh. While the oppression wrought by that ancient city's powers helps us appreciate Jonah's reluctance to preach there, Nahum's joy at their destruction must be carefully interpreted.

Both of the optional memorials bring us to Rome. Sixtus, listed in Eucharistic Prayer I, was a pope and martyr of the third century (the reading in his Office of Readings is a good example of the early Christian view of persecution). Cajetan is a much later reformer. By keeping one of these Christian leaders' memory, parishes confront the mystery of how God is with us and with all of humanity.

SAT 8 #412 white
Dominic, priest
MEMORIAL

Another rarely heard prophet, Habakkuk, appears today coupled with the thirteenth-century preacher, Dominic. Catholics are aware of the Dominicans, but the memory of their founder provides us with more to ponder than just another religious community. Over the years, those who keep this day should come to terms with Dominic's controversial career: his role in the fight against the Cathars or Albigensians, his "invention" and propagation of the rosary, his community's witness of scholarship and preaching.

✸9 #118   green
Nineteenth Sunday in Ordinary Time

See pages 176–77 for patterns of prayer and rite for this block of Sundays in Ordinary Time.

■ HEBREWS: The letter to the Hebrews is read today and on the next several Sundays. In the midst of their political parties' conventions, residents of the United States can hear today's selection with particular force. The long form is preferred because it allows listeners to go deeper into the meaning of Abraham and Sarah—strangers and foreigners on earth, looking for a better, heavenly home. The gospel today also encourages a vision of the Second Coming as formative of contemporary life-style. See page 166 for suggestions of prayers for this election period.

■ NAGASAKI: A prayerful remembrance of the atomic bombing of Nagasaki could form an important part of today's intercessions.

■ THE BLESSING OF NEW PARISHIONERS, outlined in chapter 66 of the *Book of Blessings*, could be done once a month in large parishes or at the beginning of the school year in others. This blessing could take place at a party or at Sunday Mass. The setting at Mass seems to call for the presentation of the new members (#1932) and a petition in the intercessions (#1933). The service may also take

the form of Sunday Evening Prayer.

■ THE WEEK AHEAD: The weekday congregation will read from the prophet Ezekiel for two weeks. The great feasts on Monday and Saturday will interrupt this semicontinuous proclamation. The first passage that would have been read on the weekday Monday, about the call of Ezekiel, should be appended to the first reading on Tuesday.

MON 10 #618   red
Lawrence, deacon and martyr
FEAST

A disciple of Sixtus II (whose memorial was this past Friday), Lawrence was martyred a few days after him. His *cultus* was widespread within a few decades, and his day at Rome was (and is) one of the most festive. We rejoice while singing of torture, of dead seeds, of martyrs, of bountiful life through following the witness of Deacon Lawrence.

TUE 11 #414   white
Clare, virgin
MEMORIAL

Today's passage from Ezekiel features the powerful image of eating the scroll, the word of God. Communities can reflect each year on how saints such as Clare consumed the word and how our communion with them helps us digest the good news.

WED 12 #415   green
Weekday

THU 13 #416   green
Weekday

Pontian, pope and martyr, and Hippolytus, priest and martyr, optional memorial/red. ■ Hippolytus seems to have been the chief Christian intellectual in early third-century Rome. Traditional

biographies, now contested by some, hold him up as the author of key works and reforms in liturgy and doctrine, as well as a schismatic leader who demanded a more rigorous orthodoxy than the bishops of Rome did. According to these accounts, he was reconciled to his bishop, Pontian, while both were in exile. The story suggests prayers for ecclesial unity and fidelity to liturgical reforms.

FRI 14 #417   red
Maximilian Mary Kolbe, priest and martyr
MEMORIAL

Maximilian Kolbe gets a "partial day"—Evening Prayer is always the first hour for the Assumption. Yet the few hours given for a weekday memorial can be well spent. A Conventual Franciscan who died at Auschwitz on this date 51 years ago, he was canonized less than ten years ago. Proper prayers are in the current (1985) sacramentary, proper parts of the Office (including one of his letters) are in the supplemental booklet *New Memorials for the Dioceses of the United States of America*. Scripture readings, as usual, come from the weekday lectionary (those cited in the sacramentary are for places that observe his memory as a feast or solemnity, thus omitting the weekday readings). These materials help the weekday assembly to remember Maximilian Kolbe in the light of the powerful image expounded today in Ezekiel —shame for our sins and for the Holocaust, and trust in the covenant.

S
A **15** #621–622 white
T **Assumption**
SOLEMNITY

■ HISTORY OF THE SOLEMNITY: The Council of Ephesus (431) reaffirmed Mary to be *Theotokos,* the Bearer of God. Postconciliar fervor may have spread a feast devoted to Mary's "dormition" or death. A few centuries later, the church in Rome began observing this festival, eventually giving it the title of the Assumption. Pope Pius XII, in 1950, articulated the faith of many centuries when he proclaimed the dogma of the Assumption. The liturgical texts reflect the vocabulary of that recent declaration.

Throughout its history, various levels of meaning for the day have developed. From its earliest observances, this day was filled with language of the paschal mystery expressed in the death of Mary. This way of approaching the day is still reflected in the attention to death in the liturgical texts. A second level of meaning developed from those earliest days. Not content to leave the entrance to heaven implicit in a death-day observance, the church has used language about the triumphal procession, the bridal march, the ascent of the Blessed Virgin Mary to heaven. The unique fact of Mary's bodily assumption provides a third and relatively new level of texts for the solemnity. All three levels are noble and worthy of articulation in song, word and rite.

■ LITURGY OF THE WORD: The first reading for the Day Mass is wonderful! Rarely do preachers have an opportunity to speak in such graphic images. Rarely does the lectionary provide passages that can speak so powerfully to children and adults about the hideous power of evil. The verses of Revelation 12 omitted in the lectionary might be restored by those who prepare the liturgy (even up to verse 18). The assembly, especially the children, needs to know that the church recognizes the reality of evil. To many, it seems that the scriptwriters for Saturday morning television are more acutely aware of evil and the ways one can imagine it than the church is. Some parents and catechists prefer simpler, more abstract texts to give the children comfortable feelings. Meanwhile boys and girls may feel attacked by some wicked dragon and are rarely allowed to face that fear in an ecclesial setting.

An interesting and well-crafted setting of today's Psalm 45 is "Assumption Psalm" by Howard Hughes (GIA, G-2028). The preface of today's Mass provides more good material for the homilist's interaction with the readings.

■ BLESSING OF HERBS AND PRODUCE: In many countries, this feast is inextricably linked to such blessings. *Catholic Household Blessings and Prayers,* (pp. 170–71) has a simple order for the blessing. A larger scale liturgy of blessing is found in chapter 28 of the *Book of Blessings.*

✻ **16** #121 green
Twentieth Sunday in Ordinary Time

Depending on local diocesan interpretations, the Saturday evening liturgies may be those of the Assumption, not of this Sunday—another reminder of the need to

deal honestly with such back-to-back festivals. See pages 176–77 for an outline of textual possibilities for this block of Sundays in Ordinary Time. This is the final Sunday they would be used according to this scheme.

■ BLESSING OF LITURGICAL MINISTERS: Chapters 61, 62 and 63 of the *Book of Blessings* provide copious material for blessing those who minister in the parish liturgy. This combined (or separated for each ministry) rite should probably take place in Ordinary Time. A Sunday in September, when schools reopen and activity resumes, or a Sunday in January may be appropriate. (See page 63 for ideas.) The key is to plan ahead and to be realistic about the recruitment of new ministers and their training before the blessing. If a September date is the time for this blessing, then the ministers, old and new, should be engaged now in education and practice.

M
O **17** #419 green
N **Weekday**

T
U **18** #420 green
E **Weekday**

Jane Frances de Chantal, religious, optional memorial / white. • Until new editions are published, planners will have to look in the current sacramentary and *Liturgy of the Hours* under December 12 for this saint's texts. When the optional memorial of Our Lady of Guadalupe was raised to the level of a feast in the United States, members of the order she founded (Visitation) requested this transfer. Americans can be happy that this saint is preserved on their calendar, for she and her colleague, Francis de Sales, are the most gifted and admirable representatives of the post-Reformation era. Just down the road from Calvin's Geneva, they refrained from vile polemics. Rather, they inspired their religious communities and the diocese of Annecy to model the robustness of a full sacramental life. Buried side by side in an Annecy basilica, their memory calls us to fresh enthusiasm for ecumenism and to humble love of the riches Catholicism offers.

W E D **19** #421 green **Weekday**

John Eudes, priest, optional memorial/white. ▪ The stern words to leaders in Ezekiel might be combined with the seventeenth-century witness of John, particularly in communities carrying the title of the Sacred Heart or those linked to his congregations.

T H U **20** #422 white **Bernard of Clairvaux, abbot and doctor** MEMORIAL

Bernard seems to have been everywhere in the first half of the twelfth century—preaching crusades, reinvigorating Cistercians, founding monasteries, advising popes, fighting heresy and arguing with proponents of lavish art and Gothic architecture. Unfortunately, the church seems to take less interest in his life than secular medievalists do. With only slight hyperbole, it can be said that the church owes 50 years of its existence to his moral leadership. Bernard's liturgical remembrance can be enhanced by planners and presiders reading some of his literature. For example, see the selection in his Office of Readings and the seven other excerpts published in the current volume (IV) of the *Liturgy of the Hours* (see the fourth index).

F R I **21** #423 white **Pius X, pope** MEMORIAL

Joseph Sarto served as pastor, as bishop and as patriarch of Venice before being elected pope in 1903. He is remembered as a gifted pastor who translated his prior experiences into various drives for renewal—he fostered more frequent communion, lowered the age for first communion, promoted congregational singing at liturgy, fostered the foundation of biblical institutes (see the excerpt in the Office of Readings on contemporary biblical work), reorganized the Curia and began codifying canon law. A true hero of the various movements that led to Vatican II, he is now invoked, ironically, as the "patron" of those anti–Vatican II Christians in schism from Rome. His stand against "modernism" was and continues to be controversial. Nevertheless, this saintly man, claimed by liberals and conservatives alike, brightens this late summer day with his memory and his witness to Christ. Include intercessions for continued renewal and for resolutions to our divisions.

S A T **22** #424 white **Queenship of Mary** MEMORIAL

The preface in Mass #29 of the *Collection of Masses of the Blessed Virgin Mary* would enhance the celebration of this memorial.

✳ **23** #124 green **Twenty-first Sunday in Ordinary Time**

Following the narrative of Luke, we begin a second block of Ordinary Time. For an overview of Luke and these divisions, see page 167.

Sundays 21 to 27 (August 23–October 4): Journey to Jerusalem, Part II.

With another explicit reference to the journey in Luke, congregations move into another seven Sundays learning about the "way." The first Sunday's verses about the kingdom set a tone for the rest of the block. Premonitions about the death of Jesus and the opposition to be expected by his disciples are more numerous in this block of readings.

▪ INTRODUCTORY RITES: The penitential rite invocations might be prepared in the same way as over the past two months: form C*i* can be used each week, with the scriptures of that Sunday lending a phrase to one or another of the three invocations in that set.

▪ LITURGY OF THE WORD: For all the Sundays of this block, Psalm 27 or Psalm 95 are recommended. The latter was one of the two suggested for the last block; both bring the themes of discipleship and journey to musical expression. David Haas's setting of Psalm 27 in *Psalms for the Church Year,* vol. I (GIA), wears well and has found a place in the common repertoire of many communities. A refreshing, but lesser known offering is Christopher Willcock's "The Lord is my Light" in *Psalms for Feasts and Seasons* (Cooperative Ministries). See page 176 for recommendations for Psalm 95.

Those who prepare the liturgy should select another acclamation verse from Lectionary #164 and stay with it for these weeks.

A well-worded set of intercessions can last throughout these weeks of late summer and early fall. Weekly variants, expressing particular needs or relating petition to the day's scriptures, should also be included. Many parishes will want to include petitions for a good harvest (see the *Book of Blessings* [BB], #1018), for children returning to school (samples in BB, #527), for parishioners who are moving (sample in BB, #1937), for fair and honest political campaigns, for a society of justice and peace enhanced by this season's elections, and for our Jewish sisters and brothers (especially in the later weeks near their highest holy days).

■ LITURGY OF THE EUCHARIST: See the ideas expressed with the first block of Ordinary Time (p. 176). The American campaign season, with its thoughts of justice, should highlight the possibility of using the preface "Independence Day and Other Civic Observances II" (P83). "All men" can be "all."

For the communion procession during this time, some suggestions include "Song of the body of Christ" (GIA, G-3360) by David Haas, James Chepponis's "Shepherd of our hearts" (GIA, G-3148), "In the breaking of the bread" (OCP, #8776) by Bob Hurd, and Haas's "We have been told" (GIA, G-2662).

■ HYMNODY: The scriptural call to gather the nations is echoed in the hymn "In Christ there is no east or west" and celebrated in "Jesus shall reign," sung to "Duke Street." "There's a wideness in God's mercy" can help us celebrate the stories of God's mercy and compassion. "God, whose giving knows no ending" is a strong sending-forth hymn, reminding us of our mission to "heed Christ's ageless call, healing, teaching and reclaiming, serving you by serving all."

■ THE WEEK AHEAD: Saints' days with proper readings on Monday and Saturday take precedence over the regular progression of weekday readings. The first reading this week brings a change of pace

—from prophets we turn to New Testament letters. No accommodation seems necessary, but those who are paying particular attention to Matthew may want to append the verses lost on Monday to the Tuesday gospel, thus allowing all of chapter 23 to be heard.

MON 24 #629 red Bartholomew, apostle
FEAST

Linked by tradition to Armenia, this apostle can inspire us to pray for all who live in that divided and turbulent area.

TUE 25 #426 green Weekday

Louis, optional memorial / white. ■ *Joseph Calasanz, priest, optional memorial / white.* ■ Holding fast to our traditions, as advised by Paul, we can receive encouragement from celebrating eucharist in communion with one or another of these heroes. In the election year, Louis gives witness of bringing justice to civil order. Joseph is most famous for his patience when malcontents in his new religious order plotted against him.

WED 26 #427 green Weekday

THU 27 #428 white Monica
MEMORIAL

This famous mother's memorial falls on the day we begin several weeks of listening to 1 Corinthians. Weekday homilists would do well to review available commentaries on this letter.

FRI 28 #429 white Augustine, bishop and doctor
MEMORIAL

■ NORTHERN AFRICA: Augustine looms large in any recounting of church history, but his prominence should not deflect energetic Catholics from reading and

celebrating other figures from his time—the years around 400 (for example, Paulinus of Nola, memorialized on June 22, was born and died in the same years as Augustine; they exchanged letters and were part of a scholarly network). And Augustine cannot be appreciated without understanding the man who brought him to baptism, Ambrose. Weekday planners can absorb Augustine's spirit by reading the frequent passages from his books found in the Office of Readings and the proper readings, listed in the lectionary at #633, long associated with him. They are to be used where his day is a titular or patronal festival.

■ FLORIDA: In 1992, many Americans may remember the early Catholic foundations at St. Augustine, Florida. Tracing their roots back to this feast centuries ago, local churches there proudly hold to a faith that is both Catholic and American. The focus on reconciliation when approaching recollections of Columbus should not diminish the dignity that our oldest local communities feel. The churches of Quebec, Baltimore, St. Augustine, New Orleans, Bardstown and Santo Domingo usually lead the way in showing how a sense of dignity brings one to awareness of the need for continued penance and renewal.

■ CALIFORNIA: Junipero Serra died on this day in 1784. When he was beatified in 1988, the Vatican set his feast on this day. Many publications indicate his observance on this date, and some churches around the world may observe his memorial today, but the U.S. bishops moved his day on the national calendar to July 1.

#634   red

SAT 29 Beheading of John the Baptist, martyr
MEMORIAL

All three synoptic evangelists tell of John's martyrdom, another clue as to this saint's importance. Today's intercessions from Morning and Evening Prayer are good models for the petitions at Mass.

#127   Green

☼30 Twenty-second Sunday in Ordinary Time

See the notes for this block on pages 187–88.

■ BACK TO SCHOOL! Students greet the opening of school with mixed emotions, whether it falls before Labor Day or after. This important point in the year should not pass unnoticed in church. This Sunday or next (whichever immediately precedes the opening of the school year), children and all other students should be invited to the front of the assembly (or into the center aisle) prior to the general intercessions. The intercessions given in the *Book of Blessings* (#527) can be added to the ongoing set from this block of Sundays. Then the presider extends hands over the students and says prayer #528 or #529. The first one has explicit reference to the opening of schools. If it is used, the wonderful phrase in the second prayer can be part of the intercessions, "Let them take delight in new discoveries." The final blessing at the end of this Mass might draw from two other parts of the *Book of Blessings:* #543 for a prayer over the people, or #741 for a solemn blessing.

On the day that local schools reopen, or on a nearby weekday not already taken by a saint's memorial, sacramentary texts can be drawn from Masses and Prayers for Various Needs and Occasions,

24. Beginning of the Civil Year" or "Votive Mass, 7. Holy Spirit."

■ THE CATECHUMENATE: The *Rite of Christian Initiation of Adults,* in #18 and #44, calls for each parish to schedule the rite of accepting catechumens on two or three days of the year.

Unfortunately, many parishes still organize the catechumenate on an abbreviated school year model, and thus early Advent has come to be a customary time for this rite of acceptance in many places. This has serious problems, both for the conversion/initiation process and for the liturgy. Pastoral workers (pastors, RCIA coordinators, catechists, liturgists) should review the National Statutes for the Catechumenate in the United States, printed at the back of every current (1988) edition of the *Rite of Christian Initiation of Adults.* Statute #6 calls for a catechumenate of at least 12 months.

One of the regular dates for the rite of acceptance might be at this time of year. While it might still perpetuate some notions of a "school year" program, it is better than waiting for Advent.

In the rite itself, whether for catechumens alone or combined with the welcome of previously baptized adults preparing for reception, take special note of #48 and #507. The architectural setting is of great importance, as the rite envisions everyone meeting the candidates outside the main worship space. The various dialogues and the beautiful rite of signing (of all the senses, with sung acclamations) are followed by a rite of equal importance— the congregation leading the new catechumens in for the first celebration of the liturgy of the word.

#431   green

MON 31 Weekday

The weekday gospels will be taken from Luke for the rest of the year. The pericopes follow the order of the evangelist, so they will unfold in the same way as they have over the Sunday in Ordinary Time. The "Journey to Jerusalem" section will begin on the weekdays of late September.

September

#432   green

TUE 1 Weekday

#433   green

WED 2 Weekday

#434   white

THU 3 Gregory the Great, pope and doctor
MEMORIAL

As the opening prayer suggests, this is a fitting day to pray for wisdom among church leaders.

#435   green

FRI 4 Weekday

#436   green

SAT 5 Weekday

Blessed Virgin Mary, optional memorial/white. ■ If a Marian memorial is desired, see Mass #24 in the *Collection of Masses of the Blessed Virgin Mary,* "Seat of Wisdom." These texts allow the community to pray for all who are returning to school.

#130   green

☼6 Twenty-third Sunday in Ordinary Time

See pages 187–88 for suggested prayer patterns for this Sunday and all the Sundays of the "Journey to Jerusalem."

Those who are moving to new jobs or enrolling in new schools this fall will be envious of Onesimus. What a reference letter he carried back to Philemon! It is the one appearance of this brief letter in the lectionary for Sundays and should not go unnoticed—either by homiletic interpretation of the presence of slavery or by reflections on the continuity of racism and domination.

■ THE WEEK AHEAD: The progression through 1 Corinthians and Luke will be suspended on Tuesday and perhaps on Monday. It does not seem necessary to add the omitted passages to a neighboring day.

MON 7 #437 or as noted below   green
Weekday

Labor Day. ▪ The liturgy of the hours for this day is of the regular weekday, but this American holiday presents a wide range of choices for Mass texts:

- Two sets of prayers at Masses and Prayers for Various Needs and Occasions, 25. For the Blessing of Human Labor are especially recommended. They can be combined with the weekday readings or with passages selected from lectionary #846–50 ("Blessing of Man's Labor").

- Prayers from Masses and Prayers for Various Needs and Occasions, 21. For the Progress of Peoples can be combined with the weekday readings.

- Prayers and readings from May 1 ("Joseph the Worker") can be used, most especially in places named after that saint.

- Prayers from July 4 or from appendix X.6 ("Other Civic Observances"), with readings from lectionary #831–35 ("For Peace and Justice").

Prefaces P82 and P83 (for civic observances) are appropriate for today's observance, but parishes using the May 1 texts will find a proper preface for Joseph.

■ BLESSINGS AND DOMESTIC PRAYER: The *Book of Blessings,* chapter 24, has an "Order for the Blessing of Tools or Other Equipment for Work." Several of the prayers there can be used at today's Mass: the greeting at #925, the intercessions at #932, the prayer to end the intercessions at #935 and the prayer over the people at #937.

TUE 8 #636   white
Birth of Mary

The texts for this day give it a "preparation" motif: "The birth of the Virgin Mary's Son was the dawn of our salvation. May this celebration of her birthday bring us closer to lasting peace" (opening prayer). Hymns and intercessions related to the expectations of Advent are appropriate. This does not mean borrowing the tunes long associated with Advent, but it does suggest that the joy of this feast is best expressed as a joy of expectancy. The long form of the gospel, especially if not used on Christmas eve, should be used; it puts the story of Mary into the context of salvation history.

WED 9 #439   white
Peter Claver, priest
MEMORIAL

Peter Claver spent most of his adult life serving black slaves in Colombia. The proper prayer for this American memorial notes how his witness can help all of us overcome racial hatreds. Many parishes with large numbers of black Catholics have special festivities today or on November 3 (Martin de Porres). These feasts tied to the colonial era may be the best time to celebrate a service of reconciliation in those parishes (see p. xiii).

THU 10 #440   green
Weekday

During these weeks related to harvest, prayers can come from Masses and Prayers for Various Needs and Occasions, 27. After the Harvest.

FRI 11 #441   green
Weekday

SAT 12 #442   green
Weekday

Blessed Virgin Mary, optional memorial / white. ▪ In the *Collection of Masses of the Blessed Virgin Mary,* prayers from Mass #11 ("At the Foot of the Cross") would tie this day to the great feasts to come on Monday and Tuesday.

#133   green
⊗ 13 Twenty-fourth Sunday in Ordinary Time

See pages 187–88 for suggestions on this whole block of Sundays.

■ PASTORS IN THE BIBLE: Passages from 1 and 2 Timothy will now appear with Luke. These letters, written by a disciple of Paul, sought to extend Pauline principles to the problems of a later era (perhaps around 100 AD). As Robert Wild notes in "The Pastoral Letters," *The New Jerome Biblical Commentary* (Englewood Cliffs NJ: Prentice Hall, 1990), page 893, "What the author of the Pastorals did intend was to urge church leaders to value and maintain ecclesial and societal structure and order. . . . He envisioned Christianity as a worldwide and fully unified movement that fulfilled the deepest aspirations of contemporary culture for civic and familial harmony. Titus and 1 Timothy each set forth in rather reduplicative fashion procedures for the proper maintenance of 'God's household,' the church."

■ PASTORS IN THE BREVIARY: Coincidental to this letter's unfolding, the Office of Readings for Sundays and weekdays over the next two weeks provides excerpts from Augustine's "On Pastors," a marvelous piece on shepherding and ecclesial leadership.

■ OTHER RITES AND INTENTIONS: In the United States this is "Grandparent's Day." Prayers for them, living and deceased, may be welcome. This is another Sunday fitting for the blessing of liturgical ministers and of volunteers in the wider ministries (see page 63). If new members of the pastoral staff are being introduced to the parish, this should be more than a greeting after the communion rite (see the *Book of Blessings,* chapter 60).

■ THE WEEK AHEAD: The weekday readings from 1 Corinthians and Luke will be eclipsed by the festivals on Monday and Tuesday. No combinations with neighboring days seem necessary, although a fuller appreciation of the first reading on Wednesday would be gained if the lost verses from Tuesday were read with it.

M O N **14** #638   red
Triumph of the Cross
FEAST

This feast commemorates the dedication of the church (September 13, 335) erected by Emperor Constantine over the site of Christ's crucifixion, Calvary. The annual celebration was followed by a day to venerate the relic of the true cross kept there. It is one of the few feasts kept on the same day for over 15 centuries in all Christian communities, both East and West.

■ RITES: Excellent resources for use at a school liturgy today (formally opening the year after the first few days of orientation, perhaps) are found in LTP/GIA's *Leader's Manual of the Hymnal for Catholic Students.*

The Byzantine celebration of Evening Prayer on this night concludes with the assembly coming forward to kiss the cross (which rests on a bed of September herbs and flowers) and to receive one of the flowers. Our own churches in the West developed the same custom of venerating the cross on this date. Our heritage, the liturgical texts and the enduring need for what used to be called "sacramentals" suggest the possibility of returning to this practice.

■ MUSIC: Two specific hymns should be dusted off and used on days like this (and at several moments during the next Triduum). Venantius Fortunatus composed both "Vexilla regis" and "Pange lingua" 1500 years ago. They still are printed in eminently singable formats in most hymnals. Both praise the cross and open up a wealth of the cross's symbolism. Venantius was a close friend of the abbess in Poitiers in the sixth century. When he heard that she and her abbey were receiving a large relic of the cross from the emperor, he was moved to prepare these hymns for the entrance procession of the relic into the city. We can still see the relic there, visit the abbess's tomb and sing the texts, but most importantly we can join the ages-old effort to find words to express our homage for the cross. Those who prepare the liturgy may wish to review their notes for Good Friday and, perhaps, choose some of the same texts and music.

T U E **15** #639   white
Our Lady of Sorrows
MEMORIAL

When medieval monasteries began venerating Mary under titles such as this, the observances took place just before or after Holy Week, holding up Mary as a paradigm of sharing in Christ's cross. Moved here to complement yesterday's feast, we can also celebrate Mary as a model of sharing in the triumph of the cross.

One of the few sequences left in our missal, the famous "Stabat Mater" should be sung, if at all possible. The proper gospel acclamation verse provides a memorable summary of the day, and the preface from Mass #11 ("At the foot of the cross") in the *Collection of Masses of the Blessed Virgin Mary* is quite appropriate.

W E D **16** #445   red
Cornelius, pope and martyr and Cyprian, bishop and martyr
MEMORIAL

The inclusion of these saints in Eucharistic Prayer I gives a clue to their importance in the early church. Bishops of Rome and Carthage in the mid–third century, they provided later bishops of Northern Africa, such as Augustine, vital models of good pastors. Their witness helped inspire the kind of writing we see in this week's Office of Readings.

T H U **17** #446   green
Weekday

Robert Bellarmine, bishop and doctor, optional memorial/white.
■ One of the most intelligent men ever to rise to leadership in the church, Robert maintained civility despite the tenor of the Reformation era. His memory may be

invoked on this day early in the academic year.

F R I 18 #447 green **Weekday**

S A T 19 #448 green **Weekday**

Januarius, bishop and martyr, optional memorial / red. ▪ *Blessed Virgin Mary, optional memorial / white.* ▪ The Marian commemoration should give way to the fourth-century martyr of Naples who is most well noted for the annual phenomenon of the liquefaction of his blood. Whatever the mystical or scientific explanation of this, the worshiping throngs in the Naples cathedral today (and in the Little Italy section of New York City) can remind us of the centrality of blood in our ecclesial life. The blood of martyrs is central to the liturgy. The appreciation of this symbol perhaps may deepen and broaden people's participation from the eucharistic cup.

✹20 #136 green **Twenty-fifth Sunday in Ordinary Time**

The prayer patterns discussed on pages 187–88 can continue for these autumn Sundays.

▪ BLESSING OF CATECHISTS: Many parishes bless their catechists on this Sunday or another Sunday in September. The term "blessing" is truer to liturgical form than the authoritarian term "commissioning." National and diocesan offices often send out suggestions for such a "religious education Sunday." As in many books issued by a committee, the quality of these suggestions is uneven. Often the liturgy suggestions are weak: They search for words in the assigned readings that seem to promote religious education or recommend intercessions that are verbose. See

instead the *Book of Blessings:* Chapter 4 has a fine "Order for the Blessing of Those Appointed as Catechists." The suggestions given there for inclusion in the Sunday eucharistic celebration include fine intercessions and two possible prayers of blessing over the catechists (who may stand in front of the assembly or in some other visible place during the blessing).

▪ THE WEEK AHEAD: The feast of Matthew on Monday will take precedence over the weekday readings. Congregations will miss the first of three proclamations from Proverbs, but no loss of comprehension will result.

M O N 21 #643 red **Matthew, apostle and evangelist** FEAST

Legends say that Matthew brought the gospel to Persia. Prayers for all peoples in that troubled area of the world would be appropriate this day, perhaps especially for the small and beleaguered communities of Catholics living in fundamentalist Islamic nations. We might also remember tax collectors and all civil servants.

T U E 22 #450 green **Weekday**

Masses today may use the prayer texts from Masses and Prayers for Various Needs and Occasions, 27. After the Harvest, linking Catholic communities to this human need to pause at the equinox time and praise the Giver of every good thing.

W E D 23 #451 green **Weekday**

T H U 24 #452 green **Weekday**

For three days we will listen to significant sections from the fascinating book of Ecclesiastes. This first passage includes the verses heard on the first Sunday last month (August 2).

F R I 25 #453 green **Weekday**

S A T 26 #454 green **Weekday**

Cosmas and Damian, martyrs, optional memorial / red. ▪ *Blessed Virgin Mary, optional memorial / white.* ▪ The Marian memorial should give way to these Arabian or Syrian martyrs. All corners of the early Christian world provided us with martyrs, and their memory-keeping helps us remember the worldwide presence of the Spirit, unrestrained by political and religious boundaries.

✹27 #139 green **Twenty-sixth Sunday in Ordinary Time**

See pages 187–88 for suggestions on structuring the Sunday liturgy during this block of Ordinary Time.

▪ BLESSINGS: With their materials on the blessing of the parish pastoral council and other parish societies, chapters 64 and 65 of the *Book of Blessings* should be used at least once a year, preferably in Ordinary Time. These blessings would often be used at organizational meetings, but the importance of the parish pastoral council suggests that its blessing take place at the Sunday eucharist. The simple outline given in #1900–02 can be given some local embellishments—a formal calling of the individual council members forward, a hymn such as "The church of Christ in ev'ry age" *(Worship,* GIA) before the intercessions, a reception honoring the council after Mass, and photographs and brief biographies in the bulletin or on a special program sheet.

■ THE WEEK AHEAD: Days in honor of angels, on Tuesday and Friday, impede the normal course of Job and Luke. Job does appear on two Sundays of Year B, but the six days of this 26th week in Year II provide the only semicontinuous telling of the whole story within the Catholic liturgy. The selections from Tuesday and Friday should be saved and added to the first reading the next day. The "lost" gospel passage on Tuesday sets the stage for the following weeks by explicitly stating Jesus' resolve to go to Jerusalem. It should be added to Wednesday's proclamation.

M O N 28 #455 green Weekday

Wenceslaus, martyr, optional memorial / red. ▪ *Lawrence Ruiz, and companions, martyrs, optional memorial / red.* ▪ Yes, this Wenceslaus, a Bohemian prince, is the "good king" of the carol, the one whose witness continues to inspire many in Czechoslovakia. Lawrence Ruiz and companions is a new optional memorial in the church's calendar and a new "patronal day" for Christians of Japan, the Philippines and Taiwan. The day commemorates 16 missionaries, from Europe and Asia, ordained and lay, who ministered in those countries and who were martyred in Nagasaki in the seventeenth century. If the latter memorial seems appropriate in a given church, new proper texts may be available through the diocese, or else the Common of Several Martyrs should be used.

■ ROSH HASHANAH: Pray for our Jewish brothers and sisters as they enter the year 5753. Although this is commonly called "Jewish New Year," it is also the beginning of the "ten days of awe," a period of intense reflection and repentance, and an anticipation of the day of judgment. The sending of greetings at this time of year includes the wish *L'Shanah tovah tikatevu:* "May you be inscribed (in the Book of Life) for a good year."

T U E 29 #647 white Michael, Gabriel and Raphael, archangels FEAST

This feast was, until recently, totally devoted to the memory of Michael. The added angels may not be the only "chief angels" mentioned in the scriptures (some regret the omission of Uriel), but they are the most famous in both sacred and secular literature.

This greatest of the angel days invites a sensitive reappraisal of the place of angels. See the reflection on this from the patristic era (Office of Readings) and the overview in LTP's *Leader's Manual of the Hymnal for Catholic Students* (pp. 58–62). The latter source also includes liturgical ideas applicable in general parish assemblies as well as in gatherings of school children: suggestions to identify and decorate any existing images of angels, to pay close attention to the gloria and sanctus as the angelic music already in the liturgy and to focus on angels as messengers, healers and companions. As is often the case on feasts, the intercessions in the *Liturgy of the Hours* can assist the preparation of petitions for the eucharist.

W E D 30 #457 white Jerome, priest and doctor MEMORIAL

Widely known for his hot temper, Jerome has received almost universal veneration since his death for the promethean tasks of biblical scholarship he completed. The proper prayers offer an excellent occasion for remembering the centrality of biblical reflection and study in the Christian life.

October

T H U 1 #458 white Theresa of the Child Jesus, virgin MEMORIAL

Statues, paintings and venerated photographs of Theresa proliferate in worship spaces everywhere. In grand cathedrals with tombs of saints and mosaics of great venerability, the plain statue of Theresa often receives most of the lit devotional candles and most of the visitors with their petitions. Why has her *cultus* become so popular? Perhaps one reason is the simplicity of her reception of the gospel.

F R I 2 #650 white Guardian Angels MEMORIAL

The proper prayers, scriptures and even gospel acclamation verse can shape our consciousness of what we remember this day. One cannot dismiss the biblical angels, even if one loses a liking for endearing pictures of winged companions.

S A T 3 #460 green Weekday

Blessed Virgin Mary, optional memorial / white. ▪ Today's gospel and the harvest season suggest the prayers of Mary, "Queen of Creation" (*Collection of Masses of the Blessed Virgin Mary,* #29).

#142 green
4 Twenty-seventh Sunday in Ordinary Time

See pages 187–88 for notes for the Sunday assembly for the last Sunday in this block of Ordinary Time. The mismatched metaphors in today's alternative opening prayer should be avoided. Petitions in the general intercessions might include the U.S. Supreme Court, which opens its annual session these days.

■ BLESSING AT HARVEST: Those who prepare the liturgy in many areas of the country will want to become familiar with chapter 28 of the *Book of Blessings.* The relief and jubilation over the harvest provide the setting for this service to be celebrated in the fields or in a church.

#461 green
MON 5 Weekday

#462 green
TUE 6 Weekday

Bruno, priest, optional memorial/white. ▪ *Blessed Marie-Rose Durocher, virgin, optional memorial/white.* ▪ The first Carthusian should probably give way in the dioceses of the United States and Canada to the great educator, Marie-Rose. The beautiful opening prayer sums up her life in nineteenth-century Quebec. Intercessions might include: perseverance in new undertakings (her witness of tenacity through difficulties in the early years of her religious congregation), ecclesial collaboration, help and health for religious educators.

#463 white
WED 7 Our Lady of the Rosary
MEMORIAL

When parishioners gather to pray the rosary communally in the name of the parish, often they do so immediately before or after Mass. Pastoral ministers can help them (and everyone) appreciate the difference between liturgy and devotions. At least a few minutes should lapse between the rosary (or any other devotion) and the Mass.

■ YOM KIPPUR, the Jewish Day of Atonement, is the holiest day in the Jewish calendar, a day of complete fast, a day of prayer. The liturgy is rich and complex, and includes the reading of the book of Jonah. At Mass today, announce Yom Kippur and include prayer for the Jewish people in the general intercessions.

#464 green
THU 8 Weekday

#465 green
FRI 9 Weekday

Denis, bishop and martyr, and companions, martyrs, optional memorial/red. ▪ *John Leonardi, priest, optional memorial/white.* ▪ The first option is recommended as a way to continue the procession of martyrs in our liturgy. The reading from the Office of Readings (by Ambrose) is a fine reflection on the types of martyrdom to which all of us are called.

#466 green
SAT 10 Weekday

Blessed Virgin Mary, optional memorial/white. ▪ The prayers in Mass #45 of the *Collection of Masses of the Blessed Virgin Mary* ("Queen of Peace") can mark this national holiday weekend, this time of remembering Columbus and this month when the United Nations marks its anniversary.

#145 green
11 Twenty-eighth Sunday in Ordinary Time

Another block of Ordinary Time Sundays begins today, this one considerably shorter than the previous two. For an overview of Luke and these divisions, see page 167.

Sundays 28–30 (October 11–25): Journey to Jerusalem, Part III.

As has been the case with the last two blocks, another explicit reference to the journey to Jerusalem begins a new block of Sundays. The world's opposition to Jesus' disciples has been an important aspect of the teachings along the way. Now the end of the liturgical year and the end of the journey narrative are accompanied by a miracle story (today) and two parables (the next two Sundays) that focus on the "moment of truth," the end of this world and the coming of the Son of Man.

The healing of the lepers and the gratitude of the Samaritan have strong eschatological overtones: What was promised in the Hebrew scriptures and earlier in Luke is now coming to pass, God's salvation for all peoples. The parable on October 18 is explicitly linked in its last verse to the coming of the Son of Man. The last installment on October 25 has harsh words for those who rely on their own self-righteousness as the final days approach.

■ INTRODUCTORY RITES: Once again, form C*i* (or C*viii*) can be used each week, with the scriptures of that Sunday lending a phrase to one or another of the three invocations in that set.

■ LITURGY OF THE WORD: Psalm 34, which is also the proper psalm for the 30th Sunday, is recommended for use as the seasonal psalm on all three of these Sundays. Some settings that lend themselves as responsorial psalms include Stephen Dean's crisp "Taste and see" (OCP, #7114), Stephen Somerville's tried and true "O taste and see" in *Peoples' Mass Book* (World Library Publications), Marty Haugen's setting in *Psalms for the Church Year,* Volume 1 (GIA), which requires a broad vocal range and pitch accuracy from the cantor, and the setting in the *Collegeville Hymnal* (Liturgical Press) by Robert Kreutz (#142).

Those who prepare the liturgy should select another acclamation verse from lectionary #164 and stay with it for these weeks. The verse at #509.19 may also be appropriate for these three mid-autumn Sundays.

A well-worded set of intercessions can last throughout these weeks of late summer and early fall. Weekly variants, expressing particular needs or relating petition to the day's scriptures, also should be included. Many parishes will want to include petitions for a good harvest (see the *Book of Blessings,* #1018), for a society of justice and peace enhanced by November's elections and for appropriate remembrances of Christopher Columbus (see page x).

■ LITURGY OF THE EUCHARIST: See the ideas expressed with the first block of Sundays (page 176). Once again, the American elections, with their thoughts of justice, should highlight the possibility of using the preface entitled, "Independence Day and Other Civic Observances II" (P83). "All men" can be "all."

For the communion procession, you might choose from "The bread that we break" by Stephen Dean (OCP, #7102), Robert Kreutz's "Our daily bread" (OCP, #8717) or Owen Alstott's "Gather us together" (OCP, #8725), all of which would be fine additions to your community's ritual music for the communion procession.

■ HYMNODY: A hymn of confidence and thanksgiving is "O God beyond all praising," a marvelous text combined with the tune "Thaxted" by Gustav Holst. With its two strong stanzas, it serves well as a sending-forth hymn.

■ HOLIDAY WEEKEND: In many areas of North America blessed by beautiful autumn scenery, this is a big weekend for travel. Parishes in these communities also might be accustomed to hosting summer or winter visitors. All travelers can be provided a warm welcome and whatever materials and orientation necessary to help them take an active role in the liturgical action.

M O N 12   #467   green
Weekday

■ COLUMBUS DAY: The traditional day devoted to Columbus's memory coincides in 1992 with the second Monday, the day so many states observe the holiday. See page xiii for ideas on observing this civic commemoration. This could be the date selected for the service of reconciliation suggested there. In any event, the prayers at Mass can be taken from a number of places in the sacramentary—see especially the "civic observances" ones at July 4 and in appendix X.6 of the sacramentary.

■ THANKSGIVING DAY: Canadian parishes can join their prayers to that nation's observance of Thanksgiving today, using Masses "In Thanksgiving" or "After the Harvest."

■ SUKKOT: The eight-day Jewish festival of harvest booths or shelters begins today. Catholics, especially in organized small groups, should consider visiting a synagogue or Jewish center to experience the joy of standing within a *sukkah,* (plural, *sukkot*). (*Sukkot* are the huts that harvesters build in the fields so they can work uninterruptedly.) The moon is full at this festival, just as at Passover. The harvest moon is universal in its appeal; besides the romantic associations, it affords the practical opportunity to harvest through the night.

■ A DAY FOR FREEDOM: These commemorations mentioned, so expressive of autumn, join the regular course of scriptures and its arrival at the end of Galatians 4 with the wonderful words, "It was for liberty that Christ freed us." They conclude a particularly difficult set of verses. An allegory on Christian freedom, the readings would have been more transparent to early Christians. Perhaps understanding can be facilitated by restoring the missing verses to today's passage.

T U E 13   #468   green
Weekday

W E D 14   #469   green
Weekday

Callistus I, pope and martyr, optional memorial/red.

T H U 15   #470   white
Teresa of Jesus, virgin and doctor
MEMORIAL

This doctor of the church was formerly called Teresa of Avila in the liturgical books. In 1984, the church turned to her name in the Carmelites. Today we begin to read from Ephesians.

FRI 16 #471 green
Weekday

Hedwig, religious, optional memorial/white. ▪ *Margaret Mary Alacoque, virgin, optional memorial/white.* ▪ The hope-filled words of Paul and Jesus can be linked today to one of two great women —the thirteenth-century wife, mother, widow and religious or the seventeenth-century mystic who spread devotion to the Sacred Heart.

SAT 17 #472 red
Ignatius of Antioch, bishop and martyr
MEMORIAL

One of the greatest and earliest of the martyrs we meet in Ordinary Time, Ignatius was thrown to wild animals on this date about the year 107. A harvest image from one of his better known letters (see today's Office of Readings) urges us to come to terms with the language about martyrdom so prominent in our heritage.

18 #148 green
Twenty-ninth Sunday in Ordinary Time

See pages 187–88 for prayers that can mark this section of Ordinary Time.

The Office of Readings today contains a letter by Augustine to inspire preachers and all who work with liturgy. Liturgical prayer is described as an exercising of desires, marking the progress we have made in being shaped by the sacred realities we celebrate.

▪ MISSION SUNDAY: If the diocese is using this title for today, great care needs to be taken to keep the focus on Sunday, not on "cause." Proper intercessions, a special collection and perhaps a fitting hymn should be the regular ways of incorporating the missions into an Ordinary Time Sunday. Some coordinators of this observance

press pastors to use the prayer texts from Masses and Prayers for Various Needs and Occasions, 14. For the Spread of the Gospel. The rubrics printed with those two sets of formularies also give encouragement for this. Whatever is decided about the prayer texts, no parish should drop the Sunday readings for thematic ones.

MON 19 #473 red
Isaac Jogues and John de Brebeuf, priests and martyrs, and companions, martyrs
MEMORIAL

The prayers printed in the sacramentary for Paul of the Cross are not used today in the United States and Canada. The "North American Martyrs" bring the ancient prayers about martyrdom to New York and Canada. Isaac is mentioned first in the title of the day in the U.S.A. because he is the better known here. John receives first billing in other countries (and in the opening prayer). All eight martyrs worked with Native Americans in the early seventeenth century.

The troubled years of our continent's invasion by Europeans should not be glossed over. The memories of Native Americans— those who embraced Christianity and those who did not—should be a strong part of life we call "American." See pages x–xvi for suggestions. The intercessions this day could include missionaries, a resurgence of enthusiasm for the gospel, for courage and tenacity in adversity.

TUE 20 #474 green
Weekday

Paul of the Cross, priest, optional memorial/white. ▪ This commemoration was recently moved to this date by the U.S. bishops. On his optional memorial in the universal calendar (October 19), the

American martyrs take precedence. Thus we have here the possibility of remembering this founder of the Passionists for the first time in decades. The selection in the Office of Readings captures well the content of his preaching and the spirit of the community he founded.

WED 21 #475 green
Weekday

THU 22 #476 green
Weekday

Pope John Paul II was installed on this day in 1978. Prayer texts might be taken from Masses and Prayers for Various Needs and Occasions, 2. For the Pope.

FRI 23 #477 green
Weekday

John of Capistrano, priest, optional memorial/white. ▪ Pray for lawyers, preachers and Franciscans.

SAT 24 #478 green
Weekday

Anthony Claret, bishop, optional memorial/white. ▪ *Blessed Virgin Mary, optional memorial/white.* ▪ Communities can remember this modern-day saint (died in 1870), founder of a religious order, bishop in Cuba and confessor to the Spanish Queen. Pray for Christians in Cuba.

25 #151 green
Thirtieth Sunday in Ordinary Time

This is the last of the block of Sundays described on pages 187–88.

▪ REFORMATION DAY: The intercessions should include petitions for our Protestant brothers and sisters who observe Reformation Sunday today. There is much to be angry about when reading the history of the Reformation, but most churches have let this day evolve into a prayer for ongoing reformation—a hope for all Catholics, Orthodox and Protestants.

■ DEDICATION ANNIVERSARY: Today can be a local solemnity observing the anniversary of dedication in many parishes. See page 213. Such an observance brings great liturgical options to the fore and links this Sunday celebration closely to the solemnity of All Saints.

■ THE WEEK AHEAD: The week that moves us into November starts on a suitably eschatological note. Darkness comes one hour earlier than yesterday in most zones of North America. The feast of Simon and Jude on Wednesday will interrupt the regular weekday pattern of readings, but no rearrangement for the "lost" passages seems necessary. See page 166 for suggestions of prayer texts for Masses during this week before the national elections.

M O N **26** #479   green
Weekday

T U E **27** #480   green
Weekday

W E D **28** #666   red
Simon and Jude, apostles
FEAST

Little is known about these apostles, and their proper texts are so general that a rubric after the readings notes that they can be used for any apostle or for a votive Mass of the apostles. Thus we have a feast of "apostleship" linked to All Saints' Day. In such ways we begin our liturgical movement into the November arena of death, the saints and the end of time.

T H U **29** #482   green
Weekday

F R I **30** #483   green
Weekday

S A T **31** #484   green
Weekday

Blessed Virgin Mary, optional memorial/white. ▪ See the *Collection of Masses of the Blessed Virgin Mary,* Masses #25 ("Image and Mother of the Church") and #37 ("Mother of Divine Hope") for prayers and prefaces that express the tangible sense of church and of the last things found throughout the liturgies these weeks. For notes on Halloween and this evening's liturgies, see the entry for All Saints' Day.

November

 #667   white
All Saints
SOLEMNITY

THE MONTH OF NOVEMBER

In 1992, "November" includes all the days from November 1 and its eve up to the weekday liturgy of November 28. The last two days belong to Advent and to Year A.

For centuries, Catholics have seen November as a special time for remembering the communion of saints, for praying for all the souls who have gone before us and for remembering the inevitability of death. These themes were closely related to the liturgies of November. The reformed calendar and rites of the past decades have further enhanced this attention to the dawn of the day of the

Lord, to All Saints and All Souls. These two great days still grace the entrance to the month. As the month progresses, planners are able to draw texts from the sacramentary and lectionary that express the intense fervor of the "last days" and Christian hope. New attention to local dedication festivals at this time (see page 214 for placing the anniversaries by All Saints' Day) has provided local complements to John Lateran Day and has once again reminded us that "church" is central to celebrating the communion of saints.

■ DOMESTIC PRAYER: *Catholic Household Blessings and Prayers* (pp. 178–83) includes several prayers for domestic use this month plus an order for a family's visit to a cemetery or to a grave. This order is found in expanded formats in the *Book of Blessings* and will be discussed in the November 2 entry of this *Sourcebook,* although it can be used anytime this month. Private reading and meditation will be enhanced by the use of LTP's *A Sourcebook about Death* (1989), divided into 30 sections for day-by-day reading this month.

THE MASS IN NOVEMBER

All Saints to Christ the King (November 1–22): Jesus in Jerusalem

The semicontinuous reading of Luke is interrupted on November 1 by that solemnity's own gospel. When Luke is resumed on November 8, we open to the section titled "Jesus in Jerusalem." Those who have been following most attentively during the long weeks of the journey to Jerusalem narrative know that his presence in that city was no mere accident. The climax of the story, celebrated liturgically each year at holy week, is near at hand. Here Jesus preaches in the Temple, with opposition and controversy deepening by the moment. On Sundays 32 and 33 we hear two excerpts from this section of Luke. Then on November 22, we mark Christ the King by listening to a portion of Luke's account of the passion. What these all have in common is a high intensity of eschatological imagery: the mission of the church, the identity of church as communion of saints, the death we all face, the sure hope to which we all hold.

■ INTRODUCTORY RITES: The Sundays of this block should include several consistent items so that familiarity will enhance participation. The same opening hymn might be selected for the whole month. The litany of the saints (with local patrons included) might also serve as this opening processional. The penitential invocations at C*ii* in the sacramentary are fitting. The rite of blessing and sprinkling may be used instead of the penitential rite for each of the November Sundays; this would help set a more explicitly paschal tone, especially if the sprinkling rite is part of the parish's Eastertime pattern.

■ LITURGY OF THE WORD: The common psalm for the "Last Weeks of the Year" is Psalm 122. It can be used in place of all the proper psalms, starting November 1. It is available in several fine settings, including Christopher Willcock's exuberant "Let us go rejoicing" in *Psalms for Feasts and Seasons* (Cooperative Ministries), "I rejoiced when I heard them say" (with a lovely flute part) in Robert Kreutz's collection

Psalms (OCP) and the sprightly A. Gregory Murray antiphon with a Gelineau tone as found in *Worship* (#67).

The verses of the gospel acclamation are proper on November 1 and on Christ the King. November 2 and the two Sundays before Christ the King can use a verse from the end of #164 in the lectionary (#164.15 is best since it is from Luke).

The general intercessions would best be common for the month. They could include extra petitions for the dead (see samples in the *Order of Christian Funerals* and in the sacramentary, appendix I, #11). Some places have even used the litany of the saints (suitably adapted with local patrons) as the intercessions this month. It works only if sung, and only if sung fast enough. The litany of the saints is one of the traditional ways in which the church has prayed its intercessions. For example, at the celebration of infant baptism and at ordinations the invocation of the saints and sung petitions form the general intercessions. Of course it can also be an opening processional—witness the First Sunday of Lent and the procession to the baptistry during the Easter Vigil.

■ LITURGY OF THE EUCHARIST: Note the prefaces assigned to certain occasions: All Saints, Christian Death and Christ the King. The preface for Sundays in Ordinary Time VI (P34) is appropriate for the other Sundays and also for November 2. Acclamations during the eucharistic prayer could be the same for all November assemblies.

■ CONCLUDING RITE: Solemn blessings are suggested for November 1 (note the interesting difference between the version printed with the day's texts and

the one listed at #18 in the general collection) and for November 2 (the general one for the dead, in the sacramentary at #20). The latter might be used for all the Sundays of November after All Saints. Its translation in the *Book of Blessings* (#25 in appendix II) changes "man" in the second line to "us."

■ HYMNODY FOR NOVEMBER: A review of the parish's familiar Advent hymns would be a good beginning for this month's planning. Certainly any setting of the Beatitudes could be used all month; you may want to acquaint yourself with Suzanne Toolan's setting (GIA, G-2132); its brief, easily memorized refrain "Blest, o blest indeed are you" lends itself well to the communion procession. "Christ is the King" to the bright Vulpius tune "Gelobt Sei Gott" recalls the faith of "Christ's brave saints of ancient days" and urges us to seek again their way of hope and faith; this hymn could certainly be introduced on All Saints' Day and sung throughout November, especially on the final week for the solemnity of Christ the King. Bernadette Farrell offers two pieces that speak to the mysteries of life and death that we celebrate this month: "All that is hidden" (OCP, #7161) and "Unless a grain of wheat" (OCP, #7115). Both are appropriate for the communion procession. Hymns that speak of harvesttime, such as "For the fruits of this creation" sung either to "East Acklam" or to the more familiar Welsh tune "Ar Hyd Nos" are well suited to these final weeks of fall ordinary time.

THE WORSHIP ENVIRONMENT FOR NOVEMBER

■ REMEMBERING THE DECEASED: For years, this *Sourcebook* has advocated the use of a "Book of the Dead"—a blank book in which members of the assembly may inscribe the names of the deceased. In 1991, LTP published a beautifully bound book for this purpose, *The Book of the Names of the Dead*. It (or its locally prepared equivalent) can grace the assembly space (near the baptismal font, perhaps) throughout November. All of the names of people buried from the church the past year should be inscribed on one of the pages. If "All Souls" envelopes have been put on the altar in the past, this can replace them—just enter all the names from these envelopes into the book. If the book is kept by the font, the paschal candle can be kept lit there during the Masses of November beginning on All Saints' Day. The book can be honored with incense at least on All Saints and All Souls.

■ SAINTS: The statues and icons of various saints can be enhanced with flowers and candles throughout this month, highlighting without words this central aspect of "All Saints' Month."

■ CEMETERIES will receive a lot of visitors this month. Their care is a sign of respect not only to the dead but to the bereaved and to the descendants who visit. Parishes charged with such a responsibility should think about decorating the entranceway to the cemetery, about posting signs telling the significance of November and its feasts, about leaving special prayers in weatherproof containers along walkways, and about other ways to say that this month is special.

THE SOLEMNITY OF ALL SAINTS

■ HISTORY: By the fourth century, most churches in the East observed a festival in honor of all martyrs. The date varied from region to region, but generally it was kept in relation to the great Fifty Days of Easter—Friday of the Easter Octave, May 13, or the Sunday after Pentecost (the date it has retained on the Byzantine calendar). The content of our present-day solemnity maintains this paschal style. We celebrate the many named and unnamed Christians who have followed the spotless Lamb to victory.

The observance gradually became a commemoration for all saints and was moved to November 1. This new date seems to have originated in Ireland as a replacement for a Celtic pagan feast: Druids (and their successors) celebrated New Year's Day on November 1. However, once the transfer was incorporated into Western churches, some of the paschal content was lost. People seemed to focus on the dead and the saints with too little reference to the Lamb. Many secular and "pop" religious authors study Halloween, All Saints and "Day of the Dead" customs from an anthropological or folkloric angle without also incorporating the paschal foundation of many of these customs.

We are neither Druids nor a society of folklorists. We find our roots in the Jewish and Christian communities of the Mediterranean, which have always celebrated Passover as a harvest celebration. So, when we speak of this solemnity as the "harvest of the saints," we must be careful to recognize two things: The festival began as a paschal celebration.

The "harvest of saints" designation is fitting as long as we see the paschal nature of harvest.

■ HALLOWEEN CUSTOMS: Secular cultures have turned All Saints' Eve into everything that is wicked and superstitious about humans. Even churches too often forget the Easter roots of this day and fail to pass on how ghosts and skeletons and cemeteries point to the heavenly Jerusalem.

THE LITURGY FOR ALL SAINTS

For the key image of this day, read today's preface, one of the loveliest in the sacramentary: "Today we keep the festival of your holy city, the heavenly Jerusalem, our mother. . . ."

■ VIGIL MASSES: Many parishes have tried scheduling a Mass with children for about 4:00 PM on this eve, early enough to allow youngsters to go on their rounds. Participation in costume can be fun and a kind of eschatological sign, although too much didacticism by pushing for "saints only" costumes is not necessary. The norms of the *Directory for Masses with Children* should be internalized, making this a powerful eucharistic experience. The sung litany of the saints is a good opening to Mass, or a fine form of the intercessions. Be sure to include the local saints. "When the saints go marching in" is justly popular. Parishes with a cemetery by the church building should consider a procession (with music) through it as an opening, or else a visit to it after Mass (see the notes under November 2). A cemetery visit should not be avoided as too scary for children. With adult participation and liturgical forms that do not play up the "spooky," this can be a grand experience to begin November. For other ideas, see page 64–67 of the *Leader's Manual of the Hymnal for Catholic Students.*

■ VIGIL SERVICE FOR HALLOWEEN: On this night which is both a vigil for Sunday and a vigil for a great feast, three services can be noted for those who have begun weekly or periodic vigils.

A "Vigil for the Eve of All Saints' Day" is included in *The Book of Occasional Services,* an Episcopalian liturgical book. This baptismal vigil calls for a service of light, three or more readings and psalms before the gospel (the readings are about holy men and women throughout salvation history and into eternity), then the sacraments of initiation or a renewal of baptismal vows. (Catholic tradition reserves the initiation of adults to the Easter Vigil.) The citations of the readings alone make this an important reference for preachers and those who prepare any liturgy on November 1 and its eve.

The same resource book has an exciting "Service for All Hallows' Eve," meant to be combined with "suitable festivities and entertainment" and/or a communal visit to a cemetery. The rite begins with a service of light, and continues with two or more readings and psalms (the witch of Endor, the vision of Eliphaz the Temanite, the valley of dry bones, and the war in heaven). It concludes with a homily and the Te Deum (a paschal hymn that should become one of the hallmarks of all our greatest days).

Appendix I of the *Liturgy of the Hours* contains texts proper to this night and a possible extended vigil service. The wonderful canticle of Tobit and the gospel citations commend those pages to every person who prepares the liturgy for this festival.

■ MASSES ON THE DAY: The intercessions should include the many needs related to the national elections on Tuesday. A procession through the cemetery before Mass or following the prayer after communion would be appropriate. Since this feast falls on a Sunday, the formal procession and visit to a cemetery suggested for November 2 might be accomplished to great pastoral benefit today. See the notes that follow.

■ THE WEEK AHEAD: The weekdays are of the 31st week. The regular readings from New Testament letters (Philippians) and Luke will be omitted on Monday. Since the first reading from the day forms the introduction to Tuesday's reading, it should not be lost, but rather appended to Tuesday's proclamation.

M
O **2** #789–793   white, violet or black
N **All Souls**

■ IMAGES: The customs associated with the day reveal the fullness of Christian attitudes toward death. At one extreme, death is the enemy conquered by Christ. At the other, death is a sister and a brother to us all, leading us into the heavenly reign. The rich Mexican traditions of *El Día de los Muertos* include graveside picnics, candy skulls and scathing satire showing politicians and movie idols as the playmates of Death itself. The parish has a responsibility in keeping those ethnic traditions alive that express a Christian spirit.

■ ENVIRONMENT: White, black or violet vestments may be worn. Because we still seem to be moving away from the negative and morbid, violet or white should probably be used at funerals. Many liturgists, however, have come to a realization that black was too quickly removed from the range of vesture options. This might be the right day to bring out any black sets from storage. The paschal candle should be prominent, with the Book of the Names of the Dead in front of it (see page 199).

■ INTRODUCTORY RITES: The litany of the saints may be chanted again today as an opening processional. Its solemn tone helps us gather for a liturgy that is paschal and truly expressive of the human grief we feel. The gentle Taizé ostinato "Beati in domo domine" ("Happy they who dwell in God's house") would be an effective beginning for today's liturgy; consider also a hymn from the parish's funeral repertoire.

■ LITURGY OF THE WORD: Any readings from the section "Masses for the Dead" may be used: Daniel 12:1–3; Psalm 122; Revelation 21:1–5, 6–7 and Luke 12:35–40 are particularly appropriate this day.

■ LITURGY OF THE EUCHARIST: The Prayers over the Gifts and the Prayers after Communion do not have to be used in tandem with each other, staying under one or another numerical heading. They can be drawn from the six pages of texts in the sacramentary. The Sanctus and Agnus Dei from the old funeral chants (Mass XVIII) can be used, particularly if they have also been used in Lent.

■ CONCLUDING RITE AND VISIT TO THE CEMETERY: The *Book of Blessings* (chapter 57) contains the "Order for Visiting a Cemetery on All Souls' Day." It may be used on other days, most especially on November 1 when that is a Sunday. The "Order" may be used apart from Mass, in which case all gather at the cemetery. The "Order" may include a procession after Mass from the church to the cemetery or burial vault or tombs if they are in the church building or nearby.

Suggestions for this procession include:

▪ After the prayer after communion (omitting the concluding rite), an introduction to the procession is spoken by a deacon or another person. Participants already will know about the visit to the cemetery, but these words give any practical directions and phrase the invitation in liturgical form (for example, "Let us go in peace to the cemetery . . .").

▪ The deacon or another minister draws water from the baptismal font into a vessel, and a procession is formed, led by thurifer, cross and candles. During the procession, psalms or other songs are sung by all (Psalms 25, 42, 116 and 118 are suggested in the *Book of Blessings*). The "Beati in domo domine" could be repeated; the Taizé "Jesus, remember me" also would work if it is well known. A simple setting of the Beatitudes, such as that by Toolan mentioned earlier would also be fitting.

▪ In the cemetery, the presider or deacon uses the introduction in #1742.

▪ The special litany/intercessions given at #1746 are sung (note the response, "pray for them") as the presider, ministers or members of the faithful sprinkle the graves with holy water or sign each of them with water in the form of a cross. This litany can be expanded with the names of local saints. If many participate in this signing, they can take water in small dishes from the large vessel carried in the procession from the baptismal font.

▪ The Lord's Prayer is said or sung by all. The introduction is in #1747.

▪ A closing prayer is read or chanted from #1748 or from the *Order of Christian Funerals* (#398.46 or 398.47).

▪ The words of dismissal and blessing (#1752, "Eternal rest . . .") are followed by a prayer over the people and a trinitarian blessing. The solemn blessing to be used throughout November in the parish might be used instead.

▪ A song or psalm is sung by all. Any song or psalm commonly used for funerals that can be rendered effectively without accompaniment can be used to conclude.

TUE **3** #486   green
Weekday

Martin de Porres, religious, optional memorial/white. ▪ The beautiful passage from Philippians can be joined by this saint of color from Lima, Peru. Canonized in 1962, he has become a hero to many black Catholics in the Americas and, as such, might bear particular importance in this year of Christopher Columbus. We join in the memory here of one of our hemisphere who gave humble service to all the poor (a true reflection of the first reading).

▪ ELECTION DAY: Today is also a day for fervent intercessions and other rites for justice and peace. See page 166. An evening service of reconciliation might be appropriate on this night (see page xiii) between the closing of polls and the marathon news broadcasts.

WED **4** #487   white
Charles Borromeo, bishop
MEMORIAL

Planners of church renovations, reformers of dioceses, and all pastors would do well to learn of this man's life. His norms for architecture covered all elements of the church, gave appropriate background, were keenly expressive of pastoral imperatives and were explicitly framed to further the proper celebration of the sacraments. Many of our imperatives have shifted, but the honest, consistent and clear hand of a Borromeo is needed even today in many dioceses.

THU **5** #488   green
Weekday

FRI **6** #489   green
Weekday

Today's first reading about true citizenship offers a counterpoint to this past Tuesday's elections. The votive Mass prayers at #15 (All Saints) might be used for weekdays at the beginning of November. This is a good month to schedule "memorial Masses" that have no fixed date—for example, Mass for deceased members of a parish society.

SAT **7** #490   green
Weekday

Blessed Virgin Mary, optional memorial/white. ▪ See Mass #37 of the *Collection of Masses of the Blessed Virgin Mary.*

8 #157   green
Thirty-second Sunday in Ordinary Time

See pages 197–99 for ideas on November's ritual prayer. If the relatives of those who were buried over the past year were not made a special part of a liturgy on November 1 or 2, the readings for this day suggest making one of the Sunday Masses a memorial gathering for parishioners and mourners (perhaps to be followed by lunch for all).

▪ THE WEEK AHEAD: The weekday readings will be skipped on Monday. No combinations of "lost" readings seem necessary.

M O N 9
#701–706 white
Dedication of St. John Lateran
FEAST

■ THE BUILDING: In the early fourth century, Emperor Constantine gave land on a hilltop near central Rome to the bishop of that city. The property included a large basilica, a meeting hall.

A number of buildings have come and gone in that complex of buildings that was called the Lateran. Some reports say that on this day in 324, the central basilica was dedicated to the Most Holy Savior. From then until now, it and its successively rebuilt walls have housed the *cathedra* of the bishop of Rome. A baptistry soon was added to the side of the worship space. The same 1500-year-old building is still used for baptizing the faithful of that cathedral parish.

As the worship buildings and palaces evolved, the name "the Lateran" came to carry the same weight as the name "the Vatican" does now. Growth was accompanied by a name change, from "Most Holy Savior" to "St. John (the Baptist)." Thus the name "St. John Lateran" (which, admittedly, sounds like a saint) signifies a complex of buildings that were and are (at least in terms of the pope's role as the bishop of Rome and as chief liturgist) the "Mother and Head of All Churches in the City and throughout the World," which is the inscription at the east entrance.

■ LITURGICAL CELEBRATION: The texts for this day demand careful planning. The day's entry in most editions of the lectionary takes about an inch. It sends readers to the common of the dedication of a church. There choices abound. Pick some that correlate with other November images. Isaiah and Ezekiel seem properly eschatological. Psalm 122 is the common psalm for November. The gospel from Luke seems best for this time of year; it would have been read the Sunday before last if All Saints had not fallen on Sunday.

The sacramentary's section on this day is shorter than the lectionary's. The texts for an "Anniversary outside the Dedicated Church," to which that section points, are good. See the proper preface as well.

T U E 10
#492 white
Leo the Great, pope and doctor
MEMORIAL

Only two popes are given the title "Great" by our tradition. Along with Gregory, Leo was bishop of Rome at the end of the centuries designated as "early Christian." Their writings and prayers, many of which still grace the liturgy, show the inappropriateness of the designation, "Dark Ages."

The most famous story about Leo recounts his confrontation with Attila. The king of the Huns had just completed a three year siege of Aquileia by literally burying that entire metropolis of tens of thousands of people. Early in our own century, the mosaic floors of their cathedral were uncovered, preserved by Attila's rubble. Even today, many square miles of real estate rest on top of his ruins. Knowing that the same fate could be Rome's, Leo went north to head Attila off. Whatever the veracity of the story's details, we know that Leo succeeded. Pray today for diplomats, for besieged cities,

for Aquileia and all the other communities of the world still struggling to rebuild after the devastation of war.

W E D 11
#493 white
Martin of Tours, bishop
MEMORIAL

Veteran's Day (U.S.A.). ▪ *Remembrance Day (Canada).* ▪ Martin left military service because of his commitment to Christ. He founded a monastery near Poitiers (France) and allowed himself to be schooled in the faith by that city's bishop, Hilary (see January 13). He is praised for his nonviolent witness (together with Saints Justin and Cyprian) in the U.S. bishops' pastoral letter on peace. The letter quotes Martin's decision to leave the military for Christianity: "Hitherto I have served you as a soldier. Allow me now to become a soldier of God. . . . I am a soldier of Christ. It is not lawful of me to fight."

T H U 12
#494 red
Josaphat, bishop and martyr
MEMORIAL

Today's saint stands for all the history that must be faced in the various parts of the Soviet Union. Intercessions are in order for the many Christians (those in communion with Rome and those who are not) who still carry the hurt (and hatred) from their persecution at each other's hands and for the courageous leaders on all sides who are trying to forge new collaborations.

F R I 13
#495 white
Frances Xavier Cabrini, virgin
MEMORIAL

Born in Italy and founder of a religious congregation, Frances spent the second half of her life founding schools and hospitals in American cities. She died in Chicago in 1917 and was the first citizen of the United States to be canonized. The proper opening prayer evokes well the spirit of her life.

SAT 14 #496 green
Weekday

Blessed Virgin Mary, optional memorial/white. ▪ See Mass #37 in the *Collection of Masses of the Blessed Virgin Mary.*

15 #160 green
Thirty-third Sunday in Ordinary Time

See the notes on pages 197–99 for an overview of some of the possibilities for this November Sunday. Preachers should not flinch from their eschatological task. These readings demand more than sweetly voiced emotions. The Lord's coming is the promise we cherish—as has every generation of Christians.

MON 16 #497 green
Weekday

Margaret of Scotland, optional memorial/white. ▪ *Gertrude, virgin, optional memorial/white.* ▪ Both Margaret and Gertrude deserve to be placed on the parish calendar; why not observe one or the other in alternating years? We need female saints from every century. Even if we will never meet Scottish queens and German mystics, their powerful witness can be prominent beside so many men in our calendar.

The first readings for the rest of the liturgical year will be from Revelation. These visions and images convey truths and realities of far more significance than scientific or empirical analyses. Coupled with the seasonal psalm, 122, and November's other music, these pericopes form the community in the greatness of their shared and sure future.

TUE 17 #498 white
Elizabeth of Hungary, religious
MEMORIAL

This is a feast day of the poor, with whom Elizabeth is so often pictured. As is always the case on these sanctoral days, we do not just call an old figure to mind. Through the *cultus* of the saint, we link ourselves (in dreaming and praying, in celebrating sacraments and singing) to the thousands who bear her name, to the local churches that bear her title, to the poor she served, to the ideals enshrined in the traditions about her life, to the whole cloud of witnesses who have gone before us and with whom she sings in unending praise.

WED 18 #499 or 679 green
Weekday

Dedication of the Churches of Peter and Paul, apostles, optional memorial/white. ▪ *Rose Philippine Duchesne, virgin, optional memorial/white.* ▪ Three wonderful choices are presented:

▪ Use the weekday readings (with the strong passage from Revelation) and prayers from the previous Sunday (or from other appropriate places).

▪ Elect to remember one of the newest saints on the American calendar (canonized in 1988). She died in Missouri in 1852 after spending a long life teaching in France, in United States cities and in Native American communities. Her proper prayers are not yet in the sacramentary but are probably available from your diocesan liturgy office. These prayers (or ones from the Common of Virgins, if proper prayers are not readily accessible) are to be joined to the weekday readings. In 1992, this observance is highly suggested.

▪ Keep the anniversary of the dedication of the churches, uniting the

weekday community to the basilicas of Peter (at the Vatican) and Paul (on the road to Ostia). Any dedication day lets us sing the songs of November, of Jerusalem. In this option, the readings and prayers are proper. The omission of the weekday readings should not cause any lack of comprehension on the surrounding days.

THU 19 #500 green
Weekday

FRI 20 #501 green
Weekday

SAT 21 #502 white
Presentation of Mary
MEMORIAL

Two foundations exist for what is, in Western churches, a minor memorial for Mary. It is the anniversary of the dedication of the Church of Santa Maria Nova in Jerusalem (November 21, 543). (the German calendar calls this day "Our Lady of Jerusalem.") The second source of great festivity in the East is apocryphal—the story of Mary being presented in the temple at the age of three in order to be raised there by "temple virgins." While the books that contained such stories were not made part of the canon of scripture, communities in the East often saw such stories as orthodox and as befitting a festival. A recognition of Mary as the new Temple—another "November" reference to the holy city—could be seen as underlying both foundations for this memorial.

☸22 #163   white
Christ the King
SOLEMNITY

Today's solemnity echoes Ascension Day, Epiphany, Palm Sunday—any of the ancient celebrations of Christ's royal rule.

Maintain the November vesture and environment. Continue a November-long commitment to local food banks and clothing drives—it is time for the Catholic overseas collection of clothing and financial gifts for the Campaign for Human Development. Requests for volunteers to help with homeless and battered persons or troubled teens should be given prominence this month. See the notes on pages 197–99 for an overview of some of the possibilities for all of the November Sundays.

■ THE WEEK AHEAD: Proper readings for Thanksgiving Day may replace the passages from Revelation and Luke, but no loss of comprehension in the progression will result. The three days before Thanksgiving in the United States are proposed as ember days in *Catholic Household Blessings and Prayers* (p. 188).

M O N 23 #503   green
Weekday

Clement I, pope and martyr, optional memorial/red. ▪ *Columban, abbot, optional memorial/white.* ▪ *Blessed Miguel-Agustin Pro, martyr/red.* While Clement and

Columban are important historical figures, the new commemoration of this Mexican priest seems most suitable, especially in 1992. Martyred during reprisals against the Catholic Church in 1927, he stands as a witness to the troubled history we have inherited and (because of the widely circulated photograph of him kneeling before executioners) as a twentieth-century icon of patient courage. Until proper prayers are part of the sacramentary's next edition, the Common of One Martyr can be used.

T U E 24 #504   red
Andrew Dung-Lac, priest and martyr, and companions, martyrs
MEMORIAL

The proper texts from the sacramentary and *Liturgy of the Hours,* as available, should be used. In their absence, turn to the Common of Martyrs. The second reading of the Office of Readings, from the martyr Paul Le-Bao-Tinh, expresses perfectly the sense of these late November days: "We will have the happiness of seeing each other again in the world to come, when, standing at the throne of the spotless Lamb, we will together join in singing his praises and exult forever in the joy of our triumph."

W E D 25 #505   green
Weekday

T H U 26 #506 or appendix   green
Weekday

Thanksgiving Day (U.S.A.)/white. ▪ This American day carries its own narrative that has shaped generations of Americans: the arrival of the poor pilgrims, their hard winter, the first harvest, the Thanksgiving dinner, and their special guests, the local Indians.

In Plymouth, Massachusetts, itself, the day's festivities are always linked to large demonstrations by Native Americans, always scheduled in time for the evening news. Thus descendants of the first Thanksgiving celebrators know firsthand that the *mythos* of America does not match up to the reality. On this day in 1992, we need to go beyond the nice stories to the need for reconciliation, to go through thanks-giving to the One who gives all gifts. See page x for notes on observances in 1992.

■ PRAYER TEXTS: See the special votive Mass printed after November 30 in the sacramentary. These texts can be supplemented by material in chapter 58 of the *Book of Blessings,* a blessing of food for Thanksgiving, either that to be eaten by the assembly or foods to be given to the poor; #1764 is a good greeting for any assembly today; #1760 suggests intercessions. See the preface for weekdays in Ordinary Time IV instead of the preface designated "Thanksgiving Day."

■ READINGS can be taken from the weekday lectionary (#506—compelling images to get all to "stand up straight and raise [their] heads"), from the Mass of Thanksgiving (#881–85) or the readings for the votive Mass for Thanksgiving Day in the appendix.

F R I 27 #507   green
Weekday

S A T 28 #508   green
Weekday

Blessed Virgin Mary, optional memorial/white. ▪ The scriptures this day are truly fitting for the last day of the liturgical year: Revelation's words "Remember, I am coming soon!" and the wonderful refrain of the psalm, "Marana tha! Come, Lord Jesus!"

CONCLUDING PRAYER TO THE GENERAL INTERCESSIONS

THIRTEENTH SUNDAY IN ORDINARY TIME:
Sovereign God, ruler of our hearts,
you summon us to obedience
and grace us with true freedom.

Keep us true to the ways of your Son.
Leaving behind all that hinders us,
may we fix our eyes on him
and walk surely in the paths
        of the kingdom.
Grant this through your Son, our Lord
        Jesus Christ,
who lives and reigns [with you in the unity
        of the Holy Spirit
one God] forever and ever.
— © ICEL

FOURTEENTH SUNDAY IN ORDINARY TIME:
God of the covenant,
by our baptismal vocation
you have called us to be fully responsible
for proclaiming the coming of your kingdom.
Give us apostolic courage
        and evangelical freedom,
that we may make present
        in every circumstance of life
your word of love and peace.
We ask this through your Son, our Lord
        Jesus Christ,
who lives and reigns [with you in the unity
        of the Holy Spirit
one God] forever and ever.
—Italian sacramentary

FIFTEENTH SUNDAY IN ORDINARY TIME:
In Christ you draw near to us,
God of mercy and compassion,
lifting us out of death,
binding up our wounds,
and nursing our spirits to health.

Let such a tenderness compel us
to go and do likewise.
Grant this through your Son, our Lord
        Jesus Christ,
who lives and reigns [with you in the unity
        of the Holy Spirit
one God] forever and ever.
— © ICEL

SIXTEENTH SUNDAY IN ORDINARY TIME:
God, dwelling for all eternity in
        unapproachable light,
you draw near to us in Christ
and make yourself our guest.

Amid our manifold duties and distractions,
make us aware of your daily visitation
and remind us that in others it is you
        whom we serve.
We ask this through your Son, our Lord
        Jesus Christ,
who lives and reigns [with you in the unity
        of the Holy Spirit
one God] forever and ever.
— © ICEL

SEVENTEENTH SUNDAY IN ORDINARY TIME
Provident Father,
whose bounty surpasses
all we dare hope or desire,
with the words of your Son always
        on our lips,
we ask, we seek, we knock at your door.

Whatever our need, grant us your
        Holy Spirit,
the first and best of your gifts,
the perfect answer to our every prayer.
We make our prayer through your Son,
        our Lord Jesus Christ,
who lives and reigns [with you in the unity
        of the Holy Spirit
one God] forever and ever.
— © ICEL

EIGHTEENTH SUNDAY IN ORDINARY TIME:
O God,
the giver of every gift that endures,
only by your grace can we rightly perceive
how wondrous life is
and why it is given.

By the word of your Son
challenge our folly,
confront our greed,
and shape our lives
to the wisdom of the Gospel.
We ask this through your Son, our Lord
    Jesus Christ,
who lives and reigns [with you in the unity
    of the Holy Spirit
one God] forever and ever.
    —© ICEL

NINETEENTH SUNDAY IN ORDINARY TIME:
O God,
on whom our faith rests secure
and whose kingdom we await,
sustain us by word and eucharist
and keep us alert for the Son of Man,
that we may open to him without delay.
We ask this through your Son, our Lord
    Jesus Christ,
who lives an reigns [with you in the unity of
    the Holy Spirit
one God] forever and ever.
    —© ICEL

TWENTIETH SUNDAY IN ORDINARY TIME:
O God, in your Son's cross,
the sign of contradiction,
you reveal the secrets of our hearts.
Save the human race
from its repeated and tragic rejections
    of truth and grace,
that we may discern the signs of the time
and recognize every age as your moment,
the acceptable time of salvation.
We ask this through your Son, our Lord
    Jesus Christ,
who lives an reigns [with you in the unity
    of the Holy Spirit
one God] forever and ever.
    —Italian sacramentary

TWENTY-FIRST SUNDAY IN ORDINARY TIME:
To the banquet of your kingdom,
O God of the nations,
you have invited people of every race
    and tongue.

May all who have been given a place
    at this table
come also, by the narrow way,
to the unending feast of life.

We make our prayer through your Son, our
    Lord Jesus Christ,
who lives and reigns [with you in the unity
    of the Holy Spirit
one God] forever and ever.
    —© ICEL

TWENTY-SECOND SUNDAY IN ORDINARY TIME:
O God,
to the festive assembly
    of your new covenant
you invite the poor and the sinful.
Let your Church always reverence
    the presence of your Son
in the lowly and suffering people
    of this world,
and gladly welcome all to your table
as brothers and sisters of our family.
We ask this through your Son, our Lord
    Jesus Christ,
who lives an reigns [with you in the unity
    of the Holy Spirit
one God] forever and ever.
    —Italian sacramentary

TWENTY-THIRD SUNDAY IN ORDINARY TIME:
Lord of the ages,
you call the Church to keep watch
    in the world
and to discern the signs of the times.

Grant us the wisdom which your Spirit
    bestows,
that with courage we may proclaim
    your prophetic word
and, as faithful disciples and witnesses
    of the cross,
complete the work you have given us to do.
We make our prayer through your Son, our
    Lord Jesus Christ,
who lives and reigns [with you in the unity
    of the Holy Spirit
one God] forever and ever.
    —© ICEL

TWENTY-FOURTH SUNDAY IN ORDINARY TIME:
Undaunted, you seek the lost, O God,
exultant you bring home the found.

Touch the hearts of this assembly
    with wonder
at the tenderness of your forebearing love.

May we who have been reclaimed
    by your Son
delight in celebrating the mercy
    that has found us
and draw all to rejoice at the feast
    of forgiveness.
We ask this through your Son, our Lord
    Jesus Christ,
who lives and reigns [with you in the unity
    of the Holy Spirit
one God] forever and ever.
— © ICEL

TWENTY-FIFTH SUNDAY IN ORDINARY TIME:
Rich in mercy are you, O God,
a wealth of love for your people.
Show us the treasure that endures.
When we are tempted by greed,
renew our memory of your lavish mercy.
Call us back into your service
and make us worthy to be entrusted
    with the wealth that never fails.
We ask this through your Son, our Lord
    Jesus Christ,
who lives and reigns [with you in the unity
    of the Holy Spirit,
one God] forever and ever.
— © ICEL

TWENTY-SIXTH SUNDAY IN ORDINARY TIME:
Have pity on us, O God of justice!
Hear our cry and save us.
Make us heed your word
    spoken to Moses and the prophets.
Rouse us to the demand of the Gospel
    proclaimed by your Son.
Impel us to carry it out.
We ask this through your Son, our Lord
    Jesus Christ,
who lives and reigns [with you in the unity
    of the Holy Spirit,
one God] forever and ever.
— © ICEL

TWENTY-SEVENTH SUNDAY IN ORDINARY TIME:
God, the rock of our salvation,
    whose gifts can never fail,
deepen the faith you have already bestowed
and let its power be seen in your servants.

We make our prayer through your Son, our
    Lord Jesus Christ,
who lives an reigns [with you in the unity
    of the Holy Spirit,
one God] forever and ever.
— © ICEL

TWENTY-EIGHTH SUNDAY IN ORDINARY TIME:
O God,
our life, our health, our salvation,
look with mercy on your people.

Stir up in us a saving faith,
that believing, we may be healed,
and being healed, we may worthily
    give you thanks.
We ask this through your Son, our Lord
    Jesus Christ,
who lives an reigns [with you in the unity
    of the Holy Spirit,
one God] forever and ever.
— © ICEL

TWENTY-NINTH SUNDAY IN ORDINARY TIME:
Lord, tireless guardian of your people,
ever prepared to hear the cries
    of your chosen ones,
teach us to rely, day and night, on your care.
Support our prayer, lest we grow weary.
Drive us to seek your enduring justice
    and your ever-present help.
Grant this through your Son, our Lord
    Jesus Christ,
who lives an reigns [with you in the unity
    of the Holy Spirit,
one God] forever and ever.
— © ICEL

THIRTIETH SUNDAY IN ORDINARY TIME:
O God,
who alone can probe the depths of the heart,
you hear the prayer of the humble
and justify the repentant sinner.

As we come into your presence,
grant us the gift of humility,
that we may see our own sins clearly
and refrain from judging our neighbor.
We make our prayer through your Son, our
    Lord Jesus Christ,
who lives an reigns [with you in the unity
    of the Holy Spirit,
one God] forever and ever.
— © ICEL

ALL SAINTS' DAY:
All-holy God,
you call your people to holiness.

As we keep the festival of your saints,
give us their meekness and poverty of spirit,
a thirst for righteousness,
    and purity of heart.
May we share with them the richness
    of your kingdom
and be clothed in the glory you bestow.
We make our prayer through your Son,
    our Lord Jesus Christ,
who lives an reigns [with you in the unity
    of the Holy Spirit,
one God] forever and ever.
—© ICEL

THIRTY-SECOND SUNDAY IN ORDINARY TIME:
God of all the living,
in the resurrection of Christ Jesus
you have given us the promise of life
which death itself cannot destroy.

In the strength of this unshakable promise
give us new heart to live, even now,
    as your new creation.
We ask this through your Son, our Lord
    Jesus Christ,
who lives an reigns [with you in the unity
    of the Holy Spirit,
one God] forever and ever.
—© ICEL

THIRTY-THIRD SUNDAY IN ORDINARY TIME:
Lord God of hosts,
the One who is, who was, and who is
    to come,
stir up within us a longing
    for your kingdom,
steady our hearts in time of trial,
and grant us patient endurance
    until the sun of justice dawns.
We make our prayer through your Son,
    our Lord Jesus Christ,
who lives an reigns [with you in the unity
    of the Holy Spirit,
one God] forever and ever.
—© ICEL

THIRTY-FOURTH AND FINAL SUNDAY
OF ORDINARY TIME:
SOLEMNITY OF CHRIST THE KING:
God and Father of our Lord Jesus Christ,
you gave us your Son,
the beloved one who was rejected,
the Savior who appeared defeated.
Yet the mystery of his kingship
    illumines our lives.

Show us in his death
    the victory that crowns the ages,
and in his broken body
    the love that unites heaven and earth.
We ask this through your Son, our Lord
    Jesus Christ,
who lives an reigns [with you in the unity
    of the Holy Spirit,
one God] forever and ever.
—© ICEL

TEXTS FOR THE MASS OF CHRISTIAN EDUCATION

INTRODUCTORY RITES

Opening Prayer

O God, source of life and grace,
give to educators and students
the grace to work together
    according to your plan of love,
so that all of us may form
    that school of the gospel,
the school of Christ your Son,
who is the model of the human
    person made perfect;
and who lives and reigns with
    you and the Holy Spirit,
one God, for ever and ever.

LITURGY OF THE WORD

Suggested Readings

Sirach 51:13–26
Matthew 7:13–21

Concluding Prayer to the General Intercessions

Grant to young people, O God,
a life of faith and loving service
toward you and toward
    their neighbor,
in the family and in society.

Open their hearts to listen willingly
    to your word,
the word that calls young and old
to give ourselves generously and joyously
in freedom of spirit to every good work.

We ask this through Christ our Lord.

LITURGY OF THE EUCHARIST

Prayer over the Gifts

Receive, Lord God,
    our prayers and offerings,
and inspire our young people
    to consecrate their lives
to the service of their brothers and sisters,

after the example of your Son
who gave himself for the salvation of all,
and who lives and reigns forever and ever.

Preface

Father, all-powerful and ever-living God,
we do well always and everywhere
    to give you thanks:

By your power we are fashioned
    in the image of Christ,
sublime model of all that life can be
when touched by your grace.
In Christ our humanity is born again
so that, freed from sin, we may grow
    to maturity
according to your loving plan
for the salvation of all.

You sent your Son to grow within the love
    of a family,
that he might be an example
    for educators and students,
and the source of inspiration and strength
for us to grow together, as he did,
    in wisdom and grace.

Joyful in the knowledge of your love for us,
we join the angels and saints
in their hymn of endless praise:

Holy, holy, holy Lord . . .

Prayer after Communion

Almighty and eternal God,
may the love we have received
    in this eucharist
strengthen the hearts of our students
    in faith and hope
and provide their teachers
    with the patience and love
that is necessary to educate
    by word and example.
We ask this through Christ
    our Lord.

THE LOCAL CHURCH CELEBRATES THE LOCAL CHURCH

*The history and future of a parish find full expression when it celebrates
its anniversary, its title or its patron.
Parishioners reaffirm that their community of the altar is the church, not just a branch
office. They praise God, for the space built and named by their own flesh and blood is
sacred space, the gate of heaven. Here Catholics tremble with awe and gratitude
before the sacred reality of Church, the sacred body they are.
These days give each parish its own unique calendar and make present all that is
distinctive in its life—its ethnic heritage, its civic and ecclesial ministries, its devotions, its
architecture, its future dreams.*

Proper Calendars

THE "Table of Liturgical Days" found in the front of every sacramentary lists several days which should be kept as local solemnities and feasts. This "Table," a gift from our own church tradition, sets out the way we spend our time as *ecclesia,* as the church.

The local days, listed there and described below, have always been a foundation for universal observances. Ecclesial health, good liturgy and faith itself will grow only if parishes and dioceses are marked by continual renewal. Anniversaries of dedications, local saints and titles reinforce our identity as a sacred people.

■ LOCAL CHURCH: Celebrations that are unique to a specific parish or diocese reassert important convictions: that this community of the altar is the church (and not just a branch office of Rome), that this space built by our own flesh and blood is sacred space, that the place where we pray each Sunday is the threshold of heaven.

With the universal church, we celebrate the Easter Triduum and we keep each day of the Triduum. In communion with all the other churches, we gather every Sunday. Keeping the Roman calendar, we observe the ten solemnities that usually fall on weekdays. For each parish to become a vibrant local church, it needs to

know its specific identity and its place in this universal economy. Local festivals help situate the congregation in the mystery of universality. We are the church! Salvation history unfolds in our own diocese and in our own parish!

Dedication Anniversary

AT the anniversary of the dedication of a church, assembly members beam. They get goosebumps of joy singing of their temple (and they are that temple). They find comfort and union in relating the allusions to people of every epoch dedicating their liturgical houses to their parents and grandparents who built this very place. Even if they are newcomers to the region, they can see their neighbors in the next row who are related to the donors of the stained-glass windows. Sacredness becomes palpable. History does, too. Parents and elders have a sense of handing on the work of their hands— and their wallets—to future generations. Faith has a geography and we are standing in it.

Why are observances of the anniversary of dedication so rare? Perhaps we are reluctant to call our buildings "sacred," to admit the power of architecture over us. Or perhaps we are fearful of the truth: This parish, my people, are sacred. An annual bath in this pool of images can cleanse the weary body, open the eyes of faith to see more than our imperfect neighbors and clergy, to shiver in wetness before the reality of who we are.

WHEN TO CELEBRATE

■ IF THE DATE IS KNOWN: Three options for local calendars are envisioned in our tradition (see the footnote to #3818 in *Documents of the Liturgy* [Collegeville: The Liturgical Press, 1983]):

- the actual anniversary date, if the community can really keep this day as a holy day/holiday

- the Sunday nearest the anniversary date, if it is a Sunday in Ordinary Time (except for solemnities) or a Sunday in Christmastime (except Epiphany)

- the Sunday before All Saints' Day, "in order to focus on the bond between the church on earth and the church in heaven"

Since the actual anniversary date is rarely convenient for a full-scale celebration, most parishes will want to move the celebration to the nearest Ordinary Time Sunday. Parishes whose buildings were dedicated in late November, December, February, March, April, May and early June should use the third option. Thus, about half the parishes in a diocese may be observing their anniversary on the last Sunday of October. This is the day when clocks change (in most of the country) and we give a graphic farewell to the dead summer. The time of darkness arrives. The transition to late fall and to the eschatological focus of November can be marked by several high festivals of the new Jerusalem.

■ IF THE DATE IS UNKNOWN: Parishioners who specialize in local history can search through construction records, the files of civil inspection services, ecclesiastical and secular archives and back issues of the local newspapers. The Vatican commentary notes that those who still cannot find the date of dedication have two choices for their observance: October 25, if the community will always be free on this day to make a true solemnity, or the Sunday before All Saints. In 1992, this Sunday is October 25.

PREPARING THE PARISH

■ SOURCES: Most Catholics are readily convinced of the value of keeping their dedication anniversary. Once pastoral leaders are willing to dust off this treasured festival, catechesis and preparation for the parish can draw from several sources—local histories, oral tradition regarding the church, images found in the liturgy of dedication, awareness of the ethnic groups that formed the parish when the church was built and the rite of dedication (from USCC Publications or in *Rites II* [New York: Pueblo, 1982]). If a parish history has never been written, discussion about this festival might motivate leaders to commission someone to pull the varied stories and facts together in a readable format—a gift to all the faithful and to future generations, immediately useful in homilies, catechetical sessions and bulletin articles.

Imbued with the liturgical images and local histories, pastoral leaders can use the Sunday bulletins to prepare the community. Parish newsletters and invitations to the dedication anniversary can utilize the concept of "homecoming." Materials can be prepared for reflective reading and prayer in every household.

■ RELIGIOUS EDUCATION: Instead of separate classes on the day prior to the anniversary, have a catechetical assembly with tours of significant parts of the building, with music ("Bless this house, O Lord . . ."), prayer and a history of the edifice acted out by students. Catholic school assemblies, family groups and adult education groups can be given tours of the parish church by whoever can tell about font and table, iconography and architectural design.

THE MASS

Gather the whole parish for a single eucharist. Other Masses may be celebrated in a simple style at the regular times, but the majority of parishioners probably will come to one principal gathering. If circumstances of space, climate and budget require that the central celebration take place outdoors or in a tent near the church, the disappointment about not celebrating in the place being honored can be relieved by a benefit: The assembly will be able to see the entire building. A procession around the building to begin or end the eucharist might fit in well.

One large parish with a fairly small building recently marked their sacred space's centennial with an evening Mass in a tent (1,500 people) and then a candlelight procession in which the parishioners completely surrounded the building. This action would be a fitting conclusion to Mass or Evening Prayer even if it were held inside the church building. The litany of the saints or the texts of blessings may be sung during this procession.

■ MUSIC: Two hymns that are appropriate to this celebration are "Christ is made the sure foundation" to the festive "Westminster Abbey" tune and "What is this place" with the refreshing images of Huub Oosterhuis's text and the memorable Dutch tune "Komt nu met zang." Psalm 84, "How lovely is your dwelling place," would be quite appropriate for this occasion; good choices include Michael Joncas's setting (NALR) found in *Gather* (GIA) and the setting by Jan Vermulst in *Peoples' Mass Book* (World Library Publications). Psalm 122, in the settings already mentioned on page 198, should also be considered.

■ INTRODUCTORY RITES: Taking a cue from the dedication rite, some Catholic communities meet in a separate place and then go together in joyous procession to the church. The rite of dedication includes a water blessing. With virtually no modification, this rite can also enhance the anniversary Mass on a Sunday. If the font is accessible to everyone in the assembly, the entire assembly might be invited to process there after the blessing prayer to sign themselves or each other with the water. During this procession, all may sing the parish's best baptismal or ecclesial hymn.

■ LITURGY OF THE WORD: Three readings, a psalm and a gospel verse from the lectionary (#701–6) are to be chosen. The citations for these readings might be included in an anniversary booklet. This booklet may also include pictures of the church, historical facts and anecdotes, music for liturgy, and prayers for use at home. To select from the varied readings, these values can be brought to the lectionary:

• harmony with the time of year (If the observance is just before All Saints, the Hebrews passage relates the church on earth and the assembly of the first-born.)

• harmony with the surrounding Sundays and the semicontinuous lectionary

• the use of scripture passages that contain compelling, graphic images

• the preference of the homilist

The homily could be based not just on the scriptures and liturgy of the solemnity but on the sacred place itself. The homilist could preach it from various parts of the building. For example, the homilist might speak from beside the cross about the tree of life and its place in this assembly, or reflect about gathering and welcome and mission at the entranceway, or challenge hearers about almsgiving under a window portraying Elizabeth of Hungary or Stephen.

The dismissal of the catechumens might include a word expressing the faithful's prayer for their full membership in the church. The patristic readings in the Office of Readings could be included in the time of reflection on the liturgy's readings, as might further consideration of an image or object spoken of in the homily.

Two models present themselves for the general intercessions. The wonderful petitions found in Morning Prayer and in Evening Prayer use a rich variety of divine attributes and invite a sung response. Alternatively, the dedication tradition of singing the litany of the saints can be continued on the anniversary, particularly if it is held near November 1. Those who prepare the liturgy must not omit the insertion of local saints' names (as called for in the rubrics). The city patron (if there is one), church patron (if named after a saint) and diocesan patron also deserve a place in the local litany.

■ LITURGY OF THE EUCHARIST: The inserts for Eucharistic Prayers I and III given in the rite of dedication (appendix VIII of the sacramentary) are equally appropriate for anniversary Masses.

■ CONCLUDING RITE: The solemn blessing listed as #19 in the sacramentary should be used.

HOMEBOUND PARISHIONERS

As Mass ends, eucharistic ministers should be sent, as they are every Sunday, to bring communion to the homebound. This day's visit might also include sharing any commemorative booklet about the church. Homebound parish members are living stones, too, and sharing the liturgical events with them, no matter how briefly, can lift them up in their vital role within the parish.

LITURGY OF THE HOURS AND OTHER ASSEMBLIES

Beginning with Evening Prayer I, all prayers are taken from the Common of the Dedication of a Church (even for private prayer). The entire day and its eve are a festival that should embrace the lives of all members.

■ VIGIL: Appendix I contains canticles to add to the Office of Readings, thus fashioning an extended vigil service. A vigil can be graced by a reading from the decree erecting the parish, a poetic quotation from the homily on dedication day, a dramatic account of the ceremony found in the local press or an excerpt from another document important to the parish's history. The climax of the vigil, the singing of the Te Deum, may become a treasured annual moment.

■ MORNING PRAYER AND EVENING PRAYER may be followed by breakfast, by an opportunity to tour neglected corners of the building, by an annual parish supper or by an annual parish meeting for reports on the status of the parish.

■ OTHER GATHERINGS: If there is an annual picnic, perhaps it can be moved to this day. If there is an annual talent show, stage it after Evening Prayer. If there is an annual or seasonal banquet or dinner dance, fill out the day's schedule with it. Weddings or other events that ordinarily involve less than the whole parish can be kept off this day. It is a day for the parish to spend together, for the parish to become parish.

ENVIRONMENT FOR WORSHIP

Although decorations should never eclipse the rites, they can serve the events that will unfold on the day—for example, a procession or a rich and full remembrance of baptism as described earlier. They might even set the tone for the span of Ordinary Time during which the celebration is held. Decorations should be designed with an awareness of the day's ecclesial and eschatological images. Specifically, decorations should include attention to the outdoors—to doorways, to the outline of the structure or to the tower. Everyone who passes it should know that this parish is celebrating.

The celebration of the anniversary of dedication should motivate interior designers and decorators to look at the entire building and its main worship space. This is not a day to

decorate only the sanctuary or to concentrate solely on a historical diorama near the entranceway. Three customs might help to show the whole space as holy, to enliven the senses of those gathered:

- Concentrate on the walls and corners, on the outlines of the building itself. Old consecration rites and current dedication liturgies include lighting 12 (or 4) candles on walls around the building. Even parishes without such an installation can light the walls in candlelight.

- Find a way for seasonal flowers or branches and candles to highlight the contours of the space. The four corners might be marked by brilliant arrangements.

- If Christmastime celebrations include the use of pew candles, they might be used again on this weekend.

Titular Solemnity

EVERY church and parish is given a title: the Trinity, the Holy Spirit, one or more of the angels or saints, or a title or mystery of Jesus used in the liturgy. From the earliest centuries, Christians have celebrated their local identity on the feast day of the saint or title. Such a celebration helps a parish remember and make present all that is unique to its life—its ethnic heritages, its civic and ecclesial missions, its devotions and more.

WHEN TO CELEBRATE

Once established by the parish, the date should remain the same every year. Parish customs and events can gradually migrate to this second local festival. If the titular solemnity falls during Ordinary Time, it can be moved to the preceding Sunday if this will help the community gather for the observance. When a title is celebrated in Advent, Christmas, Lent or Easter, it should be kept in the style of that season (e.g., Immaculate Conception as an Advent title, Patrick as a lenten saint).

■ DIVINE TITLES: These titles (and the mysteries such as Blessed Sacrament or Ascension) are celebrated on the day given in the universal calendar or, if the day is not on the current calendar, on the day assigned to it on older calendars. If the title is on neither list and it relates to Jesus, tradition suggests that it be celebrated on August 6.

■ MARIAN TITLES: The local solemnity is observed on the day on which the title is celebrated in the universal calendar (Visitation, Immaculate Conception, Holy Rosary, etc.). If the title is not in the calendar, then it can be celebrated on a day on which the title has traditionally been celebrated in older calendars (see the indexes of old missals). If the title still cannot be found, tradition suggests August 15.

■ OTHER SAINTS: If the title is one of the saints, observe the solemnity on the date listed in the universal calendar. If the saint is one of the thousands without a place on the current universal calendar, then celebrate on the date given by tradition (moving it to the closest available date if it now falls on a universal feast or solemnity). Traditional dates are discovered in one of these ways, listed in order of priority:

- the date given in the old calendar and now left to local observances (listed on the pages of "Variations in the Roman Calendar" [p. 115ff. in *Liturgy Documentary Series 6: Norms Governing Liturgical Calendars,* Bishops' Committee on the Liturgy, 1984] or found in the index in older missals)

- the date given in the martyrology; since the old edition is rarely available and the new one will not be issued for several years, an accessible source is the recent edition of *Butler's Lives of the Saints* (see the general index in volume 4)

- the day of death of the saint, if known

- another date traditionally associated with the saint

PREPARING THE PARISH

The *Leader's Manual of the Hymnal for Catholic Students* (p. 99) offers curriculum ideas for religious educators. Those who prepare the liturgy can provide educational and inspirational stories about the saint or title, but hagiography need not end with the religious education classroom. Parish mailings, handouts to homebound parishioners, and Sunday bulletins can include catechesis on the paschal mystery as evidenced in the title or in the life of the saint. Materials should always include any "local angle" to the title—why the parish was given this name, what the pastor said about it at the founding of

the parish, how this name is particularly welcome in 1992.

THE MASS

■ LOCATING TEXTS: The texts for saints without texts in the current sacramentary are to be taken from the "commons" of their type—Mary, apostle, martyr, pastor, doctor, virgin, holy men and holy women. (These last two are further specified as "religious," "those who worked for the underprivileged," and "teachers.") Sometimes a saint can be observed under more than one heading. In this case, select the set of texts most appropriate to the parish.

■ MUSIC: *The Summit Choir Book* (Monastery of Our Lady of the Rosary) and *Hymnal for the Hours* (GIA) are excellent sources. "God, we praise you," found in *Worship,* praises apostles, saints, prophets and martyrs, and so could serve as a "general" hymn for patrons in any of those categories. With the energetic early American hymn tune "Nettleton," "God, we praise you" would be a useful and enjoyable addition to your parish.

If no hymns in honor of the saint or title can be found, parishes could commission one. Texts can be found in works by the saint, in the entrance antiphons and communion antiphons in the various commons of saints, and in the *Liturgy of the Hours.* In lieu of commissioning, researchers might correspond with likely sources of existing texts or music: motherhouses of congregations founded by the saint, a basilica where the saint is buried, dioceses where the saint lived. The litany of the saints might be chanted if the title is that of a saint. Other litanies correlate with certain titles: Sacred Heart, St. Joseph, Blessed Virgin Mary, for example.

■ LITURGY OF THE WORD: The intercessions can take the form of the litany of the saints. They may incorporate practices encouraged by the *Book of Blessings,* chapter 59 ("Order for Blessing of Food or Drink or Other Elements Connected with Devotion: Order of Blessing within Mass on a Feast Day"). This order lists special petitions concluded by a prayer of blessing over traditional materials related to the title. If no traditions from ethnic or religious histories are known, it is hard to invent them, but the blessing and distribution of seasonal flowers to everyone would be a welcome custom.

HOMEBOUND PARISHIONERS

Here again, the many sick, infirm and elderly members must be included in the parish's life. They, too, can be inspired by the title of the parish. Communion should be brought to all of them directly from the Mass. Materials and prayers traditional to the parish's title can be brought to them also. Videos of the local solemnity might be provided after the date. If weekdays are the principal days for Masses and prayer services at local nursing homes and elderly housing complexes, the titular solemnity a good day on which to schedule them.

LITURGY OF THE HOURS AND OTHER ASSEMBLIES

The titular feast is a local solemnity, which means that there should be Evening Prayer I. Materials for an extended vigil can be found in the commons of the *Liturgy of the Hours* (appendix I).

■ VENERATION OF RELICS: One of the liturgies or gatherings might include the veneration of relics (if there are some present for a titular saint). If handled with reverence and accompanied by a strong celebration of the liturgy of the hours for the saint, this action can inspire an entire community. (Be wary both of any old pietistic superstitions that may be attached to such an action and of the impulse to deliver lectures about "right attitudes.") Of course, titular relics deserve careful placement and honor all year.

■ CATECHETICAL SESSIONS: Participants in the parish's religious education program may gather for a catechetical session celebrating the parish's name. Verbal or visual presentations can take any number of approaches: on the history of the title, on traditional devotions associated with the name, on the provenance of the church's own titular image, on the iconography in the church, on the style of life this saint or title suggests for us or on the liturgical celebrations being planned. Music that will be sung at the liturgies can be rehearsed.

■ SCHOOL CELEBRATIONS: Perhaps the festival can be a school holiday, or a festival day for all grades, with activities and prayers and field trips that fit the title. The chapter on the patronal day in the *Leader's Manual of the Hymnal*

for Catholic Students includes ideas for a liturgy with students.

■ PROCESSIONS: Many parishes, especially those with strong ties to old world heritages, schedule a procession through the streets with their patronal statue. In some areas, the secular customs, materialism and even violence that may spring up in relation to the procession are a cause for worry. If the procession has been turned over by parish ancestors to an independent association, negotiations may result in an agreement allowing the parish once again to celebrate its patron in a more ecclesial and liturgical way. This may include starting or completing the procession with a liturgy for the whole community, and eliminating the need for money or fake flowers as the only decorations for the statue, for example.

If the parish alone is responsible for the procession, then it should be scheduled on or close to the actual date of the liturgical solemnity, with the statue receiving an honored place in the church throughout the year. Indeed there should be but one titular image so that devotion receives focus and so that other liturgical elements are not overshadowed.

ENVIRONMENT FOR WORSHIP

Apart from the image of Christ's cross, no image is required in a church, but our tradition has given the image of the titular patron its highest recommendation. Not even an image of Mary receives such high honors in our liturgical tradition. For example, old laws stated that if there was an image over any "fixed" altar, it must be of the titular.

A rediscovery of patronal or titular days should motivate a parish to review its iconography. Does the name of the parish find expression in a suitable image? Can one be commissioned? Can one owned by the parish be brought out of storage? Is it properly located to attract veneration but not to interfere with the celebration of the sacred mysteries?

■ OUTDOORS: Luminarias *(farolitos)* might surround any outdoor image of the title at ground level. Spotlights might highlight stonework high on the church building. The same decorations used outdoors for the dedication anniversary might be appropriate.

Patron of a Diocese

THE unity of parishes in a diocese is not accomplished by episcopal decree. It is not even produced by the good intentions of pastors and pastoral councils. It is the work of the Holy Spirit. The building of a communion of communities in a diocese needs the work of many to allow all to be open to the Spirit's fire.

From the perspective of liturgy, several aspects of different importance form the bond: the assignment of liturgical presiders to represent the bishop, the assignment of deacons, the inclusion of the bishop's name in the eucharistic prayer, the active participation of many in good liturgies in the cathedral, the observance of the anniversary of the cathedral's dedication and the annual celebration of the diocesan patronal day. Such practices and calendar days set each diocese apart, link observant communities and form the people who are themselves the local church. While worrying about parochialism, racism and low participation in diocesan appeal collections, many dioceses and pastors have neglected these opportunities to celebrate the bonds that form individuals and parishes into a local church.

If diocesan bonds have been underplayed, ecclesial solidarity with the saints (or with a saint) has been almost ignored. The observance of the saints' days is foundational to the liturgical calendar, both universal and local. One of these days should be raised to the rank of feast (or higher) and observed in every parish of the diocese. A patron not only serves as a model and as a protector, to use two traditional words, but also as a souvenir of local history and as a guide to future unity. The founders of the diocese, or its early leaders, decided on a patron with an eye to the devotional life of the people there. Even if the demographics of a diocese have changed, the patron calls all to unity and to fidelity to the diocesan mission.

When the patron was selected because of a link to an ethnic group (Patrick, Boniface, Louis, for example), it may be difficult for the saint's feast to be perceived as a sign of unity. The diocese probably embraces many groups now, some of whom may have had to struggle for acceptance. This necessitates a broad view of saints and an understanding that a particular saint's cultural and geographic connections are less important than the witness of holiness she or he gave in that place and time. A Haitian person can respect the missionary zeal of Patrick even if she or he has had unfortunate run-ins with "sons of Patrick." A Japanese person can revere Boniface despite a German neighbor's less-than-apostolic behavior.

WHEN TO CELEBRATE

Parishes that have begun to establish local festivals should consider celebrating the diocesan patron's day in the parish in addition to participating in the celebrations held in the cathedral. Such celebrations will, of course, be related to the day assigned to the saint or title in the general calendar, the tradition or the martyrology. The calendar of each diocese will note the date each year. If the diocese is still without such a helpful tool, liturgical commissions or offices of worship can be of assistance. This will be important in those dioceses that have a saint's day that sometimes bumps into Holy Week or the Easter Octave.

LITURGY OF THE DAY

This day is a feast and thus should not be moved to an Ordinary Time Sunday. Rather, it should receive a weekday observance equivalent, at least, to other feasts in the calendar. This may mean an evening celebration either of Evening Prayer or the eucharist. It may also involve children in a celebration or catechetical assembly of prayer and song.

Since the day is a diocesan feast as well as a sanctoral one, intercessions for the diocese should be included. If there is a diocesan hymn, it should be sung. The litany of the saints can be sung. Any image of the patron present in the parish might be honored with flowers, candles or incense.

Anniversary of the Dedication of the Cathedral

THE worship space that houses the bishop's *cathedra* (seat) is more than a grand place for ceremonies. It is also the bishop's church, the sign and place of the bishop's personal care and leadership. The cathedral is the sign of diocesan unity and the place where that can be given shape and color. For all of these reasons, it should be a model of liturgical life, both in architecture and in celebration (see the *Ceremonial of Bishops,* #42ff).

Esteem and reverence for the cathedral are supported by the ancient practice of remembering the cathedral in every parish every year. Such an observance of the cathedral's anniversary of dedication, like the diocesan patron's day, helps link separate parishes as a communion of communities around their bishop.

WHEN TO CELEBRATE

This date can be found in the diocesan calendar or from the diocesan liturgical commission. Like the patronal feast of the diocese, it is not normally moved to Sunday.

LITURGY OF THE DAY

Many of the images and catechetical points noted earlier under the local solemnity of the dedication of the parish's church can be used with some benefit here.

The liturgy of the hours (even in private recitation) throughout the diocese comes from the common of the dedication of a church. The collect prayers are chosen from the selections for "outside the dedicated church,"except, of course, for liturgies celebrated at the cathedral.

The celebration of the eucharist should be held in the evening if this would help gather the largest congregation. If there is one central celebration in the cathedral itself, local observances should not impede that gathering. Parish representatives should be sent to the celebration to carry the sincerest regards of the parish to the convening of the local church.

Intercessions should be prayed for the bishop, for the bishops who occupied the *cathedra* before him, for the unity of the diocese and for the cathedral parish.

Other Local Celebrations

THE universal Roman calendar and the minimum of four local days encouraged by the liturgical books hardly exhaust the calendar entries made by parishes. Some of these other days, most of them with liturgical implications, are listed here. May this list serve as an inspiration for planners to chart the whole year before it begins, to see how to integrate such local dates into the flow of the liturgy.

- *Anniversary of the bishop:* As noted in the sacramentary and *Ceremonial of Bishops* (#1167), each parish should remember the bishop on the anniversary of his ordination as bishop. If the date is not a Sunday, solemnity or feast of the Lord, then Masses and Prayers for Various Needs and Occasions, 3. For the Bishop is to be used.

- *Anniversary of the death of the last deceased bishop:* According to the *Ceremonial of Bishops* (#1168), this is also a "longstanding tradition" and it should marked by the celebration of a Mass for the dead, if allowed by the rubrics for that day.

- *Anniversary of ordination of a priest:* The presidential prayer texts provided in the sacramentary (Masses and Prayers for Various Needs and Occasions, 7C. For the Priest Himself on the Anniversary of Ordination) seem to presume a "private" Mass, with "I" language used between the priest celebrant and God. If a special Mass of the parish notes significant anniversaries of priests (25th, 50th), then the Mass of the day should probably be used: Such Masses are often celebrated on a Sunday anyway. Whether the celebration occurs on a Sunday morning or at another time, those who prepare such a liturgy should take care not to turn it into a beatification rite.

- *Local civic day:* Most towns and cities have at least one day a year when the local heritage is remembered and celebrated—the anniversary of incorporation, the holiday named after the town, the memorial of a Civil War battle, for example. The harmony and justice of the civic community should certainly be the focus of intercessions. If the day is a simple weekday or optional memorial, special Mass texts might be of pastoral advantage. See the prayers given under Masses and Prayers for Various Needs and Occasions, II. For Civil Needs, especially those listed at #17, #21 and #22. The reconciliation service suggested for 1992 might be celebrated on this day.

- *National ember days:* Every parish, as every diocese, should take the tradition of ember days seriously. See pages 186–92 in *Catholic Household Blessings and Prayers* for background and further resources. That book and this *Sourcebook* suggest these dates as particularly appropriate for the United States: Yom Hashoah (in 1992 on April 30, p. 147), August 6 and 9 (pp. 184 and 185), the weekdays before Thanksgiving (p. 204), December 28 (p. 37). As suggested on page v, the observances of Columbus in 1992 suggest an ember day or penitential service on October 12 or on another day that links the local community to its American heritage.

- *Local ember days:* Pastoral planners can add local days that pick up on cultural propensities or local anniversaries. "Days of Repentance" once were a prized part of New England history. Pilgrim and Puritan ancestors there have a lot to teach their Catholic neighbors about spending a day, especially after harvest, in total awareness of dependency on God. Communities located near Native American centers can draw from them some awareness of the local days which should be commemorated, both the days when they celebrate their heritage and the days when all of us should enter into corporate repentance for the heritage of blood we share. Anniversaries of natural disasters and major crimes allow each locality to frame certain annual days as "ember days."

ACKNOWLEDGMENTS

─────────

Texts of original opening prayers for Mass based on the scripture readings of the day, copyright © 1983, 1986, 1987, 1988, 1990, International Committee on English in the Liturgy, Inc. (ICEL). All rights reserved.

Texts taken from the Italian sacramentary, *Messale Romano,* copyright © 1983, Liberia Editrice Vaticana, are translated by Peter Scagnelli.

─────────

Sourcebook for Sundays and Seasons, 1992, copyright © 1991, Archdiocese of Chicago. All rights reserved.

Liturgy Training Publications
1800 North Hermitage Avenue
Chicago IL 60622-1101
Editorial offices: 1-312-486-8970
Order phone: 1-800-933-1800
FAX: 1-800-933-7094

Printed in the United States
of America

ISBN 0-929650-29-8